# Selected Topics in Investment Management for Financial Planning

# Selected Topics in Investment Management for Financial Planning

*Edited by*

**Frank J. Fabozzi**

*Walter E. Hanson/Peat, Marwick, Mitchell
Professor of Business and Finance
Lafayette College*

and

**Sheri Kole**

*Director, Financial Planning Department
The Copeland Companies*

DOW JONES-IRWIN   Homewood, Illinois   60430

© DOW JONES-IRWIN, 1985

This publication is designed to provide accurate and
authoritative information in regard to the subject matter
covered. It is sold with the understanding that the
publisher is not engaged in rendering legal, accounting, or
other professional service. If legal advice or other expert
assistance is required, the services of a competent
professional person should be sought.

*From a Declaration of Principles jointly adopted by a Committee
of the American Bar Association and a Committee of Publishers.*

ISBN 0-87094-681-1

Library of Congress Catalog Card No. 85–70800

*Printed in the United States of America*

4 5 6 7 8 9 0 K 2 1 0 9 8

# Preface

This book is designed for use as a supplementary book for an undergraduate or MBA course in investment management and as a reference book for financial advisors or those who plan to be financial advisors. The topics covered in this book are those that are usually not given adequate coverage in investment textbooks.

The articles in this book are not reprints of articles from academic or professional journals. With the exception of one article, the articles have been written specifically for this book. The articles are written like chapters in a textbook. This makes it easier for the instructor to integrate the articles with the textbook material and for the student to acquire a greater appreciation of the topic.

The 19 articles in the book discuss different aspects of investment management including the tax, regulatory, and economic environments; factors to consider when selecting investment vehicles; and the fundamentals and uses of several investment vehicles. It is sometimes difficult to integrate one's knowledge of economics, investment techniques, and investment vehicles to determine an appropriate plan of action. We think this book can be useful to individuals in the investment management field as a resource to determine appropriate planning opportunities.

Investment decisions are based on several factors, including the economic, political, regulatory, and tax environment, as well as personal financial goals. The first article in the book discusses the financial institutions active in the investment marketplace. Articles Three and Four present information on taxes and regulations as they relate to investment management. Article Five presents the portfolio construction and management process for the individual investor. This article presents a framework for selecting appropriate investment vehicles to meet financial goals. Articles Six, Eight, Nine, and Eleven discuss the economic implications of investing, including the stock market, interest rates, and business cycles. Articles Two and Seven present strategies used in the investment decision-making process. Article Ten and Articles Twelve through Nineteen discuss the fundamentals, uses, and risks of several investment vehicles available in the financial markets today. Several of these vehicles are new developments created by the financial services industry to meet the needs of the investing public.

We are indebted to many individuals for their assistance in this project. To all the contributors, we extend our deep thanks and appreciation. We are grateful for the invaluable assistance provided by the three editorial advisors to this project, Darwin M. Bayston (The Institute of Chartered Financial Analysts), Donald Johnson (College for Financial Planning), and James Kuttner (College for Financial Planning). Leslie Daniels (Chase Manhattan Bank), Mark Pitts (Shearson Lehman/American Express Inc.), and James M. Peaslee (Cleary, Gottlieb, Steen & Hamilton) each reviewed one article of this book. The following students at Lafayette College provided assistance at various stages of this project: Kathy Lucas, Karen Randall, Jane Rehm, and Rob Worth.

Frank J. Fabozzi
Sheri Kole

# CONTRIBUTING AUTHORS

**Jerome B. Cohen,** Professor of Finance and Dean (Emeritus), Bernard M. Baruch College, The City University of New York

**Bruce M. Collins,** Analyst, Mortgage Research and Product Development, Drexel Burnham Lambert, Inc.

**David N. Dreman,** Managing Director, Dreman, Gray & Embry, Inc.

**Frank J. Fabozzi,** Walter E. Hanson/Peat, Marwick, Mitchell Professor of Business and Finance, Lafayette College, and Managing Editor, *The Journal of Portfolio Management*

**Sylvan G. Feldstein,** Vice President and Manager, Municipal Bond Research Department, Merrill Lynch Capital Markets

**Michael G. Ferri,** Associate Professor of Finance, University of South Carolina

**T. Dessa Garlicki,** Instructor of Finance, Rutgers University

**Joseph C. Hu,** Vice President, Salomon Brothers Inc

**Jonathan C. Jankus,** Vice President, Kidder, Peabody & Co., Inc.

**Frank J. Jones,** Vice President, Kidder, Peabody & Co., Inc.

**David S. Kidwell,** Keehn Berry Chair of Banking, Tulane University

**Sheri Kole,** Director, Financial Planning Department, The Copeland Companies, and Academic Associate, College for Financial Planning

**John C. Ritchie, Jr.,** Professor of Finance and Assistant Dean, Temple University

**Dexter Senft,** Managing Director, Fixed Income Research, The First Boston Corporation

**David A. Smilow,** Analyst, Mortgage Research and Product Development, Drexel Burnham Lambert, Inc.

**Marcia Stigum,** Stigum & Associates, New York

**Kenneth H. Sullivan,** Managing Director, Mortgage Research and Product Development, Drexel Burnham Lambert, Inc.

**Richard S. Wilson,** Vice President, Fixed Income Research Department, Merrill Lynch Capital Markets

**Nancy H. Wojtas,** Partner, Memel, Jacobs, Pierno, Gersh & Ellsworth

**Benjamin Wolkowitz,** Vice President, Morgan Stanley & Co., Inc.

**Arthur Zeikel,** President and Chief Investment Officer, Merrill Lynch Asset Management, Inc.

**Edward D. Zinbarg,** Senior Vice President, The Prudential Insurance Company of America

# Contents

*Weak form efficiency. Semistrong form efficiency. Strong form efficiency.* Investing in an efficient market.

# ONE

**———————————————————**

## Overview of the financial system

**Michael G. Ferri, Ph.D.**
*Associate Professor of Finance*
*University of South Carolina*

**David S. Kidwell, Ph.D.**
*Keehn Berry Chair of Banking*
*Tulane University*

This article presents an overview of the components that comprise the U.S. financial system. The role of the financial system is to collect savings in the economy and allocate them efficiently to the ultimate borrower for investment in productive assets or for current consumption. The flow and use of savings is complicated because in most cases savers lend funds to financial intermediaries who, in turn, lend funds to various ventures, such as building condominiums, constructing a chemical plant, or to consumers to buy automobiles or take vacations. The flow of funds is important to the economy because, the larger the flow and the more efficiently funds are allocated, the greater the accommodation of individual preferences and the greater the output of the economy. This chapter examines the nature of the flow of funds in the economy, describes types of financial institutions, examines the various financial markets, and discusses some of the innovations affecting the financial sector.

## FLOW OF FUNDS AMONG ECONOMIC SECTORS

All economic units can be classified into one of the following groups: (1) households, (2) business firms, or (3) governments (local, state, and federal). Each of these must operate within a budget constraint imposed by its total income receipts and expenditures for the period. Households typically receive income in the form of wages and make frequent expenditures for durable and nondurable goods, services, and home real estate. Businesses sell goods and services to households and businesses for revenue, and their expenditures are for wages, inventory, and other production costs. Less frequently, businesses make capital expenditures. Governments obtain income by collecting taxes and fees, and they make expenditures for a myriad of services, such as health, welfare, education, and police and fire protection.

For a given budget period, any economic unit can have one of three budget positions: (1) a *balanced budget* where income and expenditures are equal, (2) a *surplus budget* where income for the period exceeds current expenditures, or (3) a *deficit budget* where expenditures for the period exceed receipts. The financial system is concerned with funneling purchasing power from surplus spending units (SSUs) to deficit spending units (DSUs). The transfer can be accomplished by an SSU lending money to and accepting an IOU from a DSU. An IOU is a written promise to pay money and interest to the holder at a future date; it is more formally called a *financial claim*. Examples of financial claims are bonds, mortgages, Treasury bills, certificates of deposits, and commercial paper. To the DSU, the financial claim is a liability; to the SSU, the financial claim is an asset. Thus, the total financial claims issued in the economy must equal the total financial assets owned.

Households are the largest supplier of funds to financial markets. Financial institutions are also important suppliers of funds, even though their net position is not large relative to households. The reason is their role as financial intermediaries. That is, the institutions purchase funds from households and others and then sell the funds to others in the form of loans or investments. Thus, households usually do not invest directly in capital markets, but, more likely, invest through such depository institutions as commercial banks, savings and loan associations, and life insurance companies. On the deficit side, the federal government and nonfinancial corporations are consistently large deficit spending units. Most state governments operate close to a balanced budget, though at times they are, in the aggregate, deficit units.

### Transferring funds from surplus to deficit units

As was stated above, the purpose of the financial system is to facilitate the transfer of funds from SSUs to DSUs in the most efficient way possible. Efficiency requires a variety of channeling techniques, and the modern financial systems have numerous channels. For the purpose of introduction, it is possible to classify the channels as (1) direct financing or (2) indirect financing.

**Direct financing.** In direct financing, the surplus unit gives money to the ultimate deficit spending unit in exchange for financial claims that are interest-earning assets. Though some third parties may help facilitate the exchange, SSU and DSU are dealing directly with one another. For example, a business with excess cash (SSU) purchases commercial paper issued by General Motors Acceptance Corporation (DSU). Though direct credit markets increase the efficiency of the financial system, a problem with this type of financing is that the financial claim that DSUs want to sell may not precisely match the type of claim that SSUs want to buy. Nonetheless, direct financial market transactions are widely used. In the direct market, most sales are wholesale transactions (large dollar amounts), and the participants are sophisticated lenders or borrowers who are knowledgeable about the intricacies of financial markets. The top frame in Exhibit 1 shows the flow of financial claims between SSU and DSU in the direct credit market; it also shows some of the participants that help arrange the transfer of funds in the direct credit market.

The simplest form of direct financing is the *private placement* of financial claims. In this market, a deficit unit, such as a corporation, sells the entire security issue directly to a single institution or a small group of institutions. Private placements occur easily, quickly, and with few legal entanglements, compared to new issue sales in the public market, which are often

**EXHIBIT 1**  The transfer of funds from surplus to deficit spending units

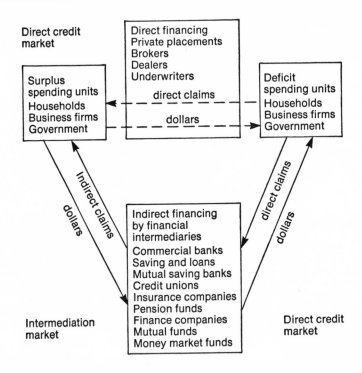

highly regulated. For example, private placements are exempt from being registered with the Securities and Exchange Commission, a process that can be costly and time consuming.

Another form of direct financing involves "matchmaking"— buyer and seller are brought together by security specialists, such as dealers or brokers. *Brokers* execute buy and sell transactions for their clients at the best possible price; they do not buy securities for their own account. Their profit is derived from charging a commission on each transaction. *Dealers,* however, own an inventory of securities and stand ready to either buy or sell a particular security at a stated price. The *bid price* is the highest price offered by the dealer to purchase securities; the *ask price* is the lowest price the dealer is willing to sell. The dealer makes a profit spread between the bid and the ask and, hopefully, a trading profit from his or her inventory of securities when they are sold to investors. Most dealers also operate as brokers and typically specialize in a particular type of market, such as the Treasury, commercial paper, or bond market.

Another specialist is the *investment banker,* who helps DSUs bring new financial claims to market. The primary economic function of investment bankers is to reduce the risk to DSUs when issuing new securities. That is, investment bankers underwrite new security issues by purchasing the entire block of securities issued by a DSU; they then resell the securities to investors. Underwriters make a profit by selling the claims for more than their purchase price. The profit is the reward the underwriters earn for bearing the risk that the securities may not be entirely sold or that there may be some delay in their purchase by the public. Thus, the underwriter is a direct supplier of funds to deficit units, but the supplying is based on the belief that the public will purchase the securities from the underwriter. Underwriters also provide other services, such as helping to prepare the prospectus, selecting the sale date, and providing general financial advice to the issuer. Issuers who frequent the direct financial markets find these services valuable.

**Indirect financing.**   Indirect financing occurs if financial intermediaries play a role in channeling funds from the surplus to the deficit units. Financial intermediaries include life insurance companies, commercial banks, savings banks, pension funds, mutual funds, and credit unions. The purpose of financial intermediation is to resolve the problems that can arise with direct financing. Specifically, DSU claims must have the same maturity, denomination, and size that SSUs are willing to buy. Otherwise, the transaction is unlikely to take place. For example, a household that temporarily has excess cash of $400 is not likely to want to buy a 20-year municipal bond with a denomination of $5,000.

Financial intermediaries overcome these problems by selling their own claims to the public, pooling the funds together, and then purchasing financial claims from DSUs. The characteristics of financial claims purchased and sold by a financial intermediary may vary sharply. Financial intermediaries are important to the economy because they transform DSU claims into more desirable forms for SSUs.

Two examples will illustrate this process of intermediation. First, households deposit cash into a savings and loan association's accounts, and the thrift uses the funds to finance mortgage loans to other households. Second, a corporation purchases the commercial paper of a consumer finance company, which then makes consumer installment loans. It is important to note that the surplus spending unit and the ultimate deficit spending unit would probably not have been able to arrange mutually satisfactory terms if left to their own devices. Hence, without the intermediary, the successful channeling of funds would have only been achieved at a much greater cost to both the DSU and SSU. The bottom half of Exhibit 1 shows the flow of funds through the intermediation market and identifies the more important financial intermediaries.

## BENEFITS PROVIDED BY
## FINANCIAL INTERMEDIARIES

Financial intermediaries transform claims in such a way as to make them more attractive to both DSUs and SSUs. If they did not serve this function, financial intermediaries would not exist. Financial intermediaries are business firms that provide financial services, such as NOW accounts, business loans, and life insurance policies. Like other business firms, they produce these products whenever they can sell them for prices that are expected to cover all their costs of production. They can do this because they can achieve economies of scale of production and because they can reduce transaction costs involved in searching for credit information.

For the above reasons, financial intermediaries are often able to produce financial commodities at a lower cost than businesses or individual consumers. If they did not, individuals or firms would enter the direct markets and produce their own financial commodities. The underlying reason financial intermediaries exist is the high transaction cost in producing many financial services in small quantities. If transaction costs are low and/or the quantity of goods produced is large, the financial commodity may be produced by the consumer.

In producing financial commodities, intermediaries perform four basic services. First, intermediaries are able to produce a wide range of denominations. By collecting and pooling the funds of individual savers, financial intermediaries are able to invest in direct securities. This funciton is of particular importance to savers who do not have enough money to purchase large-denomination securities typically sold in direct financial markets.

The second service is maturity flexibility. Financial intermediaries collect funds with short-term maturities and convert them into long-term funds. For example, a savings and loan association may obtain funds by issuing NOW accounts and a variety of short-term certificates of deposit and then invest the funds in long-term consumer mortgages. Thus, both the DSU and SSU find the maturities of their financial claims more attractive, because they dealt with a financial intermediary, than they would have if they dealt directly with each other.

A third service provided by financial intermediaries is risk diversification. Intermediaries purchase securities of varying risk and return, and then they offer claims to savers based on a diversified portfolio. To see the benefits, imagine how few securities a single household might purchase on its own and imagine the great cost of constructing a diversified portfolio. Thanks to the risk-diversification activities of the intermediary, however, such efforts are not necessary.

A final benefit of intermediation is liquidity. The intermediary offers claims that can be turned into cash easily. The ultimate deficit unit that borrows from the intermediary is not able to offer such a promise. The pooling of funds by numerous SSUs underlies the ability of financial intermediaries to offer liquid claims.

## FINANCIAL INTERMEDIARIES IN THE ECONOMY

A large number of financial intermediaries exists in the economy. Though distinctly different, financial intermediaries all have one function in common: They purchase claims with one set of characteristics from DSUs and then sell financial claims on themselves with a different set of characteristics.

Intermediaries are classified as: (1) deposit-type intermediaries, (2) contractual savings institutions, or (3) other types of financial intermediaries. Each of these institutions has major characteristics.

### Depository institutions

Depository financial institutions are the most commonly recognized intermediary because most people transact with them on a regular basis. Typically, these institutions issue a variety of checking and time deposits and use the funds to make consumer, business, and mortgage loans. Deposit accounts are insured by one of several federally sponsored insurance agencies. Also, most deposit accounts are liquid because funds can be withdrawn on very short notice, usually on demand, or they can be sold easily in secondary markets.

**Commercial banks.** Commercial banks are the largest and most diversified intermediary in the range of assets held and liabilities issued. Their liabilities are in the form of checking accounts and time deposits. Large banks issue money market liabilities, such as negotiable CDs, Eurodollar deposits, or commercial paper (through bank holding companies). On the asset side, commercial banks make a wide variety of loans to consumers, businesses, and state and local governments. In addition, banks or their holding companies have trust departments, offer some brokerage services, underwrite certain types of securities, offer credit life insurance, operate finance and mortgage companies, and run leasing companies. Finally, commercial banks are one of the most highly regulated financial intermediaries because of their vital role in the conduct of monetary policy by the Federal Reserve System.

**Savings and loan associations.** Savings and loan associations (SLAs or S&Ls) are highly specialized financial institutions that obtain most of their funds by issuing NOW accounts and consumer time deposits; they use these funds to make consumer mortgage loans. In effect, SLAs specialize in borrowing small amounts of money short-term from consumers and lending long-term on real estate collateral. This is known as maturity denomination intermediation. Recent deregulation, however, now allows SLAs to make a limited amount of consumer installment loans and business loans. One of the motivations for this deregulation was to reduce SLAs' interest rate risk by allowing them time to better match the maturities of their assets and liabilities. Currently, SLAs are the second largest financial intermediaries in the economy.

**Mutual savings banks.** Mutual savings banks (MSBs) are similar to savings and loan associations. They both collect most of their funds in the form of NOW accounts and consumer time deposits, and they invest their funds in residential mortgages. Recent deregulation has also expanded the asset and liability power of MSBs. Thus, to the consumer, MSBs and SLAs are similar institutions, though some technical differences do exist. At present, SLAs operate in only 18 states, most of them located in the northern Atlantic area. The growth of MSBs has been slower than other depositor institutions primarily because of the slow growth in residential mortgage demand in the Northeast, compared to other areas in the country.

**Credit unions.** Credit unions (CUs) are small nonprofit consumer institutions owned entirely by their members. The primary liabilities of CUs are checking accounts (called share drafts) and savings accounts (called share accounts); their investments are almost entirely short-term consumer installment loans. More recently, deregulation has allowed CUs to make a limited amount of residential mortgage and mobile home loans. Credit unions are organized by consumers having a common bond, such as employees of a given firm or union. To use any service of a credit union—for example, a passbook account or a loan—an individual must be a member. Finally, because of their cooperative nature, CUs are exempt from federal income taxes as well as from most state and local taxes.

### Contractual savings institutions

Contractual savings institutions obtain funds under long-term contractual arrangements and invest the funds in capital markets. Firms in this category are insurance companies (life and casualty) and pension funds. These institutions are characterized by a relatively steady inflow of funds from contractual commitments with insurance policyholders and pension fund participants. Thus, liquidity is not a problem for these institutions, and, as a result, they are able to invest in such long-term securities as bonds and, in some cases, common stock.

**Life insurance companies.** Life insurance companies (LICs) obtain funds by selling insurance policies that protect against loss of income due to death or retirement. Because LICs have a predictable inflow of funds and their outflows are actuarially predictable, they are able to invest primarily in higher-yielding, long-term assets, such as corporate bonds and stocks. LICs are regulated by individual states, and, compared to deposit-type institutions, their regulation is less strict. Despite less government regulation, LICs have experienced the lowest growth rate of any major financial intermediary.

**Casualty insurance companies.** Casualty insurance companies (CICs) sell protection against loss of property from fire, theft, accident, negligence, and other causes that can be actuarially predicted. The major source of funds for these firms is the premiums charged on insurance policies. Because the cash outflow on claims for casualty insurance companies is not as predictable as those on life insurance companies, CICs hold a greater proportion of their assets in short-term, highly marketable securities. To offset the lower return typically generated by these investments, CICs have invested heavily in equity securities. Also, because CICs are taxed at the full corporate tax rate, they own substantial amounts of municipal securities to shield their income from federal income taxes.

**Pension funds.** Pension funds collect contributions from employer and employee during an employee's working years and then provide a monthly income on retirement. Because the inflow into pension funds is long-term and the outflow is highly predictable, pension funds are able to invest in long-term, higher-yielding securities, such as bonds and equity obligations. The need for retirement funds and the success of organized labor in negotiating for wage packages has led to the remarkable growth of both private pensions and state and local government pension funds in the postwar period.

### Other types of financial intermediaries

The final catchall category, though diverse, includes institutions that fulfill the traditional financial intermediary role but have a different set of characteristics.

**Finance companies.** Finance companies make loans to consumers and small businesses; typically, finance company customers are of lower credit standing than the typical bank customer. Unlike depository institutions, finance companies do not accept saving deposits from consumers; they obtain most of their funds by selling commercial paper or borrowing from commercial banks. There are three basic types of finance companies: (1) consumer finance companies specializing in installment loans to households; (2) business finance companies specializing in loans and leases to many businesses; and (3) sale finance companies, which finance products sold by retail dealers. Finance companies are regulated by the state in which they operate and are also subject to many federal regulations. These regulations focus primarily on consumer transactions and deal with loan terms, rates charged, and collection practices. Because of restrictive regulations and growing competition from commercial banks, the growth rate of finance companies has been slower than that of other consumer financial institutions.

**Mutual funds.** Mutual funds sell equity shares to investors and use these funds to purchase stock, bonds, and money market securities. As intermediaries, they tend to specialize in denomination and default-risk intermediation. The advantages of a mutual fund over direct investment are that it provides investors with modest sums of money opportunities to: (1) reduce investment risk from diversification; (2) realize economies of scale in transaction cost; and (3) benefit from professional financial management. Mutual funds usually specialize within particular sectors of the market, such as debt, or in a particular type of equity security. The growth of mutual funds has closely followed that of the stock market.

**Money market mutual funds.** Money market mutual funds (MMMFs) emerged on the financial scene during the early 1970s. A MMMF is just a mutual fund that specializes in short-term financial securities with low default risk, such as Treasury bills or negotiable certificates of deposit issued by the nation's largest commercial banks, and high-grade commercial paper. These securities are issued in the direct credit market and typically sell in denominations of $1 million or more, so most investors are unable to purchase them directly. Thus, MMMFs provide investors who have small money balances with the opportunity to earn the market rate of interest without incurring a great deal of financial risk. Most MMMFs offer check-writing privileges, which makes these accounts close substitutes for NOW and Super NOW accounts offered by commercial banks or thrift institutions. However, their substitutability is somewhat limited, in that most MMMFs restrict the minimum withdrawals to $500 and the funds are not insured by a federal agency, such as the Federal Deposit Insurance Corporation (FDIC).

## FINANCIAL MARKETS

The term *financial markets* refers to that group of markets where participants buy and sell financial claims of a wide variety of economic institutions. These claims differ not only in terms of their issuers but also in terms of their maturity, default risk, tax treatment, and marketability. For the purpose of introducing financial markets, we are categorizing them into money markets, capital markets, and options and futures markets to provide the reader with a basic taxonomy of the many kinds of financial assets.

### The money markets

A money market is a wholesale market for financial claims that are close substitutes for money. The instruments traded are of large denomination, have low default risk, and are highly liquid. The major issuers of money market instruments include the U.S. Treasury, federally sponsored agencies, large domestic and foreign banks, large industrial firms, and state and local governments. Investors include these same institutions—in addition to thrift institutions, pension funds, insurance companies, mutual funds, and wealthy individuals.

There is no physical location where the money market is located, such as the New York Stock Exchange for equities. The money market is a collection of markets where such distinctly different financial instruments as Treasury bills and commercial paper are traded. Central to the activities of money markets are the dealers and brokers who specialize in particular money market instruments. Dealers who buy and sell from their inventories of securities are particularly important to the operation of the money market. Their primary function is to "make a market" for the money market instruments they trade in. They do this by standing ready to buy or sell from their inventory virtually any quantity of a security at its posted bid or offer price. The dealer function increases the liquidity of a money market instrument because the brokerage function of matching buyers and sellers in multimillion-dollar transactions would prove difficult, if not impossible, to do. Large money market dealers trade in a variety of money market instruments as well as in capital market instruments. Thus, dealers help link together the nation's money and capital markets.

The economic function of money markets is to provide an efficient means for economic units to adjust their liquidity positions. This is important because most economic units—household, business, and government—find that cash inflows and outflows are rarely perfectly timed. Money markets allow economic units to bridge the gap between cash receipts and expenditures. Article Ten discusses the major money market instruments.

### Capital markets

As discussed, money market instruments are highly liquid investments that have minimal financial risk. They are reasonably homogeneous and are held by economic units to adjust their liquidity. In contrast, capital market instruments vary widely in terms of their default risk, maturity, and marketability, and the funds are invested in productive assets that are expected to produce income for the owners. Hence the name *capital markets*. The most frequently discussed capital market instruments are common stock, preferred stock, corporate bonds, mortgages, and municipal bonds.

Equity or *common stock* represents an ownership claim on the assets of a firm. Stock differs from debt obligations in that equity holders have the right to share in a firm's profit, whereas the return of debt is fixed. The higher the firm's net income, the greater the return to the stockholders; however, common stockholders must share any losses that company may incur. A special class of equity is *preferred stock*. Preferred stockholders, though legally owners of the firm, have no voting powers in the management of the firm and receive a fixed return subject to adequate profits. The price of preferred stock is tied to interest rate movements in the economy. The price of common stock is tied to the firm's prospective earnings and fluctuates as the firm's prospects change. Most stock transactions take place in secondary markets, such as the New York or American Stock Exchanges.

*Corporate bonds* are long-term IOUs of a business firm and represent claims against a firm's assets. Unlike an equity holder, the bondholder's returns are fixed; and if the firm fails to pay as promised, the firm defaults on its debt. Corporate bonds have maturities ranging from 5 to 30 years. The secondary market for bonds is not as active as that for equity securities. Bonds come in a bewildering variety of terms and provisions. Specifically, some bonds can be retired by the issuer prior to their maturity (callable bonds). And bonds may require a portion of the bond issue to be retired systematically over the life of the issue (sinking-fund provision). Some bond issues, such as municipal bonds, are "serial" in nature, while others have the entire bond issue retire on a single date (term bonds). Finally, some bonds have options that allow them to be converted into a common or preferred stock at a predetermined price.

*Mortgages* are debt instruments secured by real estate. They are the largest segment in the capital markets in terms of the amount outstanding. More than half of all mortgage funds go into financing family dwellings, with the remainder financing business property, apartment buildings, and farm construction. Because most mortgages are relatively small and of odd denominations, are secured by collateral in various parts of the country, and are highly personal complex contracts, they are not very marketable on the secondary market. However, in recent years, mortgages in increasing numbers have been made more marketable by standardizing the contracts and by pooling individual mortgages together to form a new security backed by the original mortgage pool. These "mortgage-backed" securities trade in active secondary markets. Finally, most mortgages have fixed monthly payments. In recent years, because of volatile interest rates, mortgage issues have turned toward variable payment mortgages where the monthly payments vary in a predetermined manner with the level of interest rates. Most mortgages are made by savings and loan associations, mutual savings banks, and mortgage bankers.

*Municipal bonds* are long-term debt obligations issued by state and local governments. They are used to finance public capital expenditures, such as schools, highways, toll bridges, and airports. The most distinguishing feature of municipal bonds is that their coupon income is exempt from federal income taxes and, in many instances, from state and local taxes. As a result, municipal bonds are purchased by individuals or business firms in high tax brackets. Municipal securities are either collateralized by the full taxing power of the issuing gov-

ernment (general obligation bonds) or by the revenues generated by the capital project (revenue bonds).

### Options and futures markets

Financial markets, in general, have been scenes of innovation during the last decade. But nowhere has innovation and
creativity been more obvious or more successful than in the
markets for futures and options. These markets have forged a
new array of investment, hedging, and speculative opportunities that have changed the nature of portfolio management and
investment practice. Article Nineteen discusses these two
markets.

# TWO

## Psychology and markets*

**David N. Dreman**
*Managing Director*
*Dreman, Gray & Embry, Inc.*

London during the first days of 1524 was a city awaiting its doom. Crowds of anxious people of every social stratum gathered to listen to the numerous astrologers and fortune-tellers along bustling thoroughfares. All said the same thing: on February 1 the Thames would suddenly rise from its banks, engulf the entire city, and sweep away 10,000 homes. The vision was described in terrifying detail to increasingly larger throngs.

It had started the preceding June, when a few soothsayers began to bandy about the prophecy, which quickly permeated their ranks. Month after month the warnings were repeated with total assurance, and, as time passed, they became accepted by most of the population, even though the Thames had always been the most docile of rivers.

At first, only a handful of families began to leave the city, but, as the time grew near, people left in ever-increasing numbers. Long streams of laborers on foot, trailed by their wives and children, tramped the muddy roads to higher ground, 15 to 20 miles away. They were joined by their more prosperous neighbors whose horse-drawn carts were piled high with posses-

* Adapted from chapter 4, "The Strange World of Reality," in *The New Contrarian Investment Strategy* by David N. Dreman. Copyright © 1982 by David N. Dreman. Reprinted by permission of Random House, Inc.

sions. Nobles and clergy followed suit, fleeing to safe country estates. By the middle of January over 20,000 people had departed. London was rapidly becoming a ghost town.

Electing to stay, the prior of Saint Bartholomew's built a towerlike structure on Harrow-on-the-Hill and provisioned it for two months. He also acquired several boats manned by expert rowers—just in case.[1]

When the ill-fated day arrived, some braver souls stayed behind to watch, the soothsayers had predicted that the river would rise slowly, allowing those fleet enough to escape. The hour finally came, and, to the consternation of the watchers, nothing happened. The tide quietly ebbed and flowed, and ebbed and flowed as it always had. An awareness slowly spread over the good people that they had been had. Still, to be safe, most stayed up that night and continued their watch.

The next morning, with the Thames continuing to flow peacefully within its banks, the crowd, joined by the returning evacuees, was boiling with fury. Many shouted to throw the pack of soothsayers into the river.

Fortunately, the prophets were prepared. In a clever maneuver—seemingly not lost on present-day chartists—they said they had scrupulously rechecked their calculations the previous night and found a minute error. London was most certainly doomed, the stars were as always undeniably right. But, because of the minor oversight, the great flood would occur in 1624, not 1524. The good townspeople could go home—at least for a while.

This story, whose many variations have been replayed through history, has a great deal more to do with financial markets than you might at first think. Present-day investors employ a variety of tools to formulate investment strategies. Although these tools appear to be practical, they rest on a bed of psychological quicksand. Without understanding how investors form opinions and the psychology that affects their decision making, people's odds are considerably reduced in the marketplace.

A good place to start examining what goes wrong with established investment methods is to observe how groups or crowds affect our ability to exercise independent judgment, even in areas where we think we can be totally objective. In this article,

---

[1] Charles Mackay, *Extraordinary Popular Delusions and the Madness of Crowds* (New York: Noonday Press, 1974), p. 421. Originally published in London in 1841 by Richard Bently.

we will look at crowd behavior and how it can influence us as investors.

It is important to recognize that people in groups tend to be continually swept by one idea or trend after another. Sometimes, as in the London of 1524, they have no supporting facts and still participate in crowd action that to an impartial observer borders on the insane. On each occasion most people justify and often enthusiastically back the new thinking. While we can always look back and shake our heads at group folly in the past, it is far harder to remain unaffected by these influences in our own time.

The American Civil Liberties Union (ACLU) considered itself very brave indeed to defend the right to demonstrate of a handful of Nazis in 1978, a group who—though thoroughly repugnant—represented no real threat at the time. But at the height of McCarthyism during the early 1950s, the ACLU was swept along like most people and refused to defend suspected Communists. And while we may laugh at the absurd carryings on of the 17th-century Dutchmen who frantically sold their gold, jewelry, crops, and houses to buy tulip bulbs, investors made remarkably similar decisions in the 1960s and 1970s— only this time in stock, rather than tulip markets.[2]

To survive in the marketplace, it is essential to avoid being carried away by the current mood of the crowd. The investor must find some means of being able to withstand the tide—a task anything but simple. It is necessary first to understand exactly how these crowd influences affect investment decisions and why they are so powerful. Armed with this knowledge, you can develop strategies that should not only allow you to resist the pull of current opinion but take advantage of it.

## DR. LEBON'S CROWD

The potent force of massed human beings is a phenomenon recognized since antiquity, one often discussed by the philosopher or portrayed by the dramatists. Still, a more scientific analysis of crowd behavior, like many other such philosophical curiosities, was not undertaken until the latter part of the 19th century. Only then did rigorous investigation begin.

In 1895, a Frenchman, Gustave LeBon, wrote what continues

---

[2] For a discussion of "tulipmania," see chapters 3 and 4 in David N. Dreman, *Psychology and the Stock Market* (New York: AMACOM, 1977).

to rank as one of the most incisive works on mass psychology, *The Crowd.* According to LeBon, "the sentiments and ideas of all persons in a gathering take one and the same direction, and their conscious personality vanishes. A collective mind is formed, doubtless transitory, but presenting very clearly defined characteristics. The gathering has then become . . . a psychological crowd."[3] In such situations, the actions of individuals may be quite different from those the same individuals would consider when alone.

One of the most striking features of the crowd to LeBon was its great difficulty in separating the imagined from the real. "A crowd thinks in images, and the image itself calls up a series of other images, having no logical connection with the first . . . a crowd scarcely distinguishes between the subjective and the objective. It accepts as real the images invoked in its mind, though they most often have only a very distant relation with the observed facts. . . . Crowds being only capable of thinking in images are only to be impressed by images."[4]

At times, as LeBon saw, the image evokes cruel behavior; the belief in witches and sorcerers sent tens of thousands to the stake in the 16th and 17th centuries, and the "isms" of this century have taken tens of millions of lives. At other times, the image can inspire heroism: the crowd that swept the Bastille; or the Republican crowd that with bare hands stormed the fascist Montana Barracks in Madrid in 1936. With the benefit of hindsight, the image may become droll, as when London was abandoned to the Thames. But, to capture the crowd, the image must always be extremely simple. LeBon believed the individual regresses in a crowd and "descends several rungs in the ladder of civilization. Isolated, he may be a cultivated individual; in a crowd he is a barbarian. He possesses the spontaneity, the violence, the ferocity, and also the enthusiasm and heroism of primitive beings."[5]

LeBon was an astute, if not particularly sympathetic, observer of crowds, and his description of crowd behavior is strikingly applicable to what we can readily discover taking place in financial markets. Certainly all the elements are present: numbers of people, intense excitement, and that essential simple

---

[3] Gustave LeBon, *The Crowd* (New York: Viking Press, 1960), pp. 23–24.

[4] Ibid., pp. 41–61.

[5] Ibid., p. 70.

image. Indeed few images are more simple and yet as beguiling as *instant wealth*. Each such image carried the crowd far into the realm of fantasy, and sometimes beyond the boundaries of sanity. Despite the assumption of the rationality and omniscience of investors claimed by our academic friends, the last word on the subject often seems to be the roar of the crowd.

Each time, as LeBon foresaw, the image was not only simple and enticing, but seemingly infallible. And, as he predicted, people lost their individuality. Crowd contagion swept intellectuals, artists, nobles, and businessmen in every period as easily as it did the common people. Actually, those who should have known best often led the way. And so, to see just how strong its pull can be, we might look a little more closely at the behavior of crowds in the marketplace.

### THE MISSISSIPPI SCHEME

The French, usually pacesetters in fashion, launched one of the first of the gigantic speculative manias, beginning in 1716. The Mississippi Company, as the venture was dubbed, resembled in many ways the classic *South Sea bubble*, which was soon to develop on the other side of the Channel.[6]

The central character in the Mississippi Company was John Law, the son of a Scottish banker. A tall, dashing figure, Law had fled to the Continent with a death sentence on his head, the result of his having killed a rival in a duel over a love affair. Having studied banking in Amsterdam, Hamburg, Vienna, and Genoa, Law had a fairly sophisticated understanding of the use of credit. He was able to convince the French regent of the merits of using paper money to lower interest rates, increase employment, and expand business. A national bank was established, which issued paper money up to twice the value of the country's gold and silver. The beginnings proved sound enough, and the bank prospered.

Law's vision, however, was much grander. Two years later, in 1718, he secured the right to the development of the vast Mississippi basin, then a territory of France.

Under Law's orchestration, a gigantic speculative bubble began to take shape. The stock in the new venture was first sold to

---

[6] For a discussion of the classic South Sea bubble, see chapter 3 of Dreman, *Psychology and the Stock Market*.

the public on very attractive terms. Three quarters of the payment could be made in Louis XIV *billets des états* at face value, although this particular currency then traded at an almost 80 percent discount.

To eliminate any doubt about the prosperity of the scheme, Law promised a dividend of 40 percent of the face value of the stock in the initial year. Using the discounted Louis XIV notes to subscribe, a shareholder would receive 120 percent of his investment in dividends alone in the first 12 months! This, and the lure of the Indies, proved too much. Few were bothered by the fact that the company was just starting and had no assets. Enthusiasm easily checkmated logic; 300,000 applications were made for the first 50,000 shares. Dukes, marquises, and comtes, with their duchesses, marchionesses, and comtesses, jostled in the streets with prostitutes and peddlars seeking to subscribe. Some of the nobility took apartments while waiting their turn to avoid rubbing shoulders with the "great unwashed" around them.

The demand for the stock seemed inexhaustible. Law issued a steady stream of new shares at progressively higher prices. Only months after the original stock sale, a new issue was offered and was oversubscribed at 5,000 livres—10 times the initial price.

Law was an expert painting the canvas of concept. To make the potential even more dazzling, he acquired the tobacco monopolies, as well as the East China, India, and Africa Companies, and merged them all into the Mississippi Company. Indians were paraded through the streets of Paris, bedecked with gold and silver, to demonstrate the wealth of the territories. Engravings showing Louisianan mountains bursting with gold, silver, and precious stones were widely distributed.

The price rise of the Mississippi Company was breathtaking and in itself became almost hypnotic. "The tendency to look beyond the simple fact of increasing value to the reasons on which it depends greatly diminishes," wrote John Kenneth Galbraith of investor behavior in 1929.[7]

Professor Galbraith's wry observation is as apt for the rue de Quincampoix, where the stock was traded. Large crowds became acclimated to prices working constantly higher—day after

---

[7] John Kenneth Galbraith, *The Great Crash* (Boston: Houghton Mifflin, 1961), p. 9.

day, week after week, and month after month. Previous and now "old-fashioned" standards of value were left far behind.

It was difficult for anyone to escape the scheme's almost irresistible appeal, and few did. At the height of the frenzy in 1720, the Mississippi Company had appreciated 40 times from the initial offering price of 500 livres in 1716. The market price of the shares was now worth 80 times all the gold and silver in France.[8]

The rue de Quincampoix was packed with speculators of all classes. Every available space was used for trading. A cobbler rented his stall to traders for 10 times his normal wages. The rents for houses on the street rose 12- to 16-fold from previous levels. Fortunes, naturally, were made—a banker was said to have made 100 million livres, a waiter 30 million. The word *millionaire* came into use for the first time.

The wild speculation took on many of the aspects of a carnival. Tents were erected to trade stock, sell refreshments, and even to gamble. One man set up a roulette wheel in the midst of the packed throng and did a thriving business. The major roads leading to Paris were made almost impassable because of the masses trying to reach the city. Over 300,000 people came from the provinces to participate in the trading!

Law was idolized by the crowd. So great were the surrounding throngs anywhere he went that the prince regent provided him with a troop of lancers to clear the way. Enormous bribes were paid to his servants to get an interview with him, and even members of the aristocracy had to wait for weeks for an appointment. One lady drove around Paris for three days looking for Law, instructing her coachman to upset the carriage when he was sighted. When at last they tracked him down, the coach was driven into a post. It turned over, and the lady screamed shrilly to attract Law's attention. As Law came to her aid, she con-

---

[8] Madness perhaps in retrospect, but only a few years ago the experienced senior investment officers of America's largest and most powerful financial institutions did almost exactly the same thing. They decided that there were only 50 or so stocks to buy out of a total of 12,000 public companies, and they bid them up to astronomical prices. Avon Products, for example, was valued for more than the entire U.S. steel industry, although it was dwarfed in size and profitability. At the time, the heads of these institutions, including Morgan Guaranty, Banker's Trust, and Citibank, vigorously defended the course they were following before Congress as "most prudent." As in the case of the Mississippi Company, both expert and average opinion was convinced that they had found the new Golconda. The subsequent performance of some of the more popular stocks is found in Table 1.

fessed the ruse and asked to subscribe to the next stock issue, to which he smilingly obliged.

Although Law exaggerated the opportunities, he did make a genuine effort to develop Louisiana and was successful in increasing French shipping, establishing new industries, and sharply raising French commercial activity. Nevertheless, the soaring prices of the Mississippi Company stock had little to do with the situation. When this awareness began to spread, a panic followed, both in the paper currency and the Mississippi shares.

LeBon was well aware of how swiftly the image guiding the crowd could change. "These image-like ideas," he wrote, "are not connected by any logical bond or analogy or successor, and may take each other's place like the slides of a Magic Lantern."[9] And so they did. The Mississippi shares, which previously represented spectacular riches, now meant doom.

Law attempted to stem the tide. Anticipating Cecil B. DeMille by several centuries, he staged a spectacular in the streets of Paris. Six thousand of the city's poorest inhabitants were pressed into service, given new clothes, picks, and shovels, and marched through the streets, presumably on the way to mine Louisiana gold. However, even this major production stopped the panic for only a few days.

When the Mississippi bubble burst, the aftermath was devastating. First a few investors, then gradually more, and within weeks almost all realized that the speculative frenzy was insane. A desperate rush to sell began—but few buyers could be found. People now focused on the emptiness of the scheme. Rumor again spread through the rue de Quincampoix, this time that the company had few assets and would be forced to omit its dividend entirely.

The image had changed for good. By late 1720, the stock had fallen to 200 livres, some 99 percent below its peak only months before. Law left the country in disgrace and died in obscurity nine years later in Venice. To the end, he loved risk. No longer gambling the economic stakes of one of the two most powerful nations on earth, he was content to wager his few available shillings with passersby on whatever local action moved him.

---

[9] LeBon, *The Crowd*, p. 62.

## WHAT IS SOCIAL REALITY?

The vision of the jeweled and powdered French dukes, comtes, and marquises frantically scurrying about the rue de Quincampoix, breathlessly followed by their duchesses, comptesses, and marchionesses, décollétage aheaving, may be amusing, but are these lessons to be learned that also apply to modern markets?

History has shown that group madness need not last for only brief periods. The fear of the flooding of the Thames occurred over many months, the Mississippi bubble was in full bloom for four or five years, and the persecution of witches and sorcerers went on for centuries. In each of these cases, the image created its own reality, reshaping the perceptions, actions, and attitudes of the crowd. How were such strange realities brought into being and nurtured, and why should supposedly rational people succumb so easily to them?

By and large, historians and psychologists are the only people who have pursued the matter. Historians have helped to preserve the important record of these events, and modern psychologists have moved far beyond LeBon in their investigations of what motivates groups. Meanwhile, for most of us as investors, it has been business as usual. Despite all our "progress," the lack of results remains conspicuous. Yet it seems pretty obvious that LeBon's rampaging crowd has not ignored the marketplace either.

If we are to avoid being victimized by crowds, it is important to possess a clear understanding of the forces that drive them. Social psychologists tell us that our beliefs, values, and attitudes can be thought to lie along a continuum. At one extreme are those based on indisputable physical evidence—if I throw a crystal goblet against a wall, it will shatter; or if I point my skis straight down a long steep slope, it's pretty unlikely I'll reach the bottom intact. Such outcomes, termed physical reality, are abundantly clear and don't require other people's confirmation.

At the other end of the continuum are beliefs and attitudes that, although important to us, lack firm support. What facts are available are sparse and difficult to evaluate. In this category are such questions as the existence of God, whether there is a "best" political system, or, of primary interest here, what a stock or the market is really worth at a point in time.

Psychologists have demonstrated that the vaguer and more complex a situation, the more we rely on other people whose intelligence we respect, both for clarification and as standards against which to judge the correctness of our own views. This helps us reduce the uncertainty we have toward our own beliefs. Most investors for example, attempting to assimilate many contradictory facts to put a value on the Mississippi Company shares, undoubtedly sought the opinions of other intelligent investors to form their own assessments. When people use others as yardsticks, against which to determine the correctness of their own views, they are utilizing what psychologists call *social comparison processes.*

We can do this in very commonplace ways, rarely giving it a second thought. I was once in a Middle Eastern restaurant in New York, where the men's and ladies' rooms were marked with what to me were unintelligible symbols. I was momentarily puzzled, until a man who obviously knew where he was going strolled confidently through one of the doors, solving my problem. Or consider the case of *The Wall Street Journal* reporter who wrote of a recent dinner he and his wife had with a desert sheik. After the meal, two other distinguished Western guests sat back and belched heartily. The reporter and his wife, guessing that this was the proper sign of approval for the hearty fare, followed suit with gusto.

Similarly, a speaker may gauge the worth of his or her talk from the audience's reaction. After one of his speeches, Lincoln, judging from what he thought was the indifferent response of the crowd, turned to a friend and said: "It's a flat failure and the people are disappointed." The speech was the Gettysburg Address.[10]

The greater the anxiety and the more indeterminate the situation appears to be, the more readily we rely on the behavior of others to gauge the proper course, treating much of the information we receive from them as being no less real than if we had directly observed it from physical reality. We thus forget its personal and tentative nature.

The term *social reality* refers to how a group of people perceive reality. As Leon Festinger, who first proposed the theory, described it: "When the dependence upon physical reality is

---

[10] Carl Sandburg, *Abraham Lincoln: Volume 2, 1861–1864* (New York: Dell Publishing, 1970), p. 410.

low, the dependence on social reality is correspondingly high. An opinion, attitude, or belief is 'correct, valid, and proper' to the extent that it is anchored in the group of people with similar beliefs, opinions, and attitudes."[11] The ensuing social reality can then be a strange amalgam of objective criteria and crowd fancy. Facts, such as are available, can be twisted or distorted entirely to conform with prevailing opinions.

And this brings up back to the strange aberrations of people in crowds that we have seen in this chapter. In each instance, the information was vague, sometimes complex, and anxiety-producing to the people of the time. Few standards existed to help them. Fortunetellers may have been right in some of their earlier prophecies, establishing their credibility for the new auguries. During the Mississippi scheme, one could see the substantial gains made by those who bought early, and that noblemen, confidants of the regent, and shrewd businessmen were buying the stock—most said the price rise was only beginning.

People then as now were uncertain, sometimes anxious, and as a result wanted to compare their opinions with those of other individuals whom they respected. Great numbers were drawn by the need to verify their individual views into conformity with the group's beliefs; the larger the nucleus of the group, the greater the attraction of its beliefs to those who had initially resisted them.

Just how easily people's behavior can be influenced by others in uncertain and even mildly anxiety-producing circumstances can be seen from the following laboratory experiment of S. Schacter's.[12] Subjects were injected with a drug called epinephrine, which temporarily causes heart palpitations and hand shaking. The subjects were told that the drug was a vitamin supplement called "Suproxin." In each case, the subject was placed in a room with a stooge, planted there by the experimenters, who allegedly had also been injected with "Suproxin." With no forewarning, the subject searched for an explanation—as his heart beat faster and his hands began to tremble. He started to watch the stooge who, as you can guess, was not inactive. In one case, he behaved lightheartedly, sing-

---

[11] Leon Festinger, "A Theory of Social Comparison Processes," *Human Relations* 7 (1954), pp. 117–40.

[12] S. Schacter and J. E. Singer, "Cognitive, Social, and Psychological Determinants of Emotional States," *Psychological Review* 69 (1962), pp. 379–99.

ing, dancing, constructing and flying paper planes, in general acting in a high-spirited, zany way. Other subjects were put in a room with a stooge who was gloomy and morose, made angry remarks, complained about a questionnaire both were filling out, and, in a sudden fit of pique, ripped his up.

How did the subjects react? Feeling the effects of the drug, and watching the behavior of the stooges, the great majority adapted behavior patterns to match.

The record outside of the laboratory is not much different. Because there are so few objective guidelines, social reality has always had a merry time in the fashion world, for males and females alike. At the turn of the century, the dictate was for women's hemlines to drag along the ground; in other periods, they were well above the knee. In the late 19th century, to be *au courant* demanded an exceptionally narrow waist (17 or 18 inches), and many a poor woman had her floating rib removed to conform to the dictate. In 1943, so many women tried to imitate the hairdo covering one eye of then-reigning film queen Veronica Lake that, according to United Press International, "the Federal Government branded her a menace to the war effort; it claimed too many lady airplane workers imitating her peek-a-boo bob had scalped themselves in the machinery."[13]

Crowd fashions and fads are no different today. Take jogging, for example. It may be healthy—the jury still seems out there—but it has certainly become contagious. It has mainly taken over from the previous physical fitness exercises, such as jumping rope (very "in" several years ago, but now advised against by some doctors because it may cause shin splints), yoga, and the RCAF-X4 plan.

Whether it's on a quiet Vermont byway or early morning in Riverside Park, there is a strong likelihood of meeting someone jogging these days. Many a poor middle-aged businessman or matron goes through the motions, panting heavily, tongue hanging out, and eyes bulging, all supposedly in the name of physical fitness. Fashionable jogging outfits costing $175 or more are sold at Bergdorf Goodman and Saks Fifth Avenue. And the elegant ladies of the East Side now lunch at expensive restaurants sporting their faultlessly tailored jogging wear never for a moment meant to be sweated in. Perhaps this isn't a fad—but already numbers of books on walking are being readied for release.

---

[13] J. C. Flugel, *The Psychology of Clothes* (New York: Universities Press, 1969).

Does the same hold true of fashions in the marketplace? Uncertainty, anxiety, lack of objective reality, and sudden and violent shifts in the image of the group are certainly integral to crowd behavior here too. Each interpretation of what was realistic was established and maintained by the consensus of the group. In every mania the group was injected (in a manner not unlike the epinephrine experiment) with an image of spectacular wealth, which changed its behavior. This new social reality was fabricated of the dreams, hopes, and greed of many thousands of investors. Many watching a particular bubble saw as much clearly. Yet most could still believe that things really would be different this time . . .

## THE REALITY OF 1962

Let's next stop briefly at the Wall Street of 1962 to examine the workings of social realities on modern investment crowds. Are they any different from those of years past?

After the 1929 crash, speculative fervor burned out for a generation. In fact, the Dow didn't break its 1929 high of 381 until November of 1954, at which time the nation was prosperous, industrial activity was increasing, consumer income was rising, as were corporate earnings and dividends. The market, with only a few minor setbacks, continued to work solidly higher through the balance of the decade. "Time," Disraeli wrote, "is the Great Physician." And so it was. A new generation of investors, untutored in the lessons of disaster that their parents had learned, was now firmly at the helm. Confident of the future, they were intrigued with the tremendous investment opportunities that were present in this new dynamic economy.

Just as the 18th-century investors were propelled by the unlimited wealth of the New World, so modern investors now saw the possibility of unlimited profits through modern science. Because of these expectations, the major technology companies of the time—IBM, Xerox, Polaroid, and Texas Instruments—commanded towering prices.

Even more striking, when viewed with the hindsight of 17 years, was the 1961–62 period's enormous similarity to the English South Sea bubble of the early 18th century—in the willingness of people to buy almost any new venture. In 1720, companies that made wheels of perpetual motion or converted gold from lead were in demand. In 1961–62, esoteric technological companies exerted enormous appeal. Whether it was alchemy in the first place or science in the second didn't matter much, as investors understood the prospects of each equally well. The crowd on the cobblestones in Exchange Alley, where the bubble companies traded, or watching the action on luminous electronic tapes in the boardrooms of space-age America behaved the same.

The beginnings, as usual, were sound enough. Many small technological companies sold to the public in the 1950s showed spectacular appreciation. An investment of $1,000 in Control Data when it was first offered in 1958 was worth $121,000 by 1961. The same $1,000 put into Litton Industries in the mid-1950s moved up 50-fold during that period. Seeing these profits and believing in the unlimited wealth to be gained in anything scientific, investors scrambled to buy the shares of any small company that was being offered to the public for the first time. A frenzied new issues boom took place in 1960 and 1961. All that was required was that the company be in electronics, computers, medical technology, or pharmaceuticals. Any company ending in "ics" or "tron" was enthusiastically bid up. Nytronics, Bristol Dynamics, and Supronics shot to immediate premiums. Some of the gains were spectacular. Dynatronics was issued at 7 and rose to 25 instantly; Risitron Laboratories went from 1 to 3⅞. Simulmatics, a company incorporated only two years earlier and with a negative net worth of $21,000, was offered at 2 and immediately quoted at 9.

The public appetite for such stocks was almost insatiable. One elderly woman called her broker to buy shares in "Hebrew National Electronics." The broker explained that the company was not in electronics at all, but was a kosher meat packer and processor. She accepted the news with disappointment and a tinge of anger. Several months later, when the stock had also moved up, she again phoned the broker. "They are too in the electronics business!" she said indignantly. "They sell electronic salami slicers."[14]

As the fever spread, new issues were underwritten in many industries outside technology. The boardrooms were filled to overflowing and the talk on commuter trains and in theater lobbies was of hot new issues and the best little underwriting houses.

---

[14] "Over the Counter: Frantic, Frenetic, Frazzled," *Dun's Review* 92 (August 1968), pp. 32–37.

Promoters, not really very different animals in 1962 from what they had been in 1718, understood the appetites of the crowd and scoured the countryside for acceptable merchandise. "Why go broke, go public," the prospective underwriting client was told. Shopworn goods were rechristened with sparkling new space-age names. Many of the hottest underwriting firms were one- or two-man companies.

The mania was intensified by the underwriter's advertising of the success of their merchandise. One firm, Michael Lomasney and Company, ran an ad stating that, had an investor purchased $1,000 of each of the 16 issues it had underwritten in the past 18 months, he or she would have had $36,800 by September 1961. This was topped by another small underwriting firm, Globus, Inc., with offices, appropriately enough, on Madison Avenue. "If you bought each of Globus' issues," its ad rang, "you would have tripled your money by late 1961." The froth danced higher and higher.

This was, of course, a house of cards, but nobody seemed to notice . . . or care. With money being made at every turn, a stream of how-to literature came off the printing presses. Nicholas Darvas, a gypsy dancer, wrote a book entitled *How I Made Two Million Dollars in the Stock Market*. Another writer published a book modestly promising *How to Make a Killing on Wall Street*.[15]

The realization came, as always, that this was a fool's paradise. By the latter part of 1961, speculative ardor had cooled noticeably. In the sharp break of April–May 1962, a panic enveloped the new bubble companies. While the market recovered in short order and went on to new highs, most of the underwritings traded at pittances of the former values. An SEC study of 500 randomly selected issues offered in the 1950s and early 1960s showed that 12 percent had simply vanished, 43 percent had gone bankrupt, 25 percent were operating at a loss, while only 20 percent displayed any earnings whatever. Of the latter, there were only 12 which had any real promise. Social reality had led the crowd down the same strange path in 1962 as it had in 1720.

---

[15] Even the art world was unable to avoid the get-rich-quick craze. One service—the Art Market Guide and Forecaster—put together an average of 500 artists and called it the AMG index after its own initials. One ad read: "With the art market for paintings up 97 percent since the war—and 65 percent in the last year alone—you can lose immense profits by failing to keep informed of the monetary value of art, present and future." See Robert Sobel, *The Big Board* (New York: Free Press, 1965).

## THE COMPELLINGNESS OF CROWD OPINION

Why do social comparison processes produce an investor consensus that is often so far off the mark? Part of the answer seems to lie in how easily people's opinions are drawn together under conditions of uncertainty.

An excellent experiment to show this was devised by psychologist Muzafer Sherif.[16] Sherif took advantage of the little-known autokinetic light phenomenon. A tiny pinpoint of light beamed for a few seconds in a darkened room appears to move, although in fact it is stationary. Sherif asked his subjects to calculate the extent of the movement as carefully as possible. (Since the light appeared to be moving, the subjects believed it actually did.) With no reference points upon which to anchor judgment in the blackened room, the answers in individual trials ranged from a few inches to 80 feet—the latter subject believed he was in a gymnasium, rather than in a small room.

After 100 trial sets, the median guess of each subject was recorded. Exhibit 1 shows it ranged from approximately one to over eight inches (as the line on the extreme left of both charts indicates). However, when subjects were brought together, the judgments converged. Exhibit 1(A) indicates the amount of convergence there was in each succeeding 100-test figure with two people present; Exhibit 1(B) with three. In the latter case, from individual medians varying from under an inch to almost eight inches, the group's convergence by the third 100-set test moved to slightly over two inches.

Sherif added another variable by including a confederate. If the subject has estimated the light moved 20 inches, the confederate might estimate 2. His influence was enormous. By the end of the trials, most subject's estimates came very close to those of the confederate, which remained stable throughout.

Writing of these experiments, psychologist William Samuels noted: "The majority of subjects in such studies indicate little awareness that their perceptions have been manipulated by the estimates of others, for they maintain that they had previously made their own estimates *before the others spoke.* The influence process then may be a rather subtle phenomenon. Partners who are well liked, who have high status, who are reputed to be competent on the judgmental task, or who merely exude

---

[16] M. Sherif and C. W. Sherif, *Social Psychology* (New York: Harper & Row, 1969), pp. 208–9.

**EXHIBIT 1** Convergence of opinion in light movement experiment

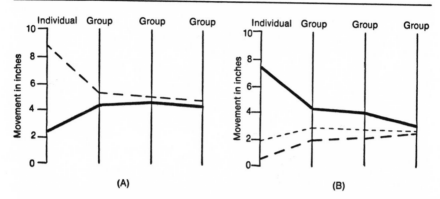

Source: Muzafer Sherif and Carolyn Sherif, *Social Psychology* (New York: Harper & Row, 1969), pp. 208–9. Copyright © 1969 by Muzafer Sherif and Carolyn W. Sherif.

self-confidence when announcing their estimates are all especially effective in influencing a subject's personal norm of movements."[17]

It is also interesting to see how far a naive subject's judgment could be shifted under subtle manipulation—as much as 80 percent or more without pressure of any sort. Because one of the prime features of the stock market is uncertainty, opinions frequently move toward a consensus and, not unlike the autokinetic light experiment, move toward the most authoritative-sounding or most outspoken points of view available at the time—usually those of the experts whose record we already know. Then throw in anxiety, another very powerful force leading toward consensus. During the best of times the stock market is uncertain and difficult, and in its worst moments can induce first-rate terror. People find it natural under such circumstances to take comfort and security in the opinions of savvy, smart money. Small wonder that the consensus of the many appears to be a refuge, not a trap.

Earlier, we saw just how elusive the anchor of objective reality and the concept of value on which it is based actually are. It is not surprising, then, given the nature of the psychological forces at work, that we, too, can often find ourselves dashing

[17] William Samuels, *Contemporary Social Psychology* (Englewood Cliffs, N.J.: Prentice-Hall, 1973), p. 10.

frantically down a rue de Quincampoix, an Exchange Alley, or a Wall Street . . . which brings me to the next wild adventure: the "go-go" market of 1967–68.

## GOD HAS BEEN GOOD TO SOLITRON DEVICES

The fascinating yet disturbing aspect of financial manias, knowing what we know about social comparison processes, is that few lessons can be learned from the past. The same mistakes made in almost the same fashion inevitably crop up again and again.

Looking back at the bizarre speculative period of a decade ago, one might feel almost as though the clock had stopped at the height of the 1961 enthusiasm and only started ticking again in 1967. Investors resumed the previous speculation at an increasingly intensified pitch, with all memory of the previous crash seemingly erased. Remarkably an even larger new-issues boom commenced, and interest again focused on many of the now-familiar technology stocks of 1962—Xerox, Polaroid, Texas Instruments, and IBM.

This was the time when youth took over Wall Street. With youth came changes in the investment game: value was no longer to be found in the stodgy blue chips favored by their elders. The action now was with new issues, growth stocks, and concept stocks. A group of sideburned, flamboyantly dressed young men in their 20s and 30s came to the helm. They were the freewheeling, high-spirited embodiment of the times, who were determined to clear out the dogma, error, and cobwebs of the past. Called "gunslingers," the new breed were out to change the world with the sureness of their instincts and the quickness of their reactions. They believed that rapid moves in and out of stocks led to exceptional results. Often entire portfolios would be turned over two or three times a year. This new style of buying or selling was called "go-go" investing. The sole objective was "performance," which meant achieving higher returns than the market averages and competing gunslingers.

In the deadly competition that soon developed, all benchmarks of fiduciary responsibility were forgotten. Criticism that the new methods were highly speculative was tossed aside, in the words of one gunslinger, "as coming from the cultural alienation of an outdated generation."

On Wall Street a new tide of folk heroes moved in—Gerald Tsai, Fred Carr, Fred Mates, Fred Alger, and John Hartwell, to name a few. They were often treated with awe by the financial press and the public—at the time it seemed with good reason. Gerald Tsai, the initial go-go star, used rapid-fire trading to increase the Fidelity Growth Fund, which he managed, by 65 percent in 1965. Starting his own Manhattan Fund in 1967, he doubled the 20 percent rise in the averages. But Tsai's performance was dull when compared with many of the others. Fred Carr's Enterprise Fund rose 118 percent in that same year as he moved stocks in and out of his portfolio at a breathtaking rate. In one quarter, Enterprise traded 200 companies, more than some staid mutual funds turned over in a decade. In late 1968, the Mates Fund of Fred Mates was up a stunning 158 percent for the year.

Many of the new breed assiduously avoided the major industrial giants, "buggywhip companies," as they were sometimes contemptuously called. At the height of the go-go market in 1968, when numbers of concept companies had gone up 25- or even 50-fold, giant AT&T made an eight-year low. One money manager summed it up in *Forbes:* "Excitement, not solidity, is what makes stocks move now." Again, social reality took hold and investors frolicked away, unfettered by the time-tested standards of the past.

The gunslingers bristled with confidence. John Hartwell, who, in 1968, managed $425 million, ignored the prudent policy of wide diversification, stating: "If you have more than half a dozen positions in an account of, say, $500,000, it only means you are not sharp enough to pick winners."[18]

All eyes were focused on relative performance. The winners of the go-go derby would receive large flows of funds from the enthusiastic public, while the losers would have the money quickly taken away. In spite of its excellent record, Gerald Tsai's Manhattan Fund had net redemptions in 1968 as the public moved into better-performing vehicles, such as those of Fred Carr and Fred Mates. As one manager phrased it: "In this market, the crowd is betting on the jockeys, not the horses."

Outstanding fund managers could make a million dollars or more a year, and they lived high—gold faucets in bathrooms, 15-room penthouses on Park Avenue or in the Dakota, and sum-

---

[18] Gilbert Kaplan and Chris Welles, *The Money Managers* (New York: Random House, 1969).

mer homes on the Adriatic. Because of the public's obsession with them, performance rankings became the go-go manager's lifeblood. Fred Alger once flew to Europe to protest to Bernie Cornfeld, then running the vast International Overseas Fund network, that one month he was ranked number two rather than number one because of a typographical error. The mistake was immediately corrected.

Performance was achieved mainly by financial sleight of hand. Substantial gains were made by buying large blocks of thinly traded companies, pushing them higher. Legions of admirers usually followed in the wake of the go-go stars, making the price rise: a self-fulfilling prophecy for a while. Because of their tremendous ability to generate commissions, the major go-go managers would get large blocks of hot new stocks at the issue price, which immediately went to substantial premiums, generating instant profits on their books. The gunslingers would also buy letter stock—stock not authorized to be traded in public markets—at a substantial discount. The discount would often be two thirds or more of the going market price. The fund immediately revalued the stock at a one-third discount from the market, and—voilà—a 100 percent profit.

It is a tribute to the power of a speculative frenzy that, though these and many other practices were widely known and sometimes criticized at the time, very few people seemed to care how questionable the gains really were. Only the "bottom line" mattered—that the funds were performing well.

The rapid trading of huge blocks of stock made this the golden age of the brokerage firm. Many an institutional salesman, who could scarcely distinguish an asset from a liability, made six figures a year from his gunslinger clients, and most fully believed they deserved it. One fellow became a brief legend by leaving a $100 tip after a single round of drinks.

The gunslinger's mode of operation was simplicity itself. One merely had to have an exciting story and a record of rapid sales and earnings growth to substantiate it. Almost no attention was paid to how real the earnings actually were. And it was again the day of the black-box operation. Companies in technology were bid up to astronomical prices as investors envisioned futures of limitless growth. The chairman of one small technology company that had multiplied 10-fold in price told his annual meeting in 1968: "God has been good to Solitron Devices."

Money managers and clients alike became intoxicated by the gains. One investor, dazzled by the sensational promises of the go-go managers, went to his investment advisor, David Babson, a crusty old New Englander, and told him his objective was no less than 40 to 60 percent a year. For the previous 10 years, Babson had increased his client's money at a not unimpressive 10 percent rate, to $126,000. To illustrate the absurdity of his client's request, Babson showed him that a 40 percent rate of growth would have resulted in this sum becoming $100 million in 20 years, while a 60 percent rate of growth would have made it $1.5 billion!

For those of us playing at the time, and I had come to Wall Street a year or so earlier, it was indeed the golden age. Everywhere the atmosphere was giddy with success. Almost any investment we tried, be it computer service, uranium exploration, or flight safety instruments, worked out and many did spectacularly. With our stocks quadrupling, several going up 10-fold, and one over 50-fold, it was hard not to attribute the gains to our intelligence and surefootedness.

The longer the odds, the more sensational the payout. The favorites went up even more than the Mississippi Company over a similar period of time. With so much money being made so quickly, it was almost impossible not to be sucked into the speculative whirlpool, and not many resisted.

All around us, thousands of professionals wrote research reports condoning the current price movements and recommending a plethora of exciting new opportunities. As experiments have shown, the expert's support of a concept more firmly locks it into place. Very often people are persuaded by a message, not because of its compelling logic but because they consider the communicator an expert.[19] (Thus, the old adage of the singer, not the song.) Not only were the experts bullish, but their record of success in the immediate past was good, further enhancing their credibility. Once again, as in the 1920s, everybody talked stocks.

Some authorities became alarmed at the level of speculation. The American Stock Exchange, on which many of the smaller

---

[19] Those interested might see, for example, S. E. Asch, "The Doctrines of Suggestion, Prestige, and Social Psychology," *Psychological Review* 55 (1948), pp. 150–77; and C. I. Hovland, I. I. Janis, and H. H. Kelley, *Communication and Persuasion* (New Haven, Conn.: Yale University Press, 1953).

and more speculative companies traded, published a list in February 1969 of 109 speculative companies in which it forbade members to trade for their own accounts.[20] Former SEC chairman Manuel Cohen said at the time: "Frankly, I would have liked the AMEX to have applied the ban to all of its securities." However, most defended the reality of the moment. As one market expert wrote in a major financial magazine:

### NEW ENVIRONMENT

I would therefore like to propose the thesis that as the result of all that has been happening in the economy, the world, and the market during the last decade, we are at least in a different—if not a new—era and traditional thinking, the standard approach to the market, is no longer in synchronization with the real world.

Possibly the market ought to be considered as having gone into a sort of orbit in outer space, in the sense that while we can see how we got where we are, we really have never been here before, and therefore cannot be certain of what happens next.[21]

This seems to most clearly summarize the thinking of all investors in all manias. When the 1968 bubble finally burst, it was the most severe crash since 1929. Forty-seven billion dollars, or three times the amount lost on Black Tuesday, 1929, vanished in 30 high fliers alone. Most of the speculative favorites fared even more poorly. National Student Marketing dropped from 140 to 3½, Solitron Devices (whom the Lord apparently no longer favored) from 286 to 10¼, Parvan Dohrman from 142 to 14, and Four Seasons Nursing Homes from 110 to zero! Gone were the performance stocks, along with most of the high-living performance managers.

## NOT VERY DIFFERENT

All manias, though separated by centuries, have had surprisingly similar characteristics. They started in prosperous economies, where people were looking for new investment opportunities and wanted to believe they existed. Each mania had sound beginnings and was based on a simple but intriguing concept. The rise in prices, in every case, became a self-fulfilling prophecy, attracting more and more people into the speculative vortex. Rumor always played a major role, at first of fortunes made and of good things to come, and later in prophecies

---

[20] "Performance in Reverse?" *Forbes,* March 15, 1969.

[21] *Forbes,* October 15, 1968.

of doom. In almost every case, the experts were caught up in the speculation, condoning the price rises and predicting much higher levels in the future. At the height of both the 1961 and 1967–68 markets, money managers stated that the valuation standards of the past no longer applied—things really were different this time. And on both occasions, the statements were uttered shortly before the end.

Another point common to all speculative manias is the "greater fool" theory. Some of the more independent or cynical thinkers were not in fact overwhelmed by the consensus thinking of the time. They believed stocks should never have reached the preposterous levels that they had, the crowd really was mad. But they thought it would get madder still. (If a portfolio had gone up 6-fold, why not 8-fold, or even 10-fold?) There would thus be a chance to profit from the folly, which would only become more outrageous. Thus wrote British Member of Parliament James Milner in 1720 after being bankrupted by the South Sea bubble: "I said indeed that ruin must soon come upon us but I owe it came two months earlier than I expected."[22] Not very different was the *Dun's Review* article at the height of the 1968 market, 248 years later: "The overriding question at the moment is: how long can a speculative boom go on? How many months, investors and dealers ask, before we see a repeat of 1962?"[23] Even knowing this, most found it impossible to stop.

As speculation grew more widespread, it became the major topic of the day. In almost every period, credit was abundant and cheap. Near the end, prices rose sharply and turnover increased markedly. Finally, there was a sudden shift in the social reality, resulting in a panic that carried prices far below those initially prevailing. It's also interesting to see the similarity in the declines in each of the speculative manias. As Table 1 shows, all are on the order of 90 percent.

Four general principles seem to emerge from a study of financial speculations. First, an irresistible image of instant wealth is always presented that draws a financial crowd into existence. Second, a social reality is created that blinds most people to the dangers of the mania. Opinions converge and become "facts." Experts become leaders approving events and strongly exhort-

---

[22] Virginia Cowles, *South Sea: The Great Swindle* (London: Crowley Feature, 1960).
[23] *Dun's Review*, August 1968, p. 36.

---

**TABLE 1**   Market favorites from different eras

---

| | High price | Low price | Price decline from high (percent) |
|---|---|---|---|
| Holland, 1637 | | | |
| Semper Augustis (tulip bulb). . . . . | 5,500* | 50* | 99% |
| England, 1720 | | | |
| South Sea Company. . . . . . . . | 1,050† | 129† | 88 |
| France, 1720 | | | |
| Mississippi Company . . . . . . . | 18,000‡ | 200‡ | 99 |
| 1929–32 | | | |
| Air Reduction . . . . . . . . . . . | 233 | 31 | 86 |
| Burroughs . . . . . . . . . . . . | 97 | 6¼ | 94 |
| Case . . . . . . . . . . . . . . . | 467 | 17 | 96 |
| General Electric. . . . . . . . . . | 201 | 8½ | 96 |
| General Motors . . . . . . . . . . | 115 | 7⅝ | 94 |
| Montgomery Ward. . . . . . . . | 158 | 3½ | 98 |
| 1961–62 | | | |
| AMF . . . . . . . . . . . . . . | 66⅜ | 10 | 84 |
| Automatic Canteen . . . . . . . . | 45⅝ | 9¾ | 79 |
| Brunswick . . . . . . . . . . . . | 74⅞ | 13⅛ | 82 |
| Lionel . . . . . . . . . . . . . | 37⅞ | 4½ | 88 |
| Texas Instruments. . . . . . . . . | 207 | 49 | 76 |
| Transition. . . . . . . . . . . . | 42⅜ | 6¼ | 85 |
| 1967–70 | | | |
| ITEK . . . . . . . . . . . . . . | 172 | 17 | 90 |
| Leasco Data Processing . . . . . . | 57 | 7 | 88 |
| Ling-Temco-Vought . . . . . . . . | 135 | 7 | 95 |
| Litton Industries. . . . . . . . . | 104 | 15 | 86 |
| National Student Marketing . . . . . | 143 | 3½ | 98 |
| University Computing . . . . . . . | 186 | 13 | 93 |
| 1971–72 | | | |
| Avon . . . . . . . . . . . . . . | 140 | 18⅝ | 87 |
| Clorox . . . . . . . . . . . . . | 53 | 5½ | 90 |
| Disney . . . . . . . . . . . . . | 119⅛ | 16⅝ | 86 |
| Levitz Furniture . . . . . . . . . . | 40¼ | 3⅞ | 90 |
| MGIC. . . . . . . . . . . . . . | 97⅞ | 6⅛ | 94 |
| Polaroid . . . . . . . . . . . . | 149½ | 14⅛ | 91 |

---

* Florins.
† Pounds sterling.
‡ Livres.

ing the crowd on. Overconfidence becomes dominant, and standards of conduct and the experience of many years are quickly forgotten. Third, the LeBon image of the magic lantern suddenly changes and anxiety replaces overconfidence. The distended bubble breaks with an ensuing panic. And fourth, we do not, as investors, learn from past mistakes—things really do seem very different each time, although in fact each set of circumstances was remarkably similar to the last.

As we have seen, even though the investors of the 1960s and 1970s were armed with exacting fundamental tools, these did not save them from behaving in a fashion almost identical to the frenzied English and French of centuries earlier.

# THREE

## Federal income tax considerations for individual investors

**Frank J. Fabozzi, Ph.D., C.F.A., C.P.A.**
*Walter E. Hanson/Peat, Marwick, Mitchell*
  *Professor of Business and Finance*
*Lafayette College*
*and*
*Managing Editor*
*The Journal of Portfolio Management*

The purpose of this chapter is to explain the provisions of the Internal Revenue Code that the investor should be cognizant of in order to make intelligent investment decisions.

### SOME DEFINITIONS

**Gross income, adjusted gross income, and taxable income**

Investors often use the term *income* in a very casual way. The Internal Revenue Code (IRC), however, provides a more precise definition of income. The IRC distinguishes between gross income, adjusted gross income, and taxable income. *Gross income* is all income that is subject to income tax. For example, interest income and dividends are subject to taxation. However, there is a statutory exemption for interest from certain types of debt obligations, as explained later in this article. For such obligations, interest income is not included in gross income.

*Adjusted gross income* is gross income minus certain business and other deductions. For example, for investors an important deduction from gross income to arrive at adjusted gross income is the long-term capital gain deduction. This deduction will be discussed later.

*Taxable income* is the amount on which the tax liability is determined. It is found by subtracting the personal exemption allowance and other permissible deductions (other than those deductible in arriving at adjusted gross income) from adjusted gross income.

### Tax basis of a capital asset, capital gain, and capital loss

The IRC provides for a special tax treatment on the sale or exchange of a capital asset. Common stock, debt obligations, preferred stock, and shares of investment companies would qualify as capital assets in the hands of a qualified owner. In order to understand the tax treatment of a capital asset, the tax *basis* of a capital asset must first be defined. In most instances the *original basis* of a capital asset is the taxpayer's total cost on the date it is acquired. The *adjusted basis* of a capital asset is its original basis increased by capital additions and decreased by capital recoveries.

The proceeds received from the sale or exchange of a capital asset are compared to the adjusted basis to determine if the transaction produced a capital gain or capital loss. If the proceeds exceed the adjusted basis, the taxpayer realized a *capital gain;* on the other hand, a *capital loss* is realized when the adjusted basis exceeds the proceeds received by the taxpayer.

### INTEREST INCOME

Interest received by a taxpayer is included in gross income, unless there is a specific statutory exemption indicating otherwise. Therefore, if a taxpayer purchases $10,000 in face value of a corporate bond that has a coupon rate of 12 percent, the taxpayer expects to receive $1,200 per year. If that amount is actually paid by the issuer in the tax year, it is included in gross income.

Interest received on debt issued by any state or political subdivisions thereof, the District of Columbia, any possession of the United States, and certain local and urban agencies operating under the auspices of the Department of Housing and Urban Development is not included in gross income.

Interest paid on debt issued by the U.S. government is exempt from income taxation by state and local governments but not from federal income taxes. Interest income by U.S. territories, the District of Columbia, and certain local urban agencies operating under HUD is also exempt from all state and local income taxes. Most states exempt the interest income from its own debt obligations, its agencies, and its political subdivisions from its state and local income taxes. States may exempt the interest income from obligations of other states and political subdivisions. State income tax treatment is discussed further in Article Fourteen.

A portion of the income realized from holding a debt obligation may be in the form of capital appreciation, rather than interest income. The tax treatment of the income component that represents capital appreciation differs depending on when the bond was issued. Prior to the The Deficit Reduction Act of 1984, any capital appreciation that did not represent original-issue discount (to be discussed later) was generally treated as a capital gain.[1] As explained later in this article, the IRC provides for favorable tax treatment for certain capital gains. The 1984 act still allows this tax treatment for bonds issued on or prior to July 18, 1984; however, for bonds issued after that date, part of the capital appreciation will be treated as ordinary income. The tax treatment of income from holding a debt instrument will have a major impact on the aftertax return realized by an investor. Because of the importance of distinguishing between income in the form of a capital gain (or loss) and interest income, the investor must be familiar with certain rules set forth in the IRC. These rules are summarized below.

### Accrued interest

Usually, bond interest is paid semiannually. The interest earned by the seller from holding the bond until the disposal date is called *accrued interest*. For example, if a corporate bond whose issuer promises to pay $60 on June 1 and December 1 for a specified number of years is sold on October 1, the seller is usually entitled to accrued interest of $40 ($60 times 4/6) for the four months that the seller held the bond.

---

[1] This is not for original-issue discount obligations of individuals.

Let us look at the tax position of the seller and the buyer, assuming that our hypothetical bond is selling for $900 in the market and that the seller's adjusted basis for this bond is $870. The buyer must pay the seller $940, $900 for the market price plus $40 of accrued interest. The seller must treat the accrued interest of $40 as interest income. The $900 is compared to the seller's adjusted basis of $870 to determine whether the seller has realized a capital gain or capital loss. Obviously, the seller has realized a capital gain of $30. When the buyer receives the December 1 interest payment of $60, only $20 is included in gross income as interest income. The basis of the bond for the buyer is $900, not $940.

Not all transactions involving bonds require the payment of accrued interest by the buyer. This occurs when the issuer of the bond is in default of principal or interest or the interest on the bonds are contingent on sufficient earnings of the issuer.[2] Such bonds are said to be quoted *flat*. The acquisition price entitles the buyer to receive the principal and unpaid interest for both past scheduled payments due and accrued interest. Generally, for bonds quoted flat, all payments made by the issuer to the buyer are first considered as payments to satisfy defaulted payments or unpaid contingent interest payments and accrued interest before acquisition. Such payments are treated as a return of capital. As such, the proceeds reduce the cost basis of the bond. On the other hand, accrued interest after the acquisition date is considered interest income when received.

For example, suppose the issuer of a corporate bond is in default of two scheduled interest payments of $60 each. The interest payments are scheduled on April 1 and October 1. The bond is sold for $500 on August 1. Assume that on October 1 of the year of acquisition the issuer pays the bondholder $120. The buyer would treat the payment as a return of capital of $120, since it represents the two defaulted interest payments. Hence the adjusted basis of the bond is $380 ($500 minus $120) and is not considered interest income. Suppose that two weeks later the issuer pays an additional $60 to the bondholder. This payment must then be apportioned between accrued interest before the acquisition date of August 1 and accrued interest

---

[2] A bond whose interest is contingent upon sufficient earnings by the issuer is called an *income bond*.

after the acquisition date. The latter is $20, since the bond was held by the buyer for two months. Thus $40 of the $60 payment reduces the adjusted basis of $380 prior to the second payment to $340 and is not treated as interest income. The $20 of accrued interest since the acquisition date is treated as interest income.

### Bond purchased at a premium

When a bond is purchased at a price greater than its redemption value at maturity, the bond is said to be purchased at a premium.[3] For a taxable bond purchased by a nondealer taxpayer, the taxpayer may elect to amortize the premium ratably over the remaining life of the security. In the case of a convertible bond selling at a premium, however, the amount attributable to the conversion feature may not be amortized. The amount amortized reduces the amount of the interest income that will be taxed. In turn, the basis is reduced by the amount of the amortization.

For a tax-exempt bond, the premium *must* be amortized. Although the amount amortized is not a tax-deductible expense since the interest is exempt from taxation, the amortization reduces the original basis.

For example, suppose on January 1, 1981, a calendar-year taxpayer purchased *taxable* bonds for $10,500. The bonds have a remaining life of 10 years and a $10,000 redemption value at maturity. The coupon rate is 7 percent. The premium is $500. The taxpayer can amortize this premium over the 10-year remaining life. If so, the amount amortized would be $50 per year ($500 divided by 10).[4] The coupon interest received of $700 ($10,000 times .07) would then be effectively reduced by $50 so that $650 would be reported as interest income. At the end of 1981, the first year, the original basis of $10,500 is reduced by $50 to $10,450. By the end of 1985 the bond would be held for five years. The adjusted basis would be $10,250 ($10,500 minus $250). If the bond is held until retired by the issuer at maturity,

---

[3] A bond will sell at a premium so that the effective interest rate of the bond is adjusted to reflect the prevailing interest rate on securities of comparable risk and remaining maturity.

[4] There is a method that provides the precise value of the amount that should be amortized each year. This is known as the constant-yield (or scientific) method. However, this method provides lower amortization in the earlier years than the straight-line method of amortization used in the example. Consequently, the straight-line method is preferred for taxable bonds if the taxpayer elects to amortize the premium.

the adjusted basis would be $10,000, and consequently there would be no capital gain or loss realized. If the taxpayer does not elect to amortize the premium, the original basis is not changed. Consequently, at maturity the taxpayer would realize a capital loss of $500.

Had our hypothetical bond been a tax-exempt bond, the premium would have had to be amortized. The coupon interest of $700 would be tax exempt, and the amortization of $50 would not be a tax-deductible expense.[5] Instead, the basis would be adjusted each year.

As an illustration of the amortization for a bond purchased some time during the tax year rather than at the beginning of the tax year, let's take an actual case. In April 1981 Albany County South Mall 10s maturing 4/1/85 sold for approximately $270,285. The redemption value at maturity per bond was $250,000. Suppose that a calendar-year taxpayer purchased the bond on April 1, 1981. The premium was $20,285 ($270,285 minus $250,000).

The number of months remaining to maturity was 48 (four years times 12 months). Consequently, the monthly amortization was $422.60. At the end of 1981 the original basis of $270,285 was reduced by the amortization corresponding to the number of months the bond was held for in 1981. Since the bond was held for nine months (April 1 to December 31), the original basis was reduced by $3,803.40 ($422.60 times nine months). Hence, the adjusted basis was $266,481.60 ($270,285 minus $3,803.40) at the end of 1981.

Suppose the bond was sold on October 31, 1982, and the taxpayer received $260,000. To determine whether there was a capital gain or loss, the adjusted basis must be ascertained. Since the bond was held for 19 months, amortization was $8,029.40 ($422.60 times 19 months) and the adjusted basis was $262,255.60 ($270,285 minus $8,029.40). Hence the taxpayer would realize a capital loss of $2,255.60, the difference between the adjusted basis of $262,255.60 and the proceeds received of $260,000.

So far in our illustration we have used the original basis and the remaining number of years to maturity to determine the

---

[5] In the case of tax-exempt bonds, the scientific method of amortization would be preferred, since the adjusted basis would be higher than if the straight-line method were used. Consequently there would be a greater capital loss or smaller capital gain if the bonds were sold before maturity.

amount to be amortized. In the case of a callable taxable bond acquired after January 1, 1957, the taxpayer must elect to compute the amortization based upon the earlier call date *if a smaller deduction results compared to using the number of years remaining to maturity.* For example, suppose an investor purchased a bond that has 10 years remaining to maturity for $1,300. The redemption value at maturity is $1,000; however, the bond may be called in six years for $1,150. If the bond is a taxable bond, then the first election the investor must make is whether or not to amortize the premium. If the investor elects to amortize the premium, then the investor must elect to base the amount of the amortization on the call price and date rather than on the redemption value at maturity if the deduction is less. If the amount amortized is based on the redemption value at maturity, then the annual amount deducted would be $30, since the premium is $300 and there are 10 years remaining to maturity. If the earlier call date is used, the amount of the premium is $150. The annual deduction is $25 per year, since there are six years to the call date.

### Bond purchased at a discount

A bond purchased at a price less than its redemption value at maturity is said to be bought at a *discount.* The tax treatment of the discount depends upon whether the discount represents *original-issue discount* or a bond that was not sold at an original-issue discount but is purchased in the secondary market at a market discount.

**Original-issue discount bonds.** When bonds are issued, they may be sold at a price that is less than their redemption value at maturity. Such bonds are called original-issue discount bonds. The difference between the redemption value and the purchase price is the original-issue discount. Each year a portion of the original-issue discount must be amortized (accrued) and included in gross income. There is a corresponding increase in the adjusted basis of the bond.

The tax treatment of an original-issue discount bond depends on its issuance date. For obligations issued prior to July 2, 1982, the original-issue discount must be amortized on a straight-line basis each month and included in gross income based on the number of months the bond is held in that tax year. For obligations issued on or after July 2, 1982, the amount of the original-issue discount amortized is based on the constant-yield method (also called the effective or scientific method) and included in gross income based on the number of days in the tax year that the bond is held. With this method for determining the amount of the original-issue discount to be included in gross income, the interest for the year is first determined by multiplying the adjusted basis by the yield at issuance. From this interest, the coupon interest is subtracted. The difference is the amount of the original-issue discount amortized for the year. The same amount is then added to the adjusted basis.

To illustrate the tax rules for original-issue discount bonds, consider a bond with a 4 percent coupon rate (interest paid semiannually) maturing in five years that was issued for $7,683 and has a redemption value of $10,000. The yield to maturity for this hypothetical bond is 10 percent. The original-issue discount is $2,317 ($10,000 − $7,683). Suppose that the bond was purchased by an investor on the day it was issued, January 1, 198X. First, assume that this hypothetical bond was issued prior to July 2, 1982. The investor is required to amortize the original-issue discount of $2,317 on a straight-line monthly basis. Since there are 60 months to maturity, the prorated monthly interest on a straight-line basis is $38.62 ($2,317÷ by 60). Since the hypothetical bond is assumed to be purchased on January 1, the annual interest that must be reported from the amortization of the original-issue discount *each year* is $464 ($38.62 × 12). The total interest reported each year from holding this bond is $464 plus the coupon interest of $400 ($10,000 × .04). Exhibit 1 shows the amortization of the original-issue discount for each six-month period. Notice that, if the bond is held to maturity, there is no capital gain or loss since the adjusted basis will equal the redemption value of $10,000. If the bond is held for two years and six months, in the third year the investor reports $232 ($38.62 × 6) of interest income from amortization of the original-issue discount. The adjusted basis is $8,844. If the proceeds from the sale of the bond exceed $8,844, the investor realizes a capital gain. A capital loss is realized if the proceeds from the sale are less than $8,844.

Suppose instead that the bond was issued after July 2, 1982. The constant-yield method is used to determine the amortization and the adjusted basis. The procedure is as follows. Each

**EXHIBIT 1**   Amortization schedule for an original-discount bond issued prior to July 2, 1982

Characteristics of hypothetical bond:
| | |
|---|---|
| Coupon | = 4 percent |
| Interest payments | = semiannual |
| Issue price | = $7,683 |
| Redemption value | = $10,000 |
| Years to maturity | = 5 |
| Yield to maturity | = 10 percent |

| | |
|---|---|
| Original-issue discount | = $2,317 |
| Monthly amortized market discount (straight-line method) | = $38.62 |
| Six-month amortized market discount | = $232 |
| Basis at time of purchase | = $7,683 |

| Period held (years) | Adjusted basis* | For the period | | |
| | | Gross income reported | Coupon interest | Original-issue discount amortized |
|---|---|---|---|---|
| 0.5 . . . . . . . | $ 7,916 | $432 | $200 | $232 |
| 1.0 . . . . . . . | 8,148 | 432 | 200 | 232 |
| 1.5 . . . . . . . | 8,380 | 432 | 200 | 232 |
| 2.0 . . . . . . . | 8,612 | 432 | 200 | 232 |
| 2.5 . . . . . . . | 8,844 | 432 | 200 | 232 |
| 3.0 . . . . . . . | 9,076 | 432 | 200 | 232 |
| 3.5 . . . . . . . | 9,308 | 432 | 200 | 232 |
| 4.0 . . . . . . . | 9,540 | 432 | 200 | 232 |
| 4.5 . . . . . . . | 9,772 | 432 | 200 | 232 |
| 5.0 . . . . . . . | 10,000 | 432 | 200 | 232 |

* Adjusted basis at the end of the period. The adjusted basis is found by adding $232 to the previous period's adjusted basis.

six months, the investor of this hypothetical bond is assumed to realize for tax purposes 5 percent of the adjusted basis. The 5 percent represents one half of the 10 percent yield to maturity. The original investment is the purchase price of $7,683. In the first six months the bond is held, the investor realizes for tax purposes 5 percent of $7,683, or $384. The coupon payment for the first six-month period that the bond is held is $200. Therefore, $184 ($384 − $200) is assumed to be realized (although not received) by the investor. This is the amount of the original-issue discount amortized. The amount that will be reported as gross income from holding this bond for six months is $200 in coupon interest plus the $184 of the original-issue discount amortized. The adjusted basis for the bond at the end of the first six months will equal the original-issue price of $7,683 plus the amount of the original-issue discount amortized, $184. Thus, the adjusted basis is $7,867.

Let's carry this out for one more six-month period. If the bond is held for another six months, the amount of interest that the investor is expected to realize for tax purposes is 5 percent of the adjusted basis. Since the adjusted basis at the beginning of the second six-month period is $7,867, the interest is $393. The coupon interest for the second six months is $200. Therefore, the amount of the original-issue discount amortized for the second six-month period is $193 ($393 − $200). The $393 reported for holding the bond for the second six months is $200 in coupon interest and $193 in amortization of the original-issue discount. The adjusted basis at the end of the second six-month period is $8,060—the previous adjusted basis of $7,867 plus $193. If this bond, which was assumed to be purchased on January 1, 198X, is sold on December 31, 198X, interest income would be $777, consisting of $400 of coupon interest and $377 of the original-issue discount amortized. If this bond is sold on December 31, 198X, for $8,200, there would be a capital gain of $140, the difference between the sale proceeds of $8,200 and the adjusted basis of $8,060.

Exhibit 2 shows the amount of the original-issue discount that must be reported as gross income for each six month period that the bond is held and the adjusted basis at the end of the period. Notice that amortization is lower in the earlier years, gradually increasing over the life of the bond on a compounding basis. For the pre-July 2, 1982, rules, the dollar amortization is constant each year. Note also that, if a bond is sold after 2.5 years, the adjusted basis is $8,700 using the constant-yield method but $8,844 (see Exhibit 1) using the straight-line method. The constant-yield method results in a greater capital gain.

The 1984 act requires the holders of original-issue discount tax-exempt bonds to amortize the original-issue discount using the constant-yield method. However, the amount of the original-issued discount amortized is not included as part of gross income because all interest is exempt from federal income taxes. The amount of the original-issue discount is added to the adjusted basis.

The original-issue discount rules do not apply in two cases. The first is the case of Series EE and E savings bonds. The

**EXHIBIT 2**    Amortization schedule for an original-discount bond issued after July 2, 1982

Characteristics of hypothetical bond:
Coupon            = 4 percent
Interest payments = semiannual
Issue price       = $7,683
Redemption value  = $10,000
Years to maturity = 5
Yield to maturity = 10 percent
Original-issue discount   = $2,317
Basis at time of purchase = $7,683
Amortization based on constant-yield method

| Period held (years) | Adjusted basis* | For the period | | |
|---|---|---|---|---|
| | | Gross income reported† | Coupon interest | Original-issue discount amortized‡ |
| 0.5 . . . . . . | $ 7,867 | $384 | $200 | $184 |
| 1.0 . . . . . . | 8,060 | 393 | 200 | 193 |
| 1.5 . . . . . . | 8,263 | 403 | 200 | 203 |
| 2.0 . . . . . . | 8,476 | 413 | 200 | 213 |
| 2.5 . . . . . . | 8,700 | 424 | 200 | 224 |
| 3.0 . . . . . . | 8,935 | 435 | 200 | 235 |
| 3.5 . . . . . . | 9,182 | 447 | 200 | 247 |
| 4.0 . . . . . . | 9,441 | 459 | 200 | 259 |
| 4.5 . . . . . . | 9,713 | 472 | 200 | 272 |
| 5.0 . . . . . . | 10,000 | 486 | 200 | 286 |

* Adjusted basis at the end of the period. The adjusted basis is found by adding the original-issued discount amortized for the period to the previous period's adjusted basis.
† The gross income reported is equal to the coupon interest for the period plus the original-issue discount amortized for the period.
‡ By the constant yield method, it is found as follows:

(Adjusted basis in previous period × .05) − $200

holders of these bonds may elect to have the original-issue discount on these bonds taxed when the bonds are redeemed rather than having the accrued interest taxed annually. The second exception is for noninterest-bearing obligations such as Treasury bills and many other taxable short-term obligations with no more than one year to maturity. When these obligations are held by investors who report for tax purposes on a *cash* rather than an accrual basis, the discount is not recognized until redeemed or sold. However, there are restrictions on the deductibility of interest to carry such obligations, as explained later in this article.

There are three more points the investor should be familiar

with when dealing with original-issue discount bonds. First, original-issue discount is treated as zero if the discount is less than one fourth of 1 percent of the redemption value at maturity multiplied by the number of complete years to maturity. For example, suppose a bond maturing in 20 years is initially sold for $990 for each $1,000 of redemption value at maturity. The discount is $10. The redemption value multiplied by the number of years to maturity is $20,000. The original-issue discount is .0005 of $20,000. Since it is less than one fourth of 1 percent (.0025), the original-issue discount is treated as zero; that is, the investor does not have to amortize the discount and report it as gross income. Instead, the rule discussed in the next section is applicable. Second, if an original-issue discount bond is sold before maturity, subsequent holders must continue to amortize the original-issue discount. The third point to keep in mind is that an investor may have to pay taxes on interest included in gross income but not received in cash. *Consequently, original-issue discount obligations are unattractive for portfolios of individual investors subject to taxation.*

**Bond purchased at a market discount with no original-issue discount.** When a bond is purchased at a market discount and there is no original-issue discount, the tax treatment depends on whether the bond was issued on or prior to July 18, 1984, or after. For bonds issued before that date, any capital appreciation is treated as a capital gain. If there is a loss, it is a capital loss. For example, suppose that the hypothetical bond used to illustrate the original-issue discount rules is not an original-issue discount bond. Instead, suppose that the bond was issued 25 years ago at par ($10,000) and 20 years later the price of the bond declined to $7,683 because of a rise in interest rates. If this bond is purchased by an investor for $7,683 and sold 2.5 years later for $9,000, the investor will realize a capital gain of $1,317. As discussed later, this capital gain would be treated as a long-term capital gain and afforded preferential tax treatment. No amortization of the discount is required even though a portion of the capital appreciation really represents a form of interest.

The 1984 act changed the tax treatment for *taxable* bonds issued after July 18, 1984. Any capital appreciation must be separated into a portion that is attributable to interest income (as represented by bond amortization) and a portion that is attributable to capital gain. The portion representing interest income is taxed as ordinary income when the bond is sold. This is called accrued market discount. Unlike original-issue discount, the amount of the market discount that represents interest income (that is, bond amortization) is not taxed until the bond is sold. Accrued market discount can be determined using either the straight-line method or the constant-yield method.

Exhibit 3 shows the tax consequences for five assumed selling prices for the hypothetical bond that has been used in the examples above. The results are shown for bonds issued before and after July 18, 1984. The results are also shown for the constant-yield and straight-line methods.

Two implications are evident from Exhibit 3. First, from a tax perspective, taxable bonds issued before July 18, 1984, and selling at a discount will be more attractive than bonds issued after that date and selling at a discount. This will be reflected in the market price of those bonds. Consequently, investors that are in low marginal tax rates will find that they may be overpaying for bonds issued before July 18, 1984. The second implication is that it is not in the best interest of the investor to select the straight-line method to compute the accrued market discount because the capital gain will be lower than if the constant-yield method is elected.

Because of the difference in the tax treatment of original-issue discount bonds and market discount bonds, prior to purchase the investor should check the type of bond and when it was issued.

## DIVIDENDS

Corporations make cash distributions to shareholders. Not all cash distributions, however, are taxed. For individual taxpayers, only that portion of the distribution representing dividends is included in gross income, subject to a $100 dividend exclusion for a single return and $200 for a joint return.

A *dividend* is defined as a payment made by a corporation out of earnings and profits in the year of distribution or earnings and profits accumulated in all years prior to the date of distribution. Dividend income is taxed as ordinary income. Any portion of a distribution that does not represent a dividend or a redemp-

**EXHIBIT 3**    Tax treatment of market discount bond for five assumed selling prices

Characteristics of hypothetical bond:
| | |
|---|---|
| Coupon | = 4 percent |
| Interest payments | = semiannual |
| Bond price | = $7,683 |
| Redemption value | = $10,000 |
| Years to maturity | = 5 |
| Yield to maturity | = 10 percent |
| Market discount | = $2,317 |
| Basis at time of purchase | = $7,683 |

Bond sold after 2.5 years

**Bond issued before July 18, 1984**

| Sale price | Accrued market discount | Capital gain (loss) |
|---|---|---|
| $9,500 | $ 0 | $1,817 |
| 9,000 | 0 | 1,317 |
| 8,700 | 0 | 1,017 |
| 7,683 | 0 | 0 |
| 7,000 | 0 | (683) |

**Bond issued after July 18, 1984, with amortization based on constant-yield method**

| Sale price | Accrued market discount | Capital gain (loss) |
|---|---|---|
| $9,500 | $1,017 | $ 800 |
| 9,000 | 1,017 | 300 |
| 8,700 | 1,017 | 0 |
| 7,683 | 1,017 | (1,017) |
| 7,000 | 1,017 | (1,700) |

**Bond issued after July 18, 1984, with amortization based on straight-line method**

| Sale price | Accrued market discount | Capital gain (loss) |
|---|---|---|
| $9,500 | $1,161 | $ 656 |
| 9,000 | 1,161 | 156 |
| 8,700 | 1,161 | (144) |
| 7,683 | 1,161 | (1,161) |
| 7,000 | 1,161 | (1,844) |

tion of stock is treated as a return of capital. No tax is paid on that portion; instead, the basis of the stock is reduced by that amount.[6]

Dividends are also paid by regulated investment companies, such as a mutual fund. Investment companies sell their own securities to the public and reinvest the proceeds in a large number of securities. The shareholder of an investment company participates in the return generated from holding and transactions involving these securities. The return earned by the investment company can therefore be in the form of interest, dividends, or capital gains. However, the dividend from an investment company to its shareholders is designated by the investment company in a written notice to its shareholders not later than 45 days after the close of the taxable year as either ordinary dividends or capital gains. Ordinary dividends are treated in the same way as cash dividends from common stock. However, any portion of the dividend that represents tax-exempt income realized by the investment company is under certain conditions tax-exempt to the shareholder. The amount classified as a capital gain is considered a long-term capital gain and treated accordingly as explained later in this article.

Not all of the long-term capital gain realized by the investment company is actually paid in cash to the shareholders. In that case, the investment company will pay the income tax on that portion retained. The shareholder, however, is deemed to have paid the tax on the undistributed capital gain, which can be refunded or credited to the shareholder. Moreover, the shareholder increases the basis of the share of the investment company by an amount equal to the excess of the long-term capital gains over the capital gains tax included in the shareholder's total long-term capital gains.

## CAPITAL GAIN AND LOSS TREATMENT

Once a capital gain or capital loss is determined for a capital asset, there are special rules for determining the impact on adjusted gross income. The tax treatment for individuals is explained in this section.

---

[6] If the distribution that is not a dividend exceeds the adjusted basis, it is treated as a capital gain.

## Capital gain and loss treatment for individuals

To determine the impact of transactions involving capital assets on adjusted gross income, it is first necessary to ascertain whether the sale or exchange has resulted in a capital gain or loss that is long term or short term. The classification depends on the length of time the capital asset is held by the taxpayer. For capital assets acquired after June 22, 1984, the general rule is that if a capital asset is held for six months or less, the gain or loss is a short-term capital gain or loss.[7] A long-term capital gain or loss results when the capital asset is held for one day more than six months, or longer. For capital assets acquired before June 22, 1984, the holding period for a long-term capital gain is one day more than one year.

Second, all short-term capital gains and losses are combined to produce either a *net short-term capital gain* or a *net short-term capital loss*. The same procedure is followed for long-term capital gains and losses. Either a *net long-term capital gain* or a *net long-term capital loss* will result.

Third, an overall *net capital gain* or *net capital loss* is determined by combining the amounts in the previous step. If the result is a net capital gain, the entire amount is added to gross income. However, net long-term capital gains are given preferential tax treatment. A deduction is allowed from gross income in determining adjusted gross income. The permissible deduction is 60 percent of the excess of net long-term capital gains over net short-term capital losses.[8] Exhibit 4 provides six illustrations of the treatment of a net capital gain.

If there is a net capital loss, it is deductible from gross income. The amount that may be deducted, however, is limited to the lesser of (1) $3,000 (but $1,500 for married taxpayers filing separate returns), (2) taxable income without the personal exemption and without capital gains and losses minus the zero bracket amount, and (3) the total of net short-term capital loss plus half the net long-term capital loss. The third limitation is

---

[7] An exception to this general rule applies to wash sales. A wash sale occurs when "substantially identical securities" are acquired within 30 days before or after a sale of the securities *at a loss*. In such cases, the loss is not recognized as a capital loss. Instead, the loss is added to the basis of the securities that caused the loss. The holding period for the new securities in connection with a wash sale then includes the period for which the original securities were held.

[8] A capital gain deduction taken by an individual could result in a minimum tax liability.

**EXHIBIT 4**   Tax treatment of a net capital gain

| | | | *Illustration number* | | | |
|---|---|---|---|---|---|---|
| | *(1)* | *(2)* | *(3)* | *(4)* | *(5)* | *(6)* |
| 1. Net long-term capital gain (loss). | $35,000 | $35,000 | $35,000 | $ 0 | ($ 3,000) | ($ 8,000) |
| 2. Net short-term capital gain (loss). | (15,000) | 15,000 | 0 | 15,000 | 15,000 | 15,000 |
| 3. Net capital gain: increase in gross income. | 20,000 | 50,000 | 35,000 | 15,000 | 12,000 | 7,000 |
| 4. Excess of net long-term capital gain over net short-term capital loss. | 20,000 | 35,000 | 35,000 | 0 | 0 | 0 |
| 5. Capital gains deduction (60 percent of line 4). | (12,000) | (21,000) | (21,000) | 0 | 0 | 0 |
| 6. Increase in adjusted gross income (line 3 minus line 5). | 8,000 | 29,000 | 14,000 | 15,000 | 12,000 | 7,000 |

# EXHIBIT 5   Tax treatment of a net capital loss

|  | | Illustration number | | | | | | | | |
| --- | --- | --- | --- | --- | --- | --- | --- | --- | --- | --- |
|  | (1) | (2) | (3) | (4) | (5) | (6) | (7) | (8) | (9) | (10) |
| 1. Net long-term capital gain (loss) | $ 0 | ($7,000) | ($ 7,000) | ($7,000) | ($3,000) | ($4,000) | $6,000 | ($4,000) | ($12,000) | $ 4,000 |
| 2. Net short-term capital gain (loss) | (5,000) | 0 | (5,000) | (2,000) | (1,000) | 0 | (7,000) | 1,000 | 2,000 | (14,000) |
| 3. Net capital loss | 5,000 | 7,000 | 12,000 | 9,000 | 4,000 | 4,000 | 1,000 | 3,000 | 10,000 | 10,000 |
| 4. Capital loss deduction* | 3,000 | 3,000 | 3,000 | 3,000 | 2,500 | 2,000 | 1,000 | 1,500 | 3,000 | 3,000 |
| 5. Long-term capital loss carryover | 0 | 1,000 | 7,000 | 5,000 | 0 | 0 | 0 | 0 | 4,000 | 0 |
| 6. Short-term capital loss carryover | 2,000 | 0 | 2,000 | 0 | 0 | 0 | 0 | 0 | 0 | 7,000 |

* Assumes that the taxpayer (1) is not married or if married is not filing a separate return and (2) has taxable income without the personal exemption and without capital gains and losses minus the zero bracket amount greater than $3,000.

the so-called $1 for $2 rule and is the basic difference between the tax treatment of net short-term capital losses and net long-term capital losses. The former is deductible dollar for dollar, but the latter requires $2 of long-term capital loss to obtain a $1 deduction.

Because of the difference in the tax treatment of net long-term capital losses and net short-term capital losses, the order in which these losses are deductible in a tax year are specified by the Treasury. First, net short-term capital losses are used to satisfy the limitation. Any balance to satisfy the limitation is then applied from net long-term capital losses using the $1 for $2 rule. Any unused net short-term or net long-term capital losses are carried over on a dollar-for-dollar basis.[9] When they are carried over, they do not lose their identity but remain either short term or long term. These losses can be carried over indefinitely until they are all utilized in subsequent tax years.

Exhibit 5 provides 10 illustrations of the net capital loss deduction rule. In the illustrations it is assumed that taxable income as defined in (2) above is greater than $3,000, and the taxpayer, if married, is not filing a separate return.

## DEDUCTIBILITY OF INTEREST EXPENSE INCURRED TO ACQUIRE OR CARRY SECURITIES

Some investment strategies involve the borrowing of funds to purchase or carry securities. Although interest expense on borrowed funds is a tax-deductible expense, the investor should be aware of the following three rules relating to the deductibility of interest expense to acquire or carry securities.

First, there are limits on the amount of current interest paid or accrued on debt to purchase or carry a market discount bond. It is limited by the amount of any income from the bond. Any interest expenses that remain can be deducted in the current year only to the extent that they exceed the amortized portion of the market discount. The amount of the interest expense that is disallowed can be deducted either (1) in future years if there is net interest income and an election is made or (2) when the bond is sold.

To illustrate this limitation, suppose that interest expense incurred to carry a market discount bond is $500 for the current

---

[9] However, in determining the amount of the net capital loss deduction in a future tax year, the $1 for $2 rule applies.

year, the coupon interest from that bond is $200, and the amortized portion of the market discount is $140. The investor is entitled to deduct $200 (the amount of the coupon interest). In addition, since the remaining interest expense of $300 ($500 − $200) exceeds the amortized portion of the market discount of $140 by $160, an additional $160 may be deducted. Thus, the total interest expense that may be deducted in the current year is $360. The $140 can be deducted in future years if it does not exceed the limit or when the bond is sold.

There is an exception to the above rule. An investor can elect to have the amortized portion of the market discount taxed each year. In that case, the entire interest expense to purchase or carry the bond is tax deductible in the current year. For example, if an investor elects to include the $140 of amortized market discount as gross income in the current year, he or she may deduct the $140 as current interest expense.

Second, the IRC specifies that interest paid or accrued on "indebtedness incurred or continued to purchase or carry obligations, the interest on which is wholly exempt from taxes," is not tax deductible. It does not make any difference if any tax-exempt interest is actually received by the taxpayer in the taxable year. In other words, interest expense is not deductible on funds borrowed to purchase or carry tax-exempt securities. The nondeductibility of interest expenses also applies to debt incurred or continued in order to purchase or carry shares of a regulated investment company (e.g., mutual fund) that distributes exempt interest dividends.

To understand why interest related to debt incurred to purchase or carry tax-exempt obligations is disallowed as a deduction, consider the following example. Suppose a taxpayer in the 50 percent marginal tax bracket borrows $100,000 at an annual interest cost of 12 percent, or $12,000. The proceeds are then used to acquire $100,000 of municipal bonds at par with a coupon rate of 8 percent, or $8,000 interest per year. If the $12,000 interest expense were allowed as a tax-deductible expense, the aftertax cost of the interest expense would be $6,000. Since the interest received from holding the municipal bonds is $8,000, the taxpayer would benefit by $2,000 after taxes.

Finally, there is also a limitation on investment interest deductions equal to $10,000 plus investment income.

# FOUR

---

## Securities regulations

Nancy H. Wojtas, J.D., LL.M.
*Partner*
*Memel, Jacobs, Pierno, Gersh & Ellsworth*

---

### INTRODUCTION

The securities industry is regulated by both the federal securities acts and the states' securities acts. The first federal securities law, the Securities Act of 1933 (the "Securities Act"), became effective on July 7, 1933, a date that roughly corresponded to the low point in the stock market and the country's general economy during the Great Depression. That statute was first administered by the Federal Trade Commission. In 1934, the Securities Exchange Act of 1934 (the "Exchange Act") was enacted. It created the Securities and Exchange Commission (SEC), which was empowered with administering the two securities laws then in existence. The SEC is an independent, bipartisan, administrative agency of the U.S. government. The commission is composed of five members, with no more than three from the same political party. Members are appointed by the president, with the advice and consent of the Senate, for five-year terms (the terms are staggered so that one expires on June 5 of each year). The Chairman of the Commission is designated by the president. The staff is composed of lawyers, accountants, engineers, security analysts, and examiners, together with administrative and clerical employees, and is divided into divisions and offices, each under the charge of officials appointed by the chairman with the concurrence of the commission.

In addition to the Securities Act and the Exchange Act, the laws administered by the SEC are the Public Utility Holding Company Act of 1935; the Trust Indenture Act of 1939, the Investment Company Act of 1940 (the "1940 Act"); and the Investment Advisers Act of 1940. In addition, the commission has a role in the administration of the Bankruptcy Act of 1978 and the Securities Investor Protection Act of 1970.

State securities regulation in this country began around the turn of the century. The first state "securities statute with teeth" was enacted in Kansas in 1911.[1] The term *blue-sky law* is generally used to refer to state securities laws. It was coined to describe both legislation aimed at promoters who "would sell building lots in the blue sky in fee simple" and to the "speculative schemes which have no more basis than so many feet of 'blue sky'."[2] By 1913, 23 other jurisdictions had adopted securities acts, and, by 1929, the year the stock market crashed, virtually all states had some form of securities law.[3]

## THE BLUE-SKY LAWS

Each state has its own blue-sky administrator or an official or commission in a similar position. Most state securities acts have three basic components.[4] First, there are provisions requiring registration of persons involved in the securities industry. Second, there are provisions requiring the registration of the securities sold within the state. Third, there are antifraud provisions. Since it is impossible in this article to consider the laws of all states and territorial jurisdictions having securities laws, the focus here will be on the Uniform Securities Act (the Uniform Act) which was drafted by Professor Louis Loss of Harvard Law School, adopted by the National Commissioners for Uni-

---

[1] Louis Loss, *Fundamentals of Securities Regulation* (Boston: Little, Brown, 1983), p. 8.

[2] Mulvey, Blue Sky Law, 36 Can. L. T. 37 (1916).

[3] *Hall* v. *Geiger-Jones Co.*, 242 U.S. 539, 550 (1917).

[4] 1 Blue Sky L. Rep. (CCH) ¶5501 (1983).

form State Laws in 1957, and adopted by 36 states, the District of Columbia, Guam, and Puerto Rico, with some modifications.[5]

**Registration of persons.** Generally, all broker-dealers, agents, and investment advisers who operate in a particular state, or sell securities, or offer advice from outside that state into the state must register annually under that state's securities laws. A broker-dealer is any person engaged in the business of effecting transactions in securities for the account of others or for his own account. An agent is any individual other than a broker-dealer who represents an issuer or broker-dealer in effecting purchases or sales of securities. And an investment adviser is any person who for compensation engages in the business of advising others about the value of securities or about the advisability of investing in, purchasing, or selling securities, or who for compensation and as a part of a regular business issues reports or analyses concerning securities.

Any registered broker-dealer may act as an investment adviser without registering separately in that capacity if his or her application so states and the state administrator does not condition the broker-dealer registration. Each state administrator, by rule, may require broker-dealers and investment advisers to maintain a minimum capital, may require security bonds for all registrants, and may require applicants to take examinations. Registration as a broker-dealer, agent, or investment adviser may be denied, suspended, or revoked by a state administrator provided that 1 of 11 grounds is met (e.g., lack of qualification) and the administrator finds such denial, suspension, or revocation in the public interest. Failure to register as a broker-dealer, agent, or investment adviser in a state is a felony. Further, failure to register as a broker-dealer or agent constitutes grounds for rescision of the transactions by the purchaser of the securities.

**Registration of securities.** The Uniform Act requires that every security offered or sold in the state must be registered or must qualify under one of the exemptions contained in the Uniform Act.

Registration under the Uniform Act can be accomplished in

---

[5] J. C. Long, "Development in State Securities Regulation" 1–1, *1985 Blue Sky Law Handbook* (New York: Clark Boardman Company, Ltd., 1984).

one of three ways. The first method of registration is *registration by coordination.* This method can only be used when a full registration statement is filed with, and declared effective by, the SEC. It is not available when an issuer is seeking to avail itself of certain SEC regulations that do not require the filing of registration statements. The coordination procedure provides that, if the registration statement is filed in the state, then the registration statement becomes effective automatically at the state level the moment it is declared effective by the SEC, unless the state administrator institutes a stop-order proceeding. The coordination procedure streamlines the content of the state's registration statement and the procedure by which it becomes effective but not the substantive standards governing its effectiveness.

The second method of registration is *registration by qualification.* It may be used by anyone, whether the transaction involves a primary distribution by the issuer or an offering in the secondary market. This form is used frequently by the small issuer who is relying on one of the exemptions from registration under the Securities Act. Under the qualification procedure, the administrator has plenary power to require information about the issuer and to decide when the registration statement becomes effective, as well as to require the use of a prospectus.

Finally, the third form of registration is known as *registration by notification,* which is generally available only for certain specified issuers and nonissuers. The registration statement in a notification case is substantially limited and becomes effective automatically at a fixed hour on the second full business day after filing, unless the administrator accelerates or institutes a stop-order proceeding. Several states have deleted this method of registration.

Exemptions from registration may be available under the Uniform Act. In that connection, there are two basic types of exemptions found under the Uniform Act: the securities exemptions and the transactional exemptions. Under the securities exemptions, certain securities because of their nature never need to be registered. The rationale for the exemptions is that regulation of these securities is not necessary or is supplied by another governmental agency. Among the more important exemptions in this group are: (1) the governmental securities exemptions, (2) the financial institutions exemptions, (3) the listed securities exemption, and (4) the charitable or nonprofit institutions exemption.

The transactional exemptions are on a transaction-by-transaction basis, exempting a particular transfer from registration. Thus, when the purchaser under a transactional exemption wishes to sell his or her securities, he or she will either have to register the securities or find another exemption. The more important transactional exemptions are: (1) the isolated nonissuer exemption, (2) the institutional buyers' exemption, and (3) the limited offering exemption.

While these provisions exempt securities and transactions from the registration provisions of the Uniform Act, they do not constitute exemptions from the coverage of the Uniform Act itself. Thus, the offer or sale of an exempt security is still subject to the coverage of the antifraud provisions of the Uniform Act.

In the event that a security is sold in violation of the Uniform Act, such sale constitutes a felony offense. Such an offense imposes absolute liability—it is no defense that the seller did not know that he or she was selling a security or that it needed to be registered. Such a sale will result in civil liability on the part of the person selling the security, as well as the officers, directors, agents, and control persons of the "seller" (i.e., persons whose securities are sold, the broker-dealer who sells the securities on behalf of the owner, the registered representatives that handle the sales, and persons involved in the selling process who have no direct contact with the buyer). Generally, the purchaser is entitled to the return of all the consideration he or she paid for the securities plus interest and attorney's fees.

**Antifraud provisions.** The Uniform Act proscribes fraudulent practices in connection with the sale or purchase of a security and with investment advisory activities. The sanctions that may be imposed are criminal prosecution in the event of a willful violation, injunction, and administrative proceedings to deny, suspend, or revoke registration when the violator is a broker-dealer, agent, or investment adviser. Further, there is civil liability in the case of sales made through fraud or misstatement.

## THE SECURITIES ACT OF 1933

The Securities Act, which deals principally with the distribution of new issues, has two basic objectives: first, to require that investors receive adequate and accurate disclosure regarding the securities distributed to the public; and, second, to prohibit fraudulent acts, practices, mispresentations, and deceit in the sale of any securities whether or not the offering of the securities is required to be registered under the Securities Act.

The Securities Act requires that, before an issuing company or any person in a control relationship to such company makes a public offering of securities, the issuer must file a registration statement with the SEC setting forth the required information. In general, the SEC's registration forms require the disclosure of such information as a description of the significant provisions of the security to be offered for sale and its relationship to the registrant's other securities, a description of the registrant's properties and business, information regarding the management of the registrant, and financial statements certified by independent public accountants.

Once the registration statement has been filed with the SEC, offers to sell the securities may be made with a preliminary prospectus (i.e., a red herring). The preliminary prospectus must contain substantially the information required to be included in the full prospectus, except for the omission of such information as offering price, underwriting commissions or discounts, account of proceeds, conversion rates, commissions or discounts to dealers, prices, or other matters dependent on the offering price. Further, a legend must appear in red ink (and thus the name red herring) on the outside front cover stating that a registration statement has been filed but not declared effective, that securities may not be sold until that time, that the prospectus does not constitute an offer to sell or solicitation of an offer to buy, and that no sale of securities may be made in any state in which such an offer, solicitation, or sale would be unlawful prior to registration or qualification in that state.

The purpose of the registration of securities offerings is to provide adequate and accurate disclosure of material facts concerning the issuer and the securities it proposes to sell. Investors must be furnished a prospectus containing the most significant information in the registration statement so they can make informed investment decisions about a particular securities offering. The registration process, however, neither insures investors against loss in their investment nor guarantees the accuracy of the facts presented in the registration statement and prospectus. Further, the SEC does not have the power to disapprove an offering of securities due to lack of merit, unlike some state securities laws (e.g., California). The fairness of the terms of the offering, the issuer's prospects for successful operation, and other factors concerning the merits of the securities have no bearing on whether a registration statement may be filed with the SEC and subsequently declared effective. The SEC does have the authority to refuse or suspend the effectiveness of a registration if, after hearing, the SEC finds that material representations contained in the registration statement are inaccurate, incomplete, or misleading.

Although securities of both domestic and foreign private issuers and foreign governments or their instrumentalities are subject to the registration requirement, there are certain exemptions from the requirement. Such exemptions include: (1) private offerings to a limited number of persons or institutions who have access to the kind of information registration would provide and who do not propose to redistribute such securities;[6] (2) offerings limited to residents of the state in which the issuer is organized and doing business; (3) securities of municipal, state, federal, and other government instrumentalities, of charitable institutions, banks, and carriers subject to the Interstate Commerce Act; (4) offerings not in excess of a certain dollar amount and made in compliance with the SEC's regulations;[7] and (5) offerings of small business investment companies made in accordance with the SEC's rules and regulations.

The second objective of the Securities Act is to prohibit false and misleading statements in the sale of securities. In the event an investor suffers a loss in the purchase of a security in an offering, whether or not the offering is the subject of a registration statement filed with the SEC, the Securities Act provides the investor, in certain circumstances, with rights against the issuer, its directors and officers, the underwriters, controlling persons, the sellers of the securities, and others for the losses sustained if the investor can prove that there was incomplete or

---

[6] The SEC has adopted rules allowing certain domestic and foreign issuers to offer and sell their securities, in varying amounts without registration, to an unlimited number of accredited investors (defined to include certain institutions, private business development companies, tax-exempt organization, persons buying large dollar amounts, and certain wealthy individuals), and to 35 other purchasers providing that certain conditions are met. Depending on the amount of securities to be sold (i.e., less than $500,000, less than $5 million, and no amount limitation), certain other conditions must be complied with in connection with these private offerings.

[7] The SEC's Regulation A provides that certain domestic and Canadian companies may make exempt offerings not exceeding $1,500,000, provided certain information is filed with the SEC and provided to the purchaser.

inaccurate disclosure of material facts in the registration statement or prospectus.[8]

## THE SECURITIES EXCHANGE ACT OF 1934

As originally enacted, the Exchange Act addressed itself to five principal areas: (1) disclosure provisions designed to provide current material information on securities listed and registered for public trading on national securities exchanges and to prevent abuses in the areas of proxy solicitation and insider trading; (2) the control of credit in the securities markets; (3) the prohibition of market manipulation, primarily on the exchanges; (4) the regulation of exchanges and exchange trading; and (5) the regulation of trading in the over-the-counter markets.[9] Congress has amended the Exchange Act several times since its original enactment, thereby gradually enlarging the SEC's power in the securities area.

In 1936, Congress amended the statute to provide for the registration of brokers and dealers and for the revocation or denial of such registration on stated grounds. In addition, Congress enacted a section of the Exchange Act that imposes on certain issuers registering securities under the Securities Act the obligation to file periodic reports and disclosures required of listed companies.[10] In 1938, Congress again amended the statute to provide for the creation and registration of national securities associations, thereby providing an organization for self-regulation in the over-the-counter market to perform a function somewhat comparable to that required of the exchanges. Only one national securities association is registered with the SEC, the National Association of Securities Dealers (NASD). At that time, Congress also expanded the SEC's rule-making power to define and prescribe means reasonably designed to prevent fraudulent, deceptive, or manipulative acts and practices by brokers and dealers, and to provide rules with reference to the financial responsibility of brokers and dealers. In 1964, Congress amended the statute to again extend the

---

[8] As defined in Section 2(10) of the Securities Act, a prospectus, with certain defined exceptions, can be any notice, circular, advertisement, letter, or communication that offers any security for sale or that confirms the sale of any security.

[9] Transactions effected, other than on national securities exchanges, are referred to as over-the-counter transactions.

[10] A listed company is one that is listed for trading on a national securities exchange.

disclosure and reporting requirements to equity securities of hundreds of companies traded over-the-counter, provided that the company's assets exceeded $1 million and its shareholders numbered 500 or more. In 1968, Congress amended the Exchange Act to extend the reporting and disclosure provisions to situations where control of a company is sought through a tender offer or other stock acquisition of over 10 percent of a company's equity securities (the amount was reduced to 5 percent by an amendment in 1970).

In 1975, Congress enacted the Securities Acts Amendments of 1975, which, in large part, amended the Exchange Act. These amendments substantially revised the regulation of securities exchanges and securities associations and created a regulatory environment for municipal securities professionals, transfer agents, clearing agencies, and securities information processors. The SEC was also directed to facilitate the establishment of a national market system for securities and a national system for the prompt and accurate clearance and settlement of securities transactions.

In 1977, Congress enacted the Foreign Corrupt Practices Act (FCPA), which added certain sections to the Exchange Act. The FCPA prohibits issuers from making payments to officials of foreign governments in order to induce an official to use his or her authority or influence to obtain business in the country for the issuer. The FCPA also requires issuers to maintain an adequate system of books and records, as well as a system of internal accounting controls.

In 1984, Congress enacted the Insider Trading Sanctions Act of 1984 (ITSA), which made certain revisions to the Exchange Act. The ITSA provides the SEC with an additional treble civil penalty enforcement tool to use in insider trading cases. The SEC may seek a civil penalty, in certain cases, against (1) any person who purchases or sells securities while in possession of material, nonpublic information in violation of the Exchange Act and (2) any person who aids and abets another in the purchase or sale of securities while in possession of material, nonpublic information, by communicating material, nonpublic information to such other person.

**Insider trading.**  Provisions of the Exchange Act, the Holding Company Act, and the 1940 Act are designed to provide other shareholders and investors with information on insider securities transactions. These provisions are designed to prevent unfair use of nonpublic information by insiders who might then profit from short-term trading in a company's securities. To accomplish this objective, each officer and director of a registered company and each beneficial owner of more than 10 percent of any class of equity securities that is registered under the Exchange Act must file an initial report with the SEC and the exchange on which the stock may be listed, showing his or her holdings of each of the company's equity securities. In addition, such persons must file reports for any month during which there was a change in their holdings. Further, any profits obtained by those persons from purchases and sales of such equity securities within any six-month period, with certain exceptions, may be recovered by the company or by a securities holder on its behalf. Finally, insiders are prohibited from making short sales of the company's equity securities.

**Reporting obligations.** At the time a company becomes registered with the SEC under Section 12 of the Exchange Act, that company must file with the SEC (and the stock exchange, if such company is listed) such information as the SEC requires to keep all previous information reasonably current, and annual and quarterly reports.

Each registered company is required to file an annual report (Form 10-K), normally within 90 days after the close of the fiscal year, for each year after the last full fiscal year for which financial statements were filed in the application for registration.

Every registered company required to file an annual report on Form 10-K (with a few exceptions) must file a quarterly report on Form 10-Q within 45 days after the end of its first three fiscal quarters and a current report on a Form 8-K within 15 days after the occurrence of specified events not reported previously. The quarterly report must include condensed financial data (with a management analysis of financial condition, specified information with respect to legal proceedings, material changes in registered securities, defaults on senior securities, and matters submitted to a vote of security holders). Events requiring the filing of a current report on Form 8-K are a change in control, the acquisition or disposition of a significant amount of assets, bankruptcy or receivership proceedings, a change of auditors, and a director's resignation because of a policy dispute.

## REGISTRATION OF SECURITIES EXCHANGES, SECURITIES ASSOCIATIONS, BROKERS AND DEALERS, AND MUNICIPAL SECURITIES DEALERS

In addition to the disclosure provisions, the Exchange Act imposes on the SEC broad regulatory responsibilities over the securities markets and over persons conducting business in securities. The Exchange Act provides for the registration of securities exchanges, provides for SEC supervision of the self-regulatory responsibilities of registered exchanges, permits registration of self-regulatory associations of brokers or dealers, and provides for SEC supervision of the self-regulatory responsibilities of registered associations. The Exchange Act also requires registration of brokers and dealers in securities and contains provisions designed to prevent fraudulent, deceptive, and manipulative acts and practices on the exchanges and in the over-the-counter markets.

**The national securities exchanges.** The Exchange Act provides that an exchange shall not be registered as a national securities exchange unless it is able to carry out the purposes of the Exchange Act; is able to enforce compliance by its members and persons associated with members with the provisions, rules, and regulations of the Exchange Act, and of the exchange; and has rules containing other specific provisions. Although the Exchange Act provides for self-regulation by each exchange, it imposes on the SEC the responsibility for reviewing proposed changes in exchange rules and for determining whether a proposed change is consistent with the purposes of the Exchange Act.

**Securities associations.** The Exchange Act also provides that any association of brokers or dealers may be registered with the SEC as a national securities association if it meets the standards and requirements for registration that are similar to those applicable to national securities exchanges. Only one such association—the NASD—is registered with the commission. The Exchange Act considers such associations to be vehicles for self-regulation of over-the-counter brokers and dealers.

Congress provided an incentive for brokers and dealers to join such associations by permitting the association to adopt rules that preclude any members from dealing with a nonmember broker or dealer except on the same terms, conditions, and prices as the member deals with the general public. Prior to 1983, not all broker-dealers were NASD members. The SEC was responsible for establishing and administering rules on qualification standards and business conduct of non-NASD broker-dealers (referred to as SECO broker-dealers). In 1983, Congress amended the Exchange Act to eliminate the SEC's direct regulation of SECO broker-dealers and to require any broker-dealer engaged in the over-the-counter securities business to join a registered securities association (i.e., the NASD).

**Brokers and dealers.** The Exchange Act requires that brokers and dealers who use the facilities of national securities exchanges or the mails or any means of interstate commerce in conducting an interstate over-the-counter securities business to register with the SEC. The SEC has the authority to censure, place limitations on, suspend (for a period not exceeding 12 months), or revoke the registration of any broker or dealer, after notice and opportunity for a hearing, if it is in the public interest and if the SEC finds that the broker or dealer (1) filed a false or misleading registration application; (2) was convicted, within 10 years of filing such application, of any felony or misdemeanor (involving certain crimes); (3) is enjoined by a court from acting in the capacity of various positions relating to the securities, banking, and insurance businesses, such as an investment adviser, underwriter, broker, dealer, municipal securities dealer, or an affiliate to a bank or insurance company; (4) has willfully violated, is unable to comply with, aided, abetted, counseled, commanded, induced, procured, or failed reasonably to supervise another person if that person is subject to his or her supervision, with respect to any provision of the Securities Act, Exchange Act, Investment Company Act, Investment Advisers Act, or any rules and regulations thereunder, or the rules of the Municipal Securities Rulemaking Board; or (5) is subject to an SEC order barring or suspending the right of such person to be associated with a broker or dealer.

**Municipal securities dealers.** The Exchange Act, as amended in 1975, also provides for the registration and regulation of brokers, dealers, and banks that buy, sell, or effect transactions in municipal securities[11] as part of their regular business in other than a fiduciary capacity. Issuers of municipal securities are exempt from the registration provisions of the federal securities laws. The Exchange Act directed the SEC to create a Municipal Securities Rulemaking Board, which prescribes rules regulating the activities of brokers, dealers, and municipal securities dealers that comprise the municipal securities business.

**Margin trading.** The Exchange Act also contains provisions that govern trading of securities on margin. The board of governors of the Federal Reserve System is authorized to set limitations on the amount of credit that may be extended for the purpose of purchasing or carrying securities, thereby restricting excessive use of credit in the securities markets. Presently, the required margin for each security held in a margin account is, in the case of a margin security (i.e., any registered security, OTC margin stock or bond, any OTC security designated in the National Market System, or any security issued by either an open-end investment company or unit investment trust that is registered under the Investment Company Act) 50 percent of the current market value of the security, and, in the case of an exempted security, registered nonconvertible debt security, or OTC Margin bond, the margin required by the creditor in good faith (i.e., the amount a creditor, exercising sound credit judgment, would customarily require for a specified security position established without regard to the customer's other assets or other securities positions). The margin requirements vary for options positions and short sales of exempted and nonexempted securities. Although credit restrictions are set by the Federal Reserve Board, the SEC is responsible for the enforcement of such provisions.

---

[11] The Exchange Act defines municipal securities as securities that are "direct obligations of, or obligations guaranteed as to principal or interest by, a State or any political division thereof, or any agency or instrumentality of a State or any political subdivision thereof, or any municipal corporate instrumentality of one or more states or any security which is an industrial development bond. . . ." Section 3(29) of the Exchange Act.

## THE INVESTMENT COMPANY ACT OF 1940

The 1940 Act provides a regulatory framework within which investment companies must operate. The act provides several definitions of the term *investment company,* two of which will be discussed. First, an investment company is defined as any being that is, or proposes to be, primarily engaged in the business of investing, reinvesting, or trading in securities. Second, an investment company is any issuer that is, or proposes to be, engaged in the business of investing, reinvesting, owning, holding, or trading in securities, and that acquires or proposes to acquire investment securities (i.e., all securities except government securities, securities issued by majority-owned subsidiaries provided they are not investment companies, and securities issued by employees' securities companies) exceeding 40 percent of the issuer's total assets (exclusive of government securities and cash). Several categories of issuers are excluded from the definition. The most notable exception is an issuer whose outstanding securities (other than short-term paper) are beneficially owned by not more than 100 persons and who is not making and does not propose to make a public offering of its securities.

The 1940 Act is designed to regulate public investment companies and to provide honest and unbiased management, adequate and feasible capital structures, sound financial statements and accounting practices, and greater participation in management by security holders.

Offerings of the securities of investment companies must be registered under the Securities Act, and the companies are required to file periodic reports and are subject to the SEC's proxy and insider trading rules. Such companies are required to register with the SEC and to disclose their financial conditions and investment policies to provide investors full and complete information about such companies' activities. In addition, the 1940 Act prohibits changes in the nature of an investment company's business or in its investment policies without the approval of its shareholders; protects shareholders against management self-dealing, embezzlement, or abuse of trust; provides specific controls to eliminate or mitigate inequitable capital structures; provides that management contracts be submitted to the shareholders for approval and that provision be made for the safekeeping of assets; and establishes controls to protect against unfair transactions between an investment company and its affiliates.

## THE INVESTMENT ADVISERS ACT OF 1940

The Investment Advisers Act requires that persons or firms (including advisers to registered investment companies) that are in the business of advising others about securities transactions must register with the SEC; but the act does not require registration of (1) a bank or certain bank holding companies; (2) any lawyer, accountant, engineer, or teacher whose performance of such services is solely incidental to his or her professional practice; (3) any broker or dealer whose investment advisory services are solely incidental to the conduct of his or her business as a broker or dealer and who receives no special compensation for such services; (4) certain newspaper and magazine publishers; and (5) any person whose advice relates to securities that are direct obligations or obligations guaranteed as to principal or interest by the United States, or securities issued or guaranteed by a corporation in which the United States has an interest, or securities designated by the Secretary of the Treasury as exempt.

Certain investment advisers, however, are exempted from the registration requirement with the SEC. For example, any investment adviser, who during the course of the preceding 12 months has had fewer than 15 clients, and who neither holds himself out generally to the public as an investment adviser nor acts as an investment adviser to any business development company, need not register with the SEC. Further, an investment adviser whose clients are residents in the state where the adviser maintains his principal office and place of business, and who does not furnish advice or issue analyses about securities listed or admitted to unlisted trading privileges on any national securities exchange need not register with the SEC. Finally, an investment adviser whose only clients are insurance companies is not subject to the registration requirement.

Under the Investment Advisers Act, the SEC is charged with extensive regulatory and supervisory responsibilities over investment advisers. The SEC may deny, suspend, or revoke the registration of an investment adviser if it finds, after notice and hearing, that such action is in the public interest. Statutory disqualifications include a conviction for certain financial crimes or securities violations, the existence of injunctions based on such crimes or violations, a conviction for violation of the Mail Fraud Statute, the willful filing of false reports with the SEC, willful violations of the Investment Advisers Act, the 1940 Act, the Securities Act, the Exchange Act, or any rules and regulations thereunder, or the rules of the Municipal Securities Rule-making Board, or failure to reasonably supervise, with a view to preventing violations of the provisions of such statutes, rules and regulations, another person who commits such a violation, if such other person is subject to his or her supervision.

The Investment Advisers Act contains antifraud provisions and provides the SEC with the authority to adopt rules defining fraudulent, deceptive, or manipulative acts and practices. The act also requires that investment advisers disclose the nature of their interests in transactions executed for their clients, and it imposes on investment advisers that are subject to the registration requirement the duty to maintain books and records in accordance with the SEC's rules.

The so-called brochure rule adopted under the Investment Advisers Act requires advisers to deliver a specified disclosure statement to each client and prospective client initially within certain time parameters and to offer annually in writing to deliver a current disclosure document on request to such clients without charge. The disclosure document discusses the adviser's background and business practices.

## SECURITIES INVESTOR PROTECTION ACT OF 1970

The passage of the Securities Investor Protection Act of 1970 was designed to give investors who dealt with brokers and dealers additional protections for their funds and securities in the event of the insolvency of a broker or dealer. The act requires that every broker or dealer registered with the SEC must be a member of the Securities Investor Protection Corporation (SIPC), which was created by Congress and is under some supervision of the SEC. SIPC insures customers against their brokers' insolvency up to $500,000 for each account, except that maximum is $100,000 to the extent the claim is made for cash rather than securities. SIPC is funded through an annual assessment of its members and the backing of the United States Treasury up to $1 billion.

# FIVE

## The portfolio construction and management process*

**Sheri Kole**
*Director, Financial Planning Department*
*The Copeland Companies*
*and*
*Academic Associate*
*College for Financial Planning*

### INTRODUCTION

A substantial amount of information is available on portfolio construction and management for pension funds and mutual funds. However, because the goals of these large portfolios differ from the goals of an individual, the literature available on portfolio construction and management is not always applicable to the individual. The objective of this article is to focus on a portfolio construction and management framework for the individual. The purpose of portfolio construction and management for an individual is to create and maintain, through a logical sequence of steps, optimal combinations of investment vehicles to achieve stated goals.

The portfolio construction and management process begins with the ranking of goals in order of importance. The client's available resources are identified, including existing assets and

* Reprinted with permission from the College for Financial Planning, Denver, Colorado.

discretionary income. Then, the client's constraints are identified for each goal. Next, current and forecasted economic conditions are identified. The constraints are used as guidelines for
selecting appropriate asset categories and investment vehicles
for each goal. An asset category contains investment vehicles
with similar characteristics. Investment vehicles are selected
on the basis of criteria that match the constraints and in light of
current and forecasted economic conditions. Investment strategies are used to implement the overall plan. The process continues with the allocation of resources available. Existing assets
may need to be repositioned to achieve the rate of return necessary to meet the stated goals or to reduce risk in the portfolio.

The process requires continuous monitoring as goals are
achieved, new goals created, and as the variables affecting the
portfolio change. Changes in economic conditions, portfolio
performance, or the client's circumstances can result in the
need to restructure or modify the portfolio. Thus, portfolio construction and management is a dynamic process wherein the
risk/return trade-off concepts are applied to formulate an efficient portfolio.

Before constructing a portfolio, the client should have an adequate emergency fund and risk-management program. An
emergency fund of at least three months' living expenses
should be established in a liquid investment vehicle, such as a
money market fund. An appropriate risk-management program
includes adequate coverage for all major life, health, property,
and liability exposures.

## STEP 1: ESTABLISH GOALS

After the prerequisites are established (risk-management
program and emergency fund), the portfolio construction and
management process begins. The client should establish realistic goals and quantify them in time frames and dollar amounts.
Vague and nebulous goals, such as "to do well" or "to suc-
ceed," may not produce efficient results because of a lack of
commitment on the part of the client.

Goals may include the purchase of a new car, a vacation, or a
down payment on a house, all of which can be quantified in
dollar amounts and time frames. Admittedly, some goals are
difficult to quantify in these terms. For example, the desire to
accumulate wealth independent of other goals within one's life-

time may not involve definitive time frames or dollar amounts. But this goal can be assessed by analyzing the client's risk tolerance level and available resources. All financial goals involve either the acquisition, preservation, or distribution of capital.

Clients often have many goals they would like to attain; therefore, goals should be ranked in order of priority. Existing assets and/or cash flow are utilized to achieve goals. If the client does not have sufficient assets or cash flow to meet all goals, the financial planner should concentrate on the priority goals first. There can be problems, however, with ranking goals in terms of priority and necessity. For example, suppose a client has as a top priority a private college education for his children, who are now 17 and 15 years old. The client's second goal is to purchase a new car immediately because the existing one is 10 years old. The client may not have sufficient assets or cash flow at the present time to meet both goals. Even though the children's education is top priority, the purchase of a car must be the first goal. The client can modify his goals by purchasing a less expensive car or sending his children to a public university. The financial planner helps the client identify available resources and, if necessary, modify goals.

## STEP 2: IDENTIFY RESOURCES

This step involves identifying the client's available resources. The client's statements of financial position (balance sheet) and cash flow are used to determine available resources for constructing the investment portfolio. The statement of financial position is a profile of what is owned (assets), what is owed (liabilities), and the net worth of the client on a specific date. This statement indicates the invested assets available for repositioning. Available resources may include: CDs, savings accounts, money market funds, life insurance cash values, stocks, bonds, or equity in a house. The client's emergency fund is usually included under the cash/cash equivalents category and is not considered an available resource. In addition, assume, for example, a client inherited from deceased parents a gem collection worth $25,000. If the client wants to keep this investment for sentimental reasons, it should not be considered as an available resource.

The cash flow statement reveals the client's sources of funds (inflows) and allocation of funds (outflows). The client's planned savings/investment program or discretionary income is available to achieve goals. Anticipated resources may also be included as resources available for investments. These may include a bonus, an increase in salary, or an inheritance, although these resources may be difficult to count on for planning purposes. In addition, if a client is expected to finish paying for an automobile in three months, these funds can be considered for use in the near future.

The client's available resources are identified as lump sum and annual discretionary income available. Once the resources are assessed, the financial planner identifies the constraints of the client and economic conditions and selects appropriate asset categories and investment vehicles for each goal.

## STEP 3: IDENTIFY CONSTRAINTS

After goals have been established and resources identified, the next step in the portfolio construction process is to determine parameters for the constraints that relate to the client's overall situation and goals. Constraints are factors that restrict the selection of asset categories and investment vehicles. The parameters for the constraints are the specifics unique to a client's situation that qualify or quantify the constraints. Constraints affecting portfolio construction and management include the following:

Time horizon
Liquidity
Marketability
Tax consequences
Risk-tolerance level
Diversification

The parameters for each constraint are identified for each goal. For example, the parameters for the liquidity constraint would include the degree of liquidity required by the goal and the client's overall situation. The parameters for the tax consequences constraint include the client's marginal tax bracket, need for long-term capital gains, or need for tax-exempt income. These parameters are used as the guidelines to (1) select appropriate asset categories, such as fixed-income securities, and (2) select appropriate investment vehicles (e.g., corporate, government, or municipal bonds).

The parameters for all six constraints are identified for each goal; however, the more important constraints have a greater influence on the selection of asset categories and investment vehicles. Assume, for example, that a client's priority goal is to obtain current income to fund a child's education for four years. The parameters for this goal may be expressed as follows:

1. Time horizon: four years
2. Liquidity: high degree essential
3. Marketability: moderate degree needed
4. Tax consequences: 50 percent marginal tax bracket; need for tax-exempt income
5. Risk-tolerance level: safety of principal essential
6. Diversification: important to diversify portfolio

An appropriate asset category is selected based on these parameters, the client's goal, and economic conditions. The liquidity, tax consequences, and risk-tolerance level constraints are most important to this goal; therefore, these constraints will have a greater impact on the selection of asset categories and investment vehicles. The relative importance of the constraints affects the selection of asset categories and investment vehicles for each client goal.

### Time horizon

Time horizon can be defined as the investment holding period or the time in which a specific financial goal is expected to be attained. The time horizon of each client goal influences the selection of asset categories and investment vehicles. Ideally, vehicles selected will yield the desired return within the specified time frame. If a goal cannot be attained, because the desired return is not achievable and there are insufficient resources available, the goal or the time horizon should be modified.

Fluctuating market conditions also have a major effect on the time horizons of certain goals. Goals that have long time horizons are better suited for more volatile investments, such as growth common stock versus short-term bonds. Other goals that have a shorter time horizon are better suited for less volatile investments, such as Treasury bills. Thus, the time horizon constraint is an important variable in the portfolio construction and management process.

### Liquidity and marketability

Liquidity and marketability are important in constructing a portfolio, especially when market conditions are unstable. Liquidity is the ability to readily convert an investment into cash without losing any of the principal invested. Marketability is the degree to which there is an active market in which an investment can be readily traded. The client goal dictates the degree of liquidity or marketability needed. For example, if the goal is to accumulate funds for a down payment on a house in nine months, a high degree of liquidity and marketability is essential. On the other hand, if the goal is to fund a child's education in six years, the degree of liquidity and marketability required may not be important depending upon the client's overall situation.

Marketability can be used as a measure of risk because investments with limited marketability tend to be more risky and consequently should offer more return. For example, many corporate bonds and all municipal bonds are traded on the OTC market; these bonds might have a low degree of marketability, as volume in these issues can be very limited at times. However, many listed securities may also have limited marketability if they are not actively traded. In addition, because art objects and many collectibles are usually traded at auctions or through dealers, their marketability is severely limited.

Liquidity also affects the risk/return relationship of investment vehicles (i.e., a lower expected return is a tradeoff for a more highly liquid investment). However, there are periods of economic activity when the most liquid securities offer a greater return than less liquid securities, as was the case in January 1981, when the yield on money market funds exceeded the yield on long-term corporate bonds.

### Tax consequences

Tax considerations are an integral part of investment planning and are an important consideration in selecting asset categories and investment vehicles. Examples of tax-favored vehicles include municipal bonds, which offer tax-exempt income; real estate investments, which offer cost-recovery benefits; and common stock and certain discount bonds, which offer long-term capital gain potential. If current income is a goal, the client's marginal tax bracket affects the decision of selecting between municipal bonds and corporate bonds. The marginal tax bracket is the rate affecting the last dollar of income that is added to taxable income.

Because tax laws favor long-term capital gains over short-term capital gains and short-term capital losses over long-term capital losses, the timing of capital transactions can be an important criterion to the client in achieving a desired aftertax return and reducing tax liability. Another consideration is the possibility of incurring the alternative minimum tax because of excess long-term capital gains or excess deductions from tax shelters.

The expected or realized performance of an investment on an aftertax basis should be calculated and compared with other investment alternatives. The aftertax return should be compared with other vehicles because there is a different tax treatment for short-term and long-term capital gains/losses. For example, assume that a client is in the 30 percent marginal tax bracket and receives a 20 percent short-term capital gain return on an investment. The aftertax return can be calculated as follows:

$$r_{at} = r[1 - (t)(g)]$$

where:
$r_{at}$ = Aftertax return
$r$ = Return on investment
$t$ = Marginal tax bracket
$g$ = Portion of capital gain that is taxable

Thus, the client's aftertax return is 14 percent, where: .14 = .2[1 − (.3)(1.0)]. If the return above represented a long-term capital gain, the aftertax return would be 17.6 percent, where: .176 = .2[1 − (.3)(.4)], because only 40 percent of the long-term gain is taxable. Further, assume this client receives an 18 percent long-term capital gain and a 15 percent short-term capital gain. The client's total aftertax return is 26.34 percent, where: .2634 = .15[1 − (.3)(1.0)] + .18[1 − (.3)(.4)]. To assure proper measurement of performance, it is apparent that the potential or realized return on investments must be compared on a total aftertax basis.

### Risk-tolerance level

The risk-tolerance level is an intangible and subjective constraint based upon the client's emotional temperament and attitudes. The level of risk the client is willing to assume affects the types of investment vehicles relevant for that client's portfolio and, in turn, the level of return that can be expected. It is important to recognize that some clients will assume only a given level of risk, regardless of the potential return. The objective of rational investment management is to select investment vehicles that maximize expected return for a given level of risk or minimize risk for a given level of expected return. The client's risk-tolerance level, among other constraints, affects the selection of asset categories and investment vehicles.

Risk-tolerance levels can be generalized by examining life cycles in terms of the need for current income and capital appreciation. Exhibit 1 generalizes the risk-tolerance levels generally assumed throughout the client's life cycle.

A 35-year-old single person with no dependents may be aggressive in investment decisions and include vehicles that offer

**EXHIBIT 1**

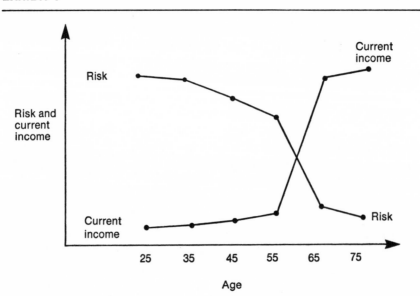

capital appreciation in a portfolio. On the other hand, a 65-year-old retired person may be defensive in investment decisions and include vehicles that offer only current income in a portfolio. The desire for capital appreciation usually entails a risk of principal, and there are two distinct risks involved: the risk of principal impairment and the risk of principal volatility. The risk of principal impairment is the exposure to, or probability of, a permanent loss of all or part of the principal. Investments in futures contracts and puts and calls are subject to a total loss of principal. The risk of principal volatility is the probability of loss of principal or an adverse rate of return during an interval of time. For example, investments in long-term bonds, common stock, or gold are subject to a certain degree of principal volatility. Almost every investment vehicle will have some degree of exposure to the risk of principal volatility. The risk of principal volatility is noticeable when there is a need to liquidate investments before the desired return has been met. The financial planner must identify the client's disposition toward these two types of risk.

Risk-tolerance levels are also influenced by the degree of investment risk the client is willing to accept. Total investment risk can be divided into two parts—systematic risk (referred to as beta) and unsystematic risk. Economic, political, and sociological changes are factors affecting systematic risk. Systematic risk has three component sources: interest rate risk, purchasing power risk, and market risk. Interest rate risk is caused by fluctuations in the general level of interest rates. Purchasing power risk refers to the impact of changes in the price level within the economy—the impact of inflation or deflation on an investment. Market risk is the loss or gain of capital resulting from changes in the prices of investments caused by investor reaction to tangible as well as intangible events.

Unsystematic risk represents the portion of investment risk that can be reduced through diversification. It is the portion of total investment risk that is unique to a firm, an industry, or a property. Unsystematic risk is composed of two sources: business risk and financial risk. Business risk is the risk associated with the nature of the enterprise itself. Financial risk is the risk associated with the mix of debt and equity used to finance a firm or property. Standard & Poor's and Moody's advisory services can be used to estimate the business and financial risks of stocks and bonds. Securities with limited financial and business risks often are subject to interest rate and purchasing power risks. For example, U.S. government securities are subject to interest rate and purchasing power risks. Growth common stocks are affected to a lesser degree by interest rate and purchasing power risks, but they are subject to business, financial, and market risks.

It is important for the financial planner to understand the sources of investment risk for each investment vehicle when constructing and managing a portfolio. In addition, the financial planner must identify the client's disposition towards risk to select an efficient portfolio that maximizes expected return and minimizes the level of risk.

### Diversification

Diversification can be thought of as a strategy for portfolio management in that a defensive strategy generally involves diversification. However, diversification can also be considered a constraint. The major purpose of diversification is to reduce the risk exposure in a portfolio by constructing a portfolio with assets whose returns are not influenced by the same factors. Assume that a client has all his or her investable assets in residential real estate, and there is a downturn in the residential real estate market. The client's entire portfolio is now subject to an adverse condition that may decrease expected return. However, if the portfolio had been diversified among asset categories, the expected return might be partially protected against this adverse condition. Diversification is a risk-reducing strategy that can reduce the opportunity for maximizing the expected return on a portfolio. However, depending upon economic conditions, a diversified portfolio may produce greater realized returns than a single-asset portfolio.

Unsystematic risk (business and financial risk) can be reduced through diversification of investment vehicles. By constructing a portfolio with securities and other assets that are not subject to the same kind of adverse developments, unsystematic risk can be reduced. Examples of this reduction include (1) diversifying real estate investment properties by selecting investments in different geographical locations, both domestically and internationally; (2) diversifying among different real estate investment properties, such as commercial, industrial and residential real estate properties, and raw land; (3) diversifying common stocks among several industry groupings whose returns are affected differently by the stages of the business cycle; and (4) diversifying among different asset categories, such as stocks, fixed-income securities, real estate, and physical assets.

Six major constraints have been identified as guidelines to use in selecting asset categories and investment vehicles. These constraints—time horizon, liquidity, marketability, tax consequences, risk-tolerance level, and diversification—should be viewed simultaneously and ranked by degree of relative importance for each goal. Because portfolio construction and management is a dynamic process, the parameters of these constraints are subject to change. Factors that affect the client's constraints include phases and magnitude of the business cycle, the client's investment experience, a change in the client's marginal tax bracket, or a change in the client's goal and personal situation. The financial planner should be aware of changes in the client's constraints in order to construct and maintain an efficient portfolio.

## STEP 4: IDENTIFY ECONOMIC CONDITIONS

An understanding of economic, political, social, and financial market conditions is essential to portfolio construction and management. These factors influence portfolio construction and management, because changes in these factors have a major impact on the performance of asset categories and investment vehicles. The level and direction of economic output, interest rates, inflation, energy costs, financial market indexes, and changes in monetary and fiscal policy all are essential variables that affect investment decision making. An appraisal of the economic outlook should include an analysis of the past, current, and forecasted performance of economic indicators and of the nature and cause of fluctuations in these indicators. Changes in the investment environment can contribute to achieving portfolio performance goals; however, they can also impede the attainment of these goals.

The most widely-used measure of total economic activity is the Gross National Product (GNP). This indicator measures the market value of the nation's output of final goods and services. Often a forecast of total GNP is derived by estimating expenditures on final output made by each of the following four broad groups of purchasers: consumers (durable and nondurable goods), businesses (fixed capital goods and changes in inventory), foreigners (excess of sales abroad over U.S. purchases abroad), and governments (federal, state, and local). The GNP is published in current dollars and in 1972 dollars (real GNP), which is nominal output adjusted for price changes (inflation or deflation). The percentage change in the real GNP from quarter-to-quarter or year-to-year is an important indicator of economic growth. (See Exhibit 2 for historical data on real GNP.)

---

**EXHIBIT 2**     GNP, PPI, and CPI 1973–1983

| | Real GNP (dollars in billions, 1972) | Annual rate of change | PPI (1967 = 100) | Annual rate of change | CPI (1967 = 100) | Annual rate of change |
|---|---|---|---|---|---|---|
| 1973 . . . . | $1,254.3 | 5.8% | 127.9 | 9.1% | 133.1 | 6.2% |
| 1974 . . . . | 1,246.3 | −0.6 | 147.5 | 15.3 | 147.7 | 11.0 |
| 1975 . . . . | 1,231.6 | −1.2 | 163.4 | 10.8 | 161.2 | 9.1 |
| 1976 . . . . | 1,298.2 | 5.4 | 170.6 | 4.4 | 170.5 | 5.8 |
| 1977 . . . . | 1.369.7 | 5.5 | 181.7 | 6.5 | 181.5 | 6.5 |
| 1978 . . . . | 1,438.6 | 5.0 | 195.9 | 7.8 | 195.4 | 7.7 |
| 1979 . . . . | 1,479.4 | 2.8 · | 217.7 | 11.1 | 217.4 | 11.3 |
| 1980 . . . . | 1,474.0 | −0.3 | 247.0 | 13.5 | 246.8 | 13.5 |
| 1981 . . . . | 1,502.6 | 2.6 | 269.8 | 9.2 | 272.4 | 10.4 |
| 1982 . . . . | 1,485.4 | −1.89 | 280.7 | 4.0 | 289.1 | 6.1 |
| 1983 . . . . | 1,534.8* | 3.3* | 285.2* | 1.6* | 298.4 | 3.2 |

\* Preliminary as of February 1984.
Source: *Economic Report of the President*, February 1983.

---

The behavior of economic indicators is related to changes in business cycles. A business cycle as defined by the National Bureau of Economic Research (NBER) "consists of expansions occurring at about the same time in many economic activities, followed by similarly general recessions, contractions, and revivals which merge into the expansion phase of the next cycle."[1] Business cycles are alternating and recurring movements, although no period of expansion or contraction is identical with earlier business cycles. Business cycle indicators used to analyze current economic conditions include housing

---

[1] Elizabeth W. Angle, *Keys for Business Forecasting* (Richmond, Va.: Federal Reserve Bank of Richmond, 1980).

starts, domestic auto sales, business inventories, the federal budget surplus (deficit), and the unemployment rate.

Measures of price movements, such as the purchasing power of a dollar, are used to interpret economic conditions. Price changes affect the purchasing power of consumers, business firms, and government entities. For instance, a rise in prices means a decline in the quantity of goods and services that a given amount of money will buy.

Two widely used measures of price changes are the Producer Price Index (PPI) and the Consumer Price Index (CPI). The PPI, formerly the Wholesale Price Index, measures changes in prices of commodities sold in U.S. primary markets. This index measures prices at the production level, encompassing raw materials and finished goods. The index base was established as 100 for the year 1967. The CPI measures changes in prices for a fixed market basket of goods and services that are purchased by a selected group of urban consumers. The market basket includes goods and services such as food, medical expenses, entertainment and housing. As with the PPI, 1967 is the base for the index (100). (See Exhibit 2 for historical data on the PPI and CPI.)

Price changes affect the level of spending by consumers, businesses, and government; however, the decision to spend is also influenced by the availability and cost of money and credit. A responsibility of the Federal Reserve Board is to pursue economic goals through regulation of the supply of credit and money. As the country's central bank, the Federal Reserve exercises control over the growth of the money supply as the availability of money and credit strongly influences the level of aggregate economic activity. The Fed and the U.S. government attempt to enhance or curtail economic growth through changes in monetary and fiscal policy. For example, changes in the growth rate of the money supply and new tax bills passed by Congress are factors having significant economic implications. These factors influence construction of the portfolio, and changes in these factors may indicate that modifications are warranted.

Interest rates are measures of the cost of credit. There are many different indicators of interest rate levels, such as the prime rate, the federal funds rate, the rate on triple-A corporate bonds, the rate differential between triple-A corporate bonds and triple-B corporate bonds, and the rates on U.S. government securities. The client needs to be aware of how changes in these interest rates affect economic activity and if interest rates are at a relatively high, normal, or low level. The level and trend of interest rates are important considerations when selecting asset categories and investment vehicles for a financial goal. (See Exhibit 3 for historical data on interest rates of various securities.)

---

**EXHIBIT 3**      Interest rates—Money and capital markets, 1978–1983, averages

| | Prime rate | 3-month treasury bills | 20-year treasury bonds | General obligation Aaa municipal bonds | General obligation Baa municipal bonds | Corporate bonds Aaa | Corporate bonds Baa |
|---|---|---|---|---|---|---|---|
| 1978 . . . . | 9.06% | 7.19% | 8.48% | 5.52% | 6.27% | 8.73% | 9.45% |
| 1979 . . . . | 12.67 | 10.07 | 9.33 | 5.92 | 6.73 | 9.63 | 10.69 |
| 1980 . . . . | 15.27 | 11.43 | 11.39 | 7.85 | 9.01 | 11.94 | 13.67 |
| 1981 . . . . | 18.87 | 14.03 | 13.72 | 10.43 | 11.76 | 14.17 | 16.04 |
| 1982 . . . . | 14.86 | 10.61 | 12.92 | 10.88 | 12.48 | 13.79 | 16.11 |
| 1983 . . . . | 10.79 | 8.61 | 11.34 | 8.80 | 10.17 | 12.04 | 13.55 |

Source: *Federal Reserve Bulletins.*

---

Several indicators measure the forces within financial markets and the level of economic activity. These indexes can be used as a measure of performance of the investment portfolio. There are other indexes used to measure the performance of asset categories and investment vehicles. Measures of common stock prices include the Dow Jones Averages, S&P 500 Index, NYSE Index, Value Line Index, AMEX Index, NASDAQ Index, and the Wilshire 5000 Equity Index. (See Exhibit 4 for historical data on several security indexes.)

Indexes for bond prices include the Dow Jones Bond Average, Lehman indexes, and the Salomon Brothers indexes. These latter include several bond categories, such as short-term and long-term U.S. government securities and short-term and long-term corporate bonds.

The Sotheby Index measures a variety of art works such as 19th century European paintings, Continental ceramics, and modern paintings. The National Association of Realtors has devised an index measuring the performance of REITs, although

**EXHIBIT 4**     Measures of security prices, 1973–1983, at year-end

| | Dow Jones Industrial Average | NYSE Index (12/31/65 = 50) | S&P Index (1941–43 = 10) | Value Line Index (6/30/61 = 100) | AMEX Index (8/31/73 = 100) | NASDAQ Index (2/5/71 = 100) |
|---|---|---|---|---|---|---|
| 1973 . . . . . . | 850.86 | 51.82 | 97.35 | 73.04 | 90.33 | 92.19 |
| 1974 . . . . . . | 616.24 | 36.13 | 68.56 | 48.94 | 60.32 | 59.82 |
| 1975 . . . . . . | 852.41 | 47.64 | 90.19 | 70.69 | 83.48 | 77.62 |
| 1976 . . . . . . | 1,004.65 | 57.88 | 107.46 | 93.47 | 109.84 | 97.88 |
| 1977 . . . . . . | 831.17 | 52.50 | 95.10 | 93.92 | 127.89 | 105.05 |
| 1978 . . . . . . | 805.01 | 53.62 | 96.11 | 97.97 | 150.56 | 117.98 |
| 1979 . . . . . . | 838.74 | 61.95 | 107.94 | 121.91 | 247.07 | 151.14 |
| 1980 . . . . . . | 963.99 | 77.86 | 135.76 | 144.20 | 348.99 | 202.34 |
| 1981 . . . . . . | 875.00 | 71.11 | 122.55 | 137.81 | 320.63 | 195.84 |
| 1982 . . . . . . | 1,046.54 | 81.03 | 140.64 | 158.94 | 340.60 | 232.41 |
| 1983 . . . . . . | 1,258.94 | 95.18 | 164.93 | 194.35 | 223.01* | 278.60 |

* Reflects two-for-one split on May 7, 1983.
Source: *Securities Industry Yearbook 1984.*

there is no other widely used measure for other types of real estate investments.

If an adequate index of prices does not exist for a given asset category or investment vehicle, historical data can be used to determine the current direction and trend in that market. Because the selection of asset categories and investment vehicles is affected by economic conditions, trends in economic activity and in financial markets are an essential element to consider when constructing a portfolio.

## STEP 5: SELECT ASSET CATEGORIES

After the client's resources and constraints have been identified for each goal and economic conditions evaluated, the next step is to select appropriate asset categories. The client's constraints and economic conditions affect the selection of asset categories for each goal. Typical asset categories include the following:

Money market instruments

Fixed-income securities

Common stock

Real estate

Options

Physical assets

Direct investments/limited partnerships

Futures

Within each asset category are investment vehicles that may be selected for the investment portfolio. For example, money market securities include Treasury bills, commercial paper, and repurchase agreements. Fixed-income securities include U.S. government and agency securities, municipal bonds, preferred stock, and corporate bonds. Common stock includes listed securities (NYSE, AMEX), over-the-counter stock, and international stock. Real estate includes REITs, raw land, and commercial, industrial, and residential properties. Options include puts and calls and convertible securities. Physical assets include collectibles, metals, gemstones, gold, and other physical assets. Direct investments and limited partnerships include investments in oil and gas, equipment leasing, cattle breeding, and other limited partnerships. Futures include commodities and financial contracts.

There may be several appropriate asset categories for each goal because of different appraisals of present and future economic conditions and because of different perceptions one may have of individual asset categories. For example, assume a client would like to purchase a new car in one year for $16,000. He would like to put down 50 percent of the purchase price and currently has $7,000 to invest; he needs approximately a 14 percent return in one year to accumulate $8,000. In determining the most appropriate asset category for the client at this time, the financial planner needs to identify the client's constraints such as marginal tax bracket, attitudes towards risk, resources available, and trends in the economic environment. Alternatives available to attain this goal may include the following asset categories: fixed-income securities, common stock, options, and money market securities. If the goal cannot be met within one year, modification may be required (e.g., lengthening the time horizon, purchasing a less costly car, or making a higher monthly payment). Therefore, the alternatives available must be reviewed carefully and analyzed as to whether they are appropriate for the client, based on an evaluation of the constraints, the current and forecasted economic outlook, and the potential for fulfilling the goal.

Selecting asset categories is a significant step in the portfolio construction and management process. The selection of asset categories is influenced by historical returns, current and forecasted economic conditions, and the constraints of each goal. The availability of measurements of security prices is useful in comparing performance results. Thus, the process of selecting asset categories depends upon the analysis, evaluation, and synthesis of a multitude of factors.

## STEP 6: IDENTIFY INVESTMENT STRATEGIES

An investment strategy is a plan of action used in portfolio construction and management to implement the overall plan. Strategies are considered after asset categories have been identified for each client goal and while the client's overall situation is being reviewed. Investment strategies involve techniques that maximize returns, protect returns, or reduce risk exposures.

The following is a brief discussion of several techniques available.

Investing in mutual funds is a technique used frequently; mutual funds may offer some advantages over investments in individual stocks or bonds. Because clients often use discretionary income as a source of funds to accomplish goals, investing in mutual funds is a convenient approach to accumulating funds with periodic purchases. Periodic contributions may be inconvenient when the client invests in individual stocks or bonds. Other advantages of mutual funds include professional management, low unit cost, and diversification of investment vehicles within each fund. In addition, dollar cost averaging and other formula plan techniques can be implemented with the use of mutual funds.

Another technique available is purchasing securities on margin. The economic environment and the client's risk-tolerance level, among other variables, should be considered before utilizing this technique. The use of margin can help the client attain a greater desired rate of return not available otherwise; however, this technique has the potential of magnifying losses. The use of margin allows the client to either (1) increase the total amount purchased in one security or (2) invest a certain amount in one security and use borrowed funds to diversify into other investment vehicles. For example, assume a client has $25,000 to invest. The client would like to purchase ABC stock, which is currently selling for $25 a share. The client can purchase 1,000 shares with the $25,000. On the other hand, if she opens a margin account with her broker (50 percent equity), she can increase her position in ABC stock to 2,000 shares for a total value of $50,000 ($25,000 of her funds, plus $25,000 of borrowed funds). Another alternative is to invest $25,000 in ABC using a margin account to purchase a total of 1,000 shares ($12,500 of her funds plus $12,500 of borrowed funds). Then she may diversify into other investment vehicles with the remaining $12,500.

Various investment strategies may be utilized to maximize the rate of return consistent with the client's risk-tolerance level. For example, assume a client needs current income but is not willing to assume the interest rate risk associated with a single maturity long-term bond. The financial planner can construct a portfolio consisting of bonds with staggered maturities. This technique reduces the risk exposure at the long end of the maturity spectrum. Maturities are spread out and the portfolio offers the client an average available interest rate, thus reducing the client's exposure to interest rate risk.

Hedging is another technique available to the client. Hedging can be accomplished through the use of warrants, puts, calls, stock index futures, and interest rate futures. Hedging involves combining two or more securities into a single investment position for the purpose of reducing risk. A principal objective of hedging is to protect profits and reduce the risk of loss on investments or portfolios. For example, assume a client has $50,000 invested in the stock market. Further assume the economic environment is bearish and the client does not want to sell these securities. The financial planner might suggest selling stock index futures contracts to offset the potential loss on the stock portfolio. Thus, the client is able to keep the portfolio and also earn a profit on the futures contracts if there is a decline in the market. Selling stock index futures contracts can be utilized at any time to hedge a stock portfolio against unforeseen events.

The financial planner should consider alternative investment strategies when reviewing the client's overall situation. Changes in economic conditions affect the techniques selected and increase the need for monitoring the portfolio. The number of techniques available for portfolio construction is limited only by the creativity of the financial planner.

## STEP 7: SELECT INVESTMENT VEHICLES

Selecting investment vehicles is a crucial step in the portfolio construction and management process. The financial planner chooses appropriate investment vehicles within the asset category selected (Step 5 above). The selection of investment vehicles is influenced by the client's goals and constraints, and by economic conditions. Trends in the economic indicators presented in Step 4 also affect this selection. For example, the direction and level of interest rates, GNP, and housing starts may affect the selection of a fixed-income security, common stock, or real estate investment. The investment vehicles selected in the portfolio construction and management process presented below are generic vehicles. When specific investment vehicles are chosen, the financial planner should apply valuation and analysis techniques for each vehicle.

The six constraints identified in Step 3 are the guidelines used to select appropriate asset categories and investment vehicles for the portfolio. In addition, there are several criteria within each asset category that are used as a checklist to determine if the selection of a given investment vehicle matches the client's constraints and goals. The following is a summary of the criteria used to evaluate the selection of investment vehicles within each asset category.

## CRITERIA:

### Money market instruments

> Objective: current income, safety of principal, defensive strategy
> Taxable or tax exempt
> Degree of liquidity and marketability
> Sources of investment risk
> Effect of diversification

### Fixed-income securities

> Advisory service ratings
> Par value, discount, or premium bond
> Type of bond: corporate, municipal, or government
> Type of corporate bond: mortgage, equipment trust, debenture
> Type of municipal bond: revenue, general obligation
> Maturity of security
> Retirement features: call feature, sinking fund requirement
> Degree of liquidity and marketability
> Sources of investment risk
> Effects of diversification

### Common stock

> Advisory service ratings
> Type of stock: income, growth, speculative
> Exchange or market where stock is traded
> Degree of liquidity and marketability

Sources of investment risk

Effects of diversification

**Real estate**

Objective: current income, capital appreciation, tax shelter

Type of real estate: commercial, industrial, residential, REITs

New property or existing property

Degree of leverage

Degree of liquidity and marketability

Sources of investment risk

Effects of diversification

**Options**

Expiration date of put or call

Buying or selling puts or calls

Selling uncovered or covered calls

Maturity of convertible securities

Advisory service ratings of convertible securities

Degree of liquidity and marketability

Sources of investment risk

Effects of diversification

**Physical assets**

Type: collectibles, gemstones, metals

Type of gold medium: Krugerrands, bullion, stock, futures

Objective: income-in-kind, capital appreciation

Degree of liquidity and marketability

Sources of investment risk

Effects of diversification.

**Futures**

Settlement date of contract

Type: commodity, financial

Hedging or speculating
Degree of liquidity and marketability
Sources of investment risk
Effects of diversification

Criteria for each asset category are used as a checklist to match the constraints identified in Step 3. The six constraints are directly or indirectly included in the criteria listed within each asset category. In some cases, however, the constraints themselves serve as the criteria. For example, the selection of the asset category, futures, implies a short time horizon. On the one hand, if futures are selected as an asset category, it is assumed that a short time horizon is consistent with the client's goal. On the other hand, if common stock is the asset category selected, further criteria are necessary to determine if the time horizon constraint is being met.

The following examples consider each constraint and show how a criterion within an asset category relates to the constraint.

*Constraint:* **time horizon**
   Asset category: **fixed-income securities**
   Criterion: **maturity**

The maturity of a bond should correlate to the client's time horizon. If the client needs a steady flow of income for the next 15 years, the call features and sinking fund requirements of the security affect the bonds selected.

*Constraint:* **liquidity**
   Asset category: **common stock**
   Criterion: *type of stock:* **high-grade growth, speculative**

The type of stock chosen should correspond to the client's liquidity constraint. In this example, a high-grade growth stock is usually more liquid than a speculative stock because the speculative stock may fluctuate more in price.

*Constraint:* **marketability**
   Asset category: **fixed-income securities**
   Criterion: *type of bond:* **corporate, municipal, or government**

A good proxy for marketability is the volume traded on a security. In this example, Treasury bills have a higher degree of marketability than corporate or municipal bonds because there is a very active secondary market.

*Constraint:* **tax consequences**
> Asset category: **fixed-income securities**
> Criterion: *type of bond:* **corporate, municipal, or government**

The type of bond chosen should correspond to the client's marginal tax bracket. The level of interest rates affects the decision when taxable and nontaxable yields are compared.

*Constraint:* **risk-tolerance level**
> Asset category: **real estate**
> Criterion: **new property or existing property**

The purchase of newly constructed real estate investment property generally involves more risks than purchasing an existing property. The client's risk-tolerance level should correspond to the vehicle selected. The risk-tolerance level constraint encompasses many of the criteria outlined. Sources of investment risk are identified for each vehicle selected as a means of correlating them to the client's risk-tolerance level. In addition, the risk of principal volatility and principal impairment are considerations when selecting vehicles to match the client's disposition towards risk.

*Constraint:* **diversification**

Diversification is used to reduce unsystematic risk in the portfolio. The client's portfolio can be diversified in several ways such as within asset categories and among asset categories. The selection of an investment vehicle, then, may have several effects on the diversification of the portfolio. It is important that the effects of diversification be considered for each investment vehicle selected in relation to the existing portfolio.

An assessment of the constraints and economic conditions is used to select appropriate investment vehicles for the client's goals. The criteria are then used to determine if the selection is consistent with the constraints. There are numerous vehicles available within each asset category. In addition, as the financial services industry develops new, innovative products, there will be many vehicles available to meet the needs of clients.

## STEP 8: PORTFOLIO APPROPRIATE?

After appropriate vehicles have been selected, the next step in the process is to consider the client's existing investment portfolio. If the vehicle selected in Step 7 is already included in the client's portfolio, repositioning may not be necessary. The financial planner should be certain that the quality and expected return are appropriate and the vehicle is not earmarked for other purposes. If the vehicle in the existing portfolio matches the vehicle selected in Step 7, monitoring is necessary to be sure the expected return is realized. If the existing portfolio is not consistent with the appropriate vehicles selected in Step 7, repositioning of the client's available resources is necessary.

## STEP 9: RESOURCES AVAILABLE?

Once appropriate vehicles are selected for client goals, resources are allocated in an efficient manner. The financial planner identifies resources remaining after allocation of each goal. If sufficient resources are not available, goals may need to be modified or delayed until there are available resources. The modification of goals may involve a change in time horizons or a change in dollar amounts. The revision process begins at Step 1 and continues through Step 9.

## STEP 10: ALLOCATE RESOURCES

The next step in the process is to allocate the resources to the appropriate investment vehicles. These resources are allocated by goals in order of their priority. Time value of money concepts are used to determine if goals can be achieved with the appropriate investment vehicles. As the client's resources may consist of both existing assets and cash flow, the present value and future value of a single sum and of an annuity are used in the analysis. In addition, the periodic payments needed to attain the goal is utilized in the analysis.

Often, net inflows are the only resource available to meet goals. Many times, goals are achieved by investing small incremental increases, rather than by investing a lump sum. Mutual fund investments are particularly suitable for periodic investing, as contributions can be made periodically into a fund that is most appropriate for the client goal. A decision to use mutual funds is made after reviewing available resources. If the client's resources are mainly from cash flow, if there are not sufficient funds to invest in individual investment vehicles, or if there is a need to dissipate the principal to achieve a goal, mutual fund investments may be appropriate for the portfolio. A fund that correlates as closely as possible to the investment vehicles selected in Step 7 should be chosen. The planner should review the fund's policies, restrictions, and investment portfolio to ascertain whether the fund matches the client's constraints.

Frequently, a goal can be attained by using a combination of lump-sum and periodic payment. Time value of money concepts are used to allocate resources in an efficient manner. It may become apparent during the allocation process that there are insufficient resources to achieve all the client's goals. The goals may need to be modified or delayed until more resources become available.

## STEP 11: ON TARGET?

Once the client resources are allocated, the financial planner evaluates the portfolio to determine if goals can be attained based on the realized or expected aftertax return on investment vehicles. Economic conditions play a major role in determining if the required rate of return can be attained. For example, assume growth common stock was selected to achieve a client's goal of capital appreciation. Due to unexpected changes in the stock market, the expected rate of return is unattainable and the goal cannot be achieved. When a goal cannot be attained due to changes in economic conditions, resources are evaluated again and so allocated that the goals, in order of priority, can be attained. If there are insufficient resources to meet the goal, modification may be necessary or the goal may be delayed until more resources are available.

Time value of money concepts are used to determine what modifications are necessary to attain a goal. Calculating the number of years, the rate of return, and the payment needed to attain a goal are required in this analysis. For example, assume a client wants to accumulate $19,500 in four years and is depositing $4,000 per year to attain this goal. If the expected aftertax return on the vehicle selected becomes 5 percent instead of 8 percent, the goal may have to be modified. The goal may take four and a half years to attain instead of the desired four years, or it may require an additional $300 deposit every year.

When resources are allocated for the first time in the portfolio construction process, this "on target" step is merely a check since the vehicles were selected in light of current economic conditions. This step becomes crucial in the monitoring process when changes in economic conditions occur. In addition, assume a client's goal can be achieved only if an 8 percent aftertax return is attained, and there are no other resources available. This goal requires continuous monitoring, because economic conditions must stay the same or improve in order for the goal to be achieved. The financial planner continuously monitors the portfolio to be sure goals can be met with changes in economic conditions and changes in the rate of return available in the marketplace.

## STEP 12: GOALS ATTAINED?

Step 12 entails determining if a given goal has been attained. This step is obviously disregarded when the portfolio is initially constructed. However, when a goal has been attained, the process begins again with Step 1. If there are resources remaining after the goal has been attained these resources can be used to attain other priority goals or new goals. If a given goal has not been attained, the financial planner continues to monitor the portfolio for changes in variables.

## STEP 13: CHANGES?

The final and most crucial step in the portfolio construction and management process is to monitor the existing portfolio for changes in variables. Portfolio monitoring is a continuous, ongoing assessment of the existing portfolio. Responding to the changes that occur involves portfolio revision. Portfolio revision involves a set of actions in response to the assessment derived from monitoring. The process of portfolio revision is systematic and parallel to the portfolio construction process. The revision process is simply a modification of the initial construction process.

Factors to monitor that could prompt portfolio revision are (1) changes in the client's goals, (2) changes in the client's constraints, and (3) changes in market conditions and expectations. For example, the death of the family breadwinner may cause the priority goal of retirement planning to be changed to current income. In this instance, the existing portfolio may need to be revised to match the client's new priority goal. An increase in inflows may affect the client's risk-tolerance level and tax constraints; therefore, the financial planner should assess the existing portfolio to determine its appropriateness. Changes in tax laws and in monetary and fiscal policy may also affect the appropriateness of the existing portfolio. For example, an unanticipated change in the inflation rate may affect the client's risk tolerance and liquidity constraints, which may prompt a modification in the portfolio. Unexpected changes involving specific vehicles in the portfolio may cause a need for revision. A change in management or in the expected earnings and dividend growth rate of a firm may affect the expected rate of return on a security needed to attain a given goal.

The monitoring process involves periodic review with the client so the financial planner is aware of changes in the goals and constraints. However, the monitoring process requires continuous review of economic conditions and expectations. Through monitoring the client's circumstances, the market conditions, and portfolio performance, the process comes full circle when changes in these variables result in the need to revise the portfolio. Ideally, the planner should maintain an efficient portfolio at all times, which maximizes the return for a given level of risk or minimizes the risk for a given level of return. If there are no changes in the variables affecting the portfolio, as in the case when the portfolio is initially constructed, the financial planner periodically reviews the portfolio to determine if the expected rate of return is on target.

Although the portfolio construction and management framework presented in this article focuses on investment planning, the process can also be applied to tax, retirement, and estate planning.

## SUMMARY OF THE PORTFOLIO CONSTRUCTION AND MANAGEMENT PROCESS

The following is a brief synopsis of the steps included in the portfolio construction and management process. A graphic presentation of the process is presented in Exhibit 5.

**Step 1.** Establish realistic **goals** and rank them in order of priority.

**Step 2.** Identify the client's **resources** available for use in portfolio construction.

**Step 3.** Identify the parameters for the six **constraints** that relate to the client's overall situation and goals.

**Step 4.** Identify current and forecasted **economic conditions.**

**EXHIBIT 5**     The portfolio construction and management process

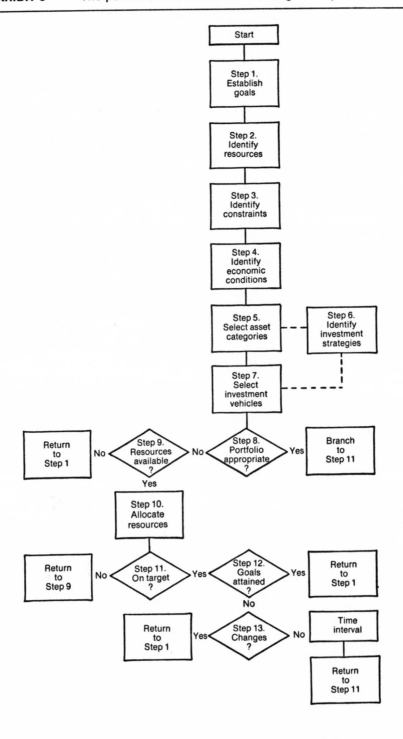

**Step 5.** Select appropriate **asset categories** based on the client's goals and constraints and current and forecasted economic conditions.

**Step 6.** Consider **investment strategies** available for the client's goals and overall situation.

**Step 7.** Select appropriate **investment vehicles** within asset categories. Use the criteria as a checklist to verify that the vehicles selected correspond to the client's goals and constraints.

**Step 8.** Determine if the client's existing **portfolio is appropriate.** If the vehicles selected in Step 7 are already included in the client's existing portfolio, determine if the quality and expected return are appropriate to meet the goal. If the vehicles selected in Step 7 are not included in the portfolio, reposition the client's resources.

**Step 9.** Identify **resources available** after allocation for each goal. If resources are not available, return to Step 1. The client may have to delay goals until resources become available.

**Step 10.** **Allocate resources** identified in Steps 2 and 9 to the appropriate vehicle by goal, in order of priority. Use time value of money concepts to allocate the resources efficiently.

**Step 11.** Evaluate the expected or realized aftertax return on the portfolio to determine if it is **on target** to attain goals. If the goal cannot be attained due to changes in the expected or realized return, evaluate available resources and reallocate. If sufficient resources are not available, return to Step 1.

**Step 12.** If the **goal is attained,** proceed to Step 1. The process begins again with other priority goals or new goals.

**Step 13.** Monitor the portfolio for **changes** in market conditions and expectations and in the client's goals and constraints. If there are changes, return to Step 1 to revise the portfolio. If there are no changes, periodically review the portfolio to determine if the expected or realized return is on target to attain client goals.

# SIX

## Stock market indicators

**Frank J. Fabozzi, Ph.D., C.F.A., C.P.A.**

*Walter E. Hanson/Peat, Marwick, Mitchell*
  *Professor of Business and Finance*
*Lafayette College*
*and*
*Managing Editor*
*The Journal of Portfolio Management*

**Jonathan C. Jankus, C.F.A.**
*Vice President*
*Kidder, Peabody & Co., Inc.*

Stock market indicators have come to perform a variety of functions, from serving as benchmarks for sophisticated performance analyses to answering the question "How did the market do today?" Thus, stock market indicators have become a part of everyday life for the investment practitioner. Even though many of the market indicators are used interchangeably, each measures a quite different facet of the "market."

In this article, we will explain the nature of the various indicators: the New York Stock Exchange (NYSE) Composite Index, the Standard & Poor's (S&P) 500 Composite Index, the Value Line Average Composite (VLA), the Dow Jones Industrial Average, the American Stock Exchange Market Value Index, the NASDAQ Composite Index, and the Wilshire 5000 Equity Index. We will also discuss three popular mutual fund indices published by Lipper Analytical Services.

## CONSTRUCTION OF STOCK MARKET INDICATORS

In general, the indicators rise and fall in unison. There are, however, important differences in the magnitude of these moves. To understand the reasons for these differences, it is necessary to understand how indicators are constructed.

Three factors differentiate stock market indicators:

1. The universe of stocks represented by the indicator.
2. The relative weights given to the stocks.
3. The method of averaging used.

Each of these factors is discussed below.

### The universe of stocks represented

An index or average can be designed from all publicly traded stocks or from a sample of publicly traded stocks. The NYSE Composite Index consists of about 1,520 stocks, the S&P 500 consists of 500 stocks, and the VLA consists of about 1,700 stocks. The breadth of coverage differs for each market indicator. The NYSE Composite Index, first computed in 1965, reflects the market value of all issues traded on the NYSE. Table 1 presents summary information on the composition of the stocks in this index.

The indicator series computed by Standard & Poor's represents selected samples of stocks chosen from both the major exchanges—NYSE and the American Stock Exchange

---

**TABLE 1**     Composition of indexes (percentage weighting) as of September 1982

|  | S&P 500 | NYSE | Value Line | Wilshire 5000 |
|---|---|---|---|---|
| Consumer nondurables | 28% | 26% | 29% | 25% |
| Consumer durables | 3 | 3 | 6 | 3 |
| Materials and services | 10 | 11 | 20 | 11 |
| Raw materials | 5 | 5 | 9 | 5 |
| Technology | 14 | 12 | 10 | 12 |
| Energy | 19 | 18 | 8 | 17 |
| Transportation | 2 | 3 | 5 | 3 |
| Utilities | 13 | 15 | 11 | 13 |
| Finance | 6 | 7 | 2 | 10 |

Source: Wilshire Associates.

(AMEX)—and the over-the-counter market. The universe represented is determined by a committee, which may occasionally add or delete individual stocks or entire industry groups from the universe. The aim of the committee is to capture present overall stock market conditions representing a very broad range of economic indicators. Table 1 compares the composition of this index with that of three other broad market indexes.

The VLA, produced by Arnold Bernhard & Co., covers a broad range of widely held and traded issues selected by Value Line. Table 1 gives summary information about the composition of the stocks in this market indicator.

The most commonly quoted indicator, the Dow Jones Industrial Average (DJIA), monitors 30 of the largest blue-chip companies traded on the NYSE. Table 2 shows the companies in-

---

**TABLE 2**     The 30 stocks in the Dow Jones Industrial Average (as of September 1983)

| | |
|---|---|
| Allied Corporation | International Business Machines Corp. |
| Aluminum Co. of America | International Harvester Co. |
| American Brands, Inc. | International Paper Co. |
| American Can Company | Merck & Co., Inc. |
| American Express Company | Minnesota Mining & Manufacturing |
| American Telephone & Telegraph | Co. |
| Company | Owens-Illinois, Inc. |
| Bethlehem Steel Corp. | Procter & Gamble Co. |
| Du Pont | Sears Roebuck & Co. |
| Eastman Kodak Co. | Standard Oil Co. of California |
| Exxon Corporation | Texaco Inc. |
| General Electric Co. | Union Carbide Corp. |
| General Foods Corp. | United States Steel Corporation |
| General Motors Corporation | United Technologies Corp. |
| The Goodyear Tire & Rubber Company | Westinghouse Electric Corporation |
| Inco | F. W. Woolworth Co. |

---

cluded in the DIJA. These companies change over time as companies are dropped due to mergers, bankruptcy, or a very low level of trading activity.[1] When a company is replaced by

---

[1] When the DJIA was originally published, in 1897, it was based on 12 stocks. Eight stocks were added in 1916, and in October 1928 the DJIA was expanded to 30 stocks. Of the original 12 stocks comprised by the DJIA, only two are now included—American Brands (formerly American Tobacco) and General Electric. Of the 30 companies in the DJIA in 1928, when the sample was expanded to its present size, only 15 are now included.

another company, the average is readjusted in such a way as to provide comparability with earlier values.

The American Stock Exchange Market Value Index, introduced in September 1973, reflects the market value of all issues traded on that exchange. This index generally includes companies with smaller capitalization than the universe of companies traded on the NYSE and has a proportionally greater foreign and energy-related orientation.

The NASDAQ Composite Index, introduced in February 1971, reflects changes in the market value of the over-the-counter stocks traded by the National Association of Securities Dealers (NASD). The NASDAQ Composite Index represents companies with much smaller capitalization than that of the companies represented by the two exchange indexes and has proportionally greater representation of banks and insurance companies.

The Wilshire 5000 Equity Index is a comprehensive index that represents all actively traded companies. The index is published daily by Wilshire Associates of Santa Monica, California. Table 1 compares the industry distribution of the firms in the Wilshire 5000 index as of September 1982 to that of the three other indicators.

### Relative weights

The stocks comprised by an indicator must be combined to construct the index or average. Each stock, therefore, must be assigned some relative weight. There are three ways in which weights can be assigned: (1) weighting by the market value of the company, (2) weighting by the price of the company's stock, and (3) weighting each company equally, regardless of its price or value.

With the exception of the VLA, the DJIA, and a newly developed index by the American Stock Exchange called the Major Market Index, all other market indicators are market value-weighted. The VLA is an equally weighted index. The DJIA is a price-weighted average. Each of these relative weighting schemes will be illustrated later in this article.

### Method of averaging

Given the stocks that will be used to create the sample and the relative weights to be assigned to each stock, it is then necessary to average the individual components. Two methods of averaging are possible—arithmetic and geometric. With the exception of the VLA, all of the market indicators discussed in this article are based on an arithmetic average.

Although the computation of an indicator based on the geometric averaging technique will be demonstrated in the next section, a brief discussion of the mathematical properties of the geometric mean is appropriate. The arithmetic mean of multiple returns will always be greater than their geometric mean. Consequently, as long as there is any variability of returns among the stocks comprised by the indicator, an indicator constructed by using geometric averaging will always grow more slowly, or decline more rapidly, than an indicator constructed by using arithmetic averaging.

### Selecting the base year value for the indicator

To gauge the movements in the stocks comprised by the indicator, some time period must be designated as the base period and a value assigned to the indicator at that time. For example, the base period for the Consumer Price Index is 1967. The value of the index assigned for the base period is 100. The CPI in November 1984 was 315. This means that the CPI was 215 percent greater in November 1984 than it was in the base period, 1967.

However, the value assigned to the base year of an index need not be 100. For the NYSE Composite Index, the base year is 1965 and the value assigned to the index for that year is 50. Since the value of the NYSE Composite Index was 94.30 on November 30, 1984, this means that the value of the index increased by 89 percent compared to 1965. The base selected for the S&P 500 is the period 1941–43. The average prices over that period are assigned an index value of 10.

Although an arbitrary value can be assigned to the base year of a value-weighted and equally weighted index, this cannot be done with a price-weighted market indicator, such as the DJIA. This is so because price-weighted indicators are not really indexes but are an *average* of the prices included in the indicator after making adjustments for stock splits.

Table 3 summarizes for all the indicators the type of relative weighting scheme, method of averaging, base year, and value of index or average in the base year, number of stocks in

**TABLE 3**

| | S&P 500 | NYSE Composite | VLA | DJIA | AMEX | NASDAQ Composite | Wilshire |
|---|---|---|---|---|---|---|---|
| Relative weighting scheme | Market value-weighted | Market value-weighted | Equally weighted | Price weighted | Market value-weighted | Market value-weighted | Market value-weighted |
| Method of averaging | Arithmetic | Arithmetic | Geometric | Arithmetic | Arithmetic | Arithmetic | Arithmetic |
| Base year | 1941–1943 | 1965 | 1961 | N/A | 1973 | 1971 | 1980 |
| Value of indicator in base year | 10 | 500 | 100 | N/A | 50[a] | 100 | 1,404.596 |
| Number of stocks in indicator | 500 | 1,520 approx. | 1,700 approx. | 30 | 830 approx. | 3,500 approx. | 5,500 approx. |
| Markets where stocks in indicator are traded | NYSE, AMEX, OTC | NYSE | NYSE, AMEX, OTC, CANADIAN | NYSE | AMEX | OTC | All U.S. stocks |

N/A = not applicable.
[a] Two-for-one split in July 1983 to make option trading more convenient.

the indicator, and markets where stocks in the indicator are traded.

## IMPLICATIONS FOR ASSET ALLOCATION STRATEGY

An important consideration for the financial planner (investor) is the asset allocation strategy that corresponds to each of the computational methods discussed in this article.

A value-weighted index is an appropriate benchmark for an index fund that attempts to invest in "the market." Certainly, all investors in aggregate define the market. With commissions ignored, a value-weighted index represents the performance achievable by investing in all possible stocks in proportion to their market value.

A price-weighted indicator is an appropriate benchmark for an investor who apportions his or her wealth among stocks in ratios that correspond to their current prices. For example, an investor would invest five times as much in stock A as in stock B, simply because the price of stock A is five times that of stock B. Equivalently, this strategy implies that the investor invests in an equal number of shares of each stock, regardless of the price.

The equally weighted arithmetic index is an appropriate benchmark for an investor who apportions his or her wealth in equal dollar amounts among all stocks selected.

These examples cannot be extended to a comparable asset allocation strategy for the equally weighted geometric index. Proponents of this type of index claim that arithmetic averages overstate attainable results. However, it is important to understand that the results described by a geometric index are simply unattainable by means of any portfolio strategy. That is, an investor could not (*ex ante*) construct a portfolio of stocks whose total appreciation would equal the geometric mean of the percentage appreciation of all.

## COMOVEMENTS OF STOCK MARKET INDICATORS

There is a high correlation between the monthly movements of each indicator in Table 3, usually greater than .80. It is almost surprising that the relationship should be so close, in particular for the Dow Jones Averages, in light of the sizable computational differences in a few cases. A moment's reflection on the universe biases involved gives some explanation. At present, the DJIA, although only 30 companies, represents approximately 21 percent of the total capitalization of NYSE stocks and approximately 28 percent of the total capitalization of the S&P 500. These are precisely the huge issues that have the heaviest impact on the value-weighted NYSE and Standard & Poor's indicators. This makes it easier to understand why these indicators should follow each other so closely.

The NASDAQ indicators are much more volatile than the NYSE and S&P indicators. The reason is that the small-capitalization stocks that comprise the NASDAQ indicators tend to be more volatile than large capitalization stocks.

It is worthwhile to investigate the price changes of various stock market indicators over different periods in the recent past. Table 4 shows the percentage changes in the various indicators over recent 1-month, 3-month, 12-month, and two-year periods ending in February 1982.

**TABLE 4**    Performance of selected indicators (percent change in price)*

|  | 1 Month | 3 Months | 12 Months | 2 Years |
|---|---|---|---|---|
| S&P 500 . . . . . . . . . . . . . . . | −6.1% | −10.5% | −13.8% | −0.6% |
| S&P 400 . . . . . . . . . . . . . . | −6.7 | −10.9 | −15.9 | −2.8 |
| DJIA . . . . . . . . . . . . . . . . | −5.4 | −7.3 | −15.4 | −4.5 |
| NYSE Composite . . . . . . . . . . | −5.9 | −11.0 | −13.0 | 0.6 |
| AMEX Composite . . . . . . . . . . | −10.0 | −20.0 | −21.5 | −12.4 |
| NASDAQ OTC Industrials . . . . . . | −6.8 | −13.6 | −18.1 | 5.7 |
| Value Line Average Composite. . . . . | −5.0 | −10.3 | −11.8 | 2.0 |

* For periods ended February 26, 1982.
Source: *Current Investment Policy and Strategy Implementation*, April 1982, Kidder, Peabody Investment Policy Group.

It is apparent from the results reported in Table 4 that, over time, considerable differences arise among the selected indicators. Moreover, these differences increase with time, to the point where over the two-year period half of the indicators show positive returns and half show negative returns. Even over the 12-month period, although all returns are negative, the relative magnitudes of the differences are dramatic.

The investor will no doubt be interested in the percentage changes in the indicators during market cycles. These results

**TABLE 5**     Comparison of cyclical percentage changes for selected indicators: 1966 through 1980*

| Cycle period | VLA | NYSE | S&P 500 | DJIA |
|---|---|---|---|---|
| 2/66–10/66 | −24.7% | −22.7% | −22.7% | −24.7% |
| 10/66–10/67 | 47.2 | 37.3 | 32.9 | 24.8 |
| 10/67– 3/68 | −10.7 | −9.3 | −9.1 | −11.1 |
| 3/68–12/68 | 35.4 | 24.3 | 21.7 | 18.8 |
| 12/68– 7/70 | −54.1 | −35.0 | −32.2 | −29.8 |
| 7/70– 4/71 | 43.6 | 44.5 | 42.6 | 36.7 |
| 4/71–11/71 | −20.3 | −11.7 | −11.6 | −13.3 |
| 4/71– 4/72 | 26.8 | 21.2 | 19.5 | 18.5 |
| 4/72– 1/73 | −7.6 | 6.7 | 9.1 | 8.2 |
| 1/73–12/74 | −58.9 | −45.6 | −44.0 | −42.5 |
| 12/74– 2/76 | 87.7 | 54.4 | 52.1 | 64.0 |
| 2/76– 3/78 | 1.2 | −10.9 | −14.3 | −24.3 |
| 3/78– 9/78 | 31.6 | 23.8 | 22.1 | 21.5 |
| 9/78–12/78 | −17.8 | −11.0 | −10.0 | −11.3 |
| 12/78–10/79 | 27.8 | 18.2 | 15.8 | 11.5 |
| 10/79–11/79 | −11.6 | −8.9 | −8.8 | −10.2 |
| 11/79– 2/80 | 18.3 | 17.0 | 16.2 | 11.1 |
| 2/80– 3/80 | −20.1 | −15.9 | −14.6 | −13.2 |
| 3/80–12/80 | 37.9 | 37.8 | 35.6 | 24.3 |

* Based on end-of-week closing values.
Source: *Value Line Composite Average: The Index behind the Futures,* by the Kansas City Board of Trade.

are reported in Table 5 for the NYSE Composite Index, the S&P 500, the VLA, and the DJIA for successive intermediate peaks and troughs from February 1966 through December 1980.

Although the geometric averaging process understates the percentage changes compared to arithmetic averaging, the VLA, which is an equally weighted geometric index, usually shows greater percentage swings in market cycles compared to the other three indicators. The reason is that the VLA consists of a greater portion of more volatile small-company stocks whose prices are generally more sensitive to market direction. Consequently, the VLA tends to move up farther when the market rises and to move down farther when the market declines.

To continue the investigation Table 6 shows the high for the DJIA, the S&P 500 Index, and the NASDAQ Index during the recent bull market from August 12, 1982, to November 29, 1983. Table 6 indicates that the smaller capitalized stocks, as repre-

**TABLE 6**   Highs for three stock market indicators: August 12, 1982 to November 29, 1983

| Indicator | Level as of 8/12/82 | High during bull market | Date high was reached | Percentage change |
|---|---|---|---|---|
| DJIA . . . . . . . . . . . . . | 776.92 | 1287.20 | 11/29/83 | +65.7% |
| S&P 500 Index . . . . . . . . | 102.42 | 172.65 | 10/7/83 | +68.6 |
| NASDAQ Composite Index . . . . . . . . . . . | 159.84 | 329.91 | 6/24/83 | +106.4 |

sented by the NASDAQ Index, peaked earlier than the stocks of larger capitalized companies. Furthermore, the NASDAQ Index made a greater gain than the DJIA and S&P 500 Index and in a shorter time. After June 24, 1983, the DJIA and the S&P 500 went on to make new highs about three to five months later, while the NASDAQ Index started to decline.

Table 7 indicates the level of these three indicators through July 25, 1984, and shows the percentage change since the highs in 1983. The table indicates, as expected, that the NASDAQ Index had the greatest percentage loss.

**TABLE 7**   Highs for three stock market indicators through July 25, 1984

| Indicator | High | Date high was reached | Low | Date low was reached | Percentage change |
|---|---|---|---|---|---|
| DJIA . . . . . . . | 1287.20 | 11/29/83 | 1086.57 | 7/24/84 | −15.6% |
| S&P 500 Index. . . | 172.65 | 10/7/83 | 147.82 | 7/24/84 | −14.4 |
| NASDAQ Composite Index . . . . . . | 329.91 | 6/24/83 | 225.30 | 7/25/84 | −31.7 |

## MUTUAL FUND INDICATORS

Lipper Analytical Securities Corporation has devised several indexes for the mutual fund industry. These indexes are used to compare the performance of funds owned by an investor. The three most popular are the Lipper Growth Fund Index, the Lipper Growth & Income Fund Index, and the Lipper Balanced Fund Index. All three indexes are based at 100 on December 31, 1968, and are value-weighted based on net asset values. As of year-end 1983, the number of funds in these three indexes represented under 11 percent of all funds tracked by Lipper Analytical Services, and represented 41.4 percent of the industry's assets.

Table 8 shows the funds that comprise each index. These indexes are published very Monday in *The Wall Street Journal* and weekly in *Barron's* and *Business Week*.

Table 9 shows the level of the indexes as of December 13, 1984, and the percentage change from the previous year.

## ILLUSTRATION OF THE CONSTRUCTION OF STOCK MARKET INDICATORS AND THE EFFECTS OF COMPUTATIONAL DIFFERENCES

To illustrate the construction of an index based on the three relative weighting schemes and the two methods of averaging and the computational effects on the various indexes, we will use a hypothetical example. We begin by assuming that the various indicators reflect the same population of stocks, so we may focus on the biases produced by computational differences, as opposed to differences in the stocks comprised by the indicator.

We begin with three stocks, A, B, and C, whose prices in the base or initial period *(0)* and some future time period *(t)* are given in Table 10. The value assigned to the indicator in the base year is 100 for all but the price-weighted indicator.

### Market value-weighted indicator

The total market value of each stock in the indicator is computed by simply multiplying the price of each by the corresponding number of shares outstanding. The market value–weighted index is then computed by dividing the current total market value of all the stocks used to construct the index by the total market value of all these stocks in the initial or base period. The quotient is then multiplied by the value assigned to

---

**TABLE 8**    Funds comprising the three popular Lipper indexes

---

### Growth Fund Index

| | | | |
|---|---|---|---|
| (1) | Amcap Fund | (16) | Lord Abbett Value Appreciation |
| (2) | American General Enterprise Fund | (17) | Mass. Investors Growth Stock Fd. |
| (3) | Chemical Fund | (18) | Mass. Capital Development Fund |
| (4) | Dreyfus Growth Opportunity Fund | (19) | W. L. Morgan Growth Fund |
| (5) | Elfun Trusts | (20) | Oppenheimer Special Fund |
| (6) | Fidelity Destiny Fund | (21) | T. Rowe Price Growth Stock Fund |
| (7) | Fidelity Magellan Fund | (22) | Putnam Growth Fund |
| (8) | Fidelity Trend Fund | (23) | Putnam Investors Fund |
| (9) | General Electric S & S Programs | (24) | Seligman Growth Fund |
| (10) | Growth Fund of America | (25) | Sequoia Fund |
| (11) | Hutton Invest Series Growth Fund | (26) | Technology Fund |
| (12) | IDS Growth Fund | (27) | Twentieth Century Select Fund |
| (13) | IDS New Dimensions Fund | (28) | United Accumulative Fund |
| (14) | IDS Variable Payment | (29) | United Vanguard Fund |
| (15) | Keystone S-4 | (30) | Value Line Spec. Situations Fund |

### Growth & Income Fund Index

| | | | |
|---|---|---|---|
| (1) | Affiliated Fund | (16) | Mutual Shares Corp. |
| (2) | American Mutual Fund | (17) | National Securities Stock Fund |
| (3) | Delaware Fund | (18) | Nationwide Fund |
| (4) | Dreyfus Fund | (19) | One William Street Fund |
| (5) | Fidelity Fund | (20) | Pioneer Fund |
| (6) | Financial Industrial Fund | (21) | Pioneer II |
| (7) | Fundamental Investors Fund | (22) | T.Rowe Price Gr. & Inc. Fund |
| (8) | Guardian Mutual Fund | (23) | Putnam Investors Fund |
| (9) | Hamilton Fund | (24) | Seligman Common Stock Fund |
| (10) | IDS Investors Stock Fund | (25) | Sentinel Common Stock Fund |
| (11) | Investment Co. of America | (26) | State Street Investment Fund |
| (12) | Mass. Financial Development Fund | (27) | Trustees' Commingled Equity Fd. |
| (13) | Mass. Investors Trust Fund | (28) | Vanguard Index Trust |
| (14) | Merrill Lynch Basic Value Fund | (29) | Washington Mutual Fund |
| (15) | Merrill Lynch Capital Fund | (30) | Windsor Fund |

### Balanced Fund Index

| | |
|---|---|
| (1) | American Balanced Fund |
| (2) | Axe-Houghton Fund B |
| (3) | Eaton Vance Investors |
| (4) | Investors Mutual Fund |
| (5) | Kemper Total Return |
| (6) | Loomis-Sayles Mutual Fund |
| (7) | Massachusetts Fund |
| (8) | George Putnam Fund of Boston |
| (9) | SteinRoe Total Return |
| (10) | Wellington Fund |

---

Source: Lipper Analytical Securities Corporation.

**TABLE 9**     Level of Lipper Indexes and change over previous year: As of December 31, 1984

|  | As of 12/13/84 | Percentage change from previous year |
|---|---|---|
| Growth Index . . . . . . . . . . . | 206.38 | −6.25% |
| Growth & Income Index . . . . . | 331.72 | + .59 |
| Balanced Index . . . . . . . . . | 278.73 | +3.14 |

**TABLE 10**     The effect of various computational techniques on indicator values

| Stock | Base year price (0) | No. of shares | Market value | Price at time t | Price change (percent) | New market value | Percent change in market value |
|---|---|---|---|---|---|---|---|
| A | $100 | 50 | $ 5,000 | $110.00 | 10% | $ 5,500 | 10% |
| B | 20 | 400 | 8,000 | 21.00 | 5 | 8,400 | 5 |
| C | 50 | 200 | 10,000 | 50.00 | 0 | 10,000 | 0 |
| Total |  |  | $23,000 |  |  | $23,900 |  |

|  | Base year index (0) | Value of index at time t | Change in index (percent) |
|---|---|---|---|
| Market value-weighted indicator | 100 | 103.91 | 3.91% |
| Price-weighted indicator | 56.67 | 60.33 | 6.47 |
| Equally weighted arithmetic indicator | 100 | 105.00 | 5.00 |
| Equally weighted geometric indicator | 100 | 104.92 | 4.92 |

the index in the base period. Mathematically, this is expressed as follows.

Market value-weighted indicator

$$= \frac{\text{Total market value in period } t}{\text{Total market value in base period}} \times \frac{\text{Index value}}{\text{in base period}}$$

Using the data for the hypothetical three-stock index given in Table 10, the total market value is $23,000 in the base year and $23,900 in time period $t$. Assuming that the index value in the base year is set at 100, then the market value–weighted index in time period $t$ is 103.91, as shown below:

$$\frac{\$23,900}{\$23,000} \times 100 = 103.91$$

Had the value of the index in the base period been set at 40 instead of 100, the market value–weighted index in period $t$ would be 41.57. Regardless of the value assigned to the index in the base period, the percentage change is 3.91 percent, which reflects an increase from $23,000 to $23,900 in the aggregate wealth in this hypothetical market portfolio.

In the preceding computation, the arithmetic mean was used to construct the index.

### Price-weighted indicator

A price-weighted indicator reflects changes in the average price of the stocks used to construct the index, adjusting for stock splits. Assuming no stock splits between the base period and period $t$ for any of the three stocks in Table 10, the average price of the three stocks changed from $56.67 [(100 + 20 + 50)/ 3] to $60.33 [(110 + 21 + 50)/3], or an increase of 6.47 percent.

Note that relative to the market value–weighted indicator, the price-weighted indicator considerably overstates the overall market portfolio change in this illustration. The reason is that the price-weighted indicator overweights the movement of stock A, simply because stock A had the highest price. Aggregate market value is not considered.

In this illustration the method of averaging is the arithmetic average. This is the method used to compute the DJIA, which is a price-weighted average. Alternatively, a price-weighted average based on the geometric mean of the prices could be computed.

Let's drop the assumption that all three stocks in Table 10 did not have a stock split between the base period and time period $t$. Instead, assume that, in time period $t$, stock A split two for one and the market price of stock A fell from $110 per share, the price it would have had in the absence of the stock split, to $55 per share. The average price in time period $t$ is $42 [(55 + 21 + 50)/3] as a result of the stock split. This is less than the base period average price of $56.67 and implies that the average stock price has declined. Of course, this is ridiculous. An adjustment is required so that the indicator will not be misleading as a result of the stock split.

The adjustment is made by changing the divisor that is used to compute the average. In the absence of the stock split, the sum of the three prices in time period $t$ is divided by 3, the number of stocks in our hypothetical indicator. The average price is $60.33. The sum of the three prices in time period $t$ after the stock split is $126. If the divisor is 2.089 (126 divided by 60.33), the average price would be $60.33 and the indicator in time period $t$ would be 106.47, just as before the stock split.

Revising the divisor is the procedure currently employed by Dow Jones to adjust for stock splits. Consequently, the computation of the DJIA can be expressed mathematically using the following formula:

$$\text{DJIA} = \frac{\text{Sum of the price of the 30 industrials}}{\text{Divisor}}$$

The divisor takes into consideration not only stock splits but also changes in the composition of the stocks used to compute the DJIA. As noted earlier, occasionally companies are dropped from the DJIA and replaced by other companies. For example, in 1979 Chrysler was replaced by IBM and Esmark was replaced by Merck.

Notice that an adjustment for stock splits is not necessary for a market value–weighted index. The market value–weighted index would still be 103.91 after the two-for-one split of stock A.

It would seem that the adjustment factor can be relied on to provide comparability with previous years after a stock split. This, however, would not be a proper conclusion. Recall that the adjustment factor is computed by looking for the value that will preserve the average price after the stock split. An alternative approach is to reweight the price of the split stock. For example, in our illustration of a two-for-one stock split for stock A, the weight for stock A would be doubled in determining the numerator of the price-weighted indicator, leaving the numerator unchanged before and after the stock split. This approach was in fact used for the DJIA prior to 1928.[2]

---

[2] The approach was dropped by the successor of Charles H. Dow, first editor of *The Wall Street Journal* (Robert D. Milne, "The Dow Jones Industrial Average Re-Examined," *Financial Analysts Journal*, December 1966).

Although the two approaches will give identical results at the time of the stock split, critics of the way in which Dow Jones currently adjusts for stock splits argue that this method produces a downward bias in subsequent years. As Hartman L. Butler, Jr., and J. Devon Allen point out:

> The new procedure reduces the importance of a successful company by reducing its weighting in the average every time expanding earnings occasion a stock split. Conversely, a laggard company with a disappointing earnings record (hence no split) receives increased arithmetic importance for at least a few years, although over time this bias will be at least partially offset as earnings disappointment reduces market price, hence weighting in the index.[3]

### Equally weighted arithmetic indicator

In an equally weighted arithmetic indicator, an equal dollar amount is assumed to be invested in each stock comprised by the indicator. For example, suppose that in the base year $1,000 is invested in each of the three stocks in Table 10. Given the same prices in the base year as used in the example above (i.e., 100, 20, and 50), the number of shares of stocks A, B, and C that could be purchased for $1,000 each is 10, 50, and 20, respectively. Thus the investment in the base year is $3,000. In time period $t$, as prices changed to 110, 21, and 50, respectively, the portfolio value of those shares would be equal to $3,150 [(110 × 10) + (21 × 50) + (50 × 20)]. The value of the portfolio therefore increased by 5 percent [(3,150/3,000) − 1]. If the base year index was 100, the index at time period $t$ would be 105 (100 × 1.05).

An alternative way of viewing the construction of this indicator is to note that the index percentage change equals the arithmetic average of the percentage changes in the prices of each of the three stocks, which is also 5 percent [(10 percent + 5 percent + 0 percent)/3]. This property will always be true when the current period is compared to the base period, but not for subsequent period-to-period comparisons.

### Equally weighted geometric indicator

As just noted, the equally weighted arithmetic indicator reflects the arithmetic average percentage change in the stocks

---

[3] Hartman L. Butler, Jr., and J. Devon Allen, "The Dow Jones Industrial Average Re-Reexamined," *Financial Analysts Journal*, November–December 1979, pp. 24 and 26.

comprised by the indicator calculated between the current period and the base period. The equally weighted geometric indicator has a similar interpretation. The difference is that the geometric mean is used to compute the average percentage change in the stocks comprised by the indicator.

The following steps are used to compute the geometric mean of the percentage change in the price of $N$ stocks comprised by an indicator.

**Step 1.** Compute the ratio of the price in period $t$ to the base period price for each of the $N$ stocks comprised by the indicator. (Prices must be adjusted for stock splits and dividends. Notice that the ratio represents 1 plus the percentage price change.)

**Step 2.** Multiply the ratios obtained from Step 1.

**Step 3.** Find the $N$th root of the product computed in Step 2. (The $N$th root is the value that produces the value computed in Step 2 if multiplied by itself $N$ times.)

**Step 4.** Subtract 1 from the value found in Step 3.

Using the three stocks in Table 10, the geometric mean return is found as follows:

**Step 1.** The ratio for each stock is:

$$A = 110/100 = 1.10$$
$$B = 21/20 \quad = 1.05$$
$$C = 50/50 \quad = 1.00$$

**Step 2.** Multiply the three ratios:

$$1.10 \times 1.05 \times 1.00 = 1.155$$

**Step 3.** Find the third root of 1.155, that is, $(1.155)^{1/3}$. The value we seek is 1.0492 since

$$1.0492 \times 1.0492 \times 1.0492 = 1.155$$

**Step 4.** Subtract 1 from the value found in Step 3:

$$1.0492 - 1 = .0492, \text{ or } 4.92 \text{ percent}$$

Notice that the geometric mean return is less than the arithmetic mean return of 5 percent. This is consistent with the mathematical property of the geometric mean discussed earlier in this article. The small difference between the geometric mean and the arithmetic mean in this illustration is due to the relatively small variation in the individual returns.

The equally weighted geometric index is found by multiply-ing 1 plus the geometric mean return by the value of the index in the base period. Assuming the value of the index in the base period to be 100, then the equally weighted geometric index for our hypothetical three-stock index would be 104.92 (1.0492 × 100).

A property of the geometric index is that both the period-to-period and the current period-to-base period percentage changes will be the same for the index and the individual stocks.

The VLA is the only indicator discussed in this article that is an equally weighted geometric indicator.

### Reworking the DJIA

The DJIA is a popular stock market indicator often quoted in the financial press.[4] A psychologically significant value for the DJIA is 1000. Some of the best parties on Wall Street have followed a market closing above 1000. The DJIA broke 1000 for the first time on January 18, 1966, when it reached 1001. Not until November 14, 1972, did it break the 1000 barrier again, closing at 1003.16.

Let us look at what would have happened if the DJIA were computed using the three other approaches discussed in this section instead of being price-weighted.

At the end of 1965, the DJIA was 969.26. Had the market value-weighted index approach been used to compute the aver-age for the 30 industrials in the DJIA since 1945, the indicator would have had a value of 1026.84 at the end of 1965. The equally weighted arithmetic index and the equally weighted geometric index approaches would have resulted in 1965 year-end DJIAs of 1096.92 and 813.40, respectively.[5] The lower value for the equally weighted geometric index compared to the equally weighted arithmetic index should not be surprising. It follows from the mathematical property of the geometric mean discussed earlier.

---

[4] Hartman L. Butler, Jr., and J. Devon Allen relate an anecdote about a successful stock trader who, when asked why the DJIA was always mentioned when people talked about the recent behavior of the stock market, replied: "The Dow Jones has been around a long time. It is literally available at my fingertips. *It is the only stock average I understand*" (emphasis added) (Butler and Allen, "The Dow Jones Industrial Average Re-Reexamined," p. 23).

[5] Milne, "The Dow Jones Industrial Average Re-Examined," p. 86.

We also mentioned the downward bias that results from the practice employed by Dow Jones to adjust the divisor. If the constant-divisor approach had been used instead of the current approach from the end of 1945 to the end of 1965, the DJIA would have been 1086.59 rather than 969.26.[6]

Substitution of companies also had an impact on the DJIA. In 1939 IBM was removed from the DJIA and replaced by AT&T. Had this substitution not taken place, the DJIA would have been 1017.39 in December 1961 rather than 734.91![7]

## SUMMARY

In a popular investment management textbook, the author begins the chapter on stock market indicator series with the following statement: "A fair statement regarding stock market indicator series is that everybody talks about them, but few people know how they are constructed and what they represent."[8] In view of this observation, an understanding of how stock indicators are constructed and what they represent is necessary to design and implement an investment strategy and, finally, to evaluate performance. In this chapter we discussed the various factors that differentiate stock market indicators and provided some empirical evidence on the comovements of the various major stock market indicators.

---

[6] Ibid.

[7] Ibid.

[8] Frank K. Reilly, *Investment Analysis and Portfolio Management* (Hinsdale, Ill.: Dryden Press, 1979), p. 119.

# SEVEN

## Stock market strategies

**Frank J. Fabozzi, Ph.D., C.F.A., C.P.A.**
*Walter E. Hanson/Peat, Marwick, Mitchell
    Professor of Business and Finance
Lafayette College
and
Managing Editor
The Journal of Portfolio Management*

**T. Dessa Garlicki**
*Instructor of Finance
Rutgers University*

There is no shortage of strategies about how to "beat the stock market." In this article, we discuss several stock market strategies that researchers have found may be successful in beating the market. However, we must first explain exactly what we mean by beating the market. This, in turn, will require that an appropriate measure of risk be defined. In the final section of this article, we explain the strategies an investor can employ if markets are too efficient to beat.

### BEATING THE MARKET

When an investor claims that he or she beat the market, what the investor often means is that he or she earned a rate of return greater than some general market index, such as the Standard & Poor's Composite 500 Index.[1] For example, if an investor

---

[1] Market indexes are discussed in Article Six.

earned a return of 12 percent on a portfolio of stocks, while the return on the Standard & Poor's 500 for the same time period was 10 percent, an investor often claims to have outperformed or beat the market. Is this claim justified?

Not necessarily. We must first know the degree of risk that characterized her portfolio of stocks before we can make any determination of relative investment performance. It is necessary to adjust her return for the degree of risk taken before we can accept her claim that she beat the market. To see why, let's draw an analogy to an individual's physical characteristics. Suppose that a man weighs 150 pounds. Is that man overweight, underweight, or the normal weight? It's impossible to answer this correctly without knowing his height. If the man was four feet tall, he would be overweight. If he was the seven-foot center for your favorite basketball team, he would clearly be underweight. If he was five feet six inches tall, standard health tables would categorize his weight as normal.

Just as we must know the height of an individual to assess whether that person is overweight, underweight, or the normal weight, we must know the degree of risk to which an individual is exposed to determine if he beat the market. Consequently, in professional money management, beating the market does not just mean earning a return greater than the Standard & Poor's 500—it means earning a rate of return greater than this index after adjusting for the risk associated with the portfolio. So if money manager A earned a rate of return of 10 percent, and money manager B earned a rate of 12 percent, and if the return on the Standard & Poor's 500 for the same period was 11 percent, it is *possible* that money manager B underperformed the market despite the fact that the "raw" return (i.e., return unadjusted for risk) was greater than the market, while money manager A beat the market despite the fact that the raw return was less than that of the market. We can't tell, without knowing, what levels of risk were accepted by the two money managers.

However, we still see the popular press comparing raw returns to some general market index when making statements about the relative investment performance of professional money managers.

## MEASURING RISK

To determine whether an investor beat the market, we must first be able to measure the degree of risk associated with his or her portfolio. Once we know how to measure the degree of risk, we need a model that tells us what return we should expect to earn for that level of risk. The expected return is the risk-adjusted return that the investor should earn. We then compare the actual return to the expected return. If the actual return is greater than the expected return, then the investor is said to have outperformed the market on a risk-adjusted basis. This is precisely what is meant by beating the market. If the actual return is less than the expected return, then the investor underperformed the market on a risk-adjusted basis.

First let's tackle the problem of how to measure risk. When we commonly think about risk, we think in terms of the chance of realizing a return less than the return we had expected to earn. One measure of risk is the variability of a stock's return around its expected return. In statistics, variance is used to measure the variability of some variable around its expected value. However, variance is not the correct measure of risk associated with a portfolio, as we will soon explain.

Variance is a measure of total risk of a stock. But the total risk of a security is comprised of two distinct types—nondiversifiable and diversifiable risk. Nondiversifiable risk is a measure of how a security's return is affected by factors common to all securities in the market. Examples of factors affecting all securities are inflation, the general level of interest rates, and the state of the economy. The impact of these factors on a portfolio cannot be avoided, since they are common to all securities in the portfolio. For this reason, other names for nondiversifiable risk are "market risk" or "systematic risk."

However, diversifiable or unsystematic risk is risk associated with a specific security. This risk can be avoided by holding a portfolio of different securities, since it is specific to the security in question. This risk is often called "company specific risk" and may include such things as a strike or lawsuit against a specific firm. Empirical studies using randomly selected portfolios have shown that, by holding a portfolio of about 10 to 12 different securities, an investor can diversify away virtually all unsystematic or company specific risk. Therefore, the only risk present in a well-diversified portfolio is nondiversifiable or market risk. It is only this risk that investors will be compensated for accepting.

A proxy measure for market risk is known as *beta*, which is a measure of how a stock moves relative to the market. For example, a beta equal to 1 means that if the market increases (de-

## EXHIBIT 1    Sample listing from Value Line

**MAGIC CHEF** NYSE-MGC

| RECENT PRICE **34** | P/E RATIO **6.2** (Trailing: 7.8 / Median: 8.5) | EARN'S YLD **16.2%** | DIV'D YIELD **2.6%** | 141 |

BUSINESS: Magic Chef, Inc. is one of the five major full-line appliance manufacturers in the U.S. The company produces gas and electric ranges, dishwashers, refrigerators, freezers and laundry equipment; and soft-drink vending machines, heating and air conditioning units. Acquired Norge (laundry equip't.) and Admiral (refrigerators & freezers) in 1979, Toastmaster in 1983. Montgomery Ward accts. for 20% of sales. Est'd wage costs, 20%. '83 deprec. rate: 7.1%. Est'd plant age: 6 yrs. Has 7,400 empls., 5,380 shrhldrs. Insiders own 5% of common. Chrmn. & Pres.: S.B. Rymer, Jr. Inc.: Del. Address: 740 King Edward Ave., Cleveland, TN 37311.

**Magic Chef's sales are soaring.** All divisions are up, but the major home appliance group is outstanding. Its 43% revenue growth in the first half (ended December 31st) was well ahead of industry figures, indicating a further gain in market share. MC's second quarter shipments of microwave ovens were more than double those of the 1982 period—and enough to earn a profit despite aggressive price competition. About the only item lagging the industry was refrigerators, and that was due to capacity limitations.

**Toastmaster is helping to heat up results.** The acquisition was completed in time to be included in Magic Chef's second quarter. That was good scheduling because Toastmaster's line has many products that sell well at Christmas. The new subsidiary added over $30 million to the quarter's sales and was a plus to share earnings.

**Capital investment is a key ingredient in Magic Chef's recipe for profits.** Especially important has been the expansion of refrigerator production capacity. An $8 million project to automate the Admiral factory's paint system took a little longer to finish than expected, but it's now speeding production and reducing unit costs so the company will be able to meet refrigerator demand profitably. Under way is a several-year program to automate Norge's laundry equipment manufacturing; it has already helped bring this operation into the black.

**Share earnings are growing like magic.** Management has, in less than five years, converted Magic Chef into a full-line appliance business. It has also brought the air conditioning and soft drink vending divisions into solidly profitable territory. Earnings jumped to a new record in fiscal 1983 and, we think, will almost double that achievement in 1984. Gains will quite naturally slow down after this year, but the current momentum is likely to carry share profits more than 20% higher in 1985. Magic Chef stock is ranked Above Average for Timeliness and is a good 3-to-5-year holding as well. *R.C.S./M.S.*

(A) Fiscal year ends about June 30 of calendar year. Includes Admiral and Norge from '79. (B) Based on avg. shs. outst'g. Excl. extraord. charges: '68, 27¢; '71, 17¢; '72, 7¢. Next eqs. rep't due late Apr. Est'd current cost eqs. per share: '83, $2.40. (C) Next dividend meet'g about May 18. Goes ex about May 25. Div'd paym't dates: Jan., Mar. 15, June 15, Sept. 15. (D) Div'd reinvest. plan av'ble. (D) In mill., adj. for stock splits & div'ds.

Company's Financial Strength: B
Stock's Price Stability: 35
Price Growth Persistence: 60
Earnings Predictability: 35

Factual material is obtained from sources believed to be reliable but cannot be guaranteed.

Source: *The Value Line Investment Survey.* © Value Line Inc. Reprinted by permission.

creases) by $x$ percent, the stock will, on average, increase (decrease) by $x$ percent. Therefore, the stock has the same risk as the market. If a stock has a beta greater than 1 and the market increases (decreases) by $x$ percent, the return on the stock will increase (decrease) by more than $x$ percent. Therefore, the stock is said to be aggressive or to have more risk than the market. If the stock has a beta less than 1, an $x$ percent increase in the market would result in an increase (decrease) of less than $x$ percent in the stock's return. This stock is said to be defensive or to have less risk than the market.

The beta of a portfolio is simply the weighted average of the betas of the individual stocks comprising the portfolio, where the weights are equal to the market value of the stock divided by the market value of the total portfolio of stocks. For example, if a portfolio with a total market value of $100,000 consists of two stocks, A and B, with $60,000 invested in stock A, which has a beta of 1.5, and $40,000 invested in stock B with a beta of .9, the beta of the portfolio will be equal to 1.26 (= 1.5 × .6 + .9 × .4).

Empirical tests have found a positive relationship between a portfolio's return and its beta. This means that the more risk an investor accepts in her portfolio (measured by beta), the higher the return she can expect from the portfolio.

Although the computation of beta is beyond the scope of this article, it should be mentioned that an estimate of beta is published in *The Value Line Investment Survey*, which is available in most public libraries. Exhibit 1 is a sample page from *The Value Line Investment Survey*. The beta is reported in the box in the upper right corner. It is also possible for professional money managers to obtain estimates of beta through some investment banking firms. Merrill Lynch, for example, publishes estimates of beta in a book titled *Security Risk Evaluation Service*.

## THE RISK/RETURN MODEL: THE CAPITAL ASSET PRICING MODEL

Now that we have what we believe to be the appropriate measure of risk, we need a model that tells us what the relationship between risk and expected return should be. That is, given the beta of a portfolio, what should be the expected (risk-adjusted) return?

There is considerable controversy about the appropriate model for measuring risk and return. The most commonly employed model, and the one that dominates investment theory, is the capital asset pricing model.[2] The capital asset pricing model specifies the following relationship between risk (as measured by beta) and expected return:

Expected return = Risk-free rate + [Beta
      × (Expected market return − Risk-free return)]

That is, the expected (risk-adjusted) return is equal to the risk-free rate of return (such as the rate on U.S. Treasury obligations) plus a risk premium. The risk premium consists of the quantity of risk (as measured by beta) times the market price of risk (as measured by the difference between the expected market return and the risk-free return). To illustrate, if the expected market return is 12 percent and the risk-free return is 8 percent, then, if a portfolio has a beta of 1.5, the expected return for the portfolio is 14 percent, as shown below:

$$.08 + [1.5 \times (.12 - .08)] = .14$$

The expected return for the portfolio is greater than the expected return for the market because the portfolio has greater risk than the market since its beta is greater than 1. If, instead, beta is .5, the expected portfolio return is 10 percent, as shown below:

$$.08 + .[5 \times (.12 - .08)] = .10$$

The expected return for the portfolio is less than that expected for the market because the beta is less than 1. Notice that, if the beta for the portfolio is 1, the expected return for the portfolio would be equal to 12 percent, the expected return for the market.

As mentioned earlier, to determine whether an investor beat the market the expected return should be compared to the actual return. For example, assuming the values above for the expected market return and the risk-free rate, if an investor's portfolio has a beta of 1.5 percent, then the expected return is 14 percent. If the investor realized a return of 14 percent and the market rate of return was 12 percent, then this investor

[2] William F. Sharpe, "Capital Asset Prices: A Theory of Market Equilibrium under Conditions of Risk," *Journal of Finance*, September 1964, pp. 425–42.

neither beat nor underperformed the market. He realized the expected return for the level of risk accepted. If the investor had realized a return greater than 14 percent, the investor can legitimately boast that he beat the market. The investor would have underperformed the market if the realized return was less than 14 percent. Notice also, if an investor realized a return of 13 percent even though the market return was 12 percent, the investor would have underperformed the market.

Now you should be able to understand why we said that just looking at the raw return (a return unadjusted for risk) will not tell us whether an investor beat the market. Moreover, you cannot compare the performance of individual money managers without considering the risks that each one accepted in constructing his or her portfolio.

The capital asset pricing model is not the only model that has been proposed to explain the risk/return trade-off.[3] Another model that recently has been receiving considerable attention is the *arbitrage pricing model.*[4] Basically, this model states that more than one factor systematically affects the price of all securities. Investors want to be compensated for accepting each of these different systematic risks. That is, the arbitrage pricing model states that the expected return is equal to:

Expected return = Risk-free return
+ Beta$_1$ × (Expected return for factor 1 − Risk-free return)
+ Beta$_2$ × (Expected return for factor 2 − Risk-free return)
+ . . . .
+ Beta$_k$ × (Expected return for factor $k$ − Risk-free return)

where there are $k$ systematic factors and the subscript for the Beta is the systematic risk measure for the security with respect to systematic factor $k$. The expected return for factor $i$ is the rate of return expected by investors if factor $i$ was the only factor affecting security returns.

The problem has been to empirically identify the number of systematic factors that affect security returns—that is, $k$—and to define these factors. One empirical study suggests there may be

---

[3] Theoretical criticisms of using the capital asset pricing model for evaluating investment performance have been raised by Professor Richard Roll in several articles. See, for example, Richard Roll, "A Critique of the Asset Pricing Theory's Tests," *Journal of Financial Economics,* March 1977, pp. 129–76.

[4] Stephen A. Ross, "The Arbitrage Theory of Capital Asset Pricing," *Journal of Economic Theory,* December 1976, pp. 343–62.

two, three, or possibly four systematic factors.[5] However, what those factors are has not yet been identified.

## MARKET EFFICIENCY

The principal question that we now address is whether it is possible to legitimately beat the market. There are many market participants who believe that the market is too "efficient" to beat on a *consistent* basis. An efficient market refers to a market in which prices at any given point in time fully reflect all available information that is relevant to the value of a security. In an efficient market, any active stock market strategies based on the analysis of relevant information available cannot be exploited to beat the market on a consistent basis after considering transaction costs.

There are three forms of market efficiency—weak, semistrong, and strong. The distinction between these three forms is the relevant set of information that is believed to be impounded into the price of the security at any given time. If stock prices quickly reflect that relevant information, then a stock market strategy using that information will not beat the market because stock prices already have discounted it.

Weak efficiency means that the price of the security fully reflects the trading volume and price history of the security. Semistrong efficiency means that the price of the security fully reflects all publicly available information about the security, such as financial statements of a company and analyst's earnings forecasts, as well as price and volume information. Strong efficiency means that the price of the security reflects all information about the security regardless of whether it is publicly available.

### Weak form efficiency

Empirical studies have found that the stock market is efficient in the weak form.[6] That is, an investor can't beat the market on a consistent basis by "charting" price or volume patterns

---

[5] Richard Roll and Stephen A. Ross, "An Empirical Investigation of the Arbitrage Pricing Theory," *Journal of Finance*, December 1980, pp. 1073–1103.

[6] The only empirical study that found that technical analysis can produce superior long-term performance is a study of *Lowry's Reports* by E. L. Bishop and J. R. Rollins, "Lowry's Reports: A Denial of Market Efficiency," *The Journal of Portfolio Management*, Fall 1977, pp. 21–27.

and following trading strategies based on such charts. Most professional money managers believe that the market is efficient in the weak form.

### Semistrong form efficiency

A good deal of the early research found that the market is efficient in the semistrong form. The implication is that those who attempt to analyze stocks by looking at the fundamental economic factors expected to influence the price of a company's stock would not be able to consistently beat the market. However, several recent empirical studies have uncovered what is believed to be active stock market strategies that appear to have consistently beat the market. These strategies, referred to by academicians as "market anomalies," are summarized below.

**The Value Line enigma.** The Value Line Investment Survey ranks securities using a scale of 1 to 5, where 1 is the most favorable. (See Exhibit 1.) The ranking is based on a complex computerized system using several criteria. The forecasting ability of the Value Line ranking system has been the subject of extensive research since 1970, when a study by Value Line suggested that employing an investment strategy based on its ranking system would have resulted in superior investment performance.

The results of such studies are mixed. A study by Black showed that an investment strategy based on the ranking system did provide a risk-adjusted return that outperformed the market after taking transaction costs into consideration.[7] However, Kaplan and Weil question Black's results.[8] Holloway found that, if transaction costs are ignored, superior performance was obtained.[9] Yet, after adjusting for transaction costs, trading strategies using Value Line's recommendation did not provide superior investment results. However, he found that a buy-and-hold strategy using Value Line's recommendations did provide superior performance even after accounting for transac-

---

[7] Fisher Black, "Yes, Virginia, There Is Hope: Tests of the Value Line Ranking System," *Financial Analysts Journal*, September 1973, pp. 10–14.

[8] Robert S. Kaplan and Roman L. Weil, "Rejoinder to Fisher Black," *Financial Analysts Journal*, September 1973, pp. 14–15. See also, "Risk and the Value Line Contest," *Financial Analysts Journal*, July/August 1973, pp. 56–60.

[9] Clark Holloway, "A Note on Testing an Aggressive Investment Strategy Using Value Line Ranks," *The Journal of Finance*, June 1981, pp. 711–19.

tion costs. Copeland and Mayers found superior investment performance, but the degree of the superior performance was much less than that found by Black.[10]

**The small-firm effect.** Several empirical studies have shown that portfolios of small firms (as measured by total market value) have earned higher rates of return after adjusting for risk than large firms. Most of these studies have been confined to the smallest firms on the New York Stock Exchange.[11] For firms listed on the New York Stock Exchange, a small firm has been defined as one whose total market value is in the lower 20 percent of all stocks traded on the exchange. This would include firms that have a total market value of less than $70 million.

Simple strategies for exploiting this finding have been proposed by Reinganum.[12] He showed that, if an investor had purchased at the end of 1962 a $1,000 portfolio comprised of the smallest firms, at the end of 1980 that same portfolio would have been worth more than $46,000. If, instead, the investor acquired a $1,000 portfolio consisting of large firms, it would have been worth only a little more than $4,000 by the end of 1980.

Moreover, Reinganum investigated two strategies involving the investment in small firms. The first strategy was a passive strategy; it involved purchasing a portfolio of small firms at the end of 1962 and holding that portfolio to the end of 1980. The second strategy was an active strategy, in which a portfolio of small firms was purchased at the end of 1962, *rebalanced annu-*

---

[10] Thomas E. Copeland and David Mayers, "The Value Enigma (1965–1978): A Case Study of Performance Evaluation Issues," *The Journal of Financial Economics*, November 1982, pp. 289–321.

[11] Marc R. Reinganum, "Abnormal Returns in Small Firm Portfolios," *Financial Analysts Journal*, March/April 1981, pp. 52–56; Marc R. Reinganum, "Misspecification of Capital Asset Pricing: Empirical Anomalies Based on Earnings Yields and Market Values," *Journal of Financial Economics*, March 1981, pp. 19–46; and Rolf W. Banz, "The Relationship Between Return and Market Value of Common Stocks," *Journal of Financial Economics*, March 1981, pp. 103–26. These results have been questioned by Roll, who argued that the explanation lies in the underestimation of the beta of small firms. (See: Richard Roll, "A Possible Explanation of the Small Firm Effect," *Journal of Finance*, September 1981, pp. 879–88.) Reinganum demonstrated that this could not completely explain the superior investment results. (Marc Reinganum, "A Direct Test of Roll's Conjecture on the Firm Size Effect," *Journal of Finance*, March 1982, pp. 27–35.)

[12] Marc R. Reinganum, "Portfolio Strategies Based on Market Capitalization," *The Journal of Portfolio Management*, Winter 1983, pp. 29–36.

*ally*,[13] and held until the end of 1980. Although superior investment performance resulted from both the passive strategy and the active strategy, the latter strategy clearly outperformed the passive strategy despite the higher transaction costs.

**The low P/E effect.**  The price-earnings (P/E) ratio of a stock is the ratio of the stock's market price to earnings per share. Several studies, particularly that of the late Professor Sanjoy Basu, have found that portfolios consisting of stocks with low price-earnings ratios have outperformed portfolios consisting of stocks with high price-earnings ratios, after adjusting for risk. As in the small-firm effect, which defines small relative to the other firms listed on the New York Stock Exchange, a stock with a low P/E is defined as those that fall within the 20 percent lowest P/E ratios on the New York Stock Exchange. Furthermore, these findings hold even after transaction costs necessary to rebalance the portfolio to implement this strategy as price-earnings ratios change are taken into account.[14]

An explanation for the superior performance of low P/E stocks has been suggested by Dreman.[15] He argues that stocks trade at low P/E ratios because they are currently out of favor with market participants. Since fads do change, companies not in vogue at the current time will rebound in the future. The psychological reasons for this are explained in Article Two.

A recent study by Lehrman and Levy, however, found that, although the low P/E strategy does produce superior risk-adjusted results before transaction costs were considered, when transaction costs were taken into account the superior performance disappeared.[16]

**The neglected-firm effect.**  Not all firms receive the same degree of attention from security analysts. Arbel and Strebel have demonstrated that firms neglected by security analysts tend to

---

[13] Rebalancing means that each year, as the total market value of firms change, stocks of firms in the portfolio that are no longer classified as small firms are sold and those that are not included in the portfolio but are classified as small firms are purchased.

[14] Sanjoy Basu, "Investment Performance of Common Stocks in Relation to their Price-Earnings Ratios: A Test of the Efficient Market Hypothesis," *Journal of Finance*, June 1977, pp. 663–82.

[15] David Dreman, *Contrarian Investment Strategy: The Psychology of Stock-Market Success* (New York: Random House, 1979).

[16] Haim Levy and Zvi Lerman, "Testing P/E Ratio Filters with Stochastic Dominance," *The Journal of Portfolio Management*, Winter 1985, pp. 31–40.

outperform firms that receive considerable attention from analysts.[17] For example, for the period 1970 to 1979, they found the average annual return for neglected stocks was 7 percent higher than for firms that were more highly researched.[18] These findings suggest that an investment strategy based on the level of security analysts' attention and changes in the level of attention devoted by security analysts may lead to superior investment returns.

**The January effect.** Studies have consistently demonstrated that stock returns decline at year-end and rebound in January.[19] Further research has found that this January effect is particularly pronounced for small firms.[20] These findings appear to be due to the year-end selling of stocks that have declined significantly in value during the year in order to realize a tax savings from the resulting capital loss in the current year.[21] This implies that it might be possible to beat the market by buying such stocks at year-end and selling them in January.

### Strong form efficiency

Studies of the strong form of market efficiency have examined whether individuals trading on the basis of insider information can beat the market. Insiders are usually individuals who are either on the board of directors, major officers of the company, or major stockholders. When insiders transact in the company's

---

[17] Avner Arbel and Paul Strebel, "Pay Attention to Neglected Firms!" *The Journal of Portfolio Management,* Winter 1983, pp. 37–42.

[18] Arbel and Strebel measure the degree of analysts' attention for a given company based on (1) the number of analysts that regularly follow the stock as reported in surveys by Drexel Burnham Lambert and (2) the number of analysts reporting earnings forecasts as compiled in *Earnings Forecaster* published by Standard & Poor's.

[19] Edward Dyl, "Capital Gains Taxation and Year-End Stock Market Behavior," *Journal of Finance,* March 1977, pp. 165–75; Ben Branch, "A Tax Loss Trading Rule," *Journal of Business,* April 1977, pp. 198–207; and Josef Lakonishof and Seymour Smidt, "Trading Bargains in Small Firms at Year-End," forthcoming in *The Journal of Portfolio Management.*

[20] Donald B. Keim, "Size-Related Anomalies and Stock Market Seasonality: Further Empirical Evidence," *Journal of Financial Economics,* June 1983, pp. 13–32; Richard Roll, "Vas Ist Das?" *The Journal of Portfolio Management,* Winter 1983, pp. 18–28; and Lakonishof and Smidt, "Trading Bargains in Small Firms at Year-End."

[21] Roll, "Vas Ist Das?" and Marc R. Reinganum, "The Anomalous Stock Market Behavior of Small Firms in January: Empirical Tests for Tax-Loss Selling Effects," *Journal of Financial Economics,* June 1983, pp. 89–104.

securities, they are required to file a report with the SEC. The report of insiders activity is made public about six weeks later.

Studies that have investigated insider trading generally have found that insiders consistently beat the market.[22] Moreover, if investors follow the insiders by trading after the report is first made available to the public, it has been found that investors can earn a greater return than a simple buy-and-hold strategy even after adjusting for transaction costs.[23]

## INVESTING IN AN EFFICIENT MARKET

If an investor does not believe that the market can be beat because it is too efficient, then a passive strategy should be followed. There are two types of passive strategies: buy-and-hold and indexing.

The buy-and-hold strategy involves purchasing a diversified portfolio and holding it over an investment horizon. There is no attempt to find undervalued stocks because none are believed to exist in an efficient market. Moreover, no trading strategies are used to try to time the market or take advantage of perceived market anomalies.

The index approach is best described as the "if you can't beat'em join'em approach." The objective of the index approach is to duplicate the performance of some general market index. According to modern portfolio theory, the "market" portfolio offers the highest level of return per unit of risk in an efficient market.[24] By combining securities in a portfolio with characteristics similar to the market, the efficiency of the market will be captured.

From a practical point of view, it is difficult for an individual to construct a portfolio that will replicate a general market, such

[22] Jeffrey Jaffe, "Special Information and Insider Trading," *Journal of Business*, July 1974, pp. 410–28; and Joseph E. Finnerty, "Insiders and Market Efficiency," *Journal of Finance*, September 1976, pp. 1141–48.

[23] One of the earlier studies showed that this can be done even up to four months after the publication of the report. See Shannon P. Pratt and Charles W. DeVere, "Relationship Between Insider Trading and Rates of Return for NYSE Stocks, 1960–1966," in *Modern Developments in Investment Management*, ed. James Lorie and Richard Brealey (New York: Praeger Publishers, 1972).

[24] Harry M. Markowitz, "Portfolio Selection," *Journal of Finance*, March 1952, pp. 71–79; and William F. Sharpe, "Capital Asset Prices: A Theory of Market Equilibrium under Conditions of Risk," *Journal of Finance*, September 1964, pp. 425–42.

as the Standard & Poor's 500. This would require buying all 500 stocks in the index. Pension funds are better equipped to handle the problems associated with constructing an index fund. For an individual, the best alternative is to purchase shares in a mutual fund whose investment objective is to index. The Vangaurd Index Trust is an example of a no-load mutual fund that is indexed based on the Standard & Poor's 500.

# EIGHT

## Business cycles and investment strategy*

Jerome B. Cohen, Ph.D.
*Professor of Finance and Dean (Emeritus)*
*Bernard M. Baruch College*
*The City University of New York*

Edward D. Zinbarg, Ph.D.
*Senior Vice President*
*The Prudential Insurance Company of America*

Arthur Zeikel
*President and Chief Investment Officer*
*Merrill Lynch Asset Management, Inc.*

This article surveys the relationships between stock prices, interest rates, and the broad movements of economic activity which are referred to as the business cycle. The survey suggests that an ability to anticipate forthcoming changes in business conditions can be used to improve the timing of security purchases and sales.

### BUSINESS CYCLES AND STOCK PRICES

Many investors assume that an accurate forecast of turning points in the business cycle will improve their ability to man-

---

* Adapted by the editors from chapter 7 of Jerome B. Cohen, Edward D. Zinbarg, and Arthur Zeikel, *Investment Analysis and Portfolio Management* (Homewood, Ill.: Richard D. Irwin, 1982).

age portfolios better. There is substantial evidence suggesting that an ability to foresee business cycle turning points for several months ahead improves the ability to foresee major turning points in the general level of stock prices. The evidence does not imply that every bear market must be accompanied by an economic recession or vice versa. However, the tendency for stock prices to decline prior to an economic downturn has been so pronounced that, if a recession or a slowdown of economic growth appears to lie ahead, the investor should consider that the odds are high it will be preceded by a significant stock market downturn some months in advance. For example, a recent study concluded that the best time to sell stocks is probably one to three months before a recession begins.[1]

It is essential to stress the fact that stock price peaks and troughs typically have preceded turning points of general business activity. Many investors are invariably surprised when, in the midst of rather dreary business news, stock prices rise, and, in the midst of prosperity, stock prices fall. But such is the nature of the stock market.

Several theories have been offered to explain the stock market's apparent forecasting ability. One is that investors collectively have good foresight and that they act on the basis of what they think is going to happen to business activity, rather than on the basis of what they currently see happening. Another argument is that investors act on the basis of current, rather than anticipated future, developments, but that the chief current indicators they watch—corporate profits and profit margins—tend to turn in advance of general business activity. Therefore, profit-oriented investors coincidentally bid stock prices up and drive them down in advance of general business activity. Yet a third theory is that stock price reversals help cause subsequent economic reversals by affecting consumer and business confidence and spending decisions. Finally, various monetary explanations for the stock price lead have been offered, as will be noted in later sections. Perhaps the truth lies closest to a combination of all these hypotheses. Exhibit 1 depicts the movement of the S&P 500 Index, before, during, and after recessions from 1948–1983.

---

[1] Raymond Piccini, "Stock Market Behavior Around Business Cycle Peaks," *Financial Analysts Journal*, July–August 1980, p. 55.

**EXHIBIT 1**  Stock market performance before, during, and after recessions

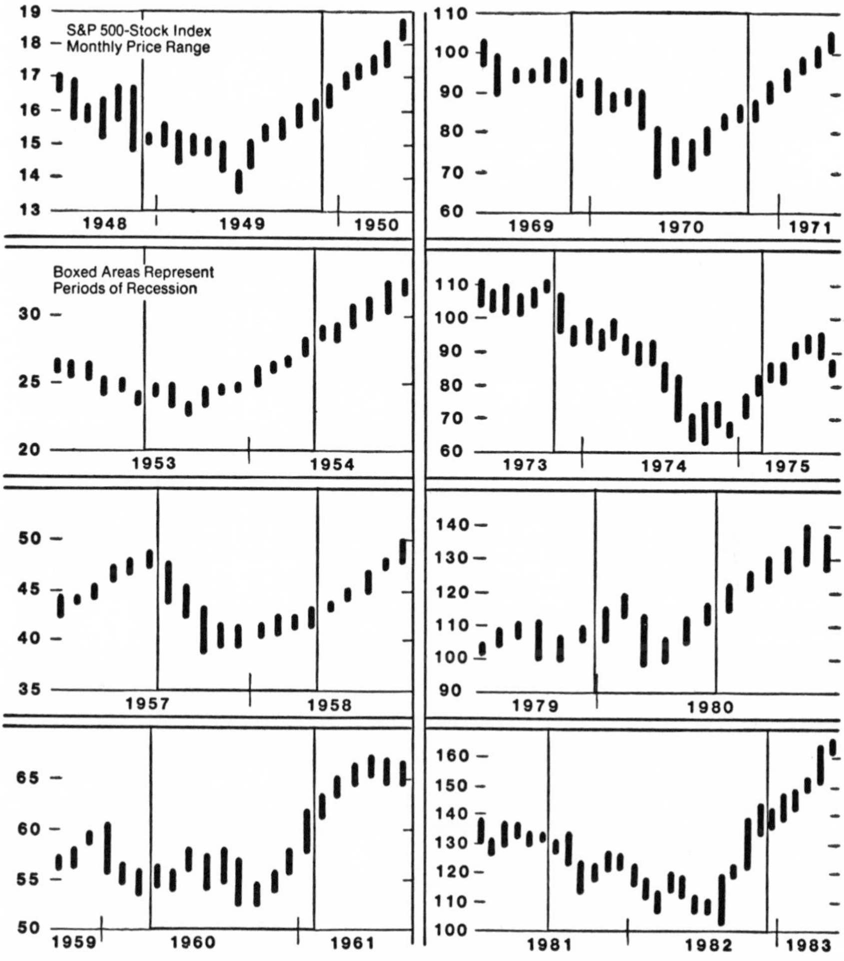

# FROM THE GENERAL TO THE SPECIFIC

Since an ability to foresee business cycle turning points normally would improve one's ability to foresee major turning points in the stock market as a whole, would it also improve one's ability to select the particular stocks to be most affected by the change in overall trend? The answer is sometimes yes, sometimes no. The relative price changes of individual stocks over short time periods reflect many factors. These include relative changes in company sales, earnings, and dividends; but the factors also include the degree to which different stocks had been overpriced or underpriced prior to the turning point of the general market. To the extent that accurate forecasts of the overall economy can improve forecasts of relative changes in the prosperity of different industries, forecasts of relative price changes of stocks in different industries should be improved.

Some industry groupings typically (but not always) achieve earnings gains in years when overall profits decline. Table 1 shows those S&P industry categories which have produced higher earnings in general during years when profits on the S&P 500 have declined. From an investment strategy viewpoint, some of these industry groupings consistently perform well early in the economic cycle when most stocks are declining. For example, Goldman Sachs has identified a list of early-cycle industries which have fairly consistently outperformed the market during the six months after an economic peak.[2] See Table 2.

Several interesting observations emerge from the listing. First, financial (interest-rate related) and retail-oriented securities dominate. Of the 19 S&P groups listed in Table 1, six are interest-rate sensitive (electric and telephone utilities, New York City and regional banks, property and casualty insurance companies, and life insurance companies) and three are retail merchandisers (department stores, food chains, and the general merchandise categories).

Second, industries with below-average earnings sensitivity to the business cycle have consistently performed well. Soft drink and tobacco companies, for example, outperformed the market in the six-month period after a peak in five of the last six economic cycles; food and soap firms outperformed the market in all six cycles.

Third, while all of the industries listed in Table 2 outperformed the market on a relative basis over the measurement period, only five (aerospace, food chains, food companies, soaps, and tobacco) actually advanced in price during this interval. Importantly, most of these same groupings exhibited an

---

[2] Goldman Sachs' analysts who conducted the study excluded those industries generally viewed as not large enough for substantial institutional investor participation.

**TABLE 1**   S&P industry groups registering earnings gains when overall profits decline

| | Earnings | | | | | | | | | | |
|---|---|---|---|---|---|---|---|---|---|---|---|
| | 1980 | 1975 | 1970 | 1967 | 1961 | 1960 | 1958 | 1957 | 1956 | 1952 | 1951 |
| S&P 500 Composite | -0.5% | -10.5% | -11.2% | -4.0% | -2.4% | -3.5% | -14.2% | -1.2% | -5.8% | -1.6% | -14.1% |
| Office and business equipment | +9.6 | +5.1 | +1.6 | +22.8 | +18.4 | +13.2 | +21.5 | +15.2 | +9.0 | -1.3 | +3.6 |
| Electric utilities | +4.8 | +7.5 | +0.6 | +5.8 | +5.0 | +6.3 | +6.6 | +3.1 | +3.2 | +8.5 | -7.9 |
| Soft drinks | +4.2 | +22.8 | +15.2 | +9.3 | +7.2 | +3.7 | +2.2 | +7.0 | -1.1 | +2.9 | -11.7 |
| Small loans | -15.4 | -7.8 | +1.6 | +2.9 | +4.9 | +4.5 | -5.4 | +10.2 | +21.3 | +5.7 | +8.8 |
| Drugs | +14.1 | +9.7 | +4.2 | +1.9 | +1.2 | -0.4 | +6.5 | +25.7 | +22.5 | -13.1 | -1.4 |
| Oil-international | +14.5 | -28.3 | +0.2 | +6.8 | +8.6 | +9.0 | -22.6 | +10.2 | +15.4 | 0.0 | +24.0 |
| Tobacco | +16.5 | +6.9 | +18.5 | +8.8 | +8.6 | +5.2 | +19.0 | +12.4 | +5.8 | -5.9 | -23.9 |
| Coal | +20.2 | +53.0 | +89.2 | +28.8 | +1.1 | +1.3 | -37.4 | +20.2 | +18.5 | -22.3 | +10.7 |
| Electronics—instrumentation* | +1.7 | +2.4 | -7.3 | +6.7 | -14.4 | +2.5 | +18.7 | -14.4 | +11.9 | +7.9 | +21.2 |
| Electronics—semiconductor* | +21.7 | +21.7 | -7.4 | -6.6 | +28.9 | +10.9 | +4.4 | +14.2 | 0.0 | -8.5 | -24.8 |
| Soaps | +3.0 | -7.4 | +7.4 | +16.8 | 0.0 | +4.1 | -1.4 | +16.0 | +2.3 | +9.7 | -28.5 |
| Retail food | -9.2 | +254.7 | +8.3 | -6.6 | -1.7 | +7.3 | +7.2 | -2.7 | +16.3 | -6.7 | -5.1 |
| Natural gas distributors | +5.0 | +3.8 | +4.1 | +5.1 | +7.3 | +7.7 | +6.2 | +4.1 | +25.4 | -3.9 | +11.0 |
| Machinery—oil well service | +36.0 | +61.9 | -4.6 | +9.3 | +21.4 | -7.7 | -49.2 | -3.2 | +6.8 | -6.1 | +11.0 |
| Food composite | +7.9 | +15.4 | +11.3 | +4.2 | +1.2 | +3.2 | +5.2 | N.A. | N.A. | N.A. | N.A. |
| Natural gas pipelines | +13.5 | +3.9 | +7.2 | +4.3 | -0.7 | +7.4 | -3.6 | N.A. | N.A. | N.A. | N.A. |
| Cosmetics | +3.6 | +17.5 | +8.1 | +26.1 | -1.3 | +9.7 | +27.8 | N.A. | N.A. | N.A. | N.A. |
| Banks—regional | +1.4 | +10.2 | +9.5 | +6.6 | -2.3 | +11.6 | +4.5 | N.A. | N.A. | N.A. | N.A. |
| Banks—New York City | +14.2 | +2.4 | +17.3 | +8.6 | -0.5 | +10.0 | -4.6 | N.A. | N.A. | N.A. | N.A. |
| Buildings—air conditioning | +855.0 | +42.2 | +17.4 | +5.0 | +6.2 | -3.0 | -8.6 | -21.1 | N.A. | N.A. | N.A. |
| Telephone | +1.7 | -3.8 | -1.1 | +2.9 | +0.8 | +2.5 | +4.2 | N.A. | N.A. | N.A. | N.A. |

N.A. = Not available.
* Originally one category—now divided into two groups.
Source: Calculated from Standard & Poor's industry data.

**TABLE 2** Market performance of selected industries following peaks in economic activity

| Industry | November 1948 to May 1949 | July 1953 to January 1954 | July 1957 to January 1958 | May 1960 to November 1960 | November 1969 to May 1970 | November 1973 to May 1974 | Average of annual changes |
|---|---|---|---|---|---|---|---|
| Aerospace | 6.0% | 25.6% | (3.5)% | 9.2% | (29.9)% | (2.1)% | 0.8% |
| **Banks** | | | | | | | |
| New York City | 0.4 | 5.0 | (0.9) | (33.5) | (24.4) | 18.8 | (5.6) |
| Regional | 5.2 | 9.9 | (4.0) | 5.2 | (19.7) | (12.9) | (2.7) |
| Beverage—soft drinks | (4.7) | 6.5 | (3.4) | 15.6 | (18.7) | (26.3) | (4.9) |
| Chemicals | 1.9 | 9.8 | (13.0) | 9.4 | (14.8) | 10.2 | (2.6) |
| Drugs | 14.1 | 11.9 | (6.9) | (2.4) | (18.6) | (10.4) | (2.1) |
| Food composite | 3.4 | 6.6 | 5.2 | 20.3 | (18.4) | (5.4) | 1.9 |
| **Insurance** | | | | | | | |
| Life | 7.2 | 25.1 | (13.5) | 6.9 | (29.4) | (28.2) | (5.3) |
| Property—casualty | 6.1 | 16.3 | (8.2) | 4.7 | (28.5) | (27.0) | (6.0) |
| Office equipment | 6.6 | 10.2 | (12.2) | 14.5 | (27.2) | (19.2) | (4.6) |
| Retail—department stores | (1.9) | 5.2 | 0.0 | 2.8 | (23.9) | (5.3) | (3.9) |
| Retail—food chains | 6.5 | 9.6 | 8.6 | (5.1) | (17.7) | 9.4 | 1.9 |
| Retail—general merchandise | (5.5) | 3.3 | (7.0) | 1.9 | (17.6) | (4.7) | (4.9) |
| Soap | (0.5) | 11.0 | 13.8 | 25.9 | (20.6) | (5.8) | (4.0) |
| Tire and rubber | (0.1) | 16.0 | (13.0) | (16.0) | (29.3) | 0.7 | (7.0) |
| Tobacco | 7.1 | (16.7) | 17.1 | 23.0 | (15.4) | (4.1) | 1.8 |
| **Utilities** | | | | | | | |
| Electric | 6.4 | 9.9 | 6.4 | 4.9 | (14.1) | (20.1) | (1.1) |
| Natural gas | 7.3 | 9.5 | (10.2) | 8.8 | (6.5) | (12.6) | (0.4) |
| Telephone | (6.1) | 2.2 | (2.0) | 5.1 | (14.6) | (4.4) | (3.3) |
| S&P 500 | (3.3) | 4.8 | (15.3) | 0.5 | (20.9) | (11.1) | (7.6) |

Source: Goldman Sachs.

earnings performance resilient to overall economic trends as shown previously in Table 1.

Because recession years and the beginning stages of an economic recovery tend to be good periods of stock market performance,[3] substantial research efforts are directed towards identifying industry groups and individual stocks likely to outperform the broad market averages during the early stages of a new bull market. Merrill Lynch, for example, studied relative stock group performance during the first six months of bull market cycles and the last four months of bear market cycles. As a basis for this study, Merrill Lynch used industry classifications for the S&P 500 and the market cycle segments of 1966–67, 1970, and 1974–75. Table 3 is a convenient reference listing of Merrill Lynch's major conclusions. Exhibit 2 shows the relationship of common stock group performance to the economic cycle.

The important findings of the Merrill Lynch study were:

1. Industries that outperform the market in the early phase of a bull market are those that are characterized by superior growth qualities or that are especially sensitive to the expected turning of the business cycle. Credit-sensitive stocks, excluding utilities,[4] stand out among those sensitive to the business cycle as beneficiaries of the anticipated decline in interest rates.

2. Industries that outperform other groups in the early phase of a bull market usually have high betas. Industries that outperform the average in the late phase of a bear market usually have low betas. The beta correlations are extremely high.

3. Basic industries are especially poor early bull market performers, because they usually do not meet the criteria noted above.

---

[3] According to Goldman Sachs, for example, "The average level of the market in the 12 months subsequent to an economic trough has, since 1948, been higher than the average stock price level in the 12 months preceding an economic trough." For further details, see "Investment Strategy Highlights Update," Goldman Sachs Research, December 1978.

[4] It is interesting to comment that utility issues, generally considered among the most interest-sensitive groups, were not found to be early bull market performers. While these issues tend to do well *immediately* following turns in interest rates, utility stocks lose relative momentum fairly quickly because, according to Merrill Lynch analysts who conducted the study, of their low beats (which offset the momentum created by the sensitivity to lower interest rates).

**TABLE 3**    Group performance in the business cycle

| Master group | Dominant investment characteristics | Best relative performance | Worst relative performance |
|---|---|---|---|
| **Cyclical stocks** | | | |
| Credit cyclicals | Sensitive to interest rates—performance best when interest rates low. Most groups building-related. | Early and middle bull markets. | Early and middle bear markets, with the exception of forest products. |
| Consumer cyclicals | Consumer durables and nondurables. Profits vary with economic cycle. | Early and middle bull markets. | Early and middle bear markets. Exception is hotel/motel. |
| Capital goods (cyclicals only) | Many groups depend on capacity utilization. | Middle and late bull markets. | Late bear markets. |
| Energy (cyclicals only) | Closely tied to economic cycle. | Early bull markets. | Early bear markets. |
| Basic industries | Profits depend on industrial capacity utilization. Prices may benefit from supply shortages near economic peaks. | Early and middle bear markets. Economic peaks. | Early or middle bull markets, depending on source of demand for products. |
| Financial | Banks, insurance, and gold mining. | Late bull and late bear markets. Economic troughs. | Early bull markets. |
| Transportation | Surface transportation. | Early bull markets. | Early bear markets. |
| **Defensive stocks** | | | |
| Defensive consumer Staples | Nonvolatile consumer goods. | Late bear markets. | Early bull markets. |
| Energy (defensive only) | Major international and domestic oils. Volatility introduced by OPEC power. | Late bear markets. | Early bull markets. |
| Utilities | Large liquidity and operating stability. | Late bear markets. | Early bull markets. |
| **Growth stocks** | | | |
| Consumer growth | Combination of growth and defensive characteristics. Several subgroups: offer high yields. | Cosmetics, soft drinks and drugs: late bear markets. Other subgroups: early bull markets. | Cosmetics, soft drinks, and drugs do not vary in any regular cyclical pattern for this group. Other subgroups: late bear markets. |
| Capital goods—technology Capital goods (growth only) | Linked to capital investment spending cycle, which tends to lag behind the economic cycle. | Early and middle bull markets. | Late bear markets. |
| Energy (growth only) | Linked to economic cycle and to OPEC. | Early bull markets but varies. | Varies. |

Source: Merrill Lynch, Pierce, Fenner & Smith.

**EXHIBIT 2**    Business cycle and relative stock performance

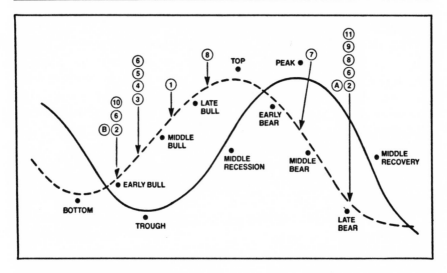

**Key:**
Solid line = economic cycle.
Broken line = stock market cycle.
 1 = Capital Goods.
2a = Consumer growth—cosmetics, soft drinks, drugs.
2b = Consumer growth—other subgroups.
 3 = Consumer cyclicals.
 4 = Credit cyclicals.
 5 = Capital goods—technology.
 6 = Energy.
 7 = Basic industries.
 8 = Financial.
 9 = Defensive consumer staples.
10 = Transportation.
11 = Utilities.
Source: Merrill Lynch, Pierce, Fenner & Smith.

4. Industries with historical market patterns that suggest they should be underweighted in the early phase of a bull market are those that thrive in the economic environment of high-capacity utilization usually created in the middle or late-middle stages of a recovery. In general, those industries are classified as intermediate goods and services, and they also tend to have minimal exposure to the capital spending cycle.

We are obliged to end this portion of our discussion with some serious words of warning. Too many investors believe that timing investment decisions with business cycle changes can be reduced to some form of a mechanical decision-making process. That is, when something which has happened before happens again, it triggers a response that would have worked well the last time around. Not so.

The purpose of understanding past patterns is to establish a framework within which unfolding events must be placed. Then the goal of effective analysis is to determine whether past patterns should or should not be expected to hold. Such judgments require that investors seek to determine whether the operating characteristics of companies and industries have changed in their sensitivity to business cycle conditions. Then the assessment must be made as to whether or not expected events have already been discounted by the market pricing mechanism.

This general concept is an important one for participants in the investment process to understand clearly. Exogenous factors frequently disturb expectations based on historical experience. Let's illustrate the point with an actual example. Late in 1980, one of Wall Street's more astute business cycle observers reviewed the position of metal stocks relative to business cycle movements and concluded, "if the groups follow the pattern established after past business cycle peaks, further weakness in price performance can be expected."[5]

What actually happened was during the first quarter of 1981, the Dow Jones Industrial Average rose 4 percent; the S&P 500 was essentially flat; copper stocks rose 54 *percent;* and the aluminum and miscellaneous metal issues rose 14 percent each. Merrill Lynch explained the generally unanticipated price appreciation as follows: "The basic industries group seems to have suddenly come alive amid the excitement generated by various takeover offers in the copper and miscellaneous metals industries. The enthusiasm was magnified by the unexpected rebound in recent operating rates and by earnings gains."

## BUSINESS CYCLES AND INTEREST RATES

Interest rate cycles have been closely related to the ebb and flow of general business activity. Essentially, interest rates have tended to rise as the business cycle matures. Geoffrey H.

---

[5] Nicocles L. Michas and Henry L. Wojtyla, *Investment Strategy*, Rosenkrantz, Ehrenkrantz, Lyon & Ross, Inc., December 1980, p. 14.

Moore of the National Bureau of Economic Research, a leading business cycle research organization, recently summarized the causal factors for this pattern as follows: (1) the rising demand for business credit, both for operating purposes and for capital investment; (2) the rising demand for mortgage credit, both residential and nonresidential; (3) the rising demand for consumer credit; (4) the widening expectation of an increase in the rate of inflation, which makes lenders reluctant to lend at the same interest rate and borrowers more willing to pay a higher rate; and (5) the sluggish response of the supply of lendable funds to the pressures. During a business cycle contraction, according to Moore and others, all or most of these factors operate in reverse and (tend to) bring interest rates down.[6]

It is also clear, again in the general case, that short-term interest rates are more sensitive to business cycle pressures than long-term rates. One reason for this is that increases in inventory positions by businesses are usually financed with short-term borrowings and, hence, influence greatly, if not govern, the cost and availability of such credit. On the other hand, plant and equipment spending decisions center more on conditions in the long-term markets. Another factor is that Federal Reserve Board management of monetary policy affects short rates more than long rates. For these and perhaps other reasons, some observers believe that changes in short rates not only precede changes in long rates but tend to act as an inverse leading indicator of overall business cycle developments. There is some historical evidence to support this conclusion. Admitting that there is a good deal of variability in the timing relationships, there is also evidence, according to Ronald J. Talley, of some fairly consistent patterns: "generally, for example, short-term market rates have turned with or before the prime rate and rates on long-term securities. Also, rates on instruments of relatively low credit risk have tended to peak with or before those of higher risk instruments, with the rates on U.S. government securities among the first to peak within a given maturity classification.[7]

We should point out, however, that other researchers have

---

[6] Geoffrey H. Moore, "Business Cycles, Inflation, and Forecasting," *National Bureau of Economic Research Studies in Business Cycles No. 24* (Cambridge, Mass.: Ballinger Publishing, 1980), p. 196.

[7] Ronald J. Talley, "Identifying a Cyclical Peak in Interest Rates," *Business Economics,* January 1981, p. 6.

**EXHIBIT 3**    Indexes leading short-term interest rates

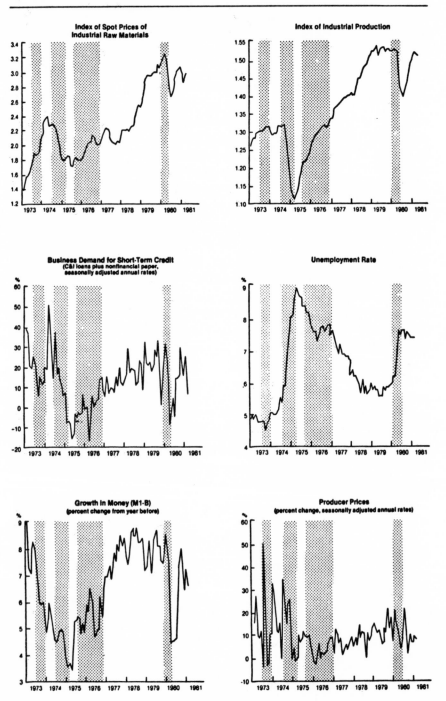

Source: Merrill Lynch, Pierce, Fenner & Smith, *Fixed Income Strategy,* April 1981.

come to different conclusions,[8] and the general subject of whether short-term interest rates turn before long-term rates remains very debatable. Furthermore, declines in economic activity no longer presuppose a drop in short-term interest rates. For example, short-term interest rates did not peak until about six months after the November 1973 peak in business activity. More recently, short-term interest rates rose throughout most of the 1980–81 period, while most indicators of general economic activity flattened and many actually declined. Most observers attribute this changed pattern to the persistence of inflation during recent recessions and the attendant inability of borrowers and institutions to rebuild liquidity.[9]

Merrill Lynch has identified six economic time series that have been somewhat reliable in identifying turning points in short-term interest rates. To be useful in this regard, according to Merrill Lynch, a series must be available on a timely basis, must shift direction decisively at or near a peak or trough in rates, and should not give off frequent false signals. Few, if any, of the series lead cyclical rate turns on a consistent basis. The six series are: Index of Spot Prices of Industrial Raw Materials, Business Demand for Short-term Credit, Yearly Percentage Change in Money (M1–B), Index of Industrial Production, Unemployment Rate, and changes in Producer Prices Index. Exhibit 3 shows the movement of each series since 1973, with the shaded areas indicating periods of declining short-term interest rates.

## INTEREST RATES AND INVESTMENT TIMING

### Stock prices

Changes in short-term interest rates are a major influence on the general level of stock prices. According to Peter Bernstein, from 1965 to 1974 the coefficient of correlation between the two was minus .85, which means that changes in short-term interest rates, as measured by yields on Treasury bills, "explained" nearly 75 percent of the variation (in opposite direction) in returns from equities. Furthermore, the relationship was not only

---

[8] John R. Brick and Howard E. Thompson, "Time Series Analysis of Interest Rates: Some Additional Evidence," *Journal of Finance* 33, no. 1 (March 1978), p. 93.

[9] See, for example, Henry Kaufman, "The Interest Rate Challenge to Portfolio Management," Salomon Brothers, January 8, 1980.

close, it was highly sensitive as well. That is, a 1 percent change in short-term yield was associated, on average, with a change of nearly 10 percent in the opposite direction in stock returns.[10]

Consequently, investors have come to recognize that the implications for stock prices are clearly positive when short-term interest rates begin to decline. Table 4 shows that, since the mid-1960s, stock prices have been higher three months after both short and long rates have peaked. With the exception of the September 1981 peak, this is also true six months later.

**TABLE 4**     Interest rate peaks and stock price performance

| Interest rate peak* | Increase in DJIA† | |
|---|---|---|
| | *Three months later* | *Six months later* |
| September 1981 . . . . . . . . | 3% | −3% |
| March 1980 . . . . . . . . . . | 10 | 19 |
| October 1974 . . . . . . . . . | 6 | 23 |
| June 1970. . . . . . . . . . . | 11 | 23 |
| September 1966. . . . . . . . | 2 | 12 |
| Average. . .   . . . . . | 7% | 19% |

\* Month when yields of both 91-day Treasury bills and Moody's AAA corporate bonds have peaked.
† Based on end-of-month prices.
Source: Wertheim & Co., Inc.

These relationships are more than a statistical coincidence. The changing spread between expected stock returns and short-term interest rates narrows as the economic advance progresses—stock yields falling and bond yields rising—gradually begin to draw income-minded investors away from stocks and into bonds. In addition, capital gains-minded investors begin selling stocks as corporate profit margins narrow and economic recession begins to threaten. The proceeds of these sales either are put into the bank or into fixed-income securities. The shifting of funds out the stock market weakens stock prices prior to the peak of business activity, but dividends are still high or rising. Therefore, stock yields begin to reverse their downward movement prior to the business peak.

---

[10] Peter L. Bernstein, "The Curious History of Stock Prices and Interest Rates," Peter L. Bernstein, Inc., September 11, 1979, p. 5.

Eventually, the economy reaches a peak and turns down. Interest rates ultimately move down as well. Dividends reach a plateau or decline, but stock prices decline faster, and stock yields, therefore, rise. The yield spread thus becomes gradually less favorable to bond investment. Income seekers begin switching back into stocks, and bargain hunters do likewise in anticipation of eventual recovery. The expansion process begins anew shortly thereafter.

There is another dimension to the impact of rising interest rates on stock prices. The discount rate, or interest factor, is an important ingredient in most common stock valuation techniques. All other things being equal, higher interest rates reduce and lower interest rates enhance the present value of long-term investments. Consequently, advancing interest rates decrease the value of common stock holdings, particularly for long-term investors.

Once again, however, we are obliged to interject some words of caution. It is erroneous to conclude that short-term, interest rate forecasting holds the key to the effective timing of equity portfolio maneuvers. It should be recognized, first, that forecasts of turning points in short-term interest rates, even by leading Wall Street experts, have not been consistently accurate. Second, close examination of stock movement behavior in the period following each of the past four major interest rate cycle peaks illustrates the presence of some unreliability surrounding the use of interest rate trends to forecast the stock market. Following peaks in interest rates during April 1980 and November 1966, the market did in fact rally sharply. However, in the period following the interest rate peaks of July 1974 and September 1969, stock prices continued to decline precipitously even as rates fell.[11]

### Bond yields

Typically, since interest rate turns have more or less coincided with business cycle peaks, the best time to buy bonds is when the crest of economic activity has been reached, not before. Bond prices under this scenario are at their lowest point, interest rates are at their highest. The best time to sell bonds is

---

[11] Alan D. Schwartz and Robert M. Sinche, "Monetary and Fiscal Discipline: Short-Run Risks, Long-Run Opportunities," Bear Stearns, *Portfolio Strategy Issues*, January 14, 1981, p. 3.

when a new economic advance begins following a recession. At such times, bond prices are usually high (interest rates low).

It is also important for fixed-income investors concerned with interest rate trends to understand the dynamics of a business cycle as it produces changes in the *yield curve*, which is discussed in Article Eleven. Briefly, the cyclical characteristics of the yield curve are as follows:

1.  Up to maturities of about three years—the "short end" of the yield curve—longer-term securities tend to have higher yields than shorter-term securities, whether the *level* of interest rates is high or low.
2.  From 3 years to about 15 years—that is, between the boundaries of relatively short-term and relatively long-term securities—the yield curve gradually changes shape as the level of rates rises. The curve moves from upward sloping, to flat, to downward sloping. Downward sloping means that longer-term securities tend to have lower yields than shorter-term securities.
3.  Beyond maturities of about 15 years, the yield usually does not change significantly as maturity is extended. That is, the long end of the yield curve typically is rather flat regardless of level.

It should also be noted that yield volatility is inversely related to maturity. When the general level of rates rises or falls, short-term rates change much more sharply than long-term rates. On the other hand, as demonstrated in Article Nine, *price* volatility is *directly* related to maturity so far as effects of changes in the level of interest rates are concerned.

A cyclical yield spread pattern has been observable not only in comparisons of yields on different types of fixed-income investments, but also in comparisons of common stock dividend yields with bond yields. As has been shown, stock prices usually rise during most of the prosperity phase of the business cycle. At the same time, dividend payments usually rise also but at a slower rate. Consequently, dividend yields on stocks fall rather steadily during prosperity. Accompanying the declining trend of dividend yields, typically, has been a rising trend of bond yields.

Thus, fixed-income investors have traditionally been encouraged to lengthen the time horizon (maturity) of their portfolios when the yield curve—the difference between short- and long-term maturities—turned negative. Rationale for this behavior has been predicated on historic experience, which indicates that cyclical interest rate declines tend to develop when short rates are higher than long ones. However, this is no longer the case. Negative spreads have not only become larger during the last 20 years, but have lasted for longer periods than heretofore. For example, at the maximum inversion, short-term governments (three months) exceeded long governments by about 40 basis points in 1959, by 70 basis points in 1966, by 140 basis points in 1969, and by 190 basis points in 1973. Consequently, some observers now believe that interest rate turns will not develop until a very large yield inversion exists and for an extended time.[12] This conclusion is based on the recognition that negative yield relationships have tended to become irregularly long in duration over the past 20 years.

These developments are intertwined with the nation's inflation problem. In the past, recessions have been associated with a diminution of inflationary pressures and economic recoveries with an acceleration of inflation. During the economic contractions since 1965, however, inflation has not diminished with the coming of recession, either in fact or in the expectations of the marketplace. If anything, the inflationary expectations generated in the late stages of prosperity have continued to spiral upward after the economy has peaked out, thus explaining the soaring level of bond yields in the face of declining industrial production. Only in the late stages of recessions have investors foreseen diminished inflationary pressures, an attitude which has tended to persist beyond the economic trough and carried bond yields down to the point where investors realized that they had been duped once again into thinking that the inflation cancer had been cured.

## BUSINESS CYCLE FORECASTING

### A business cycle chronology

For more than 50 years, the National Bureau of Economic Research, a private nonprofit organization, has sponsored the

---

[12] See, for example, Henry Kaufman, "The Interest Rate Cycle Challenge to Portfolio Management," Salomon Brothers, Bond Market Research Investment Policy, January 8, 1980, p. 4.

research efforts of America's leading students of the business cycle. Among the products of their efforts are techniques for measuring economic fluctuations and identifying major turning points of overall economic activity. Focusing on the period since the end of World War I and omitting the years of the Great Depression and World War II, Table 5 presents a chronology of American business cycles based on the National Bureau's identification system.

---

**TABLE 5**    A calendar of major economic expansions and contractions, 1920–1929, 1946–1980

| Dates of turning points | | | Duration (months) | |
|---|---|---|---|---|
| Peak | Trough | Peak | Contractions | Expansions |
| Jan. 1920 | July 1921 | May 1923 | 18 | 22 |
| May 1923 | July 1924 | Oct. 1926 | 14 | 27 |
| Oct. 1926 | Nov. 1927 | Aug. 1929 | 13 | 21 |
| Nov. 1948 | Oct. 1949 | July 1953 | 11 | 45 |
| July 1953 | May 1954 | Aug. 1957 | 10 | 39 |
| Aug. 1957 | April 1958 | April 1960 | 8 | 24 |
| April 1960 | Feb. 1961 | Dec. 1969 | 10 | 106 |
| Dec. 1969 | Nov. 1970 | Nov. 1973 | 11 | 36 |
| Nov. 1973 | March 1975 | Jan. 1980 | 16 | 58 |
| Jan. 1980 | July 1980 | July 1981 | 6 | 12 |
| July 1981 | Nov. 1982 | | 16 | |
| | | Mean: | 11 | 39 |

Source: U.S. Department of Commerce, *Business Conditions Digest*, October 1980, p. 105. Table updated by authors and editors.

---

Examination of the table suggests that the average business cycle consists of an expansion lasting over three years and a contraction lasting about a year. But even though the table excludes the atypical years of world war and catastrophic depression, considerable diversity of duration remains. These findings suggest that the timing of American business cycles has not been consistent enough to warrant purely calendar-oriented judgments as to the probability of a peak or trough occurring at any given time. Furthermore, National Bureau readings must be analyzed carefully in order to insure that the data accurately describe trends in the business picture. Frequently it does not.

For example, on June 3, 1980, the National Bureau announced that a recession had begun the previous January. Many observers question whether the "January declaration" actually described the starting date of the recession.[13] Comparative patterns of many series of economic activity strongly suggested to many observers that March 1979 would have represented a more accurate description. Comparative patterns of many economic series with movements that surround the recession of 1973–75 support this conclusion.

On another occasion early in 1981, the Index of Leading Indicators (discussed in the following section) reversed direction and rose 1.4 percent, an increase usually associated with the start of a new trend. But according to *The Wall Street Journal*, economists both in and out of government, after reviewing the data, immediately expressed doubt that the monthly reading signaled a turnaround in future economic activity.[14] It seemed that a statistical distortion was caused by a rapid rise in crude oil prices.

However, despite the need to closely monitor business cycle data for less than accurate readings, practicing analysts and investors find it very helpful to use historical analogies in their work.

### Leading economic indicators

It is a common observation that no two business cycles are exactly alike. Indeed, most modern business economists have become increasingly impressed with the almost endless variety of the cyclical fluctuations they are trying to forecast. Nevertheless, the unique aspects of each individual cycle usually fit into a common framework which has been referred to as "the cumulative process" or "the self-generating cycle." The essential characteristics of this framework can be described briefly.

If we break into a cycle as revival is beginning, we find business sales and inventories at a depressed level and considerable excess plant capacity. As sales begin to rise and profit expectations improve, business leaders start planning for production increases. They expand working hours and gradually rehire previously laid-off workers. This increases employee incomes and stimulates personal consumption expenditures. With sales and profits rising, the managers begin to expand and

---

[13] Ted T. Dahl, "NBER Says Recession Began in January, but Some Data Indicate Year-Earlier Start," *The Money Manager*, June 9, 1980.

[14] "Leading Index Increased 1.4% during March," *The Wall Street Journal*, April 30, 1981, p. 3.

modernize production facilities. These purchases from the capital goods industries create still more jobs and incomes and more consumption by workers in those industries. And so the expansion *cumulates.*

Workers, machines, and materials eventually are being utilized at capacity, and demand exerts upward pressure on prices and wages. Business leaders go increasingly into debt to finance expanding inventories, receivables, and fixed assets. Interest rates rise. Soon costs are rising faster than prices, and profit margins deteriorate. This coincides with the gradual realization that productive capacity has outstripped potential sales. Business executives become uneasy and pull in their reins. They reduce their orders for heavy equipment, cut back on the rate of inventory accumulation, repay loans, lay off marginal personnel, and even sell some of their personal common stock holdings. Caution spreads as incomes are reduced. Consumers postpone purchases of durable goods, business executives slash inventories sharply, and the cumulative process is at work in a downward direction.

As the downturn continues, credit terms ease and interest rates fall. The monetary authorities usually reinforce the ease. Housing construction often picks up as reduced mortgage rates, lowered down payments, and extended maturities bring monthly carrying charges to a level which buyers are willing to undertake despite the recessionary atmosphere. Government spending acts as a strong prop to the economy. The stock market, after a sizable shake-out, stabilizes and begins to move up. Soon consumers realize that the worst is over and begin to unloosen their purse strings. A new revival is in the making.

In recent years, observers have identified another dimension to business cycle movements known as "growth cyclical slowdowns." Geoffrey H. Moore defines this "subcyclical" development as a recurring period of slow growth in total output, income, employment, and trade, usually lasting a year or more. A growth slowdown may encompass a recession, in which case the slowdown usually begins before the recession starts but usually ends at about the same time. Slowdowns may also occur without recession, in which case the economy continues to grow but at a pace significantly below its long-run growth rate.[15]

---

[15] Geoffrey H. Moore, "Will the Slowdown Reduce the Inflation Rate? Probably," *Across the Board,* The Conference Board, September 1979, p. 3, which also contains an outstanding chronology of business cycles and inflation.

It should be clear from the brief physiology of a business cycle above that fluctuations of the whole of economic activity reflect fluctuations of the economy's many parts. Moreover, while the parts tend to move in unison, there is also a sequence observable. When one part changes direction, it pushes another part, which pushes still another. Therefore, it is logical that, if we wish to predict turning points of the whole economy, we should try to isolate and study those parts which usually turn *before* the whole.

The search for leading, coincident, and lagging indicators of general economic activity has been one of the major continuing projects of the National Bureau of Economic Research (NBER). *Business Conditions Digest* classifies indicators by their participation in the stage of economic process and their relationship to business cycle movements, as shown in Table 6. Panel A of Table 6 is a cross-classification of cyclical indicators based on an analysis of respective series involved at five business cycle peaks. Each tabulation distinguishes seven major economic processes and four types of cyclical timing. The titles in the cells identify subgroups of the given economic process with the given timing characteristic. The number of series in each such group is given in parentheses following the title.[16]

The NBER has selected 12 leaders which come closest to meeting ideal characteristics, such as smoothness of movement from month to month, and consistency and logic of relationship to the general business cycle. These 12 are identified in Table 7, which also shows the average number of months by which the indicator historically has turned in advance of general economic peaks and troughs.

As a valuable supplement to the individual indicators, there is a composite index which combines the leading indicators into a single statistical series. Most observers agree that the leading indicators have, on balance, a noteworthy record.

There also are composites of the coincident and lagging indicators. The latter are used as checks on the validity of turns in the leading index. That is, if the leading indicator index seems to have turned down, that fact should be confirmed by subsequent downturns of, first, the coincident index and, next, the lagging index.

---

[16] Complete information on how individual indicators are classified by timing at peaks, troughs, and on turns, along with selected measures, is provided in *The 1977 Handbook of Cyclical Indicators,* U.S. Department of Commerce, Bureau of Economic Analysis.

**TABLE 6**   Cross-classification of cyclical indicators by economic process and cyclical timing

**A. Timing at Business Cycle Peaks**

| Cyclical timing \ Economic process | I. Employment and unemployment (18 series) | II. Production and income (10 series) | III. Consumption, trade, orders and deliveries (13 series) | IV. Fixed-capital investment (18 series) | V. Inventories and inventory investment (9 series) | VI. Prices, costs, and profits (17 series) | VII. Money and credit (26 series) |
|---|---|---|---|---|---|---|---|
| Leading (L) Indicators (62 series) | Marginal employment adjustments (6 series)<br>Job vacancies (2 series)<br>Comprehensive employment (1 series)<br>Comprehensive unemployment (3 series) | Capacity utilization (2 series) | New and unfilled orders and deliveries (6 series)<br>Consumption (2 series) | Formation of business enterprises (2 series)<br>Business investment commitments (5 series)<br>Residential construction (3 series) | Inventory investment (4 series)<br>Inventories on hand and on order (1 series) | Stock prices (1 series)<br>Commodity prices (1 series)<br>Profits and profit margins (7 series)<br>Cash flows (2 series) | Money flows (3 series)<br>Real money supply (2 series)<br>Credit flows (4 series)<br>Credit difficulties (2 series)<br>Bank reserves (2 series)<br>Interest rates (1 series) |
| Roughly Coincident (C) Indicators (23 series) | Comprehensive employment (1 series) | Comprehensive output and real income (4 series)<br>Industrial production (4 series) | Consumption and trade (4 series) | Backlog of investment commitments (1 series)<br>Business investment expenditures (5 series) | | | Velocity of money (2 series)<br>Interest rates (2 series) |
| Lagging (Lg) Indicators (18 series) | Duration of unemployment (2 series) | | | Business investment expenditures (1 series) | Inventories on hand and on order (4 series) | Unit labor costs and labor share (4 series) | Interest rates (4 series)<br>Outstanding debt (3 series) |
| Timing Unclassified (U) (8 series) | Comprehensive employment (3 series) | | Trade (1 series) | Business investment commitments (1 series) | | Commodity prices (1 series)<br>Profit share (1 series) | Interest rates (1 series) |

**B. Timing at Business Cycle Troughs**

| Economic process / Cyclical timing | I. Employment and unemployment (18 series) | II. Production and income (10 series) | III. Consumption, trade, orders, and deliveries (13 series) | IV. Fixed-capital investment (18 series) | V. Inventories and inventory investment (9 series) | VI. Prices, costs, and profits (17 series) | VII. Money and credit (26 series) |
|---|---|---|---|---|---|---|---|
| Leading (L) Indicators (47 series) | Marginal employment adjustments (3 series) | Industrial production (1 series) | New and unfilled orders and deliveries (5 series) Consumption and trade (4 series) | Formation of business enterprises (2 series) Business investment commitments (4 series) Residential construction (3 series) | Inventory investment (4 series) | Stock prices (1 series) Commodity prices (2 series) Profits and profit margins (6 series) Cash flows (2 series) | Money flows (2 series) Real money supply (2 series) Credit flows (4 series) Credit difficulties (2 series) |
| Roughly Coincidental (C) Indicators (23 series) | Marginal employment adjustments (2 series) Comprehensive employment (4 series) | Comprehensive output and real income (4 series) Industrial production (3 series) Capacity utilization (2 series) | Consumption and trade (3 series) | Business investment commitments (1 series) | | Profits (2 series) | Money flow (1 series) Velocity of money (1 series) |
| Lagging (Lg) Indicators (40 series) | Marginal employment adjustments (1 series) Job vacancies (2 series) Comprehensive employment (1 series) Comprehensive and duration of unemployment (5 series) | | Unfilled orders (1 series) | Business investment commitments (2 series) Business investment expenditures (6 series) | Inventories on hand and on order (5 series) | Unit labor costs and labor share (4 series) | Velocity of money (1 series) Bank reserves (1 series) Interest rates (8 series) Outstanding debt (3 series) |
| Timing Unclassified (U) (1 series) | | | | | | | Bank reserves (1 series) |

Source: U.S. Department of Commerce, *Business Conditions Digest.*

**TABLE 7**    Leading indicators of economic activity

|  | | Median lead (months) | |
|---|---|---|---|
|  | | Peak | Trough |
| **1.** | Average hours in workweek of manufacturing production workers . . . . . . . . . . . . . . . . . . . . . . . . . . | 11 | 2 |
| **2.** | Layoffs of manufacturing workers (per 1,000) . . . . . . . . . . | 10 | 2 |
| **3.** | New orders of consumer products (in constant dollars). . . . . . . . . . . . . . . . . . . . . . . . . . . . . . . . . | 10 | 2 |
| **4.** | Vendor performance (i.e., percent of companies reporting slower deliveries). . . . . . . . . . . . . . . . . . | 9 | 4 |
| **5.** | Net new business formations. . . . . . . . . . . . . . . . . | 12 | 1 |
| **6.** | Permits to build new private housing units . . . . . . . . . . | 15 | 5 |
| **7.** | Contracts for new plant and equipment (in constant dollars) . . . . . . . . . . . . . . . . . . . . . . . . . | 7 | 0 |
| **8.** | Change in business inventories on hand and on order (in constant dollars) . . . . . . . . . . . . . . . . . . | 8 | 3 |
| **9.** | Common stock prices (S&P 500) . . . . . . . . . . . . . . . | 9 | 4 |
| **10.** | Change in wholesale prices of industrial raw materials . . . . . . . . . . . . . . . . . . . . . . . . . . . . . . | 9 | 4 |
| **11.** | Money supply (M–2, 1972 dollars) . . . . . . . . . . . . . . | 14 | 6 |
| **12.** | Change in total liquid assets . . . . . . . . . . . . . . . . . | 7 | 8 |
|  | Average lead of 12 indicators . . . . . . . . . . . . . . . . | 10 | 3 |

Source: U.S. Department of Commerce, *Business Conditions Digest*, June 1980, p. 104.

## A brief word on forecasting

It may be surprising to readers of this article to realize that detailed economic forecasts have been fairly inaccurate. A number of important studies call attention to the limited predictive value of detailed economic forecasts reaching out further than a few quarters.[17] Errors in turning-point forecasts—that is, the prediction that an important economic variable, or some aggregate of series, is about to change direction—are even less reliable. Part of the problem, according to a classic explanation by Victor Zarnowitz, is that "forecasters draw, to a large extent, upon the same raw materials"; that is, on information that is widely accessible and they variously influence one another. Few if any of them can be regarded as independent producers,

---

[17] *Business Week*, for example, reported that the difference between the actual performance of the economy and the consensus of more than 40 "blue-chip" forecasters for the first quarter of 1981 was an enormous 7.6 percentage points. See "Quarterly Forecasts That Aren't to Be Believed," May 4, 1981, p. 50.

though some meet this description more than others.[18] Furthermore, poor forecasting is not limited to economists in the United States. The Organization for Economic Cooperation and Development (OECD) has been publishing forecasts of the rates of economic growth and inflation for the major industrial noncommunist countries for more than 10 years. A recent study shows that not only is the OECD track record generally superior to the record of national official forecasters,[19] but also that all forecasters surveyed have tended to underpredict the rate of economic growth, except for Italy.

Thus, investors who incorporate business cycle forecasting into their portfolio management decision-making procedures are well advised to remember that the way people actually behave is captured by few—if any—forecasting models.[20] History abounds with examples of this fundamental principle, which the well-known observer of Wall Street, Ray De Voe (an appreciator of such happenings), calls the "forecasters' trap."

One of the more humorous but appropriate examples is related by Shepherd Mead in "How to Get to the Future before It Gets to You."[21] Stepping back in time to 1850, Mead engages several model builders to study the developing problems of pollution in New York City. The main causes of concern are chewing tobacco and horses; more precisely, spit and horse manure. In 1850, the spit level in the gutter was half an inch high, and the manure level in the middle of the road averaged half an inch, too.

---

[18] Victor Zarnowitz, *An Appraisal of Short-Term Economic Forecasts*, (New York: National Bureau of Economic Research, 1967), p. 7.

[19] There are two reasons to expect that the OECD should outperform the national official forecasters, other things being equal. First, as an international organization, the OECD should be more objective in analyzing and commenting on a country's economic prospects than an agency of the government of that country. Second, unlike the national official forecasters, the OECD prepares fairly detailed forecasts for all the major industrial noncommunist countries, and it should, therefore, have more information for analyzing international interactions which may affect the course of a country's economy. See Norman S. Fieleke, "The Forecasting Performances of the OECD and of National Officials in Six Major Countries," *New England Economic Review*, May–June 1979.

[20] This important point was recently reinforced by Karen Arenson of the *New York Times* when she noted that "models work best when the future resembles the past. They work least well when major shifts in economic behavior are taking place." See Karen W. Arenson, "Useful, Yes; Infallible, Hardly," *New York Times*, April 26, 1981.

[21] Shepherd Mead, *How to Get to the Future before It Gets to You* (New York: Hawthorn Books, 1974) p. 15. For those interested in going further on this point, the best compendium of inaccurate forecasts is "Erroneous Predictions and Negative Comments Concerning Exploration, Territorial Expansion, Scientific and Technological Development: Selected Statements," by Nancy T. Gamarra, May 29, 1979, available from the Library of Congress, Washington, D.C.

By 1860, each had reached a level of one inch, and using prevailing rates of growth as a basis of a forecast, levels of two inches were expected by 1870 and four inches by 1880. Looking further ahead, by 1970 it was expected that there would be 2,048 inches of spit and horse manure in the streets. That comes to 170 feet, 8 inches of each.

Clearly, investors were well advised to buy plug tobacco and horse oat company common stocks. Could growth ever be more assured?

Unfortunately, forecasts of that kind fail to recognize: (1) that people, when the spit and manure level reached the second and third story, would begin to do something about it; (2) that oat and tobacco supplies could not be made available to meet demand; and (3) most importantly, that cigarette smoking would replace chewing tobacco and automobiles would replace horses.

The point is that investors must supplement traditional forecasting methods with common sense judgments about the future.

Perhaps William Ascher summed it best:

> The rationale behind the use of judgment in economic forecasting is that the human mind is the most sensitive and comprehensive evaluator of the diverse evidence on what the future holds. The fact that all of the logic behind judgmental conclusions cannot be stated explicitly is, according to this rationale, an inevitable result of the intricacy and subtlety of human thought and intuition, rather than a limitation of the method.[22]

## SUMMARY

Historical precedent, as outlined in the first part of this article, suggests various investment strategies which may be employed profitably if investors develop an ability to forecast major economic turning points about four to six months in advance—or if they rely on the counsel of others who have such an ability. (Of course, many investors will adopt a buy-and-hold strategy which ignores cyclical swings.) The precise implementation of these strategies depends on how aggressive, self-confident, *and flexible* an investor is. For example, large institutional

---

[22] William Ascher, "Forecasting: An Appraisal for Policy-Makers and Planners," *Economic Forecasting* (Baltimore: Johns Hopkins University Press, 1979).

investors are much less flexible than individual investors. Nevertheless, the general nature of the strategies is as follows:

1. If investors suspect that the prosperity phase of the business cycle is coming to an end but are not yet firmly convinced of the fact, they might continue buying common stocks but confine purchases to companies whose sales are likely to be least vulnerable to recession and whose stocks' price-earnings ratios still seem relatively attractive.

2. When investors become convinced that a recession lies shortly ahead, even though the stock market is still strong, they should have the courage to stop making new common stock commitments. Investable funds should be kept liquid at this stage—that is, in bank time deposits or in short-term securities. Long-term bond investments probably are not yet appropriate, since interest rates are likely still to be rising. But the typical flat or downward-sloping shape of the yield curve at such times suggests that a good rate of return will be secured even on liquid investments.

3. When the recession gets under way and stock prices are falling rapidly, interest rates are likely to be at a peak, and liquid funds should be shifted into high-quality bonds of long maturity. These are likely to appreciate most in value when the cyclical decline in interest rates takes place.

4. In the midst of the recession, yield spreads between high-quality and lower-quality bonds, and between bonds and mortgages, may become relatively wide. Income-oriented investors often find it worthwhile to shift funds from high-quality bonds to these higher-yielding investments at such time.

5. When investors perceive the forthcoming end of the recession, a renewed stock buying program is in order—particularly the stocks of cyclical and *glamor-growth* companies which probably were severely depressed during the bear market. Profits on long-maturity bonds can be realized through sales, although some further rise in bond prices can be anticipated, with the proceeds of the sales to be invested in common stocks.[23]

---

[23] All of these investment operations, of course, should take place within an overall policy framework regarding the appropriate percentages of total assets to be allocated to stocks versus fixed-income investments.

It must be recognized, of course, that the business cycle approach to investment timing has faults as well as virtues. First, since many full-time professional economists have only mediocre forecasting records, investors who are not economists cannot be expected to do very well in forecasting on their own—or in evaluating the forecasts of professionals. Second, even a consistent record of perfect six-month forecasts is unlikely to result in consistently correct investment timing. For although the timing relationships among stock price, interest rate, and business cycle turning points have been reasonably stable, they have not been, and doubtless will not in the future be, unchanging.

# NINE

---

## Bond yield measures and price volatility properties

Frank J. Fabozzi, Ph.D., C.F.A., C.P.A.

*Walter E. Hanson/Peat, Marwick, Mitchell*
  *Professor of Business and Finance*
*Lafayette College*
*and*
*Managing Editor*
*The Journal of Portfolio Management*

---

To make investment decisions, the investor must be capable of determining the yield on an investment. Several measures of the yield on a bond are discussed in this article. Since a measure may not take into account all sources of income offered by a bond, the investor should understand the drawback of each measure. Special yield measures are computed for money market instruments, and they are discussed in Article Ten.

A fundamental relationship is that the price of a bond moves in the opposite direction of the change in the yield that investors require. Consequently, as market participants require a higher (lower) yield, the price of a bond falls (rises). However, not all bonds change by the same magnitude for a given change in yield. The response of bond prices to a change in yield depends upon certain characteristics of the bond. The characteristics that influence bond price volatility are discussed in this article.[1]

---

[1] To appreciate the bond yield measures and price volatility properties, the investor should understand the concepts of compound interest and present value. These concepts are discussed in most investment management textbooks.

## YIELD MEASURES

There are three potential sources of income to an investor who holds a bond: (1) the contracted interest payments, (2) income from the reinvestment of the periodic interest payments, and (3) capital gain (or loss) from disposal of the security. The four yield measures discussed below—current yield, yield to maturity, yield to call, and realized compound yield—take one or more of these sources into consideration when determining the investor's return on investment.

The following hypothetical bond will be used to illustrate the yield measures:

$$\text{Years to maturity} = 7$$
$$\text{Coupon rate} = 8 \text{ percent}$$
$$\text{Market price} = \$814.10$$
$$\text{Redemption value at maturity} = \$1,000$$
$$\text{Frequency of interest payments} = \text{Semiannual}$$

Since this bond is selling below its redemption value at maturity (or par value), the bond is said to be selling at a discount.

### Current yield

The current yield relates the annual dollar coupon interest to the market price. It can be expressed mathematically as follows:

$$\text{Current yield} = \frac{\text{Annual dollar coupon interest}}{\text{Market price}}$$

For our hypothetical bond, the current yield is:

$$\frac{\$80}{\$814.10} = .098 = 9.8 \text{ percent}$$

The current yield exceeds the coupon rate when a bond is selling at a discount. The opposite is true when a bond is selling at a premium. For example, if the market price of our hypothetical bond is $1,089, rather than $814.10, the current yield is 7.3 percent ($80 divided by $1,089).

The drawback of the current yield is that it does not take into consideration the two other sources of income—reinvestment of interest and capital gain (or loss). To illustrate the latter source, suppose the bond is held to maturity. At that time, the issuer will redeem the bond for $1,000. The investor who purchased the bond for $814.10 will realize capital appreciation of $185.90 ($1,000 minus $814.10).[2] Had the bond been purchased for $1,089, there would be a capital loss of $89.

### Yield to maturity

Unlike the current yield, the yield to maturity does take into account any capital gain or loss. The yield to maturity does consider the reinvestment of the contracted periodic payments; *however, it implicitly assumes that these payments are reinvested at a rate equal to the yield to maturity.*

The yield to maturity is the discount rate that equates the present value of the promised cash flow (coupon payments plus redemption value at maturity) to the market price.[3] Thus the yield to maturity takes the time value of money into consideration. When a yield to maturity is quoted, the market price used to make the computation is the offer price and does not include accrued interest.

Let us go through the yield-to-maturity computation once. Later it will be explained how this yield can be determined without the necessary trial-and-error computations given below. The worksheet for determining the yield to maturity for our hypothetical bond is shown as Exhibit 1. Now remember what our objective is—to determine the discount rate that equates the present value of the 14 payments of $40 every six months (beginning six months from now) plus the present value of the redemption value of $1,000 at maturity to the market price of the bond ($814.10).

An arbitrary starting point of 5 percent was selected. The present value of the promised cash flow is $901.04. This dis-

---

[2] As explained in Article Three, the tax treatment of the capital appreciation depends on whether the bond was *issued* before or after July 18, 1984.

[3] The general formula for the yield to maturity for a bond paying interest semiannually is:

$$P = \sum_{t=1}^{2n} \frac{C/2}{\left(1 + \frac{r}{2}\right)^t} + \frac{R}{\left(1 + \frac{r}{2}\right)^{2n}}$$

where

$P$ = Price of bond
$n$ = Number of years to maturity
$C$ = Annual dollar coupon interest
$r$ = Yield to maturity
$R$ = Redemption value of bond at maturity

---

**EXHIBIT 1**  Worksheet for the computation of the yield to maturity of an 8 percent coupon bond—maturing in exactly 7 years, and priced at $814.10

| Discount rate (percent) | PV of an annuity of $1 for 14 periods | PV of an annuity of $40 for 14 periods | PV of $1 14 periods hence | PV of $1,000 14 periods hence | Total PV of cash flow |
|---|---|---|---|---|---|
| 4% | $10.5631 | $422.52 | $.5775 | $577.50 | $1,000.02 |
| 5 | 9.8986 | 395.94 | .5051 | 505.10 | 901.04 |
| 6 | 9.2950 | 371.80 | .4423 | 442.30 | 814.10 |
| 7 | 8.7455 | 349.82 | .3878 | 387.80 | 737.62 |
| 8 | 8.2442 | 329.77 | .3405 | 340.50 | 669.82 |

---

count rate produces a present value that is greater than the bond's market price of $814.10. Since a higher discount rate lowers the present value, a higher discount rate must be tried. Skipping 6 percent for the moment, we see that a 7 percent discount rate produces a present value for the promised cash flow that is less than the market price. Consequently, the discount rate we are searching for must be less than 7 percent, but greater than 5 percent. When a 6 percent rate is used, the present value of the promised cash flow is equal to the market price. But 6 percent is *not* the yield to maturity because the time period in the discounting process is six months. To annualize the yield, the *convention* is to double the discount rate. The yield to maturity of our hypothetical bond is therefore 12 percent.[4]

---

[4] Technically, the yield should be annualized using the following formula:

$$(1 + \text{Discount rate})^2 - 1$$

In our example, we would find the annualized yield to be

$$(1.06)^2 - 1 = 1.1236 - 1 = .1236, \text{ or } 12.36 \text{ percent}$$

The discrepancy between the yield to maturity as conventionally computed (i.e., doubling of the semiannual discount rate) and the correct procedure for annualizing explains why bonds carrying a coupon rate equal to the prevailing market interest rate may be selling slightly below par.

This convention also presents problems when comparing bonds that do not have the same number of coupon payments per year. This can be corrected by adjusting the conventional yield to maturity as follows:

$$\text{Adjusted yield to maturity} = \left(1 + \frac{\text{Conventional yield to maturity}}{m}\right)^m - 1$$

Fortunately, it is unnecessary to go through time-consuming computations to determine the yield to maturity because tables and financial function calculators are available. The tables are part of a book usually referred to as a yield book. Sample pages from a yield book are shown in Exhibit 2.

The yield book is organized in this way. Each page corresponds to a coupon rate. A yield book may increment the coupon rate by one-eighth or one-fourth of 1 percent. Exhibits 2(a), 2(b), and 2(c) are three sample pages from a yield book for an 8 percent coupon rate. The top row of each page indicates the time remaining to maturity. The time increments can be given in terms of months, quarters, six months, or years. In the yield book from which the pages were abstracted, monthly periods are used up to 5 years, quarterly to 10 years, and semiannually to 40 years. (The bold number on the pages in Exhibit 2 refers to the number of years, and the number after the hyphen refers to the number of months.) In the first column, the yield to maturity ("yield") is given.

The values appearing within the table are the bond values expressed as a percentage of par value. For example, at the intersection of 7–0 and 10.00 is 90.10. This value is interpreted as: A bond with a coupon rate of 8 percent, seven years remaining to maturity, and priced to yield 10 percent will sell for 90.10 percent of its par value. For a bond with a par value of $1,000, this means that the bond will sell for $901.00. Notice the agreement of this value with the present value found in Exhibit 1. When the 8 percent coupon bond with seven years remaining to maturity is discounted at 5 percent, which corresponds to a 10 percent yield to maturity, the present value of the bond is $901.02.

Let us return to our original task of using the yield book to find the yield to maturity given the coupon rate, remaining time to maturity, and market price of the bond. First, locate the page

---

where

    $m$ is the number coupon interest payments per annum.

For example, if the conventional yield to maturity for a hypothetical bond that pays interest semiannually is 12 percent, the adjusted yield to maturity would be:

$m = 2$:

$$\text{Adjusted yield to maturity} = \left(1 + \frac{.12}{2}\right)^2 - 1 = .1236$$

## EXHIBIT 2 Sample pages from a yield book

**YEARS and MONTHS** 8%

| Yield | 3-5 | 3-6 | 3-7 | 3-8 | 3-9 | 3-10 | 3-11 | 4-0 |
|---|---|---|---|---|---|---|---|---|
| 4.00 | 112.65 | 112.94 | 113.23 | 113.51 | 113.79 | 114.08 | 114.36 | 114.65 |
| 4.20 | 111.97 | 112.25 | 112.51 | 112.78 | 113.05 | 113.32 | 113.59 | 113.86 |
| 4.40 | 111.30 | 111.56 | 111.81 | 112.06 | 112.31 | 112.56 | 112.82 | 113.07 |
| 4.60 | 110.63 | 110.88 | 111.11 | 111.34 | 111.58 | 111.81 | 112.05 | 112.29 |
| 4.80 | 109.97 | 110.20 | 110.41 | 110.63 | 110.85 | 111.07 | 111.30 | 111.52 |
| 5.00 | 109.31 | 109.52 | 109.72 | 109.93 | 110.13 | 110.34 | 110.55 | 110.76 |
| 5.20 | 108.66 | 108.86 | 109.04 | 109.23 | 109.42 | 109.61 | 109.80 | 110.00 |
| 5.40 | 108.01 | 108.19 | 108.36 | 108.53 | 108.71 | 108.88 | 109.06 | 109.24 |
| 5.60 | 107.36 | 107.53 | 107.69 | 107.84 | 108.00 | 108.17 | 108.33 | 108.50 |
| 5.80 | 106.72 | 106.88 | 107.02 | 107.16 | 107.31 | 107.45 | 107.60 | 107.75 |
| 6.00 | 106.09 | 106.23 | 106.36 | 106.48 | 106.61 | 106.75 | 106.88 | 107.02 |
| 6.10 | 105.77 | 105.91 | 106.03 | 106.15 | 106.27 | 106.39 | 106.52 | 106.65 |
| 6.20 | 105.46 | 105.59 | 105.70 | 105.81 | 105.93 | 106.05 | 106.17 | 106.29 |
| 6.30 | 105.14 | 105.27 | 105.37 | 105.48 | 105.58 | 105.70 | 105.81 | 105.93 |
| 6.40 | 104.83 | 104.95 | 105.04 | 105.14 | 105.24 | 105.35 | 105.46 | 105.57 |
| 6.50 | 104.52 | 104.63 | 104.72 | 104.81 | 104.91 | 105.00 | 105.11 | 105.21 |
| 6.60 | 104.21 | 104.31 | 104.39 | 104.48 | 104.57 | 104.66 | 104.75 | 104.85 |
| 6.70 | 103.90 | 104.00 | 104.07 | 104.15 | 104.23 | 104.32 | 104.40 | 104.50 |
| 6.80 | 103.60 | 103.68 | 103.75 | 103.82 | 103.90 | 103.98 | 104.06 | 104.14 |
| 6.90 | 103.29 | 103.37 | 103.43 | 103.50 | 103.56 | 103.64 | 103.71 | 103.79 |
| 7.00 | 102,98 | 103.06 | 103.11 | 103.17 | 103.23 | 103.30 | 103.37 | 103.44 |
| 7.10 | 102.68 | 102.75 | 102.79 | 102.85 | 102.90 | 102.96 | 103.02 | 103.09 |
| 7.20 | 102.38 | 102.44 | 102.48 | 102.52 | 102.57 | 102.62 | 102.68 | 102.74 |
| 7.30 | 102.07 | 102.13 | 102.16 | 102.20 | 102.24 | 102.29 | 102.34 | 102.39 |
| 7.40 | 101.77 | 101.82 | 101.85 | 101.88 | 101.92 | 101.96 | 102.00 | 102.05 |
| 7.50 | 101.47 | 101.51 | 101.54 | 101.56 | 101.59 | 101.62 | 101.66 | 101.70 |
| 7.60 | 101.17 | 101.21 | 101.22 | 101.24 | 101.27 | 101.29 | 101.32 | 101.36 |
| 7.70 | 100.88 | 100.91 | 100.91 | 100.93 | 100.94 | 100.96 | 100.99 | 101.02 |
| 7.80 | 100.58 | 100.60 | 100.60 | 100.61 | 100.62 | 100.63 | 100.65 | 100.68 |
| 7.90 | 100.28 | 100.30 | 100.30 | 100.30 | 100.30 | 100.31 | 100.32 | 100.34 |
| 8.00 | 99.99 | 100.00 | 99.99 | 99.98 | 99.98 | 99.98 | 99.99 | 100.00 |
| 8.10 | 99.70 | 99.70 | 99.68 | 99.67 | 99.66 | 99.66 | 99.66 | 99.66 |
| 8.20 | 99.40 | 99.40 | 99.38 | 99.36 | 99.35 | 99.34 | 99.33 | 99.33 |
| 8.30 | 99.11 | 99.10 | 99.07 | 99.05 | 99.03 | 99.01 | 99.00 | 99.00 |
| 8.40 | 98.82 | 98.81 | 98.77 | 98.74 | 98.72 | 98.69 | 98.68 | 98.66 |
| 8.50 | 98.53 | 98.51 | 98.47 | 98.43 | 98.40 | 98.37 | 98.35 | 98.33 |
| 8.60 | 98.24 | 98.22 | 98.17 | 98.13 | 98.09 | 98.06 | 98.03 | 98.00 |
| 8.70 | 97.96 | 97.93 | 97.87 | 97.82 | 97.78 | 97.74 | 97.71 | 97.68 |
| 8.80 | 97.67 | 97.63 | 97.57 | 97.52 | 97.47 | 97.42 | 97.39 | 97.35 |
| 8.90 | 97.39 | 97.34 | 97.28 | 97.22 | 97.16 | 97.11 | 97.07 | 97.03 |
| 9.00 | 97.10 | 97.05 | 96.98 | 96.92 | 96.85 | 96.80 | 96.75 | 96.70 |
| 9.10 | 96.82 | 96.76 | 96.69 | 96.61 | 96.55 | 96.49 | 96.43 | 96.38 |
| 9.20 | 96.54 | 96.48 | 96.39 | 96.32 | 96.24 | 96.18 | 96.11 | 96.06 |
| 9.30 | 96.26 | 96.19 | 96.10 | 96.02 | 95.94 | 95.87 | 95.80 | 95.74 |
| 9.40 | 95.98 | 95.91 | 95.81 | 95.72 | 95.64 | 95.56 | 95.49 | 95.42 |
| 9.50 | 95.70 | 95.62 | 95.52 | 95.42 | 95.34 | 95.25 | 95.17 | 95.10 |
| 9.60 | 95.42 | 95.34 | 95.23 | 95.13 | 95.04 | 94.95 | 94.86 | 94.79 |
| 9.70 | 95.14 | 95.05 | 94.94 | 94.84 | 94.74 | 94.64 | 94.55 | 94.47 |
| 9.80 | 94.87 | 94.77 | 94.66 | 94.54 | 94.44 | 94.34 | 94.25 | 94.16 |
| 9.90 | 94.59 | 94.49 | 94.37 | 94.25 | 94.14 | 94.04 | 93.94 | 93.85 |
| 10.00 | 94.32 | 94.21 | 94.08 | 93.96 | 93.85 | 93.74 | 93.63 | 93.54 |
| 10.20 | 93.77 | 93.66 | 93.52 | 93.39 | 93.26 | 93.14 | 93.03 | 92.92 |
| 10.40 | 93.23 | 93.11 | 92.96 | 92.81 | 92.68 | 92.55 | 92.42 | 92.31 |
| 10.60 | 92.69 | 92.56 | 92.40 | 92.24 | 92.10 | 91.96 | 91.82 | 91.70 |
| 10.80 | 92.16 | 92.02 | 91.84 | 91.68 | 91.52 | 91.37 | 91.23 | 91.10 |
| 11.00 | 91.63 | 91.48 | 91.29 | 91.12 | 90.95 | 90.79 | 90.64 | 90.50 |
| 11.20 | 91.10 | 90.94 | 90.75 | 90.56 | 90.39 | 90.22 | 90.06 | 89.91 |
| 11.40 | 90.58 | 90.41 | 90.21 | 90.01 | 89.83 | 89.65 | 89.48 | 89.32 |
| 11.60 | 90.06 | 89.88 | 89.67 | 89.47 | 89.27 | 89.08 | 88.90 | 88.73 |
| 11.80 | 89.55 | 89.36 | 89.13 | 88.92 | 88.72 | 88.52 | 88.33 | 88.15 |
| 12.00 | 89.04 | 88.84 | 88.60 | 88.38 | 88.17 | 87.96 | 87.77 | 87.58 |

2(a)

8% **YEARS and MONTHS**

| Yield | 6-3 | 6-6 | 6-9 | 7-0 | 7-3 | 7-6 | 7-9 | 8-0 |
|---|---|---|---|---|---|---|---|---|
| 4.00 | 121.92 | 122.70 | 123.45 | 124.21 | 124.95 | 125.70 | 126.42 | 127.16 |
| 4.20 | 120.69 | 121.42 | 122.12 | 122.84 | 123.53 | 124.23 | 124.91 | 125.59 |
| 4.40 | 119.47 | 120.16 | 120.82 | 121.49 | 122.13 | 122.79 | 123.41 | 124.06 |
| 4.60 | 118.28 | 118.92 | 119.53 | 120.15 | 120.75 | 121.36 | 121.94 | 122.54 |
| 4.80 | 117.09 | 117.69 | 118.25 | 118.84 | 119.39 | 119.96 | 120.50 | 121.05 |
| 5.00 | 115.92 | 116.47 | 117.00 | 117.54 | 118.05 | 118.57 | 119.07 | 119.58 |
| 5.20 | 114.77 | 115.28 | 115.76 | 116.25 | 116.72 | 117.21 | 117.66 | 118.14 |
| 5.40 | 113.62 | 114.09 | 114.53 | 114.99 | 115.42 | 115.86 | 116.28 | 116.71 |
| 5.60 | 112.50 | 112.93 | 113.32 | 113.74 | 114.13 | 114.53 | 114.91 | 115.31 |
| 5.80 | 111.38 | 111.77 | 112.13 | 112.51 | 112.86 | 113.23 | 113.56 | 113.92 |
| 6.00 | 110.28 | 110.63 | 110.95 | 111.30 | 111.60 | 111.94 | 112.24 | 112.56 |
| 6.10 | 109.74 | 110.07 | 110.37 | 110.69 | 110.98 | 111.30 | 111.58 | 111.89 |
| 6.20 | 109.19 | 109.51 | 109.79 | 110.10 | 110.37 | 110.67 | 110.93 | 111.22 |
| 6.30 | 108.66 | 108.95 | 109.22 | 109.50 | 109.76 | 110.04 | 110.28 | 110.56 |
| 6.40 | 108.12 | 108.40 | 108.64 | 108.91 | 109.15 | 109.41 | 109.64 | 109.90 |
| 6.50 | 107.59 | 107.85 | 108.08 | 108.33 | 108.55 | 108.79 | 109.00 | 109.2[illegible] |
| 6.60 | 107.06 | 107.30 | 107.51 | 107.75 | 107.95 | 108.18 | 108.37 | 108.59 |
| 6.70 | 106.53 | 106.76 | 106.95 | 107.17 | 107.35 | 107.57 | 107.74 | 107.95 |
| 6.80 | 106.01 | 106.22 | 106.39 | 106.60 | 106.76 | 106.96 | 107.12 | 107.31 |
| 6.90 | 105.49 | 105.68 | 105.84 | 106.03 | 106.18 | 106.36 | 106.50 | 106.68 |
| 7.00 | 104.98 | 105.15 | 105.29 | 105.46 | 105.59 | 105.76 | 105.89 | 106.05 |
| 7.10 | 104.46 | 104.62 | 104.74 | 104.90 | 105.01 | 105.16 | 105.28 | 105.42 |
| 7.20 | 103.95 | 104.10 | 104.20 | 104.34 | 104.44 | 104.57 | 104.67 | 104.80 |
| 7.30 | 103.45 | 103.57 | 103.66 | 103.78 | 103.87 | 103.99 | 104.07 | 104.19 |
| 7.40 | 102.94 | 103.05 | 103.13 | 103.23 | 103.30 | 103.41 | 103.47 | 103.57 |
| 7.50 | 102.44 | 102.54 | 102.59 | 102.68 | 102.74 | 102.83 | 102.88 | 102.97 |
| 7.60 | 101.94 | 102.02 | 102.06 | 102.14 | 102.18 | 102.26 | 102.29 | 102.37 |
| 7.70 | 101.45 | 101.51 | 101.54 | 101.60 | 101.62 | 101.69 | 101.71 | 101.77 |
| 7.80 | 100.96 | 101.00 | 101.02 | 101.06 | 101.07 | 101.12 | 101.13 | 101.17 |
| 7.90 | 100.47 | 100.50 | 100.50 | 100.53 | 100.52 | 100.56 | 100.55 | 100.58 |
| 8.00 | 99.98 | 100.00 | 99.98 | 100.00 | 99.98 | 100.00 | 99.98 | 100.00 |
| 8.10 | 99.50 | 99.50 | 99.47 | 99.47 | 99.44 | 99.45 | 99.41 | 99.42 |
| 8.20 | 99.02 | 99.01 | 98.96 | 98.95 | 98.90 | 98.90 | 98.85 | 98.84 |
| 8.30 | 98.54 | 98.52 | 98.45 | 98.43 | 98.37 | 98.35 | 98.29 | 98.27 |
| 8.40 | 98.06 | 98.03 | 97.95 | 97.91 | 97.84 | 97.81 | 97.73 | 97.70 |
| 8.50 | 97.59 | 97.54 | 97.45 | 97.40 | 97.31 | 97.27 | 97.18 | 97.14 |
| 8.60 | 97.12 | 97.06 | 96.95 | 96.89 | 96.79 | 96.73 | 96.64 | 96.58 |
| 8.70 | 96.66 | 96.58 | 96.46 | 96.39 | 96.27 | 96.20 | 96.09 | 96.03 |
| 8.80 | 96.19 | 96.10 | 95.97 | 95.88 | 95.76 | 95.67 | 95.55 | 95.47 |
| 8.90 | 95.73 | 95.63 | 95.48 | 95.38 | 95.24 | 95.15 | 95.02 | 94.93 |
| 9.00 | 95.28 | 95.16 | 95.00 | 94.89 | 94.74 | 94.63 | 94.48 | 94.38 |
| 9.10 | 94.82 | 94.69 | 94.52 | 94.40 | 94.23 | 94.11 | 93.95 | 93.84 |
| 9.20 | 94.37 | 94.23 | 94.04 | 93.91 | 93.73 | 93.60 | 93.43 | 93.31 |
| 9.30 | 93.92 | 93.76 | 93.57 | 93.42 | 93.23 | 93.09 | 92.91 | 92.78 |
| 9.40 | 93.47 | 93.30 | 93.10 | 92.94 | 92.74 | 92.58 | 92.39 | 92.25 |
| 9.50 | 93.03 | 92.85 | 92.63 | 92.46 | 92.24 | 92.08 | 91.88 | 91.73 |
| 9.60 | 92.59 | 92.39 | 92.16 | 91.98 | 91.76 | 91.58 | 91.37 | 91.21 |
| 9.70 | 92.15 | 91.94 | 91.70 | 91.50 | 91.27 | 91.09 | 90.86 | 90.69 |
| 9.80 | 91.71 | 91.49 | 91.24 | 91.03 | 90.79 | 90.59 | 90.36 | 90.18 |
| 9.90 | 91.28 | 91.05 | 90.78 | 90.57 | 90.31 | 90.11 | 89.86 | 89.67 |
| 10.00 | 90.84 | 90.61 | 90.33 | 90.10 | 89.83 | 89.62 | 89.36 | 89.16 |
| 10.20 | 89.99 | 89.73 | 89.43 | 89.18 | 88.89 | 88.66 | 88.38 | 88.16 |
| 10.40 | 89.14 | 88.86 | 88.54 | 88.27 | 87.96 | 87.71 | 87.42 | 87.18 |
| 10.60 | 88.31 | 88.01 | 87.66 | 87.38 | 87.05 | 86.78 | 86.46 | 86.21 |
| 10.80 | 87.48 | 87.16 | 86.79 | 86.49 | 86.14 | 85.85 | 85.52 | 85.25 |
| 11.00 | 86.67 | 86.32 | 85.94 | 85.62 | 85.25 | 84.94 | 84.59 | 84.31 |
| 11.20 | 85.86 | 85.50 | 85.09 | 84.75 | 84.37 | 84.05 | 83.68 | 83.38 |
| 11.40 | 85.06 | 84.68 | 84.26 | 83.90 | 83.50 | 83.16 | 82.78 | 82.46 |
| 11.60 | 84.28 | 83.88 | 83.43 | 83.06 | 82.64 | 82.29 | 81.89 | 81.56 |
| 11.80 | 83.50 | 83.08 | 82.62 | 82.23 | 81.79 | 81.43 | 81.01 | 80.67 |
| 12.00 | 82.73 | 82.29 | 81.82 | 81.41 | 80.96 | 80.58 | 80.15 | 79.79 |

2(b)

**YEARS and MONTHS** 8%

| Yield | 30-6 | 31-0 | 31-6 | 32-0 | 32-6 | 33-0 | 33-6 | 34-0 |
|---|---|---|---|---|---|---|---|---|
| 4.00 | 170.12 | 170.71 | 171.28 | 171.84 | 172.39 | 172.94 | 173.47 | 173.99 |
| 4.20 | 165.01 | 165.53 | 166.05 | 166.55 | 167.04 | 167.52 | 168.00 | 168.46 |
| 4.40 | 160.12 | 160.59 | 161.05 | 161.49 | 161.93 | 162.36 | 162.78 | 163.19 |
| 4.60 | 155.45 | 155.86 | 156.27 | 156.67 | 157.06 | 157.43 | 157.80 | 158.17 |
| 4.80 | 150.98 | 151.34 | 151.70 | 152.05 | 152.40 | 152.73 | 153.06 | 153.38 |
| 5.00 | 146.70 | 147.02 | 147.34 | 147.65 | 147.95 | 148.24 | 148.53 | 148.81 |
| 5.20 | 142.60 | 142.88 | 143.16 | 143.43 | 143.69 | 143.95 | 144.20 | 144.45 |
| 5.40 | 138.67 | 138.92 | 139.16 | 139.40 | 139.63 | 139.85 | 140.07 | 140.28 |
| 5.60 | 134.91 | 135.12 | 135.33 | 135.54 | 135.74 | 135.93 | 136.12 | 136.30 |
| 5.80 | 131.30 | 131.49 | 131.67 | 131.84 | 132.02 | 132.18 | 132.34 | 132.50 |
| 6.00 | 127.84 | 128.00 | 128.16 | 128.31 | 128.45 | 128.60 | 128.73 | 128.87 |
| 6.10 | 126.16 | 126.31 | 126.46 | 126.59 | 126.73 | 126.86 | 126.99 | 127.11 |
| 6.20 | 124.52 | 124.66 | 124.79 | 124.92 | 125.04 | 125.16 | 125.28 | 125.39 |
| 6.30 | 122.92 | 123.04 | 123.16 | 123.28 | 123.39 | 123.50 | 123.61 | 123.71 |
| 6.40 | 121.34 | 121.45 | 121.56 | 121.67 | 121.77 | 121.87 | 121.97 | 122.06 |
| 6.50 | 119.80 | 119.90 | 120.00 | 120.10 | 120.19 | 120.28 | 120.37 | 120.45 |
| 6.60 | 118.28 | 118.38 | 118.47 | 118.56 | 118.64 | 118.72 | 118.80 | 118.88 |
| 6.70 | 116.80 | 116.89 | 116.97 | 117.05 | 117.12 | 117.20 | 117.27 | 117.34 |
| 6.80 | 115.35 | 115.43 | 115.50 | 115.57 | 115.64 | 115.70 | 115.77 | 115.83 |
| 6.90 | 113.93 | 114.00 | 114.06 | 114.12 | 114.18 | 114.24 | 114.30 | 114.35 |
| 7.00 | 112.53 | 112.59 | 112.65 | 112.71 | 112.76 | 112.81 | 112.86 | 112.91 |
| 7.10 | 111.17 | 111.22 | 111.27 | 111.32 | 111.36 | 111.41 | 111.45 | 111.49 |
| 7.20 | 109.83 | 109.87 | 109.91 | 109.96 | 110.00 | 110.03 | 110.07 | 110.11 |
| 7.30 | 108.51 | 108.55 | 108.59 | 108.62 | 108.66 | 108.69 | 108.72 | 108.75 |
| 7.40 | 107.22 | 107.26 | 107.29 | 107.32 | 107.34 | 107.37 | 107.40 | 107.42 |
| 7.50 | 105.96 | 105.99 | 106.01 | 106.03 | 106.06 | 106.08 | 106.10 | 106.12 |
| 7.60 | 104.72 | 104.74 | 104.76 | 104.78 | 104.80 | 104.81 | 104.83 | 104.85 |
| 7.70 | 103.51 | 103.52 | 103.54 | 103.55 | 103.56 | 103.57 | 103.59 | 103.60 |
| 7.80 | 102.32 | 102.32 | 102.33 | 102.34 | 102.35 | 102.36 | 102.37 | 102.37 |
| 7.90 | 101.15 | 101.15 | 101.16 | 101.16 | 101.16 | 101.17 | 101.17 | 101.17 |
| 8.00 | 100.00 | 100.00 | 100.00 | 100.00 | 100.00 | 100.00 | 100.00 | 100.00 |
| 8.10 | 98.88 | 98.87 | 98.87 | 98.86 | 98.86 | 98.86 | 98.85 | 98.85 |
| 8.20 | 97.77 | 97.76 | 97.75 | 97.75 | 97.74 | 97.73 | 97.73 | 97.72 |
| 8.30 | 96.69 | 96.68 | 96.66 | 96.65 | 96.64 | 96.63 | 96.62 | 96.61 |
| 8.40 | 95.63 | 95.61 | 95.59 | 95.58 | 95.57 | 95.55 | 95.54 | 95.53 |
| 8.50 | 94.58 | 94.56 | 94.54 | 94.53 | 94.51 | 94.49 | 94.48 | 94.46 |
| 8.60 | 93.56 | 93.54 | 93.52 | 93.49 | 93.48 | 93.46 | 93.44 | 93.42 |
| 8.70 | 92.55 | 92.53 | 92.50 | 92.48 | 92.46 | 92.44 | 92.42 | 92.40 |
| 8.80 | 91.57 | 91.54 | 91.51 | 91.49 | 91.46 | 91.44 | 91.42 | 91.40 |
| 8.90 | 90.60 | 90.57 | 90.54 | 90.51 | 90.48 | 90.46 | 90.43 | 90.41 |
| 9.00 | 89.65 | 89.61 | 89.58 | 89.55 | 89.52 | 89.50 | 89.47 | 89.45 |
| 9.10 | 88.71 | 88.68 | 88.64 | 88.61 | 88.58 | 88.55 | 88.53 | 88.50 |
| 9.20 | 87.80 | 87.76 | 87.72 | 87.69 | 87.66 | 87.63 | 87.60 | 87.57 |
| 9.30 | 86.90 | 86.86 | 86.82 | 86.78 | 86.75 | 86.72 | 86.69 | 86.66 |
| 9.40 | 86.01 | 85.97 | 85.93 | 85.89 | 85.86 | 85.83 | 85.79 | 85.76 |
| 9.50 | 85.14 | 85.10 | 85.06 | 85.02 | 84.98 | 84.95 | 84.92 | 84.88 |
| 9.60 | 84.29 | 84.24 | 84.20 | 84.16 | 84.12 | 84.09 | 84.05 | 84.02 |
| 9.70 | 83.45 | 83.40 | 83.36 | 83.32 | 83.28 | 83.24 | 83.21 | 83.17 |
| 9.80 | 82.63 | 82.58 | 82.53 | 82.49 | 82.45 | 82.41 | 82.38 | 82.34 |
| 9.90 | 81.82 | 81.77 | 81.72 | 81.68 | 81.64 | 81.60 | 81.56 | 81.53 |
| 10.00 | 81.02 | 80.97 | 80.92 | 80.88 | 80.84 | 80.80 | 80.76 | 80.72 |
| 10.20 | 79.47 | 79.42 | 79.37 | 79.33 | 79.28 | 79.24 | 79.20 | 79.16 |
| 10.40 | 77.97 | 77.92 | 77.87 | 77.82 | 77.78 | 77.74 | 77.70 | 77.66 |
| 10.60 | 76.52 | 76.47 | 76.42 | 76.37 | 76.33 | 76.28 | 76.24 | 76.20 |
| 10.80 | 75.12 | 75.07 | 75.02 | 74.97 | 74.92 | 74.88 | 74.84 | 74.80 |
| 11.00 | 73.77 | 73.71 | 73.66 | 73.61 | 73.57 | 73.52 | 73.48 | 73.44 |
| 11.20 | 72.46 | 72.40 | 72.35 | 72.30 | 72.26 | 72.21 | 72.17 | 72.13 |
| 11.40 | 71.19 | 71.13 | 71.08 | 71.03 | 70.99 | 70.94 | 70.90 | 70.86 |
| 11.60 | 69.96 | 69.91 | 69.86 | 69.81 | 69.76 | 69.72 | 69.68 | 69.64 |
| 11.80 | 68.77 | 68.72 | 68.67 | 68.62 | 68.57 | 68.53 | 68.49 | 68.45 |
| 12.00 | 67.62 | 67.57 | 67.52 | 67.47 | 67.42 | 67.38 | 67.34 | 67.30 |

2(c)

Source: Reproduced from *Expanded Bond Values Tables*, Publication No. 63, Copyright 1970, by Financial Publishing Company, Boston, Ma.

in the yield book that corresponds to the coupon rate and time remaining to maturity for the bond whose yield is sought. Second, look down the column corresponding to the time remaining to maturity until the market price of the bond (expressed as a percentage of par value) is found. Finally, look across the row to obtain the yield.

The procedure can be illustrated using our hypothetical bond. Exhibit 2(b) represents the appropriate page of the yield book, since it contains bond values for a bond with a coupon rate of 8 percent and seven years remaining to maturity. The market price of our hypothetical bond is $814.10, or 81.41 percent of par. Looking down column 7–0 we find the value of 81.41 in the row corresponding to a yield of 12 percent. This, of course, agrees with our previous computation that indicated the yield to maturity for our hypothetical bond to be 12 percent.

Everything went smoothly in our illustration. The exact time remaining to maturity was on the table, and so was the exact market price. Suppose, instead, that our hypothetical bond had seven years and one month remaining to maturity and a market price of $904. Neither input needed to determine the yield to maturity is included on the sample page. What can be done in such cases? The yield to maturity can be approximated by interpolating the values presented in the yield book. Such an approach may be satisfactory for an investor with a small sum to invest. However, for a portfolio manager with substantial funds to invest, such an approach would be inadequate. In such instances, portfolio managers usually have online access to computer software that provides the yield to maturity given the three input values. For a cost of less than $40, an investor can purchase a pocket calculator that includes a feature to compute the yield to maturity.

The investor should be cognizant of the following relationships of the coupon rate, current yield, and yield to maturity:

| Price of the bond | Relationship |
|---|---|
| Selling at par | Coupon rate = Current yield = Yield to maturity |
| Selling at a discount | Coupon rate < Current yield < Yield to maturity |
| Selling at a premium | Coupon rate > Current yield > Yield to maturity |

## Yield to call

A bond may be called by the issuer before maturity. Consequently, a conservative investor will compute the yield on a bond in two ways: (1) assuming the bond is held to maturity and (2) assuming the bond is called by the issuer. The latter yield is referred to as the yield to call. A conservative investor uses the lower of the two yields in determining the promised "yield" on the bond, because it represents a minimum yield that may be realized.

At the outset, it must be noted that the yield to call, like the yield to maturity, is a traditional measure that is *not* a good measure to employ to evaluate the investment merits of alternative bonds available to the investor. This is so for two reasons. First, it assumes the coupon interest payments before the issue is called will be reinvested at a rate equal to the yield to call. Hence, it suffers from the same problem as the yield to maturity. Second, it does not recognize what will happen to the proceeds after the bond is called. Consequently, since the yield to maturity assumes a time commitment of funds greater than the yield to call, a direct comparison of these two yields is inappropriate. These drawbacks of the yield to call are discussed in the next section.

The yield to call is defined as the discount rate that equates the present value of the promised cash flow if the bond is called (coupon payments plus call price) to the market price. To illustrate the computation of the yield to call, suppose our hypothetical bond is selling for $1,089.37 instead of $814.10. Further, assume the bond is callable three years from now at 104.2 (i.e., $1,042). A 3 percent discount rate will equate the present value of the cash flow of the bond if it is called to the market price of $1,089.37. Doubling the discount rate gives the yield to call. Hence, the yield to call is 6 percent.

The yield to maturity for the bond can be found using the yield book. From Exhibit 2, we find that an 8 percent coupon bond with seven years remaining to maturity and a price of 108.91 offers a yield to maturity of 6.4 percent. Since our hypothetical bond has a market price of 108.94, its yield to maturity is approximately 6.4 percent. Therefore, a conservative investor would use the yield to call as the "yield," since it is less than the yield to maturity.

When the call price is greater than the redemption value,

which it usually is when a bond can be called, there are methods for approximating the yield-to-call.[5] Since there are specialized yield-to-call books published and pocket calculators with preprogrammed features to compute the yield on an investment, the approximation methods are not discussed here. It may not be necessary, however, to compute the yield to call. Remember, if the yield to call is greater than the yield to maturity, then the latter is the minimum "yield."

### Realized compound yield

When using the yield to maturity as a measure of investment return, it is assumed that the coupon interest can be reinvested at a rate equal to the yield to maturity. That is, if the yield to maturity is 12 percent, it is assumed that the coupon interest payments can be reinvested to yield 12 percent.

To see the importance of the interest-on-interest component of total return, consider a bond selling at par with seven years remaining to maturity and carrying a 12 percent coupon rate. The total return for this bond consists of two sources: (1) coupon interest of $60 every six months for seven years and (2) interest from the reinvestment of the coupon interest. Since the bond is assumed to be selling at par, there is no capital gain or loss.

The future value (FV) generated from the reinvestment of coupon interest at 12 percent annually can be found by multiplying the future value of an annuity of $1 by the semiannual coupon interest. Thus, for the bond under examination we have:

$$\begin{bmatrix} FV \text{ of } \$60 \text{ for } 14 \\ \text{six-month periods} \end{bmatrix} = \$60 \times \begin{bmatrix} FV \text{ of } \$1 \text{ each six months} \\ \text{at 6 percent interest} \end{bmatrix}$$
$$= \$60 \times 21.015$$
$$= \$1,261$$

The coupon interest is $840 ($60 times 14). Hence, the balance, $421 ($1,261 minus $840), represents the interest-on-interest component of the total return. For this bond, interest on interest accounts for 33 percent ($421 divided by $1,261) of the total return.

---

[5] See Sidney Homer and Martin L. Leibowitz, *Inside the Yield Book* (published jointly: Englewood Cliffs, N.J.: Prentice-Hall, and New York: New York Institute of Finance, 1972), pp. 164–67.

The importance of the interest-on-interest component becomes greater the longer the maturity. For example, if the 12 percent coupon bonds selling at par had a remaining life of 30 years instead of 7 years, the total return would be $31,987. Since coupon interest payments are $3,600 ($60 times 60 semi-annual coupon payments), interest on interest is $28,387 ($31,987 minus $3,600) or 89 percent of the total return.

For a bond selling at a discount from par, interest on interest makes up less of the total return for bonds of equal time remaining to maturity and the same yield to maturity. This can be illustrated with the hypothetical bond used to illustrate the computation of the yield to maturity. Recall that the bond carries an 8 percent coupon rate, has seven years remaining to maturity, and has a market price of $814 (rounded to the nearest dollar). The yield to maturity for this bond is 12 percent. The total return consists of (1) coupon interest payments of $560, (2) interest on interest of $281, and (3) a capital gain of $186 ($1,000 minus $814). The interest-on-interest component accounts for 27 percent of the total return ($281 divided by $1,027). For the 12 percent, seven-year par bonds, the interest-on-interest component makes up 33 percent of the total return.

The interest-on-interest component of a long-term bond selling at a discount would be a substantial portion of the bond's total return, just as in the case of a bond selling at par. In fact, the longer the term of the bond, the less important is the capital gain component, compared with the other two components. For example, a bond with 30 years remaining to maturity, carrying a coupon rate of 8 percent, and selling at $677 will have a yield to maturity of 12 percent. The total return for this bond is $21,648, consisting of: (1) coupon interest payments of $2,400, (2) interest on interest of $18,925, and (3) a capital gain of $323. The capital gain component is only 1.5 percent of the total return. For the seven-year bond selling at a discount, the capital gain component represented 18 percent of the total return. The interest-on-interest component for the 30-year bond selling at a discount is about 87 percent, which is approximately the same as in the case of the 30-year bond selling at par.

As would be expected, bonds selling at a premium are more dependent upon the interest-on-interest component of the total return.

Because of the importance of the rate that the coupon interest is assumed to be reinvested, a measure of return that can be used for investment decisions must take into account interest on interest. Homer and Leibowitz suggest a comprehensive measure that takes into consideration all three sources of a bond's return. The measure they suggest reveals the fully compounded growth rate of an investment under varying reinvestment rates. They call this measure the "realized compound yield."[6] Appendix A shows how this measure is computed.

A property of the realized compound yield is that it will be between the yield to maturity and the reinvestment rate. Therefore, when the reinvestment rate is the same as the yield to maturity, the realized compound yield is the same as the yield to maturity. When the reinvestment rate is greater than the yield to maturity, the realized compound yield will be greater than the yield to maturity. The realized compound yield will be less than the yield to maturity when the reinvestment rate is less than the latter.

The difference in basis points between the realized compound yield and the yield to maturity depends not only on the reinvestment rate but also on the remaining life of the bond and the coupon rate.[7] The longer the term to maturity, the more important will be the interest-on-interest component for a given coupon rate and yield to maturity. Consequently, the longer the term of a bond, the closer its realized compound yield will be to the reinvestment rate. However, the shorter the maturity, the closer the realized compound yield will be to the yield to maturity.

For a given term to maturity and yield to maturity, the lower the coupon rate, the less of a bond's total return depends on the interest-on-interest component. Therefore, holding all other factors constant, the realized compound yield will deviate from the yield to maturity by less basis points for a given reinvestment rate the lower the coupon rate.

Exhibit 3 shows the realized compound yield under different assumptions for the reinvestment rate for the four bonds discussed in this section. The reader can verify the properties of the realized compound yield stated in the preceding discussion.

Realized compound yield should also be used to measure the minimum yield for a callable bond selling at a premium. As

---

[6] Homer and Leibowitz, *Inside the Yield Book*.

[7] A basis point is equal to one one-hundredth of 1 percent. One hundred points are equal to 1 percent.

**EXHIBIT 3**      Realized compound yields for 7-year and 30-year bonds with a 12 percent yield to maturity: Coupon rates 12 percent and 8 percent

| | Realized compound yield* | | | |
| | 7-year bonds | | 30-year bonds | |
| Reinvestment rate | 12 percent coupon, price = 100 | 8 percent coupon, price = 81.41 | 12 percent coupon, price = 100 | 8 percent coupon, price = 677 |
|---|---|---|---|---|
| 8% | 10.8% | 11.1% | 9.3% | 9.4% |
| 10 | 11.4 | 11.6 | 10.6 | 10.8 |
| 12 | 12.0 | 12.0 | 12.0 | 12.0 |
| 14 | 12.6 | 12.5 | 13.3 | 13.3 |
| 16 | 13.2 | 13.0 | 15.0 | 14.9 |

* The yield to maturity for each bond is 12 percent.

discussed in the previous section, the selection of a minimum yield based upon the lesser of the yield to maturity and yield to call is deficient, because it does not consider the reinvestment opportunities available to the investor. A proper analysis would consider the realized compound yield assuming the bond is not called and assuming the bond is called.[8]

## BOND PRICE VOLATILITY

The price of a bond changes in the opposite direction from the change in the yield required by investors. For example, if a 9 percent coupon bond with 20 years remaining to maturity is selling at 100 (par) to yield 9 percent, the price of the bond will decrease to 91.42 if market yields increase by 100 basis points to 10 percent. The increase in market yields decreases the price of the bond by 8.58 percent. If, on the other hand, market yields decline by 100 basis points to 8 percent, the price of the bond will increase by 9.9 percent to 109.90. In addition, the change in the price of the bond will be greater the greater the change in the yield required by investors. For example, for the 9 percent coupon, 20-year bond, an increase in market yields from 9 percent to 11 percent (a 200-basis-point increase) will result in a

[8] See Frank J. Fabozzi, "Bond Yield Measures and Price Volatility Properties," in *The Handbook of Fixed Income Securities*, eds. Frank J. Fabozzi and Irving M. Pollack (Homewood, Ill.: Dow Jones-Irwin, 1983), pp. 78–79.

decrease in the price of the bond from 100 to 83.95. Hence, for a 200-basis-point increase in yield, the price of the bond will fall by 16.05 percent, compared with 8.58 percent for a 100-basis-point increase in yield.

For a given initial market yield and a given change in basis points, the percentage change in the price of the bond will depend upon certain characteristics of the bond. The relationship between bond price volatility and these characteristics of a bond are illustrated in the remainder of this article.

Before proceeding, it is important to understand that the volatility we will be discussing is the change that will result from an *instantaneous* change in market yields. Even if market yields do not change, the price of a bond selling at a premium or discount will change due to the passage of time. For example, consider a bond with a 7 percent coupon rate, 20 years remaining to maturity, and selling at 81.60 to yield 9 percent. If the bond is held for 1 year and market yields remained at 9 percent, the price of the bond would increase to 81.95, since it would have 19 years remaining to maturity. The increase in price from 81.60 to 81.95 results from an accretion process that will eventually increase the price of the bond to its par value at maturity. For a bond selling at a premium, the price of a bond decreases as it approaches maturity if market yields remain constant. Consider, for example, a bond with a coupon rate of 12 percent, 20 years remaining to maturity, and selling for 127.60 to yield 9 percent. The price of the bond after one year has passed will be 127.07 if market yields do not change. This results from the amortization of the premium. The relationship between the price of a bond and the remaining time to maturity assuming that market yields are unchanged is shown in Exhibits 4 and 5.

### Bond price volatility and coupon rate

For a given maturity and initial market yield, the volatility of a bond's price increases the lower the coupon rate. For example, for a 9 percent, 20-year coupon bond an increase in interest rates from 9 percent to 10 percent will drop the price from $1,000.00 to $914.20, or 8.58 percent. For a 5 percent coupon bond with 20 years to maturity and selling for $632 to yield 9 percent, an increase in interest rates from 9 percent to 10 percent will decrease the price by 9.65 percent to $571.

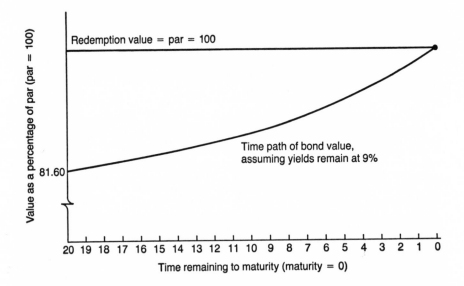

**EXHIBIT 4** Time path of the value of a 7 percent coupon, 20-year bond if the required yield begins and remains at 9 percent

Value as a percentage of par (par = 100)

Redemption value = par = 100

Time path of bond value, assuming yields remain at 9%

81.60

20 19 18 17 16 15 14 13 12 11 10 9 8 7 6 5 4 3 2 1 0

Time remaining to maturity (maturity = 0)

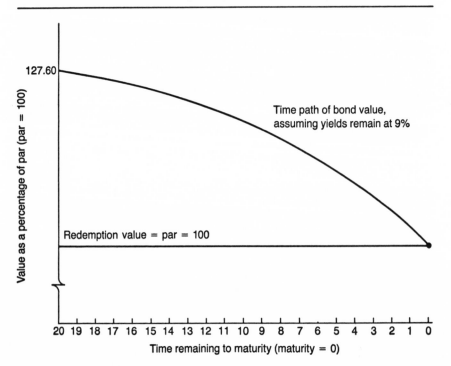

**EXHIBIT 5** Time path of the value of a 12 percent coupon, 20-year bond if the required yield begins and remains at 9 percent

Value as a percentage of par (par = 100)

127.60

Time path of bond value, assuming yields remain at 9%

Redemption value = par = 100

20 19 18 17 16 15 14 13 12 11 10 9 8 7 6 5 4 3 2 1 0

Time remaining to maturity (maturity = 0)

An implication of this property of price volatility is that bonds selling at a discount are more responsive to changes in market yield, all other factors equal, compared with bonds selling at or above par. Moreover, the deeper the discount resulting from the divergence between the coupon rate and market yield, the greater the responsiveness of the bond's price to changes in market yield. The greatest price response is offered by zero-coupon debt obligations. From a purely capital gain or loss perspective, therefore, investors would avoid bonds selling at a discount if interest rates are expected to rise; however, bonds selling at a discount rate are attractive if interest rates are anticipated to decline.

### Bond price volatility and maturity

The volatility of the price of a bond increases the longer the remaining term to maturity, all other factors constant. To see this, consider a 9 percent coupon bond with only five years to maturity and selling for $1,000 to yield 9 percent. If interest rates rise from 9 percent to 10 percent, the price of the bond will fall by less than 1 percent to $990.70. Recall that the price of the 20-year, 9 percent coupon bond would fall by 8.58 percent if interest rates increase from 9 percent to 10 percent.

An implication of this property of price volatility is that if interest rates are expected to increase, bond prices will decrease by a greater percentage for long-term bonds compared to short-term bonds, all other factors constant. Therefore, from a purely capital loss perspective, an investor will avoid long-term bonds (holding everything else constant) if interest rates are expected to rise. Conversely, since the percentage change in prices of long-term bonds will increase by a greater percentage than short-term bonds, investors will prefer long-term bonds from a purely capital gain perspective when interest rates are projected to fall.

### Bond price volatility and duration

A pitfall with using the maturity of a bond as a measure of the timing of its cash flow is that it only takes into consideration the final payment. To overcome this shortcoming, Professor Frederick R. Macaulay in 1938 suggested using a measure that would account for all cash flows expected.[9] The measure he suggested, known as duration, is a weighted-average term to maturity where the cash flows are in terms of their present value. Appendix B explains how duration is computed.

Three properties of a bond's duration should be noted. First, except for zero coupon bonds, the duration of a bond is less than its maturity. Second, the duration of a bond decreases the greater the coupon rate. Finally, as market yields increase, the duration of a bond decreases.

The specific link between a bond's duration and its bond price volatility for small changes in interest rates was demonstrated by Professors Michael Hopewell and George Kaufman.[10] They show that:

Percentage change in bond's price

$$= -(\text{Modified duration}) \times \left( \frac{\begin{array}{c}\text{Change in market yield}\\ \text{in basis points}\end{array}}{100} \right)$$

where modified duration is duration divided by (1 + market yield/the number of coupon payments per year).

For example, the duration of a 7 percent coupon bond with eight years to maturity and selling to yield 9 percent is 6.1335.[11] Hence, modified duration is 6.1335/(1 + .09/2), or 5.8694. The percentage decline in the bond's price if market yields rise by 50 basis points is 2.93 percent as shown below:

$$= -(5.8694) \times \left( \frac{50}{100} \right)$$
$$= -2.93 \text{ percent}$$

The use of duration as a measure of the responsiveness of a bond's price to a change in market yields is only one application of how this concept can be used in bond portfolio management. Another important application deals with the trade-off that arises as interest rates change over the investor's invest-

---

[9] Frederick R. Macaulay, *Some Theoretical Problems Suggested by the Movement of Interest Rates, Bond Yields, and Stock Prices in the United States Since 1865* (New York: National Bureau of Economic Research, 1938).

[10] Michael H. Hopewell and George C. Kaufman, "Bond Price Volatility and Term to Maturity: A Generalized Respecification," *American Economic Review,* September 1973, pp. 749–53.

[11] See Appendix B for the calculations.

ment horizon. As interest rates increase, the price of the bond declines, but the portion of the total return from interest on interest increases. When interest rates decrease over the investor's investment horizon, the opposite is true. The portion of the total return resulting from interest on interest decreases, but the price of the bond increases. To immunize a bond portfolio from this interest rate risk to achieve a targeted return over an investment horizon, it has been demonstrated that the duration of the portfolio should be set equal to the investment horizon.[12]

## SUMMARY

This article explained the basic elements of bond yield mathematics. In addition to illustrating how each yield measure is computed, the drawback of the conventional yield-to-maturity measure is explained and a better measure, the realized compound yield, is discussed. The investor should now understand why the yield to maturity only provides a *promised yield,* and that yield will not necessarily be equal to the return realized by the investor at the end of the investor's investment horizon. The factors that influence the volatility of a bond's price are also explained in this article. The duration of a bond is a concept with important implications for managing a bond portfolio.

## APPENDIX A

### Computation of the realized compound yield

The steps to compute the realized compound yield are as follows:

1.  Compute the total future dollars that will be received from the investment. This is equal to the sum of the coupon payments, the interest on interest from reinvesting the coupon payments at an assumed reinvestment rate, and the redemption value.
2.  Divide the amount found in the previous step by the investment. The resulting amount is the future value (FV) per dollar invested.

---

[12] For a further discussion, see H. Gifford Fong and Frank J. Fabozzi, *Fixed Income Portfolio Management* (Homewood, Ill.: Dow Jones-Irwin, 1985), chapter 6.

3. Find the interest rate that produces the future value per dollar invested. This can be done by using a future value of $1 table or by solving the following equation:

$$(\text{Future value per dollar invested})^{\frac{1}{\text{no. of periods}}} - 1$$

4. Since interest is assumed to be paid semiannually, double the interest rate found in the previous step. The resulting interest rate is the realized compound yield.

The 12 percent seven-year bond selling at par that was used to illustrate the other yield measures in this article will be used to demonstrate the computation of the realized compound yield. The reinvestment rate *assumed* is 10 percent. The steps are as follows:

1. The total future dollars to be received consists of the coupon interest and interest on interest of $1,176[13] and the redemption value of $1,000. Hence, the total future dollars to be received is $2,176.
2. Since the investment is $1,000, the future value per $1 invested is $2.176 ($2,176 divided by $1,000).
3. The interest rate that will produce a future value of $2.176 for a $1 investment made for 14 periods is between 5 and 6 percent. Using the formula, the interest rate of 5.7 percent would produce a future value of $2.17.
4. Doubling 5.7 percent, we get a realized compound yield of 11.4 percent.

## APPENDIX B

### Computation of the duration of a bond

Mathematically, duration is measured as follows

$$\text{Duration} = \frac{\text{PVCF}_1\,(1)}{\text{PVTCF}} + \frac{\text{PVCF}_2\,(2)}{\text{PVTCF}} + \cdots + \frac{\text{PVCF}_n\,(n)}{\text{PVTCF}}$$

---

[13]
$$\begin{bmatrix} FV \text{ of } \$60 \text{ for } 14 \\ \text{six-month periods} \end{bmatrix} = \$60 \times \begin{bmatrix} FV \text{ of } \$1 \text{ each six months} \\ \text{at 5 percent interest} \end{bmatrix}$$
$$= \$60 \times 19.598$$
$$= \$1,176$$

Note that, since the annual reinvestment rate is assumed to be 10 percent, a 5 percent semiannual interest rate is used in the future value computation.

where

$PVCF_t$ = The present value of the cash flow in period $t$ discounted at the prevailing yield to maturity

$t$ = The period when the cash flow is expected to be received

$n$ = Remaining number of periods until maturity

$PVTCF$ = Total present value of the cash flow from the bond where the present value is determined using the prevailing yield to maturity

For a bond in which there are no sinking fund or call effects and in which interest is paid semiannually, the cash flow for periods 1 to n − 1 is just one half of the annual coupon interest. The cash flow in period $n$ is the semiannual coupon interest

**EXHIBIT B-1** Worksheet for computation of the duration of a 7 percent coupon bond with eight years to maturity selling at $887.70 to yield 9 percent (semiannual interest payments assumed)

| Period | Cash flow | PV at 4.5 percent | PVCF | PVCF × period |
|---|---|---|---|---|
| 1 | $ 35 | .9569 | $ 33.4915 | 33.4915 |
| 2 | 35 | .9157 | 32.0495 | 64.0990 |
| 3 | 35 | .8763 | 30.6705 | 92.0115 |
| 4 | 35 | .8386 | 29.3510 | 117.4040 |
| 5 | 35 | .8025 | 28.0875 | 140.4375 |
| 6 | 35 | .7679 | 26.8765 | 161.2590 |
| 7 | 35 | .7348 | 25.7180 | 180.0260 |
| 8 | 35 | .7032 | 24.6120 | 196.8960 |
| 9 | 35 | .6729 | 23.5515 | 211.9635 |
| 10 | 35 | .6439 | 22.5365 | 225.3650 |
| 11 | 35 | .6162 | 21.5670 | 237.2370 |
| 12 | 35 | .5897 | 20.6395 | 247.6740 |
| 13 | 35 | .5643 | 19.7505 | 256.7565 |
| 14 | 35 | .5400 | 18.9000 | 264.6000 |
| 15 | 35 | .5167 | 18.0845 | 271.2675 |
| 16 | 1,035 | .4945 | 511.8075 | 8,188.9200 |
| | | | 887.6935 | 10,889.4080 |

Duration in half years $= \dfrac{10,889.4080}{887.6935}$

$= 12.2671$

Duration in years $= \dfrac{12.2671}{2}$

$= 6.1335$

plus the redemption value. The discount rate is one half the prevailing yield to maturity. The resulting value is in half years when semiannual interest payments are used in the computation. To obtain duration in terms of years, duration in half years is divided by two.[14] Since the price of a bond is equal to its cash flow discounted at the prevailing yield to maturity, PVTCF is nothing more than the current market price *including accrued interest.*

Exhibit B–1 shows how the duration of a 7 percent coupon bond with eight years to maturity and selling for $887.70 to yield 9 percent is computed assuming coupon interest is paid semiannually. The duration for this bond is 6.1335 years.

---

[14] In general, if there are $m$ coupon payments per year, then duration in years is computed by dividing the duration based upon $m$ payments per year by $m$.

# TEN

---

## Money market instruments

**Marcia Stigum, Ph.D.**
*Stigum & Associates, New York*

---

The U.S. money market is a huge and significant part of the nation's financial system in which banks and other participants trade hundreds of billions of dollars every working day. Where those billions go and the prices at which they are traded affect how the U.S. government finances its debt, how business finances its expansion, and how consumers choose to spend or save.

*The money market is a wholesale market for low-risk, highly liquid, short-term IOUs.* It is a market for various sorts of debt securities, rather than equities. The stock in trade of the market includes a large chunk of the U.S. Treasury's debt and billions of dollars worth of federal agency securities, negotiable bank certificates of deposit, bankers' acceptances, municipal notes, and commercial paper. Within the confines of the money market each day, banks, both domestic and foreign, actively trade in multimillion-dollar blocks billions of dollars of Federal funds and Eurodollars, and banks and nonbank dealers are each day the recipients of billions of dollars of secured loans through what is called the *repo market*. State and municipal governments also finance part of their activities in this market.

The heart of the activity in the money market occurs in the trading rooms of dealers and brokers of money market instruments. During the time the market is open, these rooms are characterized by a frenzy of activity. Despite its frenzied and incoherent appearance to the outsider, the money market efficiently accomplishes vital functions every day. One is shifting vast sums of money between banks. This shifting is required because the major money market banks, with the exception of the Bank of America, all need a lot more funds than they obtain in deposits, while many smaller banks have more money deposited with them than they can profitably use internally.

The money market also provides a means by which the surplus funds of cash-rich corporations and other institutions can be funneled to banks, corporations, and other institutions that need short-term money. In addition, in the money market the U.S. Treasury can fund huge quantities of debt with ease. And the market provides the Federal Reserve System (also known as *the Fed*) with an arena in which to carry out open-market operations destined to influence interest rates and the growth of the money supply. The varied activities of money market participants also determine the structure of short-term interest rates, for example, what the yields on Treasury bills of different maturities are and how much commercial paper issuers have to pay to borrow. The latter rate is an important cost to many corporations, and it influences in particular the interest rate that a consumer who buys a car on time will have to pay on the loan. Finally, one might mention that the U.S. money market is becoming increasingly an international short-term capital market. In it the oil imports of the nationalized French electric company, Electricité de France, as well as the oil imports of Japan and a lot of other non-U.S. trade are financed.

Anyone who observes the money market soon picks out a number of salient features. First and most obviously, it is not one market but a collection of markets for several distinct and different instruments. What makes it possible to talk about *the* money market is the close interrelationships that link all these markets. A second salient feature is the numerous and varied cast of participants. Borrowers in the market include foreign and domestic banks, the Treasury, corporations of all types, the Federal Home Loan Banks and other federal agencies, dealers in money market instruments, and many states and municipalities. The lenders include almost all of the above, plus insurance companies, pension funds—public and private—and various other financial institutions. And often standing between borrower and lender is one or more of a varied collection of brokers and dealers.

Another key characteristic of the money market is that it is a wholesale market. Trades are big and the people who make them are almost always dealing for the account of some substantial institution. Because of the sums involved, skill is of the utmost importance, and money market participants are skilled at what they do. In effect the market is made by extremely talented specialists in very narrow professional areas. A bill trader extraordinaire may have only vague notions on what the Euromarket is all about, and the Euro specialist may be equally vague on other sectors of the market.

Another principal characteristic of the money market is honor. Every day traders, brokers, investors, and borrowers do hundreds of billions of dollars of business over the phone and, however a trade may appear in retrospect, people do not renege. The motto of the money market is: *My word is my bond.* Of course, because of the pace of the market, mistakes do occur but no one ever assumes that they are intentional, and mistakes are always ironed out in what seems the fairest way for all concerned.

The most appealing characteristic of the money market is innovation. Compared with our other financial markets, the money market is very unregulated. If someone wants to launch a new instrument or to try brokering or dealing in a new way in existing instruments, he or she does it. And when the idea is good, which it often is, a new facet of the market is born.

In this article we examine taxable money market instruments (negotiable short-term debt securities) in which individuals and business firms invest. Treasury bills, issued by the U.S. Treasury, are the most important class of such instruments in the United States, but there are others: commercial paper, bankers' acceptances, and negotiable certificates of deposit. In Article Fourteen, short-term tax-exempt instruments are described.

Many money market instruments can be purchased through a money market fund or a money market account. By pooling the resources of many investors, these funds are able to offer high money market yields to investors who would otherwise be limited in their choices. The money market fund and account permits investors to broaden their portfolio of short-term securities and simultaneously reduce their risk, as the funds' portfolios are diversified. Money market funds consist of taxable or tax-exempt short-term securities. The investor's marginal tax bracket will dictate which type of fund is more appropriate.

## TREASURY BILLS

Treasury bills (known more familiarly as *T bills* or *bills*) represent about 40 percent of the total marketable securities issued by the Treasury. These securities are held widely by financial business firms, nonfinancial corporations, and, to some extent, by individuals.

All T bills are negotiable, noninterest-bearing securities with an original maturity of one year or less—usually 13, 26, or 52 weeks. Bills are currently offered by the Treasury in denominations of $10,000, $15,000, $50,000, $100,000, $500,000, and $1 million. Bills used to be issued by the Treasury in the form of *bearer certificates*. Accordingly, to prove ownership of a bill, the owner must produce it. The Treasury and the Federal Reserve System then made it possible to hold bills in *book-entry form;* since 1977, the Treasury has offered bills *only* in book-entry form. Exceptions are made, however, for those institutions that are required by law or regulation to hold definitive securities.

Bills are always issued at a discount from face value, with the amount of the discount being determined in bill auctions held by the Fed each time the Treasury issues new bills. At maturity, bills are redeemed by the Treasury for full face value. Thus, the investor in bills earns a return because he receives more for his bills at maturity than he paid for them at issue. This return is treated for federal tax purposes as ordinary interest income and, as such, is subject to full federal taxation at ordinary rates; it is, however, specifically *exempt* from state and local taxation. The return on other taxable money market instruments is taxed similarly, except for the exemption from state and local taxes.

In addition to normal bill issues, the Treasury periodically issues *tax anticipation bills*. TABs, as they are called, are special-issue T bills that mature on corporate quarterly income tax payment dates and can be used at face value by corporations to pay their tax liabilities.

### Determining the yield on bills

Bill dealers measure yield on a *bank discount basis;* that is, they quote yield as the percentage amount of the discount on an annualized basis. To illustrate, consider an investor who buys a bill maturing in one year at a price of $9,300 for each $10,000 of face value. The discount on this bill is $700, so yield on a bank discount basis works out to be 7 percent ($700/$10,000). In general, the formula for the yield on a bank discount basis for a bill maturing in one year is as follows:[1]

$$d = \frac{D}{F}$$

where

$d$ = Yield on a bank discount basis
$F$ = Face value in dollars
$D$ = Discount from face value in dollars

Alternatively, if the price in dollars is known, $d$ can be calculated as follows:

$$d = \left(1 - \frac{P}{F}\right)$$

where $P$ is the price in dollars.

On a bill maturing in less than one year, the discount is earned more quickly, so to get the correct annualized yield on a bank discount basis, the two general formulas above are modified as follows:

$$d = \frac{D}{F} \times \frac{360}{t_{sm}} \quad \text{or} \quad \left(1 - \frac{P}{F}\right)\frac{360}{t_{sm}}$$

where $t_{sm}$ is the number of days from settlement to maturity. Thus, if the bill selling at $9,300 had 300 days from settlement to maturity, the annual yield on a bank discount basis would be 8.4 percent, found as follows:

$$d = \frac{\$700}{\$10,000} \times \frac{360}{300} = 8.4\%$$

---

[1] The formulas presented in this section are derived in Marcia Stigum, *Money Market Calculations: Yields, Break-Evens, and Arbitrage* (Homewood, Ill.: Dow Jones-Irwin, 1981), pp. 27–35.

or equivalently:

$$d = \left(1 - \frac{\$9,300}{\$10,000}\right)\frac{360}{300} = 8.4\%$$

The simple annual interest rate that an investor earns by buying a bill is found as follows:

$$i = \frac{D}{P} \times \frac{365}{t_{sm}}$$

where $i$ is the equivalent simple interest yield. For example, the bill with 300 days from settlement to maturity and which can be purchased for \$9,300 for each \$10,000 of face value, would have an equivalent simple interest yield of 9.16 percent, as shown below:

$$i = \frac{\$700}{\$9,300} \times \frac{365}{300} = 9.16\%$$

Alternatively, given the yield on a bank discount basis $(d)$, the equivalent simple interest yield can be computed, using the following formula:

$$i = \frac{365d}{360 - d\, t_{sm}}$$

Applying this formula to our example, recall that the yield on a bank discount basis is 8.4 percent. We find:

$$i = \frac{365(0.084)}{360 - 0.084(300)} = 9.16\%$$

Notice that the yield on a bank discount basis understates the equivalent simple interest rate that an investor would realize by holding a bill. This holds for all securities offered on a discounted basis. Moreover, as Table 1 shows, the discrepancy between the two rates is greater the higher the rate of discount (i.e., the higher the yield on a bank discount basis) and the longer the time to maturity.

In the secondary market, bids for and offerings of coupon securities are quoted not in terms of yields (as in the case of discount securities) but in terms of dollar prices.[2] On a coupon quote sheet, however, there is always a number for each security stating what its yield to maturity would be if it were pur-

---

[2] An exception is municipal bonds.

**TABLE 1**    Comparisons at different rates and maturities between rates of discount and the equivalent *simple interest* rates on a 365-day-year basis

| Rate of discount (percent) | Equivalent simple interest (percent) | | |
| --- | --- | --- | --- |
| | 30-day maturity | 182-day maturity | 364-day maturity |
| 4. . . . . . . . . | 4.07 | 4.14 | 4.23 |
| 6. . . . . . . . . | 6.11 | 6.27 | 6.48 |
| 8. . . . . . . . . | 8.17 | 8.45 | 8.82 |
| 10. . . . . . . . | 10.22 | 10.68 | 11.27 |
| 12. . . . . . . . | 12.29 | 12.95 | 13.84 |
| 14. . . . . . . . | 14.36 | 15.28 | 16.53 |
| 16. . . . . . . . | 16.44 | 17.65 | 19.35 |

chased at the quoted asked or offered price. However, the yield to maturity figure on a quote sheet for coupon securities *understates* the effective yield to maturity, because it ignores the fact that interest is paid *semiannually*. That is, whatever the investor does with coupon interest, it is worth something to him to get semiannual interest payments, rather than a single year-end interest payment.

In converting the yield on a discount security to an add-on interest rate, various approaches are possible. One is to convert to an equivalent simple interest rate, as explained previously. However, the "street" in putting together quote sheets takes a slightly different tack. It restates yields on discount securities on a basis that makes them comparable to the yield to maturity quoted on coupon securities. A rate so computed is called a *coupon yield equivalent* or *equivalent bond yield.*

The street's decision to restate bill yields on a coupon yield equivalent basis creates a need to distinguish between discount securities that have six months (182 days) or less to run and those that have more than six months to run. When a coupon security is on its last leg (i.e., when it will mature on the next coupon date and thus offers no opportunity for further compounding), its stated yield to maturity equals its yield on a simple interest basis. For this reason, on discount securities with six months or less to run, bond equivalent yield is taken to be the equivalent simple interest rate offered by the instrument. Letting $d_b$ equal the equivalent bond yield, then $d_b$ can be found from the rate of discount ($d$), or the yield on a bank discount basis, by:

$$d_b = \frac{365d}{360 - d\,t_{sm}}$$

However, when a discount security has more than six months to maturity, the bond equivalent yield, denoted $d_b'$, is computed by the following formula:

$$d_b' = \frac{\dfrac{-2\,t_{sm}}{365} + 2\,\sqrt{\left(\dfrac{t_{sm}}{365}\right)^2 - 1\left(\dfrac{2\,t_{sm}}{365} - 1\right)\left(1 - \dfrac{1}{P}\right)}}{\dfrac{2\,t_{sm}}{365} - 1}$$

where $P$ is the price per $1 of face value. To illustrate how to use the foregoing formula for a bill with more than six months to run, consider a bill with an asked price of 95.0653 percent of face value and 190 days to run. The equivalent bond yield is 9.95 percent, as shown in the formula:

$$d_b' = \frac{\dfrac{-2(190)}{365} + 2\,\sqrt{\left(\dfrac{190}{365}\right)^2 - 1\left(\dfrac{2(190)}{365} - 1\right)\left(1 - \dfrac{1}{.950653}\right)}}{\dfrac{2(190)}{365} - 1}$$

$$= 9.95\%$$

## Buying bills

There is no way for an individual to invest in bills unless he has a minimum of $10,000 available or is willing and able to pool his funds with other investors. For an individual with more than $10,000 to invest, it is possible to acquire bills in amounts equal to any multiple of five by buying an appropriate mix of bills in $10,000 and $15,000 denominations. Bills can be purchased from a bank or at auction.

The easiest way for a small investor to acquire bills is to buy them from his bank. If your bank is a major bank in a large financial center, such as Chicago or New York, it may well act as a dealer in government securities; in that case, it will sell bills to you directly out of its inventory. If your bank is not a dealer bank, it will purchase the required amount of bills from a larger bank with which it has a correspondent relationship.

If you are willing to put yourself out a little, you can escape the service charge that banks impose on bill purchases by buying bills directly from the Fed during one of the periodic auctions at which the Fed sells new issues of T bills.

Naturally, a small investor can't be expected to arrive panting at the Fed just before the bid window closes with a tender tuned to the morning's developments in the money market. That is no problem, however, since the Fed has made provision for the small investor who is unsophisticated, and, worse still, has no runner at his disposal. To service such investors, the Fed accepts what are called *noncompetitive* bids for amounts up to $500,000 per investor per auction. A person submitting a noncompetitive bid gets his bills at a price equal to the average of the competitive bids accepted by the Treasury. Generally, the spread in competitive bids is not very wide, so the noncompetitive bidder does not fare badly.

## COMMERCIAL PAPER

*Commercial paper*, whoever the issuer and whatever the precise form it takes, is an unsecured promissory note with a fixed maturity. In plain English, the issuer of commercial paper (the borrower) promises to pay the buyer (the lender) some fixed amount on some future date. But the issuer pledges no assets— only his liquidity and established earning power—to guarantee that he will make good on his promise to pay. Traditionally, commercial paper resembled in form a Treasury bill; it was a negotiable, noninterest-bearing note issued at a discount from face value and redeemed at maturity for full face value. Today, however, a lot of paper is interest-bearing. For the investor, the major difference between bills and paper is that paper carries some small risk of default, because the issuer is a private firm, whereas the risk of default on bills is zero for all intents and purposes.

Firms selling commercial paper frequently expect to roll over their paper as it matures; that is, they plan to get money to pay off maturing paper by issuing new paper. Since there is always the danger that an adverse turn in the paper market might make doing so difficult or inordinately expensive, most paper issuers back their outstanding paper with *bank lines of credit;* they get a promise from a bank or banks to lend them at any time an amount equal to their outstanding paper. Issuers normally pay for this service in one of several ways: by holding at their line banks compensating deposit balances equal to some percentage of their total credit lines; by paying an annual fee equal to some small percentage of their outstanding lines; or through some mix of balances and fees.

### Issuers of paper

The large open market for commercial paper that exists in the United States is a unique feature of the U.S. money market. Its origins trace back to the early 19th century, when firms in need of working capital began using the sale of open-market paper as a substitute for bank loans. Their need to do so resulted largely from the unit banking system adopted in the United States. Elsewhere, it was common for banks to operate branches nationwide, which meant that seasonal demands for credit in one part of the country, perhaps due to the movement of a crop to market, could be met by a transfer of surplus funds from other areas to that area. In the United States, where banks were restricted to a single state and more often to a single location, this was difficult. Thus, firms in credit-scarce, high-interest-rate areas started raising funds by selling commercial paper in New York City and other distant financial centers.

Financial and nonfinancial firms (e.g., public utilities, manufacturers, retailers) issue paper. Paper issued by nonfinancial firms, referred to as *industrial paper,* accounts for about 32 percent of all paper outstanding. Such paper is issued, as in the past, to meet seasonal needs for funds and also as a means of interim financing (i.e., to obtain funds to start investment projects that are later permanently funded through the sale of long-term bonds). In contrast to industrial borrowers, finance companies have a continuing need for short-term funds throughout the year; they are now the principal borrowers in the commercial paper market, accounting for roughly 48 percent of all paper.

In the recent years of tight money, bank holding companies have also joined finance companies as borrowers in the commercial paper market. Many banks are owned by a holding company, an arrangement offering the advantage that the holding company can engage in activities in which the bank itself is not permitted. Commercial paper is sold by bank holding companies primarily to finance their nonbank activities in leasing, real estate, and other lines. However, funds raised through the sale of such paper can also be funneled into the holding company's bank, if the latter is pinched for funds, through various devices, such as the sale of bank assets to the holding company.

### Issuing techniques

All industrial paper is issued through paper dealers. Currently there are eight major paper dealers in the country; their main offices are in financial centers—New York, Chicago, and Boston—but they have branches throughout the country. Also, there are a number of smaller regional dealers. Typically, dealers buy up new paper issues directly from the borrower, mark them up, and then resell them to investors. The current going rate of markup is very small, an eighth of 1 percent per annum. Generally, paper issues are for very large amounts, and the minimum round lot in which most dealers sell is $250,000. Thus, the dealer market for commercial paper is a meeting ground for big corporate borrowers and for large investors (the latter including financial corporations, nonfinancial corporations, and pension funds).

Finance companies and banks occasionally place their paper through dealers, but most such paper (over 80 percent) is placed directly by the issuer with investors. A big finance company, for example, might place $1 million or more of paper with an insurance company or with a big industrial firm that had a temporary surplus of funds. In addition to these large-volume transactions, some finance companies and banks also sell paper in relatively small denominations directly to small business firms and individual investors, as will be discussed later in this section.

### Paper maturities

Maturities on commercial paper are generally very short— one to three months being the most common on dealer-placed paper. Generally, dealers prefer not to handle paper with a maturity of less than 30 to 45 days because, on paper of such short maturity, their markup (which is figured on a percent *per annum* basis) barely covers costs. However, to accommodate established borrowers, they will do so. Paper with a maturity of more than 270 days is rare, because issues of such long maturity have to be registered with the SEC.

Finance companies that place their paper directly with large investors generally offer a wide range of maturities—3 to 270 days. Also, they are willing to tailor maturities to the needs of investors and will often accept funds for very short periods (e.g., for a weekend). Finance companies that sell low-denomination paper to individual investors generally offer maturities ranging from 30 to 270 days on such paper. These companies also issue longer-maturity short-term notes that have been registered with the SEC.

### Paper yields

Some paper bears interest, but much does not. The investor who buys noninterest-bearing paper gets a return on his money because he buys his paper at a discount from face value, whereas the issuer redeems the paper at maturity for full face value. Yields on paper are generally quoted in eighths of 1 percent—for example, at 7⅛ percent per annum. Paper rates, whether the paper is interest-bearing or not, are quoted on a *bank discount basis,* as in the case of bills.

Bill rates vary over time, rising if business demand for credit increases or if the Fed tightens credit, falling in the opposite cases. The yields offered by paper issuers follow much the same pattern of bill yields, except that paper yields are, if anything, even more volatile than bill yields.

The reason paper rates fluctuate up and down in step with the yields on bills and other money market securities is simple. Paper competes with these other instruments for investors' dollars. Therefore, as yields on bills and other money market securities rise, paper issuers must offer higher rates in order to sell their paper. In contrast, if bill yields and other short-term rates decline, paper issuers can and do ease the rates they offer.

The volatility of paper rates has important consequences for the investor. First, it means that the attractiveness of paper as an investment medium for short-term funds varies over the interest rate cycle. It also means that the rate you get on paper bought today tells you relatively little about what rate you would get if you were to roll over that paper at maturity. Paper yields offered in the future may be substantially higher or lower than today's rates, depending on whether money is tightening or easing.

### Risk and ratings

If you are thinking of buying paper, you should consider not only the *return* it yields but also whether there is any *risk* that you will not get timely payment on your paper when it matures. Basically there are two situations in which an issuing company might fail to pay off its maturing paper: (1) it is solvent but lacks cash and (2) it is insolvent. How great are the chances that either situation will occur?

Since the early 1930s, the default record on commercial paper has been excellent. In the case of dealer paper, one reason is that, after the 1920s, the many little borrowers who had populated the paper market were replaced by a much smaller number of large, well-established firms. This gave dealers, who were naturally extremely careful about whose paper they handled, the opportunity to examine much more thoroughly the financial condition of each issuer with whom they dealt.

Since 1965, the number of firms issuing at any time a significant quantity of paper to a wide market has increased from 450 to 1,200; of these, about 130 are currently non-U.S. borrowers. Only five issuers of commercial paper have failed over the last decade. Three of these five were small domestic finance companies that got caught by tight money; in each case the losses to paper buyers were small, $2–$4 million. The fourth firm that failed was a Canadian finance company that had sold paper in the U.S. market; losses on its paper totaled $35 million. The fifth failure, one that shook the market, was that of the Penn Central, which at the time it went under had $82 million of paper outstanding.

Although the payments record on paper is good, the losses that have occurred make it clear that an individual putting money into paper has the right—more strongly, the responsibility—to ask: How good is the company whose paper I am buying? Because of the investor's very real need for an answer, and because of the considerable time and money involved in obtaining one, rating services have naturally developed. Today a large proportion of dealer and direct paper is rated by one or more of three companies: Standard & Poor's, Moody's, and Fitch.

Paper issuers willingly pay the rating services to examine them and rate their paper, since a good rating makes it easier and cheaper for them to borrow in the paper market. The rating companies, despite the fact that they receive their income from issuers, basically have the interests of the investor at heart for one simple reason: The value of their ratings to investors and thereby their ability to sell rating services to issuers depend on their accuracy. The worth to an issuer of a top rating is the track record of borrowers who have held that rating.

Each rating company sets its own rating standards, but their approaches are similar. Every rating is based on an evaluation of the borrowing company's management and on a detailed study of its earnings record and balance sheet. Just what a rating company looks for depends, in part, on the borrower's line of business; the optimal balance sheet for a publishing company would look quite different from that of a finance company. Nonetheless, one can say, in general, that the criteria for a top rating are strong management, a good position in a well-established industry, an upward trend in earnings, adequate liquidity, and the ability to borrow to meet both anticipated and unexpected cash needs.

Since companies seeking a paper rating are rarely in imminent danger of insolvency, the principal focus in rating paper is on *liquidity*—can the borrower come up with cash to pay off his maturing paper? Here what the rating company looks for is ability to borrow elsewhere than in the paper market and especially the ability to borrow short-term from banks. Today, for a company to get a paper rating, its paper must be backed by bank lines of credit.

Different rating firms grade borrowers according to different classifications. Standard & Poor's, for example, rates companies from A for highest quality to D for lowest. It also subdivides A-rated companies into three groups according to relative strength, A-1 down to A-3. Fitch rates firms F-1 (highest grade) to F-4 (lowest grade). Moody's uses P-1, P-2, and P-3, with P-1 being their highest rating.

## BANKERS' ACCEPTANCES

*Bankers' acceptances (BAs)* are an unknown instrument outside the confines of the money market. Moreover, explaining them isn't easy, because they arise in a variety of ways out of a variety of transactions. The best approach is to use an example.

Suppose a U.S. importer wants to buy shoes in Brazil and pay for them four months later, after he has had time to sell them in the United States. One approach would be for the importer to simply borrow from his bank; however, short-term rates may be lower in the open market. If they are, and if the importer is too small to go into the open market on his own, then he can go the bankers' acceptance route.

In that case he has his bank write a letter of credit for the amount of the sale and then sends this letter to the Brazilian exporter. Upon export of the shoes, the Brazilian firm, using this letter of credit, draws a time draft on the importer's U.S. bank and discounts this draft at its local bank, thereby obtaining immediate payment for its goods. The Brazilian bank, in turn, sends the time draft to the importer's U.S. bank, which then stamps "accepted" on the draft—that is, the bank guarantees payment on the draft and thereby creates an *acceptance*. Once this is done, the draft becomes an irrevocable primary obligation of the accepting bank. At this point, if the Brazilian bank did not want cash immediately, the U.S. bank would return the draft to that bank, which would hold it as an investment and then present it to the U.S. bank for payment at maturity. If, on the other hand, the Brazilian bank wanted cash immediately, the U.S. bank would pay it and then either hold the acceptance itself or sell it to an investor. Whoever ended up holding the acceptance, it would be the importer's responsibility to provide his U.S. bank with sufficient funds to pay off the acceptance at maturity. If the importer should fail for any reason, his bank would still be responsible for making payment at maturity.

Our example illustrates how an acceptance can arise out of a U.S. import transaction. Acceptances also arise in connection with U.S. export sales, trade between third countries (e.g., Japanese imports of oil from the Middle East), the domestic shipment of goods, and domestic or foreign storage of readily marketable staples. Currently most BAs arise out of foreign trade; the latter may be in manufactured goods, but more typically is in bulk commodities, such as cocoa, cotton, coffee, or crude oil, to name a few. Because of the complex nature of acceptance operations, only large banks that have well-staffed foreign departments act as accepting banks.

Bankers' acceptances closely resemble commercial paper in form. They are short-term (270 days or less), noninterest-bearing notes sold at a discount and redeemed by the accepting bank at maturity for full face value. The major difference between bankers' acceptances and paper is that payment on paper is guaranteed by only the issuing company, while payment on bankers' acceptances is also guaranteed by the accepting bank. Thus, bankers' acceptances carry slightly less risk than commercial paper. The very low risk on acceptances is indicated by the fact that to date no investor in acceptances has ever suffered a loss.

Yields on bankers' acceptances are quoted on a bank discount basis, as in the case of commercial paper. Yields on bankers' acceptances closely parallel yields on paper. Also, both rates are highly volatile, rising sharply when money is tight and falling in an equally dramatic fashion when conditions ease. This means that, when money is tight, yields on bankers' acceptances are very attractive.

The big banks through which bankers' acceptances originate generally keep some portion of the acceptances they create as investments. The rest are sold to investors through dealers or directly by the bank itself. Major investors in bankers' acceptances are other banks, foreign central banks, and Federal Reserve banks.

Many bankers' acceptances are written for very large amounts and are obviously out of the range of the small investor; certainly this includes all acceptances that pass through the hands of dealers. However, acceptances in amounts as low as $5,000 or even $500 are not uncommon. Some accepting banks offer these low-denomination acceptances to their customers as investments. An individual investing in a $25,000 acceptance may in fact be buying a single small acceptance arising out of one transaction, or he may be buying a bundle of even smaller acceptances, that have been packaged together to form a round-dollar amount. Frequently, bankers' acceptances are available in still smaller odd-dollar amounts. The investor who puts his money into an odd-dollar acceptance should be prepared to experience some difficulty in rolling over his funds. Also, the availability of bankers' acceptances varies both seasonally and over the cycle. Generally, availability is greatest when money is tight and banks prefer not to tie up funds in acceptances.

The rates offered on bankers' acceptances, like those on paper, vary from day to day. An easy way to get some idea of the general level of rates on bankers' acceptances and to see how they compare with yields on competing instruments is to check the "Money Rate" quotes in *The Wall Street Journal* or in *Barron's* "Economic and Financial Indicators." Rates on bankers' acceptances are normally quoted for maturities of 30, 60, 90, 120, and 180 days. Some dealers quote rates in eighths of 1 percent, but rate quotes to two decimal points are also common.

Since payment on acceptances is guaranteed by both the accepting bank and the ultimate borrower, investing in acceptances exposes an individual to minimal risk. For small acceptances, as for paper, there is no secondary market. Thus, an investor who needs cash cannot sell his bankers' acceptance to another investor. However, he can use it as collateral for a bank loan. Also, if his need for cash is really pressing, chances are that the accepting bank will be willing to buy back the acceptance early.

To sum up, bankers' acceptances are little known, but at times very attractive, investments for the small investor.

### NEGOTIABLE CERTIFICATES OF DEPOSIT

In the early post-World War II period, when interest rates were low, bankers were not inclined to accept corporate time deposits on which they would have to pay interest. However, in the late 1950s and early 1960s, things changed for several reasons. First, corporate treasurers, who had customarily met their liquidity needs by holding large balances of noninterest-bearing demand deposits, began to manage their money in a more sophisticated manner as short-term rates rose. They switched funds where possible out of demand deposits into liquid, income-yielding, money market instruments, such as T bills and commercial paper. Second, the large New York money market banks, which had historically enjoyed a dominant position on the national banking scene, found that their competitive position was eroding. As a result of industrial decentralization and the rapid growth of population outside the Northeast, their share of total deposits had declined by almost 50 percent between 1940 and 1960.

In response to these trends, the First National City Bank of New York announced in 1961 that it would issue large-denomination *negotiable certificates of deposit* and that a large, well-known government securities dealer, The First Boston Corporation, had agreed to create a secondary market (act as a dealer) in these securities. A negotiable CD is simply a receipt from a bank for funds deposited at that bank for some specified time at some specified rate of return.

Negotiable CDs were not a new instrument in 1961; they had been around in small volume for a long time. What made First National City's announcement the beginning of a phenomenal expansion in outstanding CDs was not its willingness to issue this instrument, but rather First Boston's intent to act as a dealer in CDs. To the corporate treasurer looking for liquidity, what is important is not *negotiability* per se, but rather *marketability*. The marketability of an instrument, which is measured in degrees, depends on the existence of a secondary market for that instrument and on the level of activity in that market. Bills and paper are both negotiable, but bills have high marketability whereas paper does not. Thus, corporations typically use bills to provide first-line liquidity, and they use paper and other less-liquid instruments to provide second-line liquidity.

Once First National City made its announcement, the other major banks quickly followed suit, and a number of other dealers joined First Boston in the secondary market. From essentially a zero base in 1961, the volume of negotiable CDs outstanding grew rapidly. Today, the major issuers of negotiable CDs are large nationally known money market banks, principally in New York and Chicago. In addition to these prime borrowers, there are also a number of less well-known regional banks that issue CDs.

Since some investors in Eurodollars wanted liquidity, banks that accepted time deposits in London began to issue Eurodollar CDs. A *Eurodollar CD* resembles a domestic CD except that, instead of being the liability of a domestic bank, it is the liability of the London branch of a domestic bank or of a British bank or another foreign bank with a branch in London. Although many of the Eurodollar CDs issued in London are purchased by other banks operating in the Euromarket, a large portion of the remainder are sold to U.S. corporations and other domestic institutional investors. Many Euro CDs are issued through dealers and brokers who maintain secondary markets in these securities.

The Euro CD market is younger and smaller than the market for domestic CDs, but it has grown rapidly since its inception. The most recent development in the Eurodollar CD market is that some large banks have begun offering such CDs through their Caribbean branches.[3]

Foreign banks issue dollar-denominated CDs not only in the Euro market but also in the U.S. market through branches established here. CDs of the latter sort are frequently referred to as *Yankee CDs;* the name is taken from Yankee bonds, which are bonds issued in the U.S. market by foreign borrowers.

CDs can have any maturity longer than 30 days, and some five- and seven-year CDs have been sold (these pay interest semiannually). Most CDs, however, have an *original maturity* of one to three months. Generally, the CD buyer, who may be attempting to fund a predictable cash need—say, provide for a tax or dividend payment—can select his own maturity date when he makes his deposit.

Until May 1973, the Fed, under Regulation Q, imposed lids on the rates that banks could pay on large-denomination CDs of different maturities. Today, these lids are past history, and the general level of yields on negotiable CDs is determined by conditions of demand and supply in the money market. Since holding a CD exposes the investor to a small risk of capital loss (the issuing bank might fail), prime-name negotiable CDs, in order to sell, have to be offered at rates approximately one eighth of a point above the rate *on T bills of* comparable maturity. Of course, in actual practice there is no one CD rate prevailing at any one time. Each issuing bank sets a range of rates for different maturities, normally with an upward-sloping yield curve. On a given day a bank at which loan demand is especially strong, and which therefore needs money, may set rates slightly more attractive than those posted by other banks. Posted rates are not fixed rates; big investors can and do haggle with banks over the rate paid.

Generally, prime-name banks can attract funds more cheaply than other banks, the rate differential being one percentage

---

[3] A CD issued, for example, in Nassau is technically a Euro CD because the deposit is held in a bank branch outside the United States.

point or less. Foreign banks pay still higher CD rates. In comparing CD rates with yields on other money market instruments, note that CDs are *not* issued at a discount. It takes $1 million of deposits to get a CD with a $1 million face value. CDs typically pay interest at maturity. Thus, rates quoted on CDs correspond to yield in the terms in which the investor normally thinks—what we call *equivalent bond yield.*

Recently, banks have introduced on a small scale a new type of negotiable CD, *variable-rate CDs.* The two most prevalent types are six-month CDs with a 30-day *roll* (on each roll date, accrued interest is paid and a new coupon is set) and one-year paper with a three-month roll. The coupon established on a variable-rate CD at issue and on subsequent roll dates is set at some amount (12.5 to 30 basis points, depending on the name of the issuer and the maturity) above the average rate (as indicated by the composite rate published by the Fed) that banks are paying on new CDs with an original maturity equal to the length of the roll period.

We can sum up our discussion of risk, liquidity, and return on negotiable CDs by saying that CDs are slightly riskier than T bills. They are also slightly less liquid since the spread between bid and asked prices is narrower in the bill market than in the secondary CD market; the reason being that in the bill market the commodity traded is homogeneous and buying and selling occur in greater volume.

CDs, however, compensate for these failings by yielding a somewhat higher return than bills do. Euro CDs offer a higher return than domestic CDs. The offsetting disadvantages are that they are less liquid and expose the investor to some extra risk because they are issued outside the United States. Yankee CDs expose the investor to the extra (if only in perception) risk of a foreign name, and they are also less liquid than domestic CDs. Consequently, Yankee CDs trade at yields close to those on Euro CDs. Although variable-rate CDs offer the investor some interest rate protection, they have the offsetting disadvantage of illiquidity because they trade at a concession to the market. During their last *leg* (roll period) variable-rate CDs trade like regular CDs of similar name and maturity.

## REPURCHASES AND REVERSES

A variety of bank and nonbank dealers act as market makers in governments, agencies, CDs, and BAs. Because dealers by definition buy and sell for their own accounts, active dealers will inevitably end up holding some securities. They will, moreover, buy and hold substantial positions in various money market instruments if they believe that interest rates are likely to fall and that the value of these securities is therefore likely to rise. Speculation and risk taking are an inherent and important part of being a dealer.

While dealers have large amounts of capital, the positions they take are often several hundred times that amount. As a result, dealers have to borrow to finance their positions. Dealers, using the securities they own as collateral, can and do borrow from banks at the dealer loan rate. For the bulk of their financing, however, they resort to a cheaper alternative, entering into *repurchase agreements (RP, or repo* for short) with investors.

Much of the RP financing done by dealers is on an overnight basis. In brief, it works as follows. The dealer finds a corporation or other investor who has funds to invest overnight. He sells this investor, say, $10 million of securities for roughly $10 million, which is paid in Federal funds to his bank by the investor's bank against delivery of the securities sold. At the same time the dealer sells the securities, he agrees to repurchase them the next day at a slightly higher price. Thus the buyer of the securities is in effect making the dealer a one-day loan secured by the obligations sold to him. The difference between the purchase and sale prices on the RP transaction is the interest the investor earns on his loan. Alternatively, the purchase and sale prices in an RP transaction may be identical; in that case the dealer pays the investor some explicit rate of interest.

Often a dealer will take a speculative position that he intends to hold for some time. In that case he might do an RP for 30 days or longer. Such agreements are known as *term* RPs.

From the point of view of the investors, overnight loans in the RP market offer several attractive features. First, by rolling overnight RPs, investors can keep surplus funds invested without losing any liquidity or incurring any price risk. Second, because RP transactions are secured by governments or other top-quality paper, investors expose themselves to little or no credit risk.

The overnight RP rate generally lies below the Fed funds rate. The reason is that the many nonbank investors who have funds to invest overnight or very short-term and who do not want to incur any price risk have nowhere to go but the RP market, because they cannot (with the exception of S&Ls) participate directly in the Fed funds market. Also, lending money through an RP transaction is safer than selling Fed funds, because a sale of Fed funds is an unsecured loan.

On term as opposed to overnight RP transactions, investors still have the advantage of their loans being secured, but they do lose some liquidity. To compensate for that, the rate on an RP transaction is generally higher the longer the term for which funds are lent.

Banks making dealer loans fund them by buying Fed funds, and the lending rate they charge—which is adjusted each day— is the prevailing Fed funds rate plus a one eighth or one quarter markup. Because the overnight RP rate is lower than the Fed funds rate, dealers can, as noted, finance their positions more cheaply by doing RPs than by borrowing from the banks.

Since the overnight RP rate is one of the lowest rates in the money market, the borrowing rate a dealer has to pay to finance securities in his position is typically much lower than the return yielded by these securities. The resulting *positive carry* is a source of profit to dealers and thus one more factor encouraging them to position securities.

A dealer who is *bullish* on the market will, as noted, position large amounts of securities.[4] If he's *bearish* because he expects interest rates to rise, he will *short* the market—that is, sell securities he does not own. Since the dealer has to deliver any securities he sells whether he owns them or not, a dealer who shorts has to borrow securities one way or another.

The most common technique these days for borrowing securities is to do what is called a *reverse RP* or simply a *reverse*. To obtain securities through a reverse, a dealer finds an investor holding the required securities; he then buys these securities from the investor under an agreement that he will resell these same securities to the investor at a fixed price on some future date. In this transaction the dealer, besides obtaining securities, is extending a loan to the investor for which he is paid some rate of interest.

As you probably noted, an RP and a reverse are identical transactions. What a given transaction is called depends on who

---

[4] A person who is *bearish* on the market expects securities prices to fall; one who is *bullish* expects them to rise. In the money market, rising interest rates depress the prices of money market instruments; falling interest rates do the opposite.

initiates it: typically, if a dealer hunting money does, it's an RP; if a dealer hunting securities does, it's a reverse.

The market in RPs and reverses is huge and rapidly growing. It is also one of the most innovative and exciting sectors of the money market.

# ELEVEN

## The term structure of interest rates

**Frank J. Jones, Ph.D.**
*Vice President*
*Kidder, Peabody & Co.*

**Benjamin Wolkowitz, Ph.D.**
*Vice President*
*Morgan Stanley & Co.*

It is often asked what determines or affects "the" interest rate as if there were a single interest rate. However, from the financial markets it is obvious that there is not one but several interest rates. And although these interest rates may move, in general, in the same direction at the same time, the amounts of their movements and at times even the direction of their movements may differ substantially. Thus, the spreads, or differences, between interest rates vary. These observations are illustrated by Exhibit 1.

This article considers the relationship between a security's interest rate and its term to maturity. This relationship is usually referred to as the *maturity structure* or *term structure* of interest rates. A common analytical construct in this context is the yield curve (or term structure curve), which is a curve illustrating the relationship between the interest rate and the maturity of securities that are identical in every way other than maturity.

**EXHIBIT 1**   Plot of interest rates

## MONEY MARKET RATES

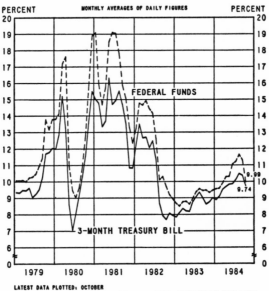

## LONG-TERM INTEREST RATES

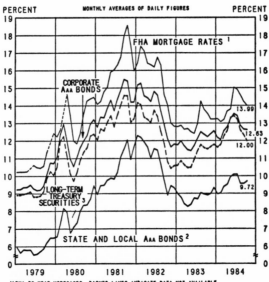

Source: *Monetary Trends*, Federal Reserve Bank of St. Louis.

There are three distinct explanations of the relationship between the maturities of securities and their interest rates.

## LIQUIDITY HYPOTHESIS

Although there are several aspects to a security's liquidity, the major aspect is the security's potential for capital gain or loss, often called *market risk*. The major determinant of a security's market risk is its maturity, since the longer the security's maturity, the greater the price change for a given change in its interest rate. For example, the prices of Treasury bonds are more volatile than the prices of Treasury bills.

Since there is a trade-off between the risk and the return on a security, investors typically require a higher return to invest in a security with higher risk. Because a security with a longer maturity has greater market risk and, for this reason, less liquidity, interest rates should increase with maturity as a compensation to investors. This relationship between the level of interest rates and the maturity of a security is called the *liquidity preference hypothesis* and is illustrated in Exhibit 2. This hypothesis does not purport to be a complete explanation of the term structure of interest rates but only a complement to the other explanations described below.

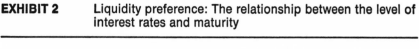

**EXHIBIT 2**    Liquidity preference: The relationship between the level of interest rates and maturity

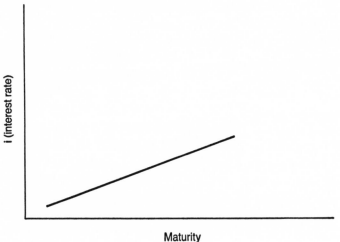

Maturity

## EXPECTATIONS HYPOTHESIS

The expectations hypothesis begins with a premise that lenders desire to maximize their return from providing funds and borrowers desire to minimize their cost of borrowing funds. However, the expectations hypothesis explicitly considers how lenders and borrowers attain their objectives over a time period, rather than just at any moment in time.

To consider the temporal aspect of maximizing investment return and minimizing borrowing cost and how these decisions affect the relationship between interest rates and maturities, consider a two-period planning horizon. Consider each period to be one year, although it could be any other discrete time. A lender considering strategy over this two-period planning horizon has two alternatives—either to purchase a security with a maturity equal to the two periods or purchase a security with a one-period maturity with the intention of reinvesting for an additional period at the end of the first period. The lender's decision will depend on a comparison of the currently available two-period interest rate with the average of the currently available one-period rate and the expected one-period rate, one period hence. Obviously, the lender will select the strategy with the higher anticipated return.

The borrower who is planning over the same two-period horizon is also faced with two alternatives—either to issue a security with a two-period maturity or to issue a one-period security with the intention of issuing another one-period security, one period hence. The borrower's decision will be based on the total cost of funds over the two periods. If the two-period interest rate is less than the average of the current one-period rate and the one-period rate expected one period hence, then the borrower will issue a two-period security. Otherwise, the borrower will sequentially issue two one-period securities.

The decisions made separately by lenders and borrowers will affect the relative interest rates over the two-period horizon. For example, if the two-period interest rate exceeds the average of the one-period rate and the expected one-period rate one period hence, then all lenders would choose to invest for two periods and all borrowers would sequentially issue two one-period securities. As a consequence, there would be an excess supply of funds in the two-period market, causing the two-period interest rate to decrease, and an excess demand for funds in the one-period market, causing the one-period interest rate to increase. According to the expectations hypothesis, the interest rates will continue to change until the current two-period rate equals the effective rate for two sequential one-period securities. Under this circumstance, both borrowers and lenders will be indifferent between a single two-period transaction and two sequential one-period transactions, and thus interest rates will be in equilibrium.

The expectations hypothesis is also applicable to a larger number of periods. However, the basic conclusion that the current long-term rate should equal the average of the current and expected future short-term rates remains the same. As a result, borrowers and lenders will be indifferent between relying on a long-term security or a series of short-term securities.

The expectations hypothesis does not imply that all interest rates will be equal, only that the average of the observed and anticipated short-term rates will equal the long-term rate. If interest rates are expected to remain so stable, however, that future short-term rates are expected to equal the currently observed short-term rate, then current interest rates across all maturities will be equal, as illustrated by the yield curve shown in Exhibit 3. This is a "flat" yield curve.

If rates are expected to increase, the shape of the yield curve will be different. With an anticipated increase in interest rates,

---

**EXHIBIT 3**     Flat yield curve

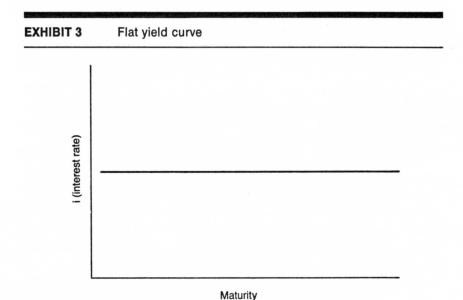

Maturity

lenders will purchase short-term securities so they can earn the higher anticipated rate after their initial short-term-maturity security matures and they subsequently reinvest in another short-term security at a higher rate, and also so they avoid the capital losses that longer-term securities would incur when interest rates rise. Borrowers, however, would be induced to issue long-term securities to lock in the currently low rates for a long time period, thereby eliminating the need for issuing new securities at the higher rates. These actions of lenders and borrowers would result in an excess demand for short-term securities, causing short-term rates to decrease, and an excess supply of long-term securities, causing long-term rates to increase. These pressures on short- and long-term interest rates would produce an upward-sloping yield curve, as illustrated in Exhibit 4.

**EXHIBIT 4**     Upward-sloping yield curve

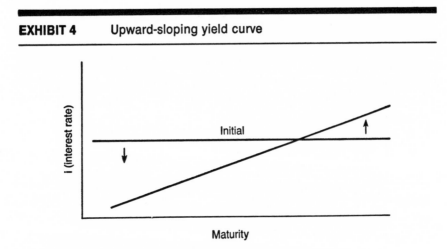

According to the expectations hypothesis, these pressures on interest rates will continue until, again, the current long-term interest rate equals the average of the current and expected short-term rates. For example, if the current one-year rate is 12 percent, the expected one-year rate one year hence is 13 percent, and the expected one-year rate two years hence is 14 percent, then the current two-year rate would be 12.5 percent, and the current three-year rate should be the average of these three one-year rates, 13 percent.[1] Thus, the yield curve based

---

[1] This example ignores the effect of compound interest.

on the current one-year, two-year, and three-year rates would be upward sloping.

The explanation is similar if interest rates are expected to decrease in the future. In this case, lenders would purchase only long-term securities in an attempt to lock in currently high interest rates before rates decrease and to reap the capital gain that would result from the decrease in interest rates. Borrowers, though, would issue only short-term securities, thereby paying currently high rates for a short period with the expectation of subsequently issuing longer-term securities when rates decrease. Consequently, there would be an excess demand for securities in the long-term market and an excess supply of securities in the short-term market, which would cause long-term interest rates to decrease and short-term interest rates to increase. These pressures on interest rates would result in a downward-sloping, or inverted, yield curve, as illustrated in Exhibit 5.

**EXHIBIT 5**    Downward-sloping yield curve

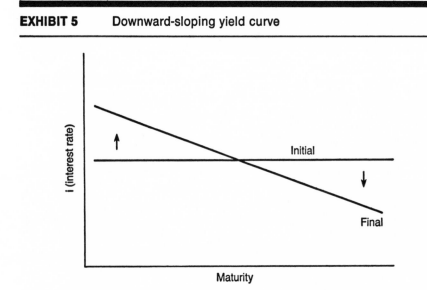

As indicated above, the liquidity hypothesis is not intended to be a complete explanation of the term structure of interest rates. Rather, it is intended to supplement the expectations hypothesis. The combined effects of the liquidity hypothesis and the expectations hypothesis are shown in Exhibit 6.

**EXHIBIT 6**   Expectations hypothesis plus liquidity hypothesis

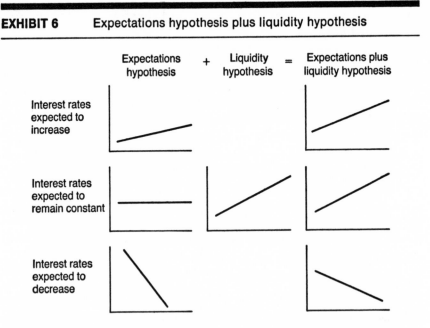

The expectations hypothesis produces a horizontal yield curve when interest rates are normal, an upward-sloping yield curve when interest rates are low, and a downward-sloping yield curve when interest rates are high. Supplementing the expectations hypothesis with the liquidity hypothesis, which always predicts an upward-sloping yield curve, provides an upward bias to a yield curve based only on the expectations hypothesis. Indeed, upward-sloping yield curves have historically been the most frequently observed, and for this reason upward-sloping yield curves are frequently referred to as *normal yield curves*. During recessionary periods, when interest rates are low and are expected to increase, the yield curve has a steep upward slope. When the economy is strong, credit is tight, and interest rates are high, however, downward-sloping yield curves are observed. Both observations are consistent with the expectations hypothesis.

## SEGMENTATION HYPOTHESIS

The basis for the segmentation hypothesis is the antithesis of the basis for the expectations hypothesis. Whereas the expectations hypothesis assumes that both borrowers and lenders are able to alter the maturity structure of their portfolios, each group shifting among the maturities of their respective borrowings or investments, the segmentation hypothesis assumes that both borrowers and lenders are constrained to particular segments of the maturity spectrum for institutional and legal reasons. For such market participants, shifting among maturities is not feasible, and, therefore, various maturity securities are not considered to be substitutes for one another, independent of the levels of the various interest rates.

In practice, there are numerous financial market participants whose borrowings or investments are, for a variety of reasons, constrained to only one portion of the maturity spectrum. For example, pension fund managers and insurance companies have a relatively small amount of their investments in short-maturity securities, whereas commercial banks and thrifts have a relatively small amount of their investments in long-term bonds.

If, indeed, the market is segmented so that borrowers and lenders active in the market for one maturity are unlikely to be active in the market for any other maturity, then the interest rate associated with a particular maturity would have to be the result of the supply and demand pressures for only that maturity. Consequently, a change in supply and demand factors in one maturity will affect the interest rate for only that maturity and have no impact on the interest rate for any other maturity.

The segmentation hypothesis and the expectations hypothesis are competing, incompatible explanations of the relationship between interest rates and maturities on securities. For technical reasons, resolving which is the more correct explanation of the relationship is an intractable problem. In reality, there are probably some elements of both theories that are correct while neither one is completely correct in explaining the relationship. In particular, it is unlikely that all borrowers and lenders are locked into one portion of the available maturity structure and unable to switch to another when interest rates dictate. Alternatively, there are undoubtedly some market participants who are restricted to particular segments of the maturity structure.

Either hypothesis could provide correct conclusions without the hypothesis holding in its extreme version. For example, for the expectations hypothesis to apply, not all borrowers and lenders have to be able to shift among maturities on the basis of relative interest rates, only enough to affect the relative interest rates. Similarly, for the segmentation hypothesis to apply, not all borrowers and lenders have to be restricted to particular segments of the maturity range, only enough so the interest rates associated with each maturity segment are influenced by different supply and demand considerations. Observers of debt markets have noted characteristics supportive of both hypotheses in their less-than-extreme versions. However, most observers tend to support the expectations hypothesis complemented by the liquidity hypothesis as the dominant explanation for the observed relationship between interest rates and maturity.

The combined expectations hypothesis/liquidity hypothesis description of the maturity structure of interest rates can be applied to the actual behavior of the financial markets. The conclusions that can be drawn from a combination of the expectations hypothesis and the liquidity preference hypothesis are that, when the level of interest rates is normal, the yield curve will have a slight upward slope—the long-term rates will be slightly greater than short-term rates. When the general level of interest rates is low, the term structure will have a steeper upward slope. Finally, when the level of interest rates is high, the term structure will have a downward slope. Pragmatically, the

**EXHIBIT 7**      Yield curve—November 29, 1984

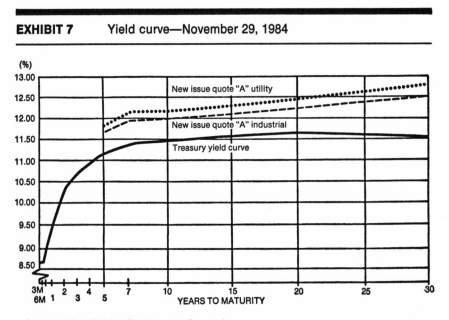

Source: Paine, Webber Fixed Income Research.

**EXHIBIT 8**     Yield curve—September 3, 1981

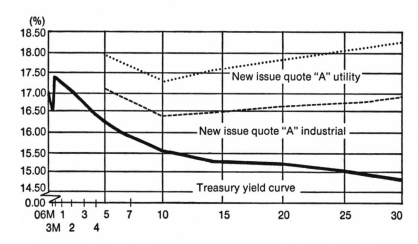

YEARS TO MATURITY

Source: Paine, Webber Fixed Income Research.

**EXHIBIT 9**     Yield curve—August 5, 1982

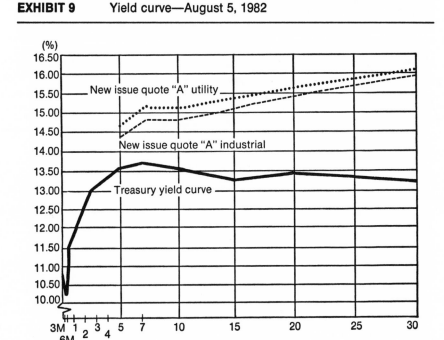

YEARS TO MATURITY

Source: Paine, Webber Fixed Income Research.

segmentation hypothesis adds nothing that either contradicts or supports this observation.

Empirical observations support conclusions derived from the expectations and the liquidity hypotheses. Exhibits 7, 8, and 9 show yield curves on different dates with various slopes. Note that the general level of interest rates is higher for the downward-sloping yield curve.

## CONCLUSIONS

The conclusions of the three maturity structures of interest rates are as follows. When the level of interest rates is low, interest rates increase with maturity (the term structure-of-interest-rate curve has a positive slope). And when the level of interest rates is high, interest rates decrease with maturity (the term structure-of-interest-rate curve has a negative slope). Thus, short-term interest rates vary through a much wider range than the long-term interest rates, as illustrated in Exhibit 10. And, thus, the spread between short-term and long-term interest rates (long-term minus short-term) varies considerably over the interest rate cycle and becomes less positive (or more negative) as interest rates increase.

**EXHIBIT 10**     Interest-rate variability by maturity

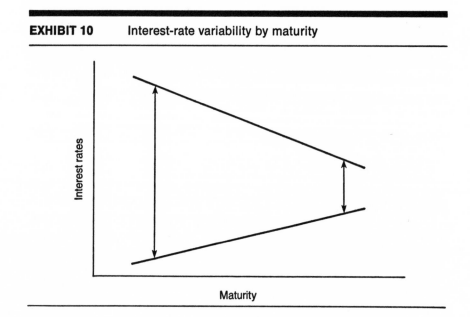

# TWELVE

## Zero-coupon bonds

**T. Dessa Garlicki**
*Instructor of Finance*
*Rutgers University*

**Frank J. Fabozzi, Ph.D., C.F.A., C.P.A.**
*Walter E. Hanson/Peat, Marwick, Mitchell*
  *Professor of Business and Finance*
*Lafayette College*
*and*
*Managing Editor*
*The Journal of Portfolio Management*

The high and volatile interest rates that prevailed in the U.S. capital market in the late 1970s and early 1980s made the cost of borrowing expensive for issuers of even the highest-quality rating. To reduce the cost of debt funds for their corporate and municipal clients, investment bankers designed debt instruments that were more attractive to investors than traditional offerings.

One type of bond introduced at the time when interest rates were at a historical peak was the zero-coupon bond. This type of bond has no coupon payments. Instead, the issuer sells the bond at a substantial discount from its maturity value. The interest received by the investor from holding this bond to maturity is the difference between the maturity value and the purchase price. The advantage of this bond from the investor's point of view is that it eliminates reinvestment risk. This risk, as we shall explain in the next section of this article, may have a substantial impact on a bond's total return.

## ELIMINATING REINVESTMENT RISK

There are three potential sources of a bond's return: (1) the coupon interest payments, (2) income from reinvestment of the coupon interest payments (known as the interest-on-interest component), and (3) capital appreciation realized when the bond is sold or redeemed. Most investors are cognizant of the first and third sources of return. The second, however, is an important source of a bond's return that is not widely recognized by investors.

The most often cited measure of a bond's total return is its yield to maturity. The yield to maturity measures a bond's total return if it is purchased today and held to maturity. It assumes that the entire coupon interest can be reinvested when it is received at the same rate as its yield to maturity. For example, the yield to maturity of an 8 percent coupon bond with 30 years to maturity selling today for 67.7 percent of par value is 12 percent. This assumes that, every six months when the coupon interest is received, the investor will reinvest the entire coupon payment for the remaining time to maturity in an investment that will produce a 12 percent return. Therein lies the weakness of the yield-to-maturity measure. Even if a bond is held to maturity, the actual return will be less than the yield to maturity promised when the bond was purchased if (1) the full coupon is not reinvested because part is spent on current consumption or used to pay taxes and/or (2) the coupon interest is reinvested at a rate that is less than the yield to maturity.

The degree of importance of the interest-on-interest component of a bond's total return depends on two factors: (1) the number of years to maturity and (2) the coupon rate. Holding the coupon rate and yield to maturity constant, the longer the number of years to maturity of the bond (i.e., the term of the bond), the more important is the interest-on-interest component. For example, for the 8 percent coupon bond with 30 years to maturity which is selling for 67.7 percent of par to yield 12 percent, the interest-on-interest component is 87 percent of the bond's total return. Yet, if a bond has only 7 years to maturity and is selling for 81.4 percent of par to offer a yield to maturity of 12 percent, the interest-on-interest component is 27 percent of the bond's total return. The lower the coupon rate for a given number of years to maturity and yield to maturity, the smaller is the interest-on-interest component. For example, the interest-on-interest component of a 12 percent, 7-year bond selling at par (to yield 12 percent) is 33 percent compared with 27 percent for the 8 percent coupon bond.

The risk associated with reinvesting the coupon payments of a bond at a rate that is less than its yield to maturity is known as reinvestment risk. One way to reduce reinvestment risk and thereby lock in the promised yield to maturity at the time of purchase (assuming, of course, that the issuer does not default) is to buy bonds with a low coupon rate. Although low-coupon bonds mitigate reinvestment risk, they do not eliminate it. The elimination of reinvestment risk is only possible with a zero-coupon bond since there are no coupons to reinvest.

## ZERO-COUPON BONDS AVAILABLE

There are zero-coupon bonds issued by corporations and municipalities. The first public issue of zero-coupon bonds by a corporation was issued on April 22, 1981, by J. C. Penney Company, Inc. The issue was priced at 33.427 percent of par (i.e., $334.27 per $1,000 par value) to yield 14.25 percent. It should be noted that, at the time of this writing, some corporate issuers are considering the issuance of zero-coupon convertible bonds.

In the municipal bond market, in addition to the zero-coupon bond, a variation of the zero-coupon bond has been developed. It is a bond that is issued at par and *does* actually have interest payments. However, the interest payments are not distributed to the holder of the bond until maturity. Rather, the issuer agrees to reinvest the undistributed interest payments at the bond's yield to maturity when it was issued. For example, suppose that a 10 percent, 10-year bond with a par value of $5,000 is sold at par to yield 10 percent. Every six months, the maturity value of the bond is increased by 5 percent of the maturity value of the previous six months. So at the end of 10 years, the maturity value of the bond will be equal to $13,267 [= $5,000 × $(1.05)^{20}$]. This type of zero-coupon bond is called a "compound interest bond" or "municipal multiplier." In the case of a 10-year zero bond priced to yield 10 percent, the bond would have a maturity value of $5,000 but sell for $1,884 when it is issued.[1]

---

[1] Variations on the zero-coupon bond were introduced to allow municipal issuers to circumvent restrictions on the amount of par value that they were legally permitted to issue.

U.S. Treasury bonds are the obligation of the U.S. government. These obligations are attractive for several reasons. First, there is no default risk. Second, although interest income is taxable at the federal level, it is exempt from state and local taxes. Finally, they are highly marketable. However, the holder of a U.S. Treasury bond is not immune to interest-rate risk.

Because of the attractiveness of an instrument that has minimal default risk and no reinvestment risk, and that is exempt from state and local taxes, about a dozen investment banking firms have effectively created zero-coupon Treasury obligations with virtually any maturity sought by the investor. They have done this by buying Treasury bonds, stripping off the future coupon payments and maturity values, and creating irrevocable trusts with a custodian bank. Each trust has one specific maturity date. The custodian bank then issues securities that represent a share in the trust. Although the investment vehicles created are not issued by the U.S. Treasury, the obligations in the trust—future coupon payments and maturity value—are obligations of the U.S. government.

These Treasury derivative securities were first offered in August of 1982. By the end of 1984, about $40 billion of these obligations were issued. Approximately $25 billion were marketed by Salomon Brothers under the name CATS (which stands for Certificates of Accrual on Treasury Securities) and about $12 billion by Merrill Lynch under the name TIGRs (which stands for Treasury Investment Growth Receipts). Other stripped Treasuries were marketed with such names as LIONs and, for canine lovers, DOGS. The degree of marketability of stripped Treasuries differs, CATS and TIGRs having the greatest marketability.

In 1984, the Treasury announced its STRIPS (Separate Trading of Registered Interest and Principal Securities) program. This program allows the stripping of designated Treasury issues for purposes of creating zero coupon Treasury securities. The zero coupon securities created are the direct obligations of the U.S. government. Thus, there is no default risk. Moreover, the securities are book-entry securities. This means that the securities are not represented by an engraved piece of paper that is sent to the buyer. Instead, evidence of ownership is maintained in computerized records at the Fed.

The term "stripped Treasuries" refers to both zero coupon

Treasury-related securities that are the direct obligations of the U.S. Treasury resulting from the STRIPS program and indirect obligations (such as CATS and TIGRs). Those securities from the Treasury's STRIPS program are referred to as STRIPS and "wireables." The Treasury derivative securities such as CATS and TIGRs are sometimes referred to as "physicals."

## DRAWBACKS OF ZERO-COUPON BONDS

There are several disadvantages that an investor should be aware of before buying zero-coupon bonds. These disadvantages are discussed below.

### Taxes

As explained in Article Three, income taxes must be paid each year on the accrued interest of original-issue discount bonds. A zero-coupon bond is an original-issue discount bond. Consequently, an investor will have to pay taxes on accrued interest each year, even though no cash is actually received, resulting in a negative cash flow for the holder of zero-coupon bonds. Because of this, zero-coupon bonds should be purchased only for IRAs, Keogh plans, and portfolios that are exempt from income taxes.

The tax disadvantage, however, does not apply to zero-coupon municipal bonds. The interest on these bonds is exempt from federal income taxes; however, if the bond is sold before maturity and there is a capital gain that is not attributed to ordinary income, that capital gain will be taxed.

### Yield sacrifice

Because there is no reinvestment risk, investors are willing to pay more for zero-coupon bonds, thereby accepting a lower return. For example, market observers estimated that the J. C. Penney zero-coupon bonds that we mentioned earlier would have had to sell for a yield of 15.90 percent rather than 14.25 percent, if they had been current-coupon bonds.[2] Thus, there

---

[2] A current-coupon bond is a bond in which the coupon rate is roughly equal to the prevailing yield to maturity of comparable bonds. A current-coupon bond sells for close to par value.

would have been a "yield give-up" by investors of 165 basis points[3] by buying this bond when it was issued, rather than buying a comparable bond with a current coupon. In general, how much the investor is willing to give up in terms of yield to eliminate reinvestment risk depends on his or her expectations of the future course of interest rates. If rates are expected to decline and remain lower, then investors would be more willing to sacrifice yield to eliminate reinvestment risk than if interest rates were anticipated to rise.

When stripped Treasuries were first issued in August of 1982, the yield on these investments for maturities of 9 to 10 years was 15 to 20 basis points less than that of Treasury coupon issues with the same maturity.[4] For the individual investor, this did not seem like a high price to pay for the elimination of reinvestment risk. For the longer maturities, the yield sacrifice was as much as 100 basis points. At the time of this writing, yields on stripped Treasuries and Treasury coupon issues are about the same in the 5- to 15-year range but higher on Treasury coupon issues for maturities in excess of 15 years. At the long end of the maturity spectrum, yields on stripped Treasuries are lower due to the substantial interest of foreign investors.[5]

In contrast to the yield sacrifice that exists in the long-term sector of the taxable zero-coupon market, municipal zero coupon long-term bonds have recently offered yields that are considerably greater than current coupon issues.

### Greater price volatility

Bond prices move in the opposite direction of changes in interest rates. If interest rates rise (fall), bond prices fall (rise). The risk that an investor faces if she must sell bonds prior to maturity is that interest rates may decline and, therefore, the bond price will decline when she goes to sell the bonds. This

---

[3] A basis point is equal to .01 percent—that is, .0001. One hundred basis points are equal to 1 percent.

[4] Technically, a comparison of yields should be based not on maturity but yields based on a theoretical yield curve for zero coupon Treasury securities. For an explanation of how this yield curve is constructed, see James L. Kochan, Maureen Mooney and Charles G. Tresca, *TIGR's: A Guide for Portfolio Managers* (Merrill Lynch, August 1984). The discussion in the text applies equally to yield comparisons using a theoretical yield curve for zero coupon Treasury securities.

[5] Favorable tax treatment of original-issue discount bonds (such as zero-coupon bonds) in other countries makes these vehicles attractive to foreign investors.

risk is called "interest rate risk" or "market risk."[6] For an investor who expects to hold a bond to maturity, there is no interest rate risk, but there is reinvestment risk if the bond is a nonzero-coupon bond.

As explained in Article Nine, not all bonds have the same interest rate risk. All other factors constant, the lower the coupon rate, the greater the interest rate risk. This means that zero-coupon bonds have the greatest interest rate risk for a given maturity. However, for an investor who intends to hold a zero-coupon bond until maturity, this risk is not important.

Some brokers and financial advisors who have recommended that their clients purchase stripped Treasuries have failed to point out that there is substantial price volatility for long-term zero-coupon Treasuries. For example, according to one story in *The Wall Street Journal* (June 1, 1984) some individual who purchased about $100,000 of 20-year stripped Treasury securities found that, four weeks later, the market value of his investment had declined to $78,000. When he purchased the stripped Treasuries, this poor fellow, according to the *Journal*, thought he was buying a money market instrument that didn't fluctuate in value.

### Default risk

For corporate and municipal zero-coupon bonds, there is greater default risk than for nonzero-coupon bonds.[7] The issuer must have funds available to pay off the entire issue at maturity. Many coupon bonds reduce default risk by requiring sinking-fund payments so that a substantial portion of the obligation is redeemed prior to maturity. Zero-coupon bonds do not have this provision.

The issuer of a long-term zero-coupon bond will be exposed to many economic cycles that can adversely effect its ability to pay off the bonds at maturity. If an investor holds a coupon bond in which the issuer subsequently defaults, at least part of the investment will have been recouped from the periodic cou-

---

[6] Some investors use the term interest rate risk to encompass both market risk and reinvestment risk. In this book, the term *interest rate risk* means only market risk.

[7] For a discussion of the credit concerns associated with zero-coupon municipal bonds, see Sylvan G. Feldstein and Frank J. Fabozzi, "Zero-Coupon Bonds," chapter 24, in Sylvan G. Feldstein, Frank J. Fabozzi, and Irving M. Pollack, eds., *The Municipal Bond Handbook*, Volume II (Homewood, Ill.: Dow Jones-Irwin, 1983).

pon payments. The holder of a zero, however, will not recover one penny of his or her investment until the bankruptcy litigation is complete.

Moreover, if an investor purchases a bond and the perceived default risk of the issuer increases since the time of purchase, a higher yield will be demanded. With both a coupon and a zero-coupon bond, the price of the bond will decline. However, the decline will be greater for the zero-coupon bond because, as we explained earlier, the lower the coupon, the greater is the price decline for a given rise in interest rates.

## CALL FEATURE OF A ZERO-COUPON BOND

One of the possible provisions in the contract between the issuer and the bondholder is that the issuer will have the right to redeem all or part of the issue before the maturity date. Issuers generally want to have this right, and investors do not want them to have it. Both parties think that, at some time in the future, interest rates may decline to a level well below that prevailing when the bonds are issued. If so, issuers want the right to redeem all of the bonds outstanding and replace them with a new bond issue at a lower interest cost. But this is exactly what investors do not want. If bonds are redeemed when interest rates are low, investors have to reinvest the proceeds received from the redemption at a lower interest rate.

The verb *to call* is commonly used with the same meaning as *to redeem*. Bonds are said to be callable if the right to redeem them early (known as the call provision) is stated in the agreement between the issuer and bondholders. As a general rule, when bonds are callable they are callable at a premium above par. Usually, the amount of the premium declines as the bond approaches maturity. The initial amount of the premium may be as much as one year's interest.

Call risk is the risk that the issuer will call the bonds and force the investor to reinvest the proceeds at the lower rate prevailing in the market at the time of the call. This risk is therefore tied to reinvestment risk. Another risk associated with call risk is that any capital appreciation potential will be truncated. For example, suppose that a 12 percent coupon bond with seven years to maturity is selling for $1,000 and is callable at $1,080. The yield to maturity for this bond is 12 percent. Suppose, also, that interest rates decline to 7 percent. The bond's price would ordinarily rise to $1,273. However, because the bond is callable at $1,080, and it may be beneficial for the issuer to call the bond because rates have declined dramatically, the bond's price will not rise to $1,273. No investor will pay this amount because, if the bond is called, the investor would receive only $1,080.

One way an investor can reduce call risk is to purchase low-coupon bonds.

When a zero-coupon bond is callable, the call price cannot be stated as a percent of the par value. Instead, it is based on the "compound accreted value" (CAV) of the issue at each possible call date. The CAV is the value of the bond at the call date if the bond grew by its yield to maturity when issued. To the CAV is added a premium determined by the issuer when the bond is first issued for each possible call date.[8]

## SUMMARY

Zero-coupon bonds are attractive because they eliminate reinvestment risk and thereby allow the investor to lock in the yield to maturity at the time the bond is purchased. However, they do expose the investor to greater interest rate risk and, in the case of corporates and municipals, to greater default risk. There is often a yield sacrifice, particularly for taxable long-term zero-coupon bonds.

---

[8] The general formula for the call premium is:

$$CAV \times [1 + (M - Y) \times R]$$

where $M$ is the maturity date, $Y$ is the year the bond may be called, and $R$ is the redemption factor. For example, suppose that a bond that matures on July 1, 2000, can be called on July 1, 1990, and that the redemption factor is .01. Then the call price will be:

$$CAV \times [1 + (2000 - 1900) \times .01] = CAV \times 1.10$$

Therefore, the call price is 110 percent of the CAV.

# THIRTEEN

## Floating-rate and adjustable-rate debt securities

Richard S. Wilson
*Vice President*
*Fixed Income Research Department*
*Merrill Lynch Capital Markets*

This article discusses the many varieties of a security called *floating-rate* or *adjustable-rate* debt. It reviews the market for senior securities, which have coupons or interest rates that adjust periodically over their stated life span, with adjustments occurring as often as once a week to as infrequently as every 11 years.

### CLASSIFICATION OF FLOATING-RATE DEBT INSTRUMENTS AND SUMMARY OF TERMS

"Floating-rate notes" (FRNs) is a phrase that embraces a number of types of securities with a similar feature—a coupon or interest rate that is adjusted periodically due to changes in a base or benchmark rate.[1] While the jargon of the investment

---

[1] The United States government issues a form of floating-rate debt, namely the Series EE Savings Bonds. The semiannual interest rate is determined each May and November, and it is based on 85 percent of the average market return for the preceding six months for five-year Treasury bonds with a constant maturity. If held at least five years, the minimum rate will be 7.5 percent. If held for less than five years, interest is earned on a fixed, graduated scale, rising from 5.5 percent after one year to the guaranteed minimum at five years.

world will continue to utilize the term to cover all manner of variable-rate debt issues (although there are 22 phrases describing the different types of debt, ranging from annual adjustable-rate notes to variable-rate senior subordinated debentures), they could very well be classified in two very broad, and at times, overlapping categories.

Thus, floating-rate notes are those instruments whose coupons are based on a short-term rate index (such as the prime rate or the three-month Treasury bill) and reset more than once a year.

Adjustable-rate notes or variable-rate notes (or debentures, bonds, and the like) are debt securities with coupons based on a longer-term index. Coupons are usually redetermined no more than once a year but often a longer time elapses between changes in the interest rates. For example, the base rate might be the two-year Treasury yield, and the coupon would then change every two years to reflect the new level of the Treasury security.

## HISTORICAL OVERVIEW

Floating-rate notes originated in Europe and made their appearance in this country in the early 1970s. To the best of our knowledge, the first publicly offered issue was $15 million Mortgage Investors of Washington Floating Rate (8 percent to 12 percent) Senior Subordinated Notes due November 1, 1980, offered on November 1, 1973. This was quickly followed by $20 million First Virginia Mortgage and Real Estate Investment Trust with similar terms.

The big impetus to the market was the Citicorp (a bank holding company) $650 million Floating Rate Notes issued July 30, 1974. The offering was originally structured with the individual investor in mind (Citicorp would be obligated to repurchase any notes offered to it every six months after issuance), and the initial demand was such that it probably could have sold close to $1 billion of the notes. However, opposition from the thrift industry, Congress, and others caused Citicorp to modify the proposed terms so that the date of the first put[2] was June 1, 1976, and semiannually thereafter. It also reduced the size of

---

[2] A put is a provision of the debt instrument that gives the holder the right to require the issuer to repurchase the security at certain prices (generally 100 percent of face value) at specific dates prior to the stated maturity.

the final offering. The interest rate on the notes was to be redetermined or readjusted each June and December at 1 percent higher than the Treasury bill rate, except that the minimum rate for the first year was 9.70 percent. The Treasury bill rate at the date of the offering was 7.7 percent.

Citicorp's offering was followed quickly by an issue of Chase Manhattan Corporation. Other corporate borrowers flocked to the trough over the next few months—by year-end 13 issues were outstanding, amounting to $1.36 billion. Issuance of floaters disappeared as rapidly as it made its mark on the investment community, and not one issue was offered for the next three years. Again, in mid-1978, Citicorp tapped the market with a $200 million, 20-year note issue. This time it did not give the holder the right to put the notes back to the company, and the interest rate was set at a spread above the six-month Treasury bill rate.

In 1979, 18 issues similar to Citicorp's (except that some could be converted into long-term fixed-rate debt) were sold. This was followed by only six offerings for $912 million over the next two years. However, increased market volatility and high interest rates whetted investors' appetites for variable-rate securities, and the market started to mushroom in 1982.

The issues range in quality from triple-A down to single-B. While most are tied in one way or another with various interest-rate bases, several have been linked to nonfinancial benchmarks, such as the price of West Texas crude oil or the share volume on the New York Stock Exchange. There have also been a few issues convertible into common shares.

## SIZE OF THE MARKET

Banks have been the largest issuers of those securities accounting for 45.9 percent of the number of issues and 47.2 percent of the total amount. Finance companies place second with 30 percent of the issues and 24.6 percent of the total amount. This is understandable, due to the floating-rate nature and turnover of their financial assets. In effect, they are trying to provide a matching of floating-rate assets with floating-rate liabilities.

The most active issuer and largest in terms of amount sold is the highly innovative Citicorp. Lagging far behind are two of its archrivals, BankAmerica Corporation and Chase Manhattan Corporation.

Table 1 shows volume details for the 170 issues that have been sold to September 30, 1984, by the basis for coupon adjustment. The largest amount—$7.625 billion, or 30.3 percent of the total—is based on the one-year and longer Treasury constant maturity.[3] The second-largest category, those based on the 91-day Treasury bill auction rate, amounts to $4.860 billion, or 19.3 percent of the total. The smallest segment of the market, $102 million, includes those securities utilizing nonfinancial benchmarks.

Some of the issues provide the holder with the option of putting the debt back to the borrower at par at certain dates prior to maturity. Generally, to exercise a put option, the holder must notify the issuer or its trustee some time prior to the put date (usually notice of 30 to 60 days is required). Often the put, once exercised, is irrevocable; but a few of the note indentures make it possible for one to withdraw the notification of redemption. This is usually found in issues for which a company might wish to forestall early redemptions by increasing the interest rate above what is determined by the interest-rate-setting mechanism. For example, an issuer might wish to delay or prevent the early redemption of the debt if it has determined that it needs the funds for business activities. By doing so, it will not have to borrow the funds from other sources, thus possibly eliminating expenses associated with another borrowing.

Also, call provisions[4] are not constant among the issues. Some are not optionally redeemable by the issuer for the life of the notes, while other issues can be called two or three years after sale. In some cases, the call provision applies to only part of the time that the issue is outstanding.

Denominations vary among the issues, ranging from a minimum of $1,000 to as large as $100,000, with increments of $1,000 to $100,000. In cases of large minimum denominations where a put is provided, it may be exercised in whole or in part,

---

[3] The Treasury constant-maturity series is described in the Federal Reserve Statistical Release, H.15(519). Yields on Treasury securities at "constant maturity" are estimated from the Treasury's daily yield curve. This curve, which relates the yield on a security to its time to maturity, is based on the closing market bid yields on actively traded Treasury securities. The constant yield values are read from the yield curve at fixed maturities, currently 1, 2, 3, 4, 5, 7, 10, 20, and 30 years. This method permits estimation of the yield for a 10-year maturity, for example, even if no outstanding security has exactly 10 years remaining to maturity.

[4] Call provisions are included in bond contracts to allow the issuer to retire the debt at its convenience. This usually occurs when the general level of interest rates is below the coupon of the subject debt security.

**TABLE 1**  Offerings of variable-rate securities by basis of coupon adjustment (par value dollars in millions—number of issues) (as of 9/30/84)

| Year | Prime rate, commercial paper and other short-term rates | 3-month LIBOR | 12-month LIBOR | 91-day Treasury bill auction rate | 3-month Treasury bill secondary market rate | 6-month Treasury bill auction rate | 6-month Treasury bill secondary market rate | One-year and longer Treasury constant maturity | Non-financial benchmarks | Total |
|---|---|---|---|---|---|---|---|---|---|---|
| 1984* | $2,000 (3) | $2,475 (20) | $125 (1) | $ 850 (6) | $2,655 (16) | — | — | $3,625 (27) | $ 25 (1) | $11,755 (74) |
| 1983 | 100 (1) | 400 (2) | — | 3,010 (19) | 100 (1) | $475 (3) | — | 1,150 (9) | — | 5,235 (35) |
| 1982 | — | — | — | 1,000 (7) | — | — | — | 2,015 (16) | — | 3,015 (23) |
| 1981 | — | — | — | — | — | — | — | 335 (2) | 25 (1) | 360 (3) |
| 1980 | — | — | — | — | 250 (1) | — | — | 250 (1) | 25 (1) | 552 (3) |
| 1979 | — | — | — | — | — | — | $2,441.5 (17) | 250 (1) | 52 (1) | 2,691.5 (18) |
| 1978 | — | — | — | — | — | — | 200 (1) | — | — | 200 (1) |
| 1974 | 7.5 (1) | — | — | — | 1,320 (10) | — | — | — | — | 1,327.5 (11) |
| 1973 | 35 (2) | — | — | — | — | — | — | — | — | 35 (2) |
| Total | $2,142.5 (7) | $2,875 (22) | $125 (1) | $4,860 (32) | $4,325 (28) | $475 (3) | $2,641.5 (18) | $7,625 (56) | $102 (3) | $25,171 (170) |

Note: Excludes those issues convertible into common stock, certificates of deposit, and those offered on a best-efforts or continuous-offering basis.
* To 9/30/84.

and, if the latter, the remaining outstanding holding must be at least equal to the required minimum denomination.

There are also some recent issues that are exchangeable either automatically at a certain date (often five years after issuance) or at the option of the issuer into fixed-rate securities. Most of these issues carry bond ratings below investment grade and must be considered to have speculative elements according to the rating definitions. Generally, the fixed-rate note that is issued on exchange will mature not later than five years after the exchange, or, in some cases, at the maturity date of the variable-rate note. The fixed-rate notes will bear interest based on a premium to the comparable Treasury constant maturity. For example, Chrysler Financial Corporation's Subordinated Exchangeable Variable Rate Notes due 1994 will be exchanged on August 1, 1989 (unless exchanged earlier), for Subordinated Fixed Rate Notes maturing August 1, 1994. These new notes will bear interest at a rate equal to 124 percent of the base rate, depending on the exchange date. If the exchange takes place prior to August 1, 1987, the new coupon will be based on the 10-year Treasury constant maturity; if between August 1, 1987, and August 1, 1989, the benchmark rate will be the 7-year Treasury; and if issued on August 1, 1989, the new interest rate will be reflective of the 5-year Treasury.

Because the terms of these floating- and variable-rate issues differ, it is suggested that the reader refer to the individual prospectuses for further details.

## DETERMINATION OF THE COUPON

As we have seen, the coupons are based on various benchmarks—ranging from short-term rates, such as the prime rate and one-month commercial paper, to one-year and longer Treasury rates, as well as nonfinancial determinants. While we cannot go into the details of how every issue's interest rate is determined, we will look at the more important sectors in the market. In many cases, the basic data can be obtained quite easily, with few calculations required. For other issues, the coupon-setting data are more difficult to obtain, and the investor must rely on the trustee or agent bank to announce the rates. The rates are usually published in a newspaper of general circulation in New York City. However, some note agreements do not require the publication of the new rates but require only that such notice be mailed to the registered holder of the security.

**91-day Treasury bill auction rate.** FRNs based on this rate first appeared in 1982 and now account for about 20 percent of the market. Interest is usually determined weekly and payable quarterly (the amount of interest payable is usually published retrospectively). Most of the issues have puts at the holders' option. The interest rate obtained may be equal to 100 basis points above the weighted per annum discount rate for the weekly auction of the 91-day Treasury bill, expressed on a bond equivalent basis (this is also known as the *investment basis* or the *coupon equivalent*) based on a 365-day year. The bond equivalent basis converts a yield quoted on a discount basis to one quoted on a coupon basis. The Treasury bill auctions are normally held each Monday, with the interest rate on the notes adjusted on the following day. This rate may be found in the financial sections of many daily newspapers as well as in the weekly report H.15(519)—*Selected Interest Rates*—published by the Board of Governors of the Federal Reserve System.

**Three-month Treasury bill secondary market.** When floaters first hit the market in 1974, the basis for the coupon was the interest yield equivalent of the secondary market yields of three-month Treasury bills calculated on a 360-day year. In these early floaters, interest was payable and the rate adjusted semiannually; they also provided the holder with a put.

Standard Oil Company of Indiana sold $150 million of floating rate notes due August 1, 1989, on August 15, 1974. The basis for the coupon is 1 percent above the interest yield equivalent of the weekly per annum discount rate for three-month Treasury bills as reported by the Federal Reserve Bank of New York during the 21 calendar days immediately preceding the twentieth day of January or July, as the case may be, prior to the semiannual period for which the interest rate on the notes is being determined. Thus the interest rate determination periods are December 30 through January 19 and June 29 through July 19 of each year.

For example, in the June/July interest rate determination period for 1984 the weekly averages for three-month Treasury bills were:

| | |
|---|---|
| Week ended Wednesday, July 4 . . . . . . . . . . . | 9.87% |
| Week ended Wednesday, July 11 . . . . . . . . . . . | 10.03% |
| Week ended Wednesday, July 18 . . . . . . . . . . . | 10.06% |

The calculation for the rate according to the prospectus is as follows:

1. Average of the above rates = 9.9867 × $10,000 (face value) = $998.67,
2. $998.67 × 91/360 = $252.44 (the amount of the discount),
3. $10,000 − $252.44 = $9,747.56 (the original sale price),
4. $252.44/$9,747.56 = 2.590%,
5. 2.590% × 360/91 = 10.246% (the interest yield equivalent of the arithmetic average of the reported per annum discount rates).

10.246% rounded to the nearest five hundredths of a percentage point is 10.25%. To this rate we add the 1 percent differential to arrive at the coupon rate of 11.25% for the period from August 1, 1984 through January 31, 1985.

The newer floaters in this category (often rated below investment grade) have a slightly different formula in which 365 days are used. Some of these issues have an alternate rate (such as the three-month LIBOR) which, if higher than the Treasury bill rate, will become the rate for the interest period (in some cases subject to a maximum rate).

**Six-month Treasury bill secondary market.** What used to be known as second-generation floaters—those issued in 1978 and 1979—are based on the interest yield equivalent of the six-month Treasury bill secondary market rates. Again, the base rates are found in the Federal Reserve Report H.15(519) and the calculations are similar to the 3-month Treasury bill secondary market, except that 182 days is used, not 91 days.

**Treasury constant maturity.** The largest issuer category is based on the Treasury constant maturity yields as reported in report H.15(519). While some issues are based on a specific constant maturity, others are based on a constant maturity that is the issuer's choice when future reset dates come about.

**LIBOR.** Floating rate notes based on the three-month London interbank offered rates (LIBOR) were first issued in the United States in 1983, although Eurodollar LIBOR-based floating-rate securities have been of increasing importance in the foreign debt markets for a number of years. LIBOR is the rate at which the major banks in London lend Eurodollar deposits of specific maturities.

## LOOKING AT YIELDS—EVALUATION METHODS

Bonds with coupons that remain constant to the next put date should be looked at on a yield-to-put basis, whether the put is five months or five years away. Instead of using the maturity date in the calculations, the optional put date is used. This method takes into acccunt any premium or discount amortized or accreted over the remaining term to the put. More than half of the presently outstanding issues have puts, but only 54 have coupons that are unchanged to the first optional maturity date.

More complex are those issues where the coupon varies over the time to put or maturity. There are numerous calculations used by investors in evaluating the relative attractiveness, and we will briefly discuss several of them. It is important when comparing issues to make sure that they have similar coupon redetermination bases and to be consistent with the method used to reduce distortions that could occur if issues with dissimilar features are analyzed. Comparing a weekly certificate of deposit-based floater with quarterly interest payments to a six-month Treasury bill secondary market-based floater paying interest semiannually would not be acceptable, nor would using one method of calculation for issue A and another for issue B be valid, in our opinion. The issue used in this discussion is a hypothetical one, and the terms and results are shown in Table 2. It should be noted that there are cases where one bond might appear to be the more attractive value under one method or set of assumptions and less attractive under another method and circumstances. Market participants will have to live with these complications.

The current yield method (current interest rate divided by market price) is not a satisfactory measurement for floaters, in our view, because it only reflects the current point in time, assuming both the coupon and the price remain unchanged. When comparing two similar issues with each other, the current yield would not provide much help in determining relative values, especially when there are different coupon reset dates involved. However, if we were to readjust or reset the coupon as of the present time we would get a better guide to the relative attractiveness (all other things being equal). Thus, the simple current yield for issue A is 13.12 percent, and the adjusted reset current yield is 12.85 percent.

While the contractual reset spread to the base rate is plus 100 basis points, the notes are selling at a discount and we are really

**TABLE 2**    Hypothetical issue A

| | |
|---|---|
| Coupon/maturity . . . . . . . . . . . . . . . | 12.15% / September 1, 1998 |
| Coupon reset and payment dates . . . . . . . | March 1 & September 1 |
| Reset spread . . . . . . . . . . . . . . . . . | + 100 basis points (1.00%) |
| Base rate. . . . . . . . . . . . . . . . . . . | 6-month U.S. Treasury bill, interest yield equivalent of the secondary market rate |
| Price. . . . . . . . . . . . . . . . . . . . . | 92.625 |
| Today's assumed base rate . . . . . . . . . . | 10.90% |
| Adjusted reset coupon . . . . . . . . . . . . | 11.90% |
| Time remaining to maturity (assuming today is 10/1/84) . . . . . . . . . | 13.917 years |
| Simple current yield. . . . . . . . . . . . . | 13.12% |
| Adjusted reset current yield . . . . . . . . . | 12.85% |
| Adjusted spread to base. . . . . . . . . . . . | 195 basis points* |
| Zero-coupon basis—spread from base . . . . . | 155 basis points |
| Simple or positive margin . . . . . . . . . . | 165 basis points |
| Reset or adjusted yield to maturity . . . . . . | 13.06% |
| Spread or reset yield to maturity over base rate . . . . . . . . . . . . . . | 216 basis points |

* A basis point is equal to one one-hundredth of a percentage point. Thus one percent is equal to 100 basis points.

getting a greater spread or margin. Subtracting the assumed reset rate (10.9 percent) from the adjusted reset current yield (12.85 percent) gives us the adjusted spread to base of 195 basis points. If the notes were selling at par, the adjusted reset spread would be 100 basis points (11.9 percent −10.9 percent).

However, floating-rate notes are not perpetual securities, as are preferred stocks (or at least most of them). For issues selling below par, we pick up the discount at maturity (or put date), and for issues selling above par we lose the premium. Therefore, other calculations are used to analyze floaters. Of course, in relative value analysis, the investor must take into consideration the quality of the debt as well as other factors, such as call, sinking fund, and subordination provisions, if any.

**MARKET COMMENT**

The first series of floating-rate debt issued in 1974 was met with good investor reception. The prices generally stayed within a few points of par because, at worst (once the put feature became effective), they could be viewed as a short-term dated instrument. Thus, when the 1979 issues were sold, they were initially met with good market reception. However, these differed from the earlier notes in that they generally lacked puts and, thus, were only intermediate- to long-term instruments with a coupon that was tied to a short-term rate (not necessarily the highest point on the yield curve) and adjusted only every six months. Many of the initial investors apparently failed to take these differences into consideration when purchasing the notes, for they were sorely disappointed by early 1980.

In the last quarter of 1979, interest rates started to rise rather sharply, and they did not peak until March of 1980. These new floaters declined despite upward adjustment of the coupon rate, with some falling to as low as the high 80s. This was due, in part, to the fact that the reset coupon lagged behind current market rates. Also, these floaters did not have put options that would allow the holder to request the issuer to repurchase the securities every six months as the earlier issues had. Just as rapidly as interest rates rose, they dropped dramatically over the next few months, causing an abrupt reversal in the price movement of the notes. Once again rates reversed direction and another sharp price decline occurred. By the end of 1980, new lows were recorded. Without the put feature, the notes failed to hold their own as the market adjusted their yields to compete with returns available on alternate investments. Adding to the pressure on prices was the fact that investors wanted to "get even" after seeing their issues recover in the rally earlier in the year. Only the issues with the puts maintained their value.

Since then, other features were added to the new offerings to reduce price volatility, such as more frequent resetting of the coupon rate and, in the case of variable rate notes, more putable issues. In the latter case, the variables would tend to trade as short- to intermediate-term securities, depending on the length of time to the put date. Generally, the more volatile security would be of a longer maturity, have less frequent coupon readjustments or fixings, and fewer opportunities for the investor to exercise the put option, if any. Also, the smaller the size of the issue and the lower the assigned rating or perceived quality of the debt, the more likely that the debt will be more volatile than larger and better-quality issues, all other things being equal.

Another important factor affecting the aftermarket for these securities (as well as any debt security) is the perceived quality of the issuer. Many of these securities have been downgraded by the rating agencies since they were originally offered. Thus, while a triple-A bank holding company reset spread might have been satisfactory at 100 basis points in 1979, the current rating of double-A might require 125 or more. Of course, if an issue comes under a dark cloud (as Continental Illinois Corporation did in the spring of 1984), investors will dump their bonds into a weak market at steadily declining prices. Despite a put operable on September 15, 1984, Continental's floating rate notes due September 15, 1989, dropped from 96 to 85 in the week ended May 25. Its convertible floaters due in 1987 declined from 87 to 81 at the same time. A month earlier, the putable bonds were at 99¾ and the convertibles at 97⅜. After the Federal Deposit Insurance Corporation stepped in, the notes recovered with most, if not all, of the 1989 issue redeemed at the holders' request in September. The 1987s rose—but not to the levels that existed earlier in the year.

## CONCLUSION

Floating-rate and variable-rate debt securities have a place in investment portfolios. In some cases, they can be regarded as a passive substitute for short-term holdings, especially the part of a short-term portfolio that is consistently maintained. For example, if a short-term portfolio fluctuates between $10 million and $50 million but does not drop below the $10 million level, then floaters can be bought for a portion of that more-or-less core or permanent $10 million minimum holding. The variables based on the one-year to seven-year Treasury constant maturity are alternatives to straight intermediate-term issues because the investor has the option of holding the notes or redeeming them. Despite the poor performance of some of the issues, many have maintained their value and fulfilled the objectives of the investor. They can generally be classed as defensive types of instruments. If one expects that short-term rates will remain relatively high or even increase from current levels, then a package of these notes may be held (depending, of course, on the portfolio's goals and parameters). With the issues that have frequent resets of the coupon, the investor is relieved of rolling over short-term paper, thus saving on transaction costs.

# FOURTEEN

## Tax-exempt securities

**Sylvan G. Feldstein, Ph.D.**
*Vice President and Manager*
*Municipal Bond Research Department*
*Merrill Lynch Capital Markets*

**Frank J. Fabozzi, Ph.D., C.F.A., C.P.A.**
*Walter E. Hanson/Peat, Marwick, Mitchell*
  *Professor of Business and Finance*
*Lafayette College*
*and*
*Managing Editor*
*The Journal of Portfolio Management*

Tax-exempt, fixed-income debt instruments, or municipal bonds as they are commonly known, come in a variety of types, redemption features, credit risks, and market liquidities. Most recent available information indicates that approximately 37,000 different states, counties, school districts, special districts, towns, and other public issuing bodies have issued municipal bonds. In this article we describe the investment characteristics of municipal bonds as well as the municipal bond industry.

### THE TAXATION OF MUNICIPAL BONDS[1]

Some individuals buy municipal bonds as a way of supporting public improvements, such as schools, playgrounds, and

---

[1] For a more detailed discussion of the federal income tax treatment of municipal bonds, the reader is referred to Article Three.

parks, but the vast majority of municipal bond buyers do so because of the tax-exempt feature of these debt instruments. Municipal bonds, in general, are exempt from federal income taxes. It should be noted that, although interest income on municipal bonds is exempt from federal income taxes, capital gains are not exempt. The maximum capital gains tax rate for individuals at the time of this writing is 20 percent. Consequently, the investor comparing municipal bonds available at discount prices in the marketplace must consider the tax implications of any capital gains tax on the aftertax return. Later in this chapter, we shall explain how this tax effect can be recognized.

The tax treatment of municipal bonds varies by state.[2] There are three types of tax that can be imposed: (1) an income tax on coupon income, (2) a tax on realized capital gains, and (3) a personal property tax.

There are 43 states that levy an individual income tax, as does the District of Columbia. Six of these states exempt coupon interest on *all* municipal bonds, whether the issue is in state or out of state. Coupon interest from obligations by in-state issuers is exempt from state individual income taxes in 32 states. Five states levy individual income taxes on coupon interest whether the issuer is in state or out of state.

State taxation of realized capital gains is often ignored by investors when making investment decisions. In many states where coupon interest is exempt if the issuer is in state, the same exemption will not apply to capital gains involving municipal bonds.

There are 20 states that levy a personal property tax. Of these, only 11 apply this tax to municipal bonds. The tax resembles more of an income tax than a personal property tax. For example, in Kansas, Michigan, and Ohio, personal property taxes are measured on the annual income generated by a bond.

In determining the effective tax rate imposed by a particular state, an investor must consider the impact of the deductibility of state taxes on federal income taxes. Moreover, in 13 states, *federal* taxes are deductible in determining state income taxes.

The total effective state and local tax rate in most states appears to be minimal. There are only eight states in which the

---

[2] The source of information for the remainder of this section is from Steven J. Hueglin, "State and Local Tax Treatment of Municipal Bonds," chapter 4, in *The Municipal Bond Handbook*, Volume I, eds., Frank J. Fabozzi, Sylvan G. Feldstein, Irving M. Pollack, and Frank G. Zarb (Homewood, Ill.: Dow Jones-Irwin, 1983).

total effective state and local tax rate exceeds 5 percent for investors in the highest tax bracket. Consequently, an investor must be sure that he or she is not sacrificing too much in yield by purchasing an in-state bond rather than an out-of-state bond.

## EQUIVALENT TAXABLE YIELD

An investor interested in purchasing a municipal bond must be able to compare the promised yield on a municipal bond with that of a comparable taxable bond. The following general formula is used to determine the equivalent taxable yield for a tax-exempt bond:

$$\text{Equivalent taxable yield} = \frac{\text{Tax-exempt yield}}{(1 - \text{marginal tax rate})}$$

For example, suppose an investor in the 50 percent marginal tax bracket is considering the acquisition of a tax-exempt bond that offers a tax-exempt yield of 12.8 percent. The equivalent taxable yield is 25.6 percent, as shown below:

$$\text{Equivalent taxable yield} = \frac{.128}{(1 - .5)} = .256$$

When computing the equivalent taxable yield, the traditionally computed yield to maturity is not the tax-exempt yield if the issue is selling below par (i.e., selling at a discount) because only the coupon interest is exempt from federal income taxes.[3] Instead, the yield to maturity after an assumed capital gains tax is computed and used in the numerator of the formula.

## DESCRIPTION OF THE INSTRUMENTS

### Bonds

In terms of municipal bond security structures, there are basically two different types. The first is the general obligation bond, and the second is the revenue bond.

General obligation bonds are debt instruments issued by states, counties, special districts, cities, towns, and school districts. They are secured by the issuers' general taxing powers.

---

[3] An investor who purchases a tax-exempt bond at a premium will not be entitled to a capital loss if the bond is held to maturity because the premium must be amortized. See Article Three.

Usually, a general obligation bond is secured by the issuer's unlimited taxing power. For smaller governmental jurisdictions, such as school districts and towns, the only available unlimited taxing power is on property. For larger general obligation bond issuers, such as states and big cities, the tax revenues are more diverse and may include corporate and individual income taxes, sales taxes, and property taxes. The security pledges for these larger issuers are sometimes referred to as being full-faith and credit obligations.

Additionally, certain general obligation bonds are secured not only by the issuer's general taxing powers to create revenues accumulated in the general fund but also from certain identified fees, grants, and special charges, which provide additional revenues from outside the general fund. Such bonds are known as being *double barreled* in security because of the dual nature of the revenue sources.

Also, not all general obligation bonds are secured by unlimited taxing powers. Some have pledged taxes that are limited to revenue sources and maximum property tax millage amounts. Such bonds are known as *limited-tax general obligation bonds*.

The second basic type of security structure is found in a revenue bond. Such bonds are issued for either project or enterprise financings in which the bond issuers pledge to the bondholders the revenues generated by the operating projects financed. Below are examples of the specific types of revenue bonds that have been issued over the years.

**Airport revenue bonds.** The revenues securing airport revenue bonds usually come from either traffic-generated sources—such as landing fees, concession fees, and airline apron-use and fueling fees—or lease revenues from one or more airlines for the use of a specific facility, such as a terminal or hangar.

**College and university revenue bonds.** The revenues securing college and university revenue bonds usually include dormitory room rental fees, tuition payments, and sometimes the general assets of the college or university as well.

**Hospital revenue bonds.** The security for hospital revenue bonds usually are dependent on federal and state reimbursement programs (such as Medicaid and Medicare), third-party commercial payers (such as Blue Cross and private insurance), and individual patient payments.

**Single-family mortgage revenue bonds.** Single-family mortgage revenue bonds usually are secured by the mortgages and mortgage loan repayments on single-family homes. Security features vary but can include Federal Housing Administration (FHA), Federal Veterans Administration (VA), or private mortgage insurance.

**Multifamily revenue bonds.** These revenue bonds usually are issued for multifamily housing projects for senior citizens and low-income families. Some housing revenue bonds are usually secured by mortgages that are federally insured; others receive federal government operating subsidies, such as under section 8, or interest-cost subsidies, such as under section 236; and still others receive only local property tax reductions as subsidies.

**Industrial development and pollution-control revenue bonds.** Bonds have been issued for a variety of industrial and commercial activities that range from manufacturing plants to shopping centers. They usually are secured by payments to be made by the corporations or businesses that use the facilities.

**Public power revenue bonds.** Public power revenue bonds are secured by revenues to be produced from electrical operating plants. Some bonds are for a single issuer, who constructs and operates power plants and then sells the electricity. Other public power revenue bonds are issued by groups of public and private investor-owned utilities for the joint financing of the construction of one or more power plants. This last arrangement is known as a "joint power" financing structure.

**Resource recovery revenue bonds.** A resource recovery facility converts refuse (solid waste) into commercially salable energy, recoverable products, and a residue to be landfilled. The major revenues for a resource recovery revenue bond usually are (1) the "tipping fees" per ton paid by those who deliver the garbage to the facility for disposal; (2) revenues from steam, electricity, or refuse-derived fuel sold to either a electric power company or another energy user; and (3) revenues from the sale of recoverable materials, such as aluminum and steel scrap.

**Seaport revenue bonds.** The security for seaport revenue bonds can include specific lease agreements with the benefiting companies or pledged marine terminal and cargo tonnage fees.

**Sewer revenue bonds.** Revenues for sewer revenue bonds come from hookup fees and user charges. For many older sewer revenue bond issuers, substantial portions of their construction budgets have been financed with federal grants.

**Sports complex and convention center revenue bonds.** These bonds usually receive revenues from sporting or convention events held at the facilities and, in some instances, from earmarked outside revenues, such as local motel and hotel room taxes.

**Student loan revenue bonds.** Student loan repayments under student loan revenue bond programs are sometimes 100 percent guaranteed either directly by the federal government—under the Federal Insured Student Loan program (FISL) for 100 percent of bond principal and interest—or by a state guaranty agency under a more recent federal insurance program, the Federal Guaranteed Student Loan program (GSL). In addition to these two federally backed programs, student loan bonds are also sometimes secured by the general revenues of the specific colleges involved.

**Toll-road and gas tax revenue bonds.** There are generally two types of highway revenue bonds. The bond proceeds of the first type are used to build such specific revenue-producing facilities as toll roads, bridges, and tunnels. For these pure enterprise-type revenue bonds, the pledged revenues usually are the monies collected through the tolls. The second type of highway bond is one in which the bondholders are paid by earmarked revenues outside of toll collections, such as gasoline taxes, automobile registration payments, and driver's license fees.

**Water revenue bonds.** Water revenue bonds are issued to finance the construction of water treatment plants, pumping stations, collection facilities, and distribution systems. Revenues usually come from connection fees and charges paid by the users of the water systems.

### Hybrid and special bond securities

Though having certain characteristics of general obligation and revenue bonds, there are some municipal bonds that have more unique security structures as well. They include the following:

**Federal Savings and Loan Insurance Corporation-backed bonds.**
In this security structure, the proceeds of a bond sale were deposited in a savings and loan association which, in turn, issued a certificate of deposit (CD). The CD was insured by the Federal Savings and Loan Insurance Corporation (FSLIC) up to a limit of $100,000 of combined principal and interest for each bondholder. The savings and loan association used the money to finance low- and moderate-income rental housing developments.

**Insured bonds.**  These are bonds that, in addition to being secured by issuer's revenues, also are backed by insurance policies written by commercial insurance companies. The insurance, usually structured as a surety insurance policy, is supposed to provide prompt payment to the bondholders if a default should occur.

**Lease-backed bonds.**  Lease-backed bonds are usually structured as revenue-type bonds with annual rent payments. In some instances, the rental payments may only come from earmarked tax revenues, student tuition payments, or patient fees. In other instances, the underlying lessee governmental unit is required to make annual appropriations from its general fund.

**Letter of credit-backed bonds.**  Some municipal bonds, in addition to being secured by the issuer's cash flow revenues, also are backed by commercial bank letters of credit. In some instances, the letters of credit are irrevocable and, if necessary, can be used to pay the bondholders. In other instances, the issuers are required to maintain investment-quality worthiness before the letters of credit can be drawn upon.

**Life-care revenue bonds.**  Life-care bonds are issued to construct long-term residential facilities for older citizens. Revenues are usually derived from initial lump-sum payments made by the residents.

**Moral obligation bonds.**  A moral obligation bond is a security structure for state-issued bonds that indicates that, if revenues are needed for paying bondholders, the state legislature involved is legally authorized, though not required, to make an appropriation out of general state-tax revenues.

**Municipal utility district revenue bonds.** These bonds are usually issued to finance the construction of water and sewer systems as well as roadways in undeveloped areas. The security is usually dependent on the commercial success of the specific development project involved—which can range from the sale of new homes to the renting of space in shopping centers and office buildings.

**New housing authority bonds.** These bonds are secured by a contractual pledge of annual contributions from HUD. Monies from Washington are paid directly to the paying agent for the bonds, and the bondholders are given specific legal rights to enforce the pledge.

**Tax allocation bonds.** These bonds usually are issued to finance the construction of office buildings and other new buildings in formerly blighted areas. They are secured by property taxes collected on the improved real estate.

**"Territorial" bonds.** These are bonds issued by United States territorial possessions, such as Puerto Rico, the Virgin Islands, and Guam. The bonds are tax exempt throughout most of the country. Also, the economies of these issuers are influenced by positive special features of the United States corporate tax codes that are not available to the states.

**"Troubled-city" bailout bonds.** There are certain bonds that are structured to appear as pure revenue bonds but in essence are not. Revenues come from general-purpose taxes and revenues that otherwise would have gone to a state or city's general fund. Their bond structures were created to bail out underlying general obligation bond issuers from severe budget deficits. Examples are the New York State Municipal Assistance Corporation for the City of New York Bonds (MAC) and the state of Illinois Chicago School Finance Authority Bonds.

**Refunded bonds.** These are bonds that originally may have been issued as general-obligation or revenue bonds but are now secured by an "Escrow Fund" usually consisting entirely of direct U.S. government obligations that are sufficient for paying the bondholders. They are among the safest of all municipal bonds when the escrow is properly structured.

### Notes

Tax-exempt debt issued for periods ranging not beyond three years usually are considered to be short term in nature. Below are descriptions of some of these debt instruments.

**Tax, revenue, grant, and bond anticipation notes: TANs, RANs, GANs, and BANs.** These are temporary borrowings by states, local governments, and special jurisdictions. Usually, notes are issued for a period of 12 months, though it is not uncommon for notes to be issued for periods of as short as 3 months and for as long as three years. TANs and RANs (also known as TRANs) are issued in anticipation of the collection of taxes or other expected revenues. These are borrowings to even out the cash flows caused by the irregular flows of income into the treasuries of the states and local units of government. BANs are issued in anticipation of the sale of long-term bonds.

**Construction loan notes: CLNs.** CLNs are usually issued for periods up to three years to provide short-term construction financing for multifamily housing projects. The CLNs generally are repaid by the proceeds of long-term bonds, which are provided after the housing projects are completed.

**Tax-exempt commercial paper.** This short-term borrowing instrument is used for periods ranging from 30 to 270 days. Generally, the tax-exempt commercial paper has backstop commercial bank agreements, which can include an irrevocable letter of credit, a revolving credit agreement, or a line of credit.

**Project notes of local housing authorities: PNs.** Project notes are secured by a contractual pledge from the United States Department of Housing and Urban Development. Monies from Washington are paid directly to the paying agent for the PNs, and the note-holders are given specific legal rights to enforce the pledge. These notes are usually given the highest available investment grade ratings by investors, underwriters, and the credit-rating companies.

### Newer market-sensitive debt instruments

Municipal bonds are usually issued with one of two debt retirement structures or a combination of both. Either a bond has a "serial" maturity structure (wherein a portion of the loan is retired each year), or a bond has a "term" maturity (wherein the loan is repaid on a final date). Usually term bonds have maturities ranging from 20 to 40 years and usually have retirement schedules (which are known as sinking funds) that begin 5 to 10 years before the final term maturity.

Because of the sharply upward-sloping yield curve that has existed in the municipal bond market since 1979, many investment bankers have introduced innovative financing instruments priced at short or intermediate yield levels. These debt instruments are intended to raise money for long-term capital projects at reduced interest rates. Below are descriptions of some of these more innovative debt structures.

**Put or option tender bonds.** A "put" or "option tender" bond is one in which the bondholder has the right to return the bond at a price of par to the bond trustee prior to its stated long-term maturity. The put period can be as short as one day and as long as 10 years. Usually, put bonds are backed by either commercial bank letters of credit in addition to the issuer's cash flow revenues or entirely by the cash flow revenues of the issuers.

**Super sinkers.** A "super sinker" is a specifically identified maturity for a single-family housing revenue bond issue to which all funds from early mortgage prepayments are used to retire bonds. A super sinker has a long stated maturity but a shorter, albeit unknown, actual life. Because of this unique characteristic, investors have the opportunity to realize an attractive return when the municipal yield curve is upward sloping on a bond that is priced as if it had a maturity considerably longer than its anticipated life.

**Variable-rate coupon bonds.** Variable-rate coupon bonds have floating interest rates that change on a weekly or monthly basis. The interest rates are tied to various indices, such as Treasury bill rates, the weekly Bond Buyer Index, or combinations of these and other indices.

**Bonds with warrants.** Municipal bonds with warrants allow their holders to buy during a specified time period—usually two years—bonds from the issuer at par and at predetermined coupon rates.

**Minicoupon and zero-coupon bonds.** The coupon interest on a minicoupon bond is below the prevailing yield in the market. The bonds are sold at issuance at a substantial discount from par. If the bonds are held to maturity, the difference between the original-issue discount price and the par value is not taxable, since it represents tax-free income.

A *zero-coupon bond* is one in which no interest coupons are paid to the bondholder. Instead, the bond is purchased at a very deep discount and matures at par. The difference between the original-issue discount price and par represents a specified compounded annual yield.

*Minicoupon bonds* reduce reinvestment risk. With zero-coupon bonds, there is no reinvestment risk. That is, the effective yield is assured, provided the issuer is able to make the payment at the time of the bond's maturity.

## THE COMMERCIAL CREDIT-RATING AGENCIES

Of the municipal bonds that were rated by a commercial rating agency in 1929 and plunged into default in 1932, 78 percent had been rated double-A or better, and 48 percent had been rated triple-A. Since then, the ability of rating agencies to assess the credit worthiness of municipal obligations has evolved to a level of general industry acceptance and respectability. In the large majority of instances, they adequately describe the financial conditions of the issuers and identify the credit-risk factors. However, a small but significant number of recent instances have caused market participants to reexamine their reliance on the opinions of the rating agencies.

As an example, the troubled bonds of the Washington Public Power Supply System (WPPSS) should be mentioned. Two major commercial rating companies—Moody's and Standard & Poor's—gave their highest ratings to these bonds in the early 1980s. Moody's gave the WPPSS Projects 1, 2, and 3 bonds its very highest credit rating of Aaa and the Projects 4 and 5 bonds its rating of A-1. This latter investment-grade rating is defined as having the strongest investment attributes within the upper medium grade of credit worthiness. Standard & Poor's also had given the WPPSS Projects 1, 2, and 3 bonds its highest rating of AAA and Projects 4 and 5 bonds its rating of A+. While these high-quality ratings were in effect, WPPSS sold over $8 billion in long-term bonds. By early 1985, over $2 billion of these bonds were in default. In fact, since 1975, all of the major municipal defaults in the industry initially had been given investment-grade ratings by these two commercial rating companies.

Of course, it should be noted that, in the majority of instances, ratings of the commercial rating companies adequately reflect the condition of the credit. However, unlike 20 years ago, when the commercial rating companies would not rate many kinds of revenue bond issues, today they seem to view themselves as assisting in the capital formation process.[4] The commercial rating companies now receive fees from issuers for their ratings that sometimes are very substantial, and they are part of large growth-oriented conglomerates. Moody's is an operating unit of Dun & Bradstreet Corporation, and Standard & Poor's is part of McGraw-Hill Corporation.[5]

Today, many of the larger institutional investors, underwriters, and traders rely on their own in-house municipal credit analysts for determining the credit worthiness of municipal bonds. However, many other investors do not perform their own credit-risk analysis but, instead, rely on credit-risk ratings by Moody's and Standard & Poor's. In this section, we discuss the rating categories of these two commercial rating companies.

### Moody's Investors Service

The municipal bond-rating system used by Moody's grades the investment quality of municipal bonds in a nine-symbol system that ranges from the highest investment quality, which is Aaa, to the lowest credit rating, which is C.

---

[4] See Victor F. Zonana and Daniel Hertzberg, "Moody's Dominance in Municipals Market Is Slowly Being Eroded," *The Wall Street Journal*, November 1, 1981, pp. 1 and 23; and Peter Brimelow, "Shock Waves from Whoops Roll East," *Fortune*, July 25 1983, pp. 46–48.

[5] By the 1980s, Moody's charged fees as high as $67,500 per bond sale, and Standard & Poor's charged up to $25,000.

The respective nine alphabetical ratings and their definitions are:

---

**Moody's municipal bond ratings**

---

| Rating | Definition |
|--------|-----------|
| Aaa . . . . . . | Best quality; carry the smallest degree of investment risk. |
| Aa . . . . . . | High quality; margins of protection not quite as large as the Aaa bonds. |
| A . . . . . . . | Upper medium grade; security adequate but could be susceptible to impairment. |
| Baa . . . . . . | Medium grade; neither highly protected nor poorly secured—lack outstanding investment characteristics and sensitive to changes in economic circumstances. |
| Ba . . . . . . | Speculative; protection is very moderate. |
| B . . . . . . . | Not desirable investment; sensitive to day-to-day economic circumstances. |
| Caa . . . . . . | Poor standing; may be in default but with a workout plan. |
| Ca . . . . . . | Highly speculative; may be in default with nominal workout plan. |
| C . . . . . . . | Hopelessly in default. |

---

Municipal bonds in the top four categories (Aaa, Aa, A, and Baa) are considered to be of investment-grade quality. Additionally, bonds in the Aa through B categories that Moody's concludes have the strongest investment features within the respective categories are designated by the symbols Aa1, A1, Baa1, Ba1, and B1, respectively. Moody's also may use the prefix *Con.* before a credit rating to indicate that the bond security is dependent on (1) the completion of a construction project, (2) earnings of a project with little operating experience, (3) rentals being paid once the facility is constructed, or (4) some other limited condition.

It should also be noted that Moody's applies numerical modifiers 1, 2, and 3 in each generic rating classification from Aa through B to municipal bonds that are issued for industrial development and pollution control. The modifier 1 indicates that the security ranks in the higher end of its generic rating category; the modifier 2 indicates a midrange ranking, and the modifier 3 indicates that the bond ranks in the lower end of its generic rating category.

The municipal note rating system used by Moody's is designated by four investment-grade categories of Moody's Investment Grade (MIG):

---

### Moody's municipal note ratings

| Rating | Definition |
|--------|------------|
| MIG 1 | Best quality. |
| MIG 2 | High quality. |
| MIG 3 | Favorable quality. |
| MIG 4 | Adequate quality. |

---

A short-term issue having a "demand" feature (i.e., payment relying on external liquidity and usually payable upon demand rather than fixed maturity dates) is differentiated by Moody's with the use of the symbols VMIG1 through VMIG4.

Moody's also provides credit ratings for tax-exempt commercial paper. These are promissory obligations (1) not having an original maturity in excess of nine months and (2) backed by commercial banks. Moody's uses three designations, all considered to be of investment grade, for indicating the relative repayment capacity of the rated issues:

---

### Moody's tax-exempt commercial paper ratings

| Rating | Definition |
|--------|------------|
| Prime 1 (P–1) | Superior capacity for repayment. |
| Prime 2 (P–2) | Strong capacity for repayment. |
| Prime 3 (P–3) | Acceptable capacity for repayment. |

---

### Standard & Poor's

The municipal bond rating system used by Standard & Poor's grades the investment quality of municipal bonds in a 10-symbol system that ranges from the highest investment quality, which is AAA, to the lowest credit rating, which is D. Bonds within the top four categories (AAA, AA, A, and BBB) are considered by Standard & Poor's as being of investment-grade quality. The respective 10 alphabetical ratings and definitions are shown at the top of the next page.

Standard & Poor's also uses a plus (+) or minus (−) sign to show relative standing within the rating categories ranging

## Standard & Poor's municipal bond ratings

| Rating | Definition |
|---|---|
| AAA | Highest rating; extremely strong security. |
| AA | Very strong security; differs from AAA in only a small degree. |
| A | Strong capacity but more susceptible to adverse economic effects than two above categories. |
| BBB | Adequate capacity but adverse economic conditions more likely to weaken capacity. |
| BB | Lowest degree of speculation; risk exposure. |
| B | Speculative; risk exposure. |
| CCC | Speculative; major risk exposure. |
| CC | Highest degree of speculation; major risk exposure. |
| C | No interest is being paid. |
| D | Bonds in default with interest and/or repayment of principal in arrears. |

from AA to BB. Additionally, Standard & Poor's uses the letter $p$ to indicate a provisional rating that is intended to be removed upon the successful and timely completion of the construction project. A double dagger (‡) on a mortgage-backed revenue bond rating indicates that the rating is contingent upon receipt by Standard & Poor's of closing documentation confirming investments and cash flows. An asterisk (*) following a credit rating indicates that the continuation of the rating is contingent upon receipt of an executed copy of the escrow agreement.

The municipal note-rating system used by Standard & Poor's grades the investment quality of municipal notes in a four-symbol system that ranges from highest investment quality, SP-1+, to the lowest credit rating, SP-3. Notes within the top-three categories (i.e., SP-1+, SP-1, and SP-2) are considered by Standard & Poor's as being of investment-grade quality. The respective ratings and summarized definitions are:

## Standard & Poor's municipal note ratings

| Rating | Definition |
|---|---|
| SP-1 | Very strong or strong capacity to pay principal and interest. Those issues determined to possess overwhelming safety characteristics will be given a plus (+) designation. |
| SP-2 | Satisfactory capacity to pay principal and interest. |
| SP-3 | Speculative capacity to pay principal and interest. |

Standard & Poor's also rates tax-exempt commercial paper in the same four categories as taxable commercial paper. The four tax-exempt commercial paper rating categories are:

---

**Standard & Poor's tax-exempt commercial paper ratings**

---

| *Rating* | *Definition* |
|---|---|
| A–1+ . . . . . . | Highest degree of safety. |
| A–1. . . . . . . | Very strong degree of safety. |
| A–2. . . . . . . | Strong degree of safety. |
| A–3. . . . . . . | Satisfactory degree of safety. |

---

### How the commercial rating companies differ

Although there are many similarities in how Moody's and Standard & Poor's approach credit ratings, there are certain differences in their respective approaches as well. As examples we shall present below some of the differences in approach between Moody's and Standard & Poor's when they assign credit ratings to general obligation bonds.

The credit analysis of general obligation bonds issued by states, counties, school districts, and municipalities initially requires the collection and assessment of information in four basic categories. The first category includes obtaining information on the issuer's debt structure so the overall debt burden can be determined. The debt burden usually is composed of (1) the respective direct and overlapping debts per capita as well as (2) the respective direct and overlapping debts as percentages of real estate valuations and personal incomes. The second category of needed information relates to the issuer's ability and political discipline for maintaining sound budgetary operations. The focus of attention here is usually on the issuer's general operating funds and whether or not it has maintained at least balanced budgets over the previous three to five years. The third category involves determining the specific local taxes and intergovernmental revenues available to the issuer, as well as obtaining historical information on both tax-collection rates, which are important when looking at property tax levies, and on the dependency of local budgets on specific revenue sources, which is important when looking at the impact of federal revenue-sharing monies. The fourth and last general category of information necessary to the credit analysis is an assessment of the issuer's overall socioeconomic environment. Questions that have to be answered here include determining the local employment distribution and composition, population growth, and real estate property valuation and personal income trends, among other economic indices.

Although Moody's and Standard & Poor's rely on these same four informational categories in arriving at their respective credit ratings of general obligation bonds, what they emphasize among the categories can result at times in dramatically different credit ratings for the same issuer's bonds.

There are major differences between Moody's and Standard & Poor's in their respective approaches toward these four categories and there are other differences in conceptual factors the two rating agencies bring to bear before assigning their respective general obligation credit ratings. There are very important differences between the rating agencies, and, while there are some zigs and zags in their respective rating policies, there are also clear patterns of analysis that exist and that have resulted in split credit ratings for a given issuer. The objective here is to outline what these differences between Moody's and Standard & Poor's actually are. Furthermore, although the rating agencies have stated in their publications what criteria guide their respective credit-rating approaches, the conclusions here about how they go about rating general obligation bonds are not only derived from these sources but also from reviewing their credit reports and rating decisions on individual bond issues.

**How do Moody's and Standard & Poor's differ in evaluating the four basic informational categories?** Simply stated, Moody's tends to focus on the debt burden and budgetary operations of the issuer, and Standard & Poor's considers the issuer's economic environment as the most important element in its analysis. Although, in most instances, these differences of emphasis do not result in dramatically split credit ratings for a given issuer, there are at least two recent instances in which major differences in ratings on general obligation bonds have occurred.

The general obligation bonds of the Chicago School Finance Authority are rated only Baal by Moody's, but Standard & Poor's rates the same bonds AA–. In assigning the credit rating of Baal, Moody's bases its ratings on the following debt- and budget-related factors: (1) the deficit funding bonds are to be retired over a 30-year period, an unusually long time for such an obligation; (2) the overall debt burden is high; and (3) the school board faces long-term difficulties in balancing its operating budget because of reduced operating taxes, desegregation program requirements, and uncertain public employee union relations.

Standard & Poor's credit rating of AA– appears to be based primarily upon the following two factors: (1) although Chicago's economy has been sluggish, it is still well diversified and fundamentally sound; and (2) the unique security provisions for the bonds in the opinion of the bond counsel insulate the pledged property taxes from the school board's creditors in the event of a school-system bankruptcy.

Another general obligation bond wherein split ratings have occurred is the bond issue of Allegheny County, Pennsylvania. Moody's rates the bonds A, whereas the Standard & Poor's rating is AA.

Moody's A credit rating is based primarily upon four budget-related factors: (1) above-average debt load, with more bonds expected to be issued for transportation related projects and for the building of a new hospital; (2) continued unfunded pension liabilities; (3) past unorthodox budgetary practices of shifting tax revenues from the county tax levy to the county institution district levy; and (4) an archaic real estate property assessment system, which is in the process of being corrected.

Standard & Poor's higher credit rating of AA also appears to be based upon four factors: (1) an affluent, diverse, and stable economy, with wealth variables above the national medians; (2) a good industrial mix, with decreasing dependence on steel production; (3) improved budget operations having accounting procedures developed to conform to generally accepted accounting principles; and (4) a rapid debt retirement schedule that essentially matches anticipated future bond sales.

**What is the difference in attitudes toward accounting records?** Another area of difference between Moody's and Standard & Poor's concerns their respective attitudes toward the accounting records kept by general obligation bond issuers. In May 1980, Standard & Poor's stated that, if the bond issuer's financial reports are not prepared in accordance with generally accepted accounting principles (GAAP), it will consider this a "negative factor" in its rating process. Standard & Poor's has not indicated how negative a factor it is in terms of credit rating changes but has indicated that issuers will not be rated at all if either the financial report is not timely (i.e., available no later than six months after the fiscal year-end) or is substantially deficient in terms of reporting. Moody's policy here is quite different. Because Moody's reviews the historical performance of an issuer over a three- to five-year period, requiring GAAP reporting is not necessary from Moody's point of view, although the timeliness of financial reports is of importance.

## MUNICIPAL BOND INSURANCE

Municipal bond insurance is a contractual agreement by an insurance company to pay the bondholder any bond principal and/or coupon interest that is due on a stated maturity date but has not been paid by the bond issuer. Once issued, this municipal bond default insurance usually extends for the term of the bond issue, and it cannot be cancelled by the insurance company. A one-time insurance premium (paid at the time of original bond issuance) generally is paid for the insurance policy and is nonrefundable.

The bondholder or trustee who has not received payments for bond principal and/or coupon interest on the stated due dates for the insured bonds must notify the insurance company and surrender to it the unpaid bonds and coupons. Under the terms of the policy, the insurance company is supposed to pay the paying agent sufficient monies for the bondholders. These monies must be enough to cover the face value of the insured principal and coupon interest that was due but not paid. Once the insurance company pays the monies, the company becomes the owner of the surrendered bonds and coupons and can begin legal proceedings to recover the monies that are now due it from the bond issuer.[6]

### The insurers

Municipal bond insurance has been available since 1971. Some of the largest American corporations are participants in

---

[6] In 1975, the IRS reversed a stand it took in 1973 and ruled that interest paid by insurers is exempt to investors.

this industry. By 1985, approximately 25 percent of all new municipals were insured. The following companies are the three largest municipal bond insurers, as of 1985:

Municipal Bond Insurance Association (MBIA).

Financial Guaranty Insurance Corporation (FGIC).

American Municipal Bond Assurance Corporation (AMBAC).

At the time of this writing, all issues insured by MBIA and FGIC have ratings of AAA from both Moody's and Standard & Poor's, and AMBAC has a AAA rating only from Standard & Poor's.

### Market pricing of insured municipal bonds

In general, although insured municipal bonds sell at yields lower than they would without the insurance, they tend to have yields substantially higher than other Aaa/AAA-rated noninsured municipal bonds such as escrowed-backed municipal bonds.

## YIELD RELATIONSHIPS WITHIN THE MUNICIPAL BOND MARKET

### Differences within an assigned credit rating

Major bond buyers primarily use the credit ratings assigned by Moody's and Standard & Poor's as a starting point for the pricing of an issue. The final market-derived bond price is composed of the assigned credit rating and adjustments by market participants to reflect their own analysis of credit worthiness and perception of marketability. For example, as we noted earlier, insured municipal bonds tend to have yields substantially higher than noninsured superior investment-quality municipal bonds. Many market participants also have geographical preferences among bonds, in spite of identical credit quality and otherwise comparable investment characteristics.

Also, not all issues are assigned the same credit ratings by the commercial rating agencies. In the case of split ratings, the issue generally has had a yield closer to the lower rating than to the higher one.

## Differences between credit ratings

Like taxable bonds, the differences in yield between credit ratings, often referred to as *quality spreads*, are not constant over time. For example, on September 25, 1981, the quality spread between A-rated and AAA-rated, 30-year general obligation bonds was roughly 150 basis points. The quality spread declined to 75 basis points on May 7, 1982.

Reasons for the change in spreads are the outlook for the economy and its anticipated impact on issuers, federal budget financing needs, municipal market supply and demand factors, and possible changes in federal tax law. During periods of relatively low interest rates, investors sometimes increase their holdings of issues with lower credit ratings to obtain additional yield. During periods in which market participants anticipate a poor economic climate, there is often a "flight to quality" as market participants pursue a more conservative credit-risk posture.

Another factor that causes shifts in quality spreads is the temporary oversupply of issues within a market sector. For example, substantial new-issue volume of high-grade state general obligation bonds may tend to decrease the quality spread between high-grade and lower-grade revenue bonds. Obviously, in a weak market environment it is easier for high-grade municipals to come to market than for weaker credits. Therefore, it is not uncommon for high grades to flood weak markets, while at the same time there is a relative scarcity of medium-grade and lower-grade municipals.

## Differences between in-state, general market, and territorial issues

Bonds of municipal issuers located in certain states (for example, New York, California, Arizona, Maryland, and Pennsylvania) usually yield considerably less than rated issues of identical credit quality coming from other states that trade in the "general market." There are three reasons for the existence of such spreads. As noted earlier, states often exempt interest from in-state issues from state and local personal income taxes, and interest from out-of-state issues is generally not exempt. Consequently, in states with high income taxes (e.g., New York and California), strong investor demand for in-state issues will reduce their yields relative to bonds of issues located in states where state and local income taxes are not important considerations (e.g., Illinois, Florida, and New Jersey). Second, in some states, public funds deposited in banks must be collateralized by the bank accepting the deposit. This requirement is referred to as *pledging*. Acceptable collateral for pledging will typically include issues of certain in-state issuers. For those issues qualifying, pledging tends to increase demand (particularly for the shorter maturities) and reduce yields relative to nonqualifying comparable issues. The third reason is that investors in some states (e.g., South Carolina) exhibit extreme reluctance to purchase issues from issuers outside of their state or region. In-state parochialism tends to decrease relative yields of issues from states where investors exhibit this behavior.

Territorial bonds such as those issued by Puerto Rico are tax exempt throughout most of the country and, therefore, are usually very marketable. Because of this feature, their yields tend to be lower than their respective credit ratings would indicate.

### Differences between maturities

The relationship between yields and term to maturity is referred to as the *maturity structure* or the *term structure of interest rates*. The graphical representation of this relationship for bonds that are identical in every other way is called the *yield curve*. In the taxable market, Treasury obligations are usually used to construct a yield curve.

At any given time, a yield curve can have a positive slope or an inverted slope. Economic theories for explaining the shape of the yield curve are discussed in Article Eleven.

Two characteristics of the municipal yield curve should be noted. First, the municipal yield curve almost always has a positive slope. Second, the yield spreads between maturities are usually wider in the municipal market, compared with maturity spreads in the Treasury market. That is, the positive slope of the municipal yield curve is usually greater than that for Treasuries.

## FORECASTING MUNICIPAL BOND YIELDS BY MONITORING TRENDS IN OTHER MARKETS

Since the 1970s, the municipal market has reacted more slowly than other fixed-income markets to economic information and other information that exert influence on interest rates. Consequently, some market observers believe that tracking money market conditions and certain interest rates can be useful in forecasting the direction of future municipal bond yields.

Alan Lerner and Philip Nathanson,[7] for example, have documented the relationship between municipal bond yields and both the federal funds rate and discount rate.[8] They find that, since 1971, these two rates have predicted the cyclical turning points in municipal bond yields.

In particular, their analysis indicates that "[i]f historical relationships are maintained, then the behavior of funds in the most recent 15 months can aid in predicting the general movement in the BBI *[Bond Buyer Index]* over the subsequent 15-month period." Since the discount rate is almost exclusively a confirming action of Federal Reserve policy, and not a leading overt indicator of policy as is the federal funds rate, they expected a shorter lag between movements in the discount rate and municipal bond yields. They did, in fact, find that municipal bond yields lagged movements in the discount rate by 10 months, compared with 15 months for the federal funds rate.

Lerner and Nathanson conclude: "The surprisingly long lags found in this study obviously may or may not be realized in the future. There are some indications, however, that participants in the municipal market already are more sensitive to conditions in other markets than previously. This alone may cause the lags to shrink, but the relationships we have analyzed could still remain an important key to the future behavior of municipal bond rates."

## THE PRIMARY AND SECONDARY MARKETS

### The primary market

A substantial number of municipal obligations are brought to market each week. A state or local government can market its new issue by offering them publicly to the investing community or by placing them privately with a small group of inves-

---

[7] Alan C. Lerner and Philip D. Nathanson, "Forecasting Municipal Rates and Spreads by Monitoring Trends in Other Markets," chapter 20, in *The Municipal Bond Handbook*, Volume I, eds. Fabozzi et al.

[8] The federal funds rate is the interest rate at which federal funds are traded by commercial banks. It is pegged by the Federal Reserve through open-market operations. The discount rate is the interest rate charged by the Federal Reserve to member banks that borrow at the discount window.

tors. When a public offering is selected, the issue is usually underwritten by investment bankers and by municipal bond departments of commercial banks. Public offerings may be marketed by either competitive bidding or direct negotiations with underwriters. When an issue is marketed via competitive bidding, the issue is awarded to the bidder submitting the lowest best bid.

Most states mandate that general obligation issues be marketed via competitive bidding; however, this is generally not required for revenue bonds. Usually, state and local governments require that a competitive sale be announced in a recognized financial publication, such as *The Bond Buyer*, which is the trade publication of the municipal bond industry. *The Bond Buyer* also provides information on upcoming competitive sales and most negotiated sales, as well as the results of the sales of previous weeks.

When an underwriter purchases a new bond issue, it relieves the issuer of two obligations. First, the underwriter is responsible for the distribution of the issue. Second, the underwriter accepts the risk that investors might fail to purchase the issue at the expected prices within the planned time period. The second risk exists because the underwriter may have incorrectly priced the issue and/or because interest rates rise, resulting in a decline in the value of unsold issues held in inventory. The underwriter spread (i.e., the difference between the price it paid the issuer for the issue and the price it reoffered the issue to the public) is the underwriter's compensation for undertaking these risks, as well as for other services it may have provided the issuer.

An official statement describing the issue and issuer is prepared for new offerings.

### The secondary market

Although municipal bonds are not listed and traded in formal institutions, as are certain common stocks and corporate bonds on the New York and American stock exchanges, there are very strong and active billion-dollar secondary markets for municipals that are supported by hundreds of municipal bond dealers across the country. Markets are maintained on local credits by regional brokerage firms, local banks, and by some of the larger Wall Street firms. General market names are supported by the larger brokerage firms and banks, many of whom have investment banking relationships with the issuers. Buying and selling decisions are often made over the phone and through municipal bond brokers. For a small fee, these brokers serve as intermediaries in the sale of large blocks of municipal bonds among dealers and large institutional investors. These brokers are primarily located in New York City and include Chapdelaine & Company, Drake & Company, the J. J. Kenny Company, and Titus & Donnelly, Inc., among others.

In addition to these brokers and the daily offerings sent out over *The Bond Buyer's* "munifacts" teletype system, many dealers advertise their municipal bond offerings for the retail market in what is known as *The Blue List*. This is a booklet of 100+ pages which is published every weekday by Standard & Poor's Corporation. In it are listed state municipal bond and note offerings and prices. A sample page from *The Blue List* is shown in Exhibit 1.

In the municipal bond market, an odd lot of bonds is $25,000 (five bonds) or less in par value for retail investors. For institutions, anything below $100,000 in par value is considered an odd lot. Dealer spreads—the difference between the dealers bid and ask prices—depend on several factors. For the retail investor, the dealer spread can range from as low as one quarter of one point ($12.50 per $5,000 of par value) on large blocks of actively traded bonds to four points ($200 per $5,000 of par value) for odd lot sales of an inactive issue. The average spread for retail investors seems to be around two points ($100 per $5,000 of par value). For institutional investors, the dealer spread rarely exceeds one half of one point ($25 per $5,000 of par value).

## REGULATION OF THE MUNICIPAL SECURITIES MARKETS[9]

As an outgrowth of abusive stock market practices, Congress passed the Securities Act of 1933 and the Securities Exchange Act of 1934. The 1934 act created the Securities and Exchange Commission (SEC), granting it regulatory authority over the issuance and trading of *corporate* securities. Congress specifi-

---

[9] This discussion is drawn from Thomas F. Mitchell, "Disclosure and the Municipal Bond Industry," and Nancy H. Wojtas, "The SEC and Investor Safeguards," in *The Municipal Bond Handbook*, Volume I, eds. Fabozzi et al.

**EXHIBIT 1**

# The Blue List
## of Current Municipal Offerings
(A Division of Standard & Poor's Corporation)

Published every weekday except Saturdays and Holidays by
The Blue List Publishing Company, 25 Broadway, New York, N. Y. 10004
Telephone 212 208-8200

Reg U S Patent Office • Printed in U S A

+ Items so marked did not appear in the previous issue of The Blue List.
· Prices so marked are changed from previous issue.
c Items so marked are reported to have call or option features. Consult offering house for full details.

ANNUAL SUBSCRIPTION RATE (approximately 250 issues): Hand Delivery (Wall Street Area) $400.00; First Class Mail $520.00

| AMT. M | SECURITY | PURPOSE | RATE | MATURITY | YIELD OR OFFERED PRICE | BY |
|---|---|---|---|---|---|---|
| | **ALABAMA** | | | | | |
| 100 | ALABAMA | | 10.25 | 9/ 1/90 | 8.00 | FIRSTENN |
| 25 | ALABAMA | | 7.25 | 9/ 1/91 | 8.40 | GRUNTAL |
| 640 | ALABAMA | | 8. | 9/ 1/95 | 8.80 | TUCKRAN |
| 425 | ALABAMA | | 8.10 | 3/ 1/96 | 9.10 | TRUSTCOG |
| 1435 | ALABAMA | | 8.25 | 3/ 1/98 | 9.40 | PRUBANY |
| 25 | ALABAMA | C/B | 8.375 | 3/ 1/01 | .91 | OPCONY |
| 25 | ALABAMA | | 8.375 | 3/ 1/01 | 9.60 | PORTER |
| 425 | ALABAMA | P/R a 103 | 11.75 | 3/ 1/88 C92 | 8.90 | BROWNCLA |
| 425 | ALABAMA HIGHWAY AUTH. | | 11.75 | 9/ 1/88 | 8.00 | BRUSTER |
| 290 | ALA.HSG.FIN.AU. | SNGL.FAM. | 10.50 | 10/ 1/99 | 10.25 | CENTBKBM |
| 125 | ALABAMA I.D.A. | | 11.25 | 3/ 1/90 | 8.50 | PORTER |
| 100 | ALA.PUB.SCH.&COL.AU. | | 6. | 6/ 1/88 | 7.30 | HOUGHMWD |
| 25 | ALA.PUB.SCH.&COL.AU. | | 6.40 | 12/ 1/90 | 6.40 | HOUGHMWD |
| 100 | ALA.PUB.SCH.&COL.AU. | | 10.60 | 12/ 1/91 | 8.70 | ROTHCHLD |
| 25 | ALA.PUB.SCH.&COL.AU. PUT | AMBAC | 7 | 7/ 1/96 C85 | 100 | MERRILNY |
| | **ALABAMA—CONTINUED** | | | | | |
| 5 | BIRMINGHAM P.B.A. | | 5.20 | 7/ 1/08 | 8.50 | AGEDWBQS |
| 300 | BIRMINGHAM | | 5 | 7/ 1/87 | 7.75 | CENTKBM |
| 95 | BIRMINGHAM N/M BD.RV. | | 10.10 | 1/ 1/08 | 9.75 | PORTEQA |
| 50 | COURTLAND I.D.R. | (CHAMP.INTL | 5.75 | 11/ 1/97 | 74 1/2 | BARRROS |
| 50 | COURTLAND I.D.R. | SER.67 | 5.75 | 11/ 1/97 | 75 | BEARSTER |
| 100 | COURTLAND I.D.R. | (CHAMPION INTL.) SERIES 67 | 5.75 | 11/ 1/97 | 74 | MABONIDB |
| 40 | E.ALABAMA HLTH.CARE AU. | | 11.25 | 9/ 1/13 | 100 | ROBINHUM |
| 65 | GADSDEN N/M & SWR.BD. | | 6.10 | 9/ 1/02 | 10.00 | FIRBIRM3 |
| 5 | HOUSTON CO.HOSP.BD. | ETM | 6 | 1/ 1/92 | 9.20 | PRESCOTC |
| 25 | LIVINGSTON | | 13.25 | 10/ 1/10 | 25 | NORRISMI |
| 10 | MARSHALL CO.HOSP.BD. (BOAZ) | | 11.75 | 1/ 1/01 | 11.50 | PORTER |
| 50 | MOBILE | | 7.25 | 2/ 1/87 | 100 | BANKBOST |
| 145 | MOBILE | | 7.50 | 2/ 1/08 | 100 | BANKBOST |

# THE BLUE LIST
## OF CURRENT MUNICIPAL OFFERINGS

October
30
1984
Tuesday

Volume
197
Number
22

cally exempted municipal securities from both the registration requirements of the 1933 act and the periodic reporting requirements of the 1934 act. However, antifraud provisions did apply to offerings of or dealings in municipal securities.

The reasons for the exemption afforded municipal securities appear to have been due to (1) the desire for governmental comity, (2) the absence of recurrent abuses in transactions involving municipal securities, (3) the greater level of sophistication of investors in this segment of the securities markets (i.e., institutional investors dominated the market), and (4) the fact that there were few defaults by municipal issuers. Consequently, from the enactment of the two federal securities acts in the early 1930s to the early 1970s, the municipal securities market can be characterized as relatively free from federal regulation.

In the early 1970s, however, circumstances changed. As incomes rose, individuals participated in the municipal securities market to a much greater extent. As a result, public concern over selling practices occurred with greater frequency. For example, in the early 1970s, the SEC obtained seven injunctions against 72 defendants for fraudulent municipal trading practices. According to the SEC, the abusive practices involved both disregard by the defendants about whether the particular municipal bond offered to individuals were in fact appropriate investment vehicles for the individuals to whom they were offered, and misrepresentation or failure to disclose information necessary for individuals to assess the credit risk of the municipal issuer, especially in the case of revenue bonds. Moreover, the financial problems of some municipal issuers, notably New York City, made market participants aware that municipal issuers have the potential to experience severe and bankruptcy-type financial difficulties.

Congress passed the Securities Act Amendment of 1975 to broaden federal regulation in the municipals market. The legislation brought brokers and dealers in the municipal securities market, including banks that underwrite and trade municipal securities, within the regulatory scheme of the Securities Exchange Act of 1934. In addition, the legislation mandated that the SEC establish a 15-member Municipal Securities Rule Making Board (MSRB) as an independent, self-regulatory agency, whose primary responsibility is to develop rules governing the activities of banks, brokers, and dealers in municipal securities.[10] Rules adopted by the MSRB must be approved by the SEC. The MSRB has no enforcement or inspection authority. This authority is vested with the SEC, the National Association of Securities Dealers, and certain regulatory banking agencies, such as the Federal Reserve Bank.

The Securities Act Amendment of 1975 does *not* require that municipal issuers comply with the registration requirement of the 1933 act or the periodic-reporting requirement of the 1934 act. There have been, however, several legislative proposals to mandate financial disclosure. Although none have been passed, there is clearly pressure to improve disclosure. Even in the absence of federal legislation dealing with the regulation of financial disclosure, underwriters began insisting upon greater disclosure as it became apparent that the SEC was exercising stricter application of the antifraud provisions. Moreover, underwriters recognized the need for improved disclosure to sell municipal securities to an investing public that has become much more concerned about credit risk by municipal issuers. Thus, it is in the best interest of all parties—the issuer, the underwriter, and the investor—that meaningful disclosure requirements be established.

---

[10] For a detailed discussion of the MSRB, see Frieda K. Wallison, "Self-Regulation of the Municipal Securities Industry," chapter 41, in *The Municipal Bond Handbook*, Volume I, eds. Fabozzi et al.

# FIFTEEN

## Convertible securities

John C. Ritchie, Jr., Ph.D.
*Professor of Finance and Assistant Dean*
*Temple University*

A bond or preferred stock may offer a conversion privilege, in which case the holder has the right to acquire the common stock of the issuing corporation under specified conditions, rather than by direct purchase in the market. One can, however, pay what later proves to be an excessive price for the privilege conferred.

This article clarifies the nature of convertible securities, discusses their advantages and disadvantages, and develops an analytical framework aimed at assessing the desirability of acquiring the security by an investor. The investor's point of view, rather than that of the issuer, is emphasized.

### CONVERTIBLE SECURITIES

The holder of a convertible bond or preferred stock can exchange the security, at his or her option, for the common stock of the issuer in accordance with terms set forth in the bond indenture. The option to convert is solely at the discretion of the holder and will only be exercised when and if the holder finds such an exchange desirable.[1]

Convertible bonds are typically subordinated debentures; this means that the claims of "senior" creditors must be settled in full before any payment will be made to holders of subordinated debentures in the event of insolvency or bankruptcy. Senior creditors typically include all other long-term debt issues and bank loans. Subordinated debentures, of course, have a priority over common and preferred stockholders. Convertible preferred stocks are equity securities with a priority to dividend payments over common stockholders that offer opportunity to share in corporate growth.

Although our discussion will consistently refer to convertible bonds, the comments and the approach to analysis of such securities is in general equally applicable to convertible preferred stocks.

### Who issues convertibles?

The issuers of convertible bonds are classified in Exhibit 1 in terms of broad groupings commonly used by bond analysts and the rating services, such as Standard & Poor's Corporation. It is interesting to note that, although utility issues account for the largest portion of total bond issues outstanding in the United States, utilities had chosen not to issue convertible bonds, except for a relatively small amount in 1976, until 1981. Industrial, finance and real estate, and commercial are the largest issuers of convertible bonds.

New cash offerings tend to be greater during periods of rising stock prices, such as in 1972, 1975–76, 1980–81 and 1983. The right to share in future price rises for the common stock is likely to be most highly valued during such a period of bullish expectations, allowing the corporation to offer such securities on favorable terms.

Smaller and more speculative firms, especially when a new venture is being undertaken, often issue convertible bonds in the form of subordinated debentures. The risks inherent in such issues tend to make it difficult to sell straight bonds or common stock at a reasonable cost. Management sweetens the

---

[1] We will later discuss the possibility of the corporation forcing conversion through exercising a call privilege.

# EXHIBIT 1    Convertible bond issues 1972–1981 (dollars in billions)

| Issuing classification | 1972 | 1973 | 1974 | 1975 | 1976 | 1977 | 1978 | 1979 | 1980 | 1981 | 1982 | 1983 | 1984E | 1985P |
|---|---|---|---|---|---|---|---|---|---|---|---|---|---|---|
| Public utility | $ 0.0 | $ 0.0 | $ 0.0 | $ 0.0 | $ 0.0 | $ 0.1 | $ 0.0 | $ 0.0 | $ 0.0 | $ 0.1 | $ 0.0 | $ 0.3 | $ 0.1 | $ 0.2 |
| Communications | 0.1 | 0.0 | 0.0 | 0.0 | 0.0 | 0.0 | 0.0 | 0.0 | 0.2 | 0.4 | 0.5 | 0.5 | 0.0 | 0.0 |
| Transportation | 0.1 | 0.1 | 0.0 | 0.0 | 0.1 | 0.1 | 0.0 | 0.2 | 0.2 | 0.0 | 0.3 | 0.6 | 0.1 | 0.1 |
| Industrial | 0.8 | 0.1 | 0.3 | 0.7 | 0.8 | 0.5 | 0.3 | 0.3 | 2.8 | 2.4 | 0.7 | 2.2 | 1.9 | 3.4 |
| Sales finance | N.A. | N.A. | N.A. | 0.0 | 0.0 | 0.0 | 0.0 | 0.0 | 0.0 | 0.0 | 0.0 | 0.1 | 0.1 | 0.3 |
| Other finance and real estate | 0.8 | 0.4 | 0.0 | 0.5 | 0.0 | 0.0 | 0.1 | 0.0 | 0.5 | 0.1 | 0.4 | 0.4 | 0.0 | 0.0 |
| Commercial and miscellaneous | 0.5 | 0.0 | 0.2 | 0.1 | 0.1 | 0.1 | 0.0 | 0.1 | 0.4 | 1.5 | 0.9 | 2.3 | 1.9 | 3.3 |
| Total cash offerings | $ 2.3 | $ 0.6 | $ 0.5 | $ 1.3 | $ 1.0 | $ 0.8 | $ 0.4 | $ 0.6 | $ 4.0 | $ 4.5 | $ 3.0 | $ 6.5 | $ 4.2 | $ 7.3 |
| Plus exchange, net conversion | −1.8 | −1.3 | 0.1 | −0.8 | −0.5 | −0.3 | −0.5 | +1.2 | +0.6 | −0.1 | +1.8 | −1.2 | −3.0 | −3.7 |
| Less calls and other retirements | −0.2 | −0.1 | −0.2 | −0.2 | −0.2 | −0.1 | −0.1 | −0.4 | −0.4 | −2.2 | −0.6 | −6.1 | −2.0 | −2.4 |
| Net issuance convertible debt | $ 0.3 | $−0.8 | $ 0.4 | $ 0.3 | $ 0.3 | $ 0.4 | $−0.2 | $ 1.4 | $ 4.2 | $ 2.2 | $ 4.2 | $−0.8 | $−0.8 | $ 1.2 |
| Net issuance all corporate bonds | $18.9 | $13.2 | $26.9 | $34.0 | $33.0 | $32.2 | $27.6 | $31.8 | $39.3 | $29.4 | $32.4 | $34.2 | $48.7 | $43.0 |
| Convertible issues as a percent of all corporate issues based on: | | | | | | | | | | | | | | |
| Total cash offerings | 12.17% | 4.55% | 1.86% | 3.82% | 3.03% | 2.48% | 1.45% | 1.89% | 10.18% | 15.31% | 9.26% | 19.01% | 8.62% | 16.98% |
| Net issuance | 1.59 | N.M. | 1.49 | 0.88 | 0.91 | 1.24 | N.M. | 4.40 | 10.69 | 7.48 | 12.96 | N.M. | N.M. | 2.79 |

N.A. = Not available.
N.M. = Not marked.
Source: Henry Kaufman, James McKeon, and David Foster, *1985 Prospects for Financial Markets* (New York: Solomon Brothers). Figures for 1972–74 were obtained from the 1978 issue.

debt issue by giving purchasers a chance to participate in potential profits (which may be large), while having a priority over equity securityholders in the event of financial difficulty.

### Advantages and disadvantages to issuing firms

Convertible issues offer two basic potential advantages to the issuer. First, a lower interest cost is incurred and generally less-restrictive convenants need be included in the indenture than for a nonconvertible bond issue. In other words, the investor pays for the privilege of speculating on future favorable price changes in the underlying common stock by accepting a lower interest return and a less-restrictive debt agreement.

The required yield to sell a convertible relative to that of a nonconvertible issue varies over time and with the issuer. A nonconvertible issue might require a yield to maturity that could range from 50 basis points (one half of 1 percent) to 4 percent or more higher than that offered by a convertible issue.[2] Convertible bonds, moreover, are typically subordinated debt issues. The rating agencies, therefore, have usually rated convertible issues one class below that of a straight debenture issue.[3] This would suggest even higher relative interest-cost savings than suggested by the differentials noted above. The interest-cost saving to a firm will, of course, be highly related to market expectations for the common stock.

Second, a firm may be able to sell common stock at a better price through a convertible bond than by a direct issue. To illustrate, assume a firm is currently earning $5 a common share and that the common stock is selling at $50 per share. The firm believes it can utilize new capital effectively and that it would be preferable to raise equity, rather than debt capital. The firm foresees, however, a potential fall in earnings per share if common stock is sold directly, because it will take time to bring the new facilities, acquired with the funds raised, on stream. The market might well also fear potential dilution of earnings per share and might not be as optimistic as management about the future of the planned investments. For these reasons, the firm might well have to sell new common stock at less than $50 a

---

[2] For example, see Eugene F. Brigham, "An Analysis of Convertible Debentures: Theory and Some Empirical Evidence," *Journal of Finance*, March 1966, pp. 35–54.

[3] George E. Pinches and Kent A. Mingo, "A Multivariate Analysis of Industrial Bond Ratings," *Journal of Finance*, March 1973, pp. 1–18.

share. However, the firm might be able to sell a convertible bond issue at par that can be converted into 20 shares of the firm's common stock. The required interest rate might result in less dilution in earnings per share currently than would a direct stock issue, since the number of shares outstanding would not increase. Further assume that the bonds would be callable at 105 ($1,050 per bond).

If the new capital investments raised earnings per share to $6.50 two years hence, the price of the common stock in the market would increase to $65 a share, assuming a price-earnings ratio of 10 continued to exist. The firm could then call the bonds, forcing conversion. The value of stock received in conversion is $1,300 ($65 per share times 20 shares), which is greater than the cash ($1,050) that would be received by allowing the issuer to call the stock. In effect, the firm sold stock for $50 a share, less issuance costs, through the convertible bonds. The firm, therefore, received a greater price per share than by a direct issue of common stock, at that time, since the market price for a direct issue is expected to be lower and the issuance cost of a common issue is typically higher than for a convertible bond issue. The firm, in other words, would have to issue fewer common shares to raise a given amount by selling convertibles and forcing conversion than by directly selling common stock. Also, interest cost is lowered, sometimes substantially, by offering the convertible privilege.

Convertible securities have possible disadvantages to the issuer. If the underlying common stock increases markedly in price, the issuer might have been better off had the financing been postponed and a direct issue made. Moreover, if the price of the common stock drops after the issue of the convertible instrument, conversion cannot be forced and will not occur. The firm, therefore, cannot be sure it is raising equity capital when a convertible issue is made.

### Advantages to the investor

An investor purchasing a convertible security supposedly receives the advantages of a senior security; that is, safety of principal in terms of a prior claim to assets over equity security-holders and relative income stability at a known rate. Furthermore, if the common stock of the issuer rises in price, the convertible instrument will usually also rise to reflect the increased value of the underlying common stock. Upside potential can be realized through sale of the convertible bond, on the one hand, without conversion into the stock. On the other hand, if the price of the underlying common stock declines in the market, the bond can be expected to decline only to the point where it yields a satisfactory return on its value as a straight bond. A convertible offers the downside protection that bonds can offer during bad economic times, while allowing one to share in the upside potential for the common stock of a growing firm.

In terms of their dividend yield, convertible bonds also typically offer higher current yield than do common stocks. If the dividend yield on the underlying common stock surpassed the current yield on the convertible bond, conversion would tend to be attractive.

Convertible bonds may have special appeal for financial institutions, notably commercial banks. Commercial banks are not permitted to purchase common stocks for their own account and, therefore, lose the possibility of capital gains through participation in corporate earnings growth. In 1957, approval was given for the purchase of eligible convertible issues by commercial banks if the yield obtained is reasonably similar to nonconvertible issues of similar quality and maturity and they are not selling at a significant conversion premium. Admittedly, commercial banks hold relatively few convertibles, and convertibles typically do sell at a conversion premium.

Convertible bonds have good marketability, as shown by active trading in large issues on the New York Exchange; whereas nonconvertible issues of similar quality are sometimes difficult to follow, since they are traded in the over-the-counter market.

### Disadvantages to the investor

The investor pays for the convertible privilege by accepting a significantly lower yield to maturity than that currently offered by nonconvertible bonds of equivalent quality. Also, a call clause can lessen the potential attractiveness of a convertible bond, since the firm may be able to force conversion into the common stock as previously discussed. The possibility of forced conversion limits the speculative appeal.

If anticipated corporate growth is not realized, the purchaser will have sacrificed current yield and may well see the market value of the convertible instrument fall below the price paid to acquire it. A rise in the price of the underlying common stock is necessary to offset the yield sacrifice. For example, prices of convertible bonds rose to very high levels in 1965; but in 1966, when both stock and bond markets declined, many convertible issues declined even more than the stocks into which they were convertible. It appears a speculative premium was built into the price of convertibles in 1965, and the market no longer believed that this premium was justified in 1966.

Investor risk can be markedly heightened by purchasing convertibles on margin. If interest rates rise after purchase, bond-holders may receive margin calls, reflecting falling prices of convertible bonds, as happened during the 1966–70 period. Many bonds had to be sold, depressing the market further than purchasers had thought possible based on their estimate of a floor price at which the bonds would sell on a pure yield or straight investment basis.

### Analysis of convertible bonds

The following factors must be considered when evaluating convertible securities:

1. The appreciation in price of the common stock that is required before conversion could become attractive. This is measured by the *conversion premium ratio.*
2. The prospects for growth in the price of the underlying stock.
3. The downside potential in the event that the conversion privilege proves valueless.
4. The yield sacrifice required to purchase the convertible.
5. The income advantage offered through acquiring the convertible bond, rather than the number of common shares that would be obtained through conversion.
6. The quality of the security being offered.
7. The number of years over which the conversion premium paid to acquire the convertible will be recouped by means of the favorable income differential offered by the convertible relative to the underlying common stock. This is the *break-even time.*

The discussion that follows will concentrate on calculations typically used by analysts to evaluate points 1, 3, 4, 5, and 7 above. Grading of bonds in terms of quality, both by the rating agencies and in terms of financial analysis, and the assessing of the prospects for growth in the price of the underlying common stock is the work of fundamental security analysis. The techniques of fundamental analysis are reviewed in several well-accepted books.[4]

### Convertible bonds: An illustrative analysis

Exhibit 2 contrasts the 8⅞s convertible debentures issued by Boeing Corporation that mature in the year 2006 with the $4.75 convertible preferred stock issued by Associated Dry Goods. Pertinent calculations contained in the exhibit are explained below.

A few basic definitions are in order before we begin to discuss Exhibit 2. The convertible bond contract will either state a conversion ratio or a conversion price. A *conversion ratio* directly specifies the number of shares of the issuing firm's common stock that can be obtained by surrendering the convertible bond. Alternatively, the conversion rate may be expressed in terms of a *conversion price*—the price paid per share to acquire the underlying common stock through conversion. The conversion ratio may then be determined by dividing the stated conversion price into the par value of the bond:

$$\text{Conversion ratio} = \frac{\text{Par of bond}}{\text{Conversion price}}$$

For example, if the conversion price were $20, a holder of such a bond would receive 50 shares of common stock in conversion, assuming a typical par value of $1,000 for the bond.

In some cases, the bond indenture may provide for changes in the conversion price over time. To illustrate, a conversion price of $20 might be specified for the first five years, $25 for the next five years, $30 for the next five years, and so on. This, of course, means that a holder of the instrument will be able to obtain fewer shares through conversion each time the conversion price increases. For example, 50 shares can be obtained when the conversion price is $20, but only 40 shares when the conversion price rises to $25. Such a provision forces investors to emphasize early conversion if they intend to convert, and the

---

[4] For example, see Herbert E. Phillips and John C. Ritchie, *Investment Analysis and Portfolio Selection,* 2d ed. (Cincinnati: South-Western Publishing, 1983), chapters 7, 17–22, and 24.

**EXHIBIT 2**   Comparative data for two convertible bonds as of November 30, 1984

|  | Boeing Corporation 8.87 percent, 2006 | Weyerhaeuser $4.50 pref. |
|---|---|---|
| **Known data:** | | |
| Conversion ratio . . . . . . . . . . . . . . | 23.67 | 1.111 |
| Market price of convertible . . . . . . . . . . | $1,340.00 | $47.00 |
| Market price of common stock . . . . . . . . | $ 54.00 | $28.00 |
| Dividend per share—common . . . . . . . . . | $ 1.40 | $ 1.30 |
| Call price. . . . . . . . . . . . . . . . . . | $1,065.00 | $53.00 |
| First call date. . . . . . . . . . . . . . . . | 6/85 | immediately |
| Yield to maturity, equivalent. . . . . . . . . . | 12.50%* | 11.00%* |
| Quality nonconvertible . . . . . . . . . . . | — | — |
| **Calculated data:** | | |
| Market conversion price† . . . . . . . . . . . | $ 56.61 | $42.30 |
| Conversion premium per common share . . . . | $ 2.61 | $14.30 |
| Conversion premium ratio‡ . . . . . . . . . . | 4.83% | 51.07% |
| Current yield—convertible. . . . . . . . . . . | 6.62% | 9.57% |
| Dividend yield—common . . . . . . . . . . . | 2.59% | 4.64% |
| Yield sacrifice on convertible§. . . . . . . . . | 6.50% | 1.43% |
| Income differential—total‖. . . . . . . . . . . | $ 55.56 | $ 3.06 |
| Income differential—per share. . . . . . . . . | $ 2.35 | $ 2.75 |
| Break-even time . . . . . . . . . . . . . . . | 1.11 years | 5.2 years |
| Estimated floor price# . . . . . . . . . . . . | $ 732.68 | $40.91 |

* The average yield to maturity for 25-year corporate bonds rated AA to A by Standard & Poor's and the yield for an outstanding issue of Atlantic Richfield preferred stock in November 1984, coupled with the writer's judgement.
† Market price of the convertible instrument divided by the conversion ratio.
‡ The conversion premium per common share divided by the market price of the common stock.
§ The yield to maturity offered by equivalent nonconvertible securities less the yield offered by the convertible security.
‖ The interest income paid by the convertible instrument less the annual dividend income that would be received by converting into the underlying common shares. This figure expresses the income advantage in holding the convertible bond, rather than the equivalent number of shares of the underlying common stock.
# The price at which the convertible would have to sell to offer the yield currently being offered by nonconvertible securities of equivalent risk.

provision would be reasonable if corporate growth had generally ied to a rising value for the common stock over time.

**Conversion premium.** The *market conversion price* of a convertible instrument represents the cost per share of the common stock if obtained through the convertible instrument, ignoring commissions. For example, the market conversion price of $56.61 calculated for the Boeing Corporation convertible bond is obtained by dividing the market price of the convertible bond ($1,340) by the number of common shares that could be obtained by converting that bond (23.67 shares). Since the market conversion price per common share is higher than the current market price of a common share, the bond is selling at a *conversion premium,* represented by the excess cost per share to obtain the common stock through conversion.

The *conversion premium ratio* shows the percentage increase necessary to reach a *parity price* relationship between the underlying common stock and the convertible instrument. *Conversion parity* is that price relationship between the convertible instrument and the common stock at which neither a profit nor a loss would be realized by purchasing the convertible, converting it, and selling the common shares that were received in conversion, ignoring commissions. At conversion parity the following condition would exist:

$$\frac{\text{Par of bond}}{\text{Conversion price}} = \frac{\text{Market price of the convertible}}{\text{Market price of the common}}$$

When the price of the common stock exceeds its conversion parity price, one could feel certain that the convertible bond would fluctuate directly with changes in the market price of the underlying common stock. In other words, gains in value of the underlying common stock should then be able to be realized by the sale of the convertible instrument, rather than conversion and sale of the stock itself. The market conversion price, incidentally, is the parity price for a share of common stock obtainable through the convertible instrument.

At the time of this comparative analysis, both instruments sold at a premium, but the premium on the Weyerhaeuser convertible preferred was substantially greater in both relative and absolute terms. If one assumes that the appreciation potentials of the common stocks of both companies were equal (a feeling the market appeared not to hold), the Boeing Corporation bond had a substantial advantage. An increase of only 4.83 percent in the common stock of Boeing was needed to ensure that further increases in the underlying common would be reflected in the price of the convertible bond. Weyerhaeuser common stock, however, would have to rise 51.07 percent before the conversion had an assured value.

There is usually, although not always, some conversion premium present on convertible instruments, which reflects the anticipation of a possible increase in the price of the underlying common stock beyond the parity price. Professional arbitrageurs are constantly looking for situations in which the stock can be obtained more cheaply (allowing for commissions) by buying the convertible instrument than through direct purchase in the market. For example, assume a bond is convertible into 20 shares and can be purchased for $1,000. If the common stock was currently selling at $55 a share, an arbitrageur would buy the convertible and simultaneously short sell the common stock. The arbitrageur would realize a gross profit (before transaction costs) of $100 calculated as follows:

---

Short sale of 20 shares at $55/share . . . . . . $1,100
Less purchase cost of bond . . . . . . . . . .   1,000
                                                $  100

---

The demand by arbitrageurs for the convertible would continue until the resultant rise in price of the convertible no longer made such actions profitable.

**Yield sacrifice.** At the time of this analysis, nonconvertible bonds of equivalent quality to the convertible issued by Boeing Corporation offered a yield of 12.5 percent, or 6.5 percent higher than the yield to maturity offered by the convertible. The yield sacrifice would have to be overcome by a rise in the price of the underlying common stock, or the investor would have been better off to purchase the nonconvertible instrument. The yield sacrifice required by the Weyerhauser preferred was significantly lower than that for the Boeing Corporation bonds, thereby requiring less attractive appreciation potential for its common stock during the holding period to make the convertible attractive. Although the Weyerhauser instrument offered an advantage in terms of the lower yield sacrifice required, this could have been offset by a more attractive price appreciation potential for the common stock of Boeing Corporation, if that was in fact the case.

**Downside risk potential.** The floor price for a convertible is estimated as that value at which the instrument would sell in the market to offer the yield of an equivalent quality nonconvertible instrument. Boeing Corporation bonds were rated AA by Standard & Poor's Corporation at the time of this analysis, and the average yield paid by AA bonds was used as the required market yield to represent the yield on a nonconvertible bonds if issued by Boeing Corporation. An Atlantic Richfield nonconvertible preferred, felt to be of equivalent quality, yielded 11 percent.

The floor price of the Weyerhaeuser convertible was calculated, therefore, by dividing the annual dividend ($4.50) by 11 percent. Present-value calculations were used to determine the price ($732.68) at which the Boeing Corporation bond would have to sell to yield 12.5 percent to maturity.

The analysis suggests a substantially greater downside risk for Boeing Corporation convertible bonds than for the Weyerhaeuser convertible.

One should not place too much emphasis on the estimated floor prices, however. The calculations assume that current yield levels will continue, and this may well not be correct. On the one hand, if yields rise to even higher levels, and the conversion privilege proves worthless, the price of the bonds could fall below the estimated floor price. On the other hand, if yield levels fall, the loss will not be as great as suggested. More importantly, one should not be purchasing convertibles (remember the yield sacrifice) unless one believes the probability is relatively high that the market price of the underlying common will rise and eventually exceed the parity price for that common stock.

**Break-even time.** Break-even time represents the number of years it will take for the favorable income differential over the common stock offered by the convertible instrument to equal the total dollar conversion premium paid to acquire that convertible instrument. For example, the break-even time for the Boeing Corporation bonds is 1.11 years, calculated as follows:

| | |
|---|---|
| Interest paid on each $1,000 bond at 8⅞ percent . . . . . . . . . . | $88.70 |
| Dividend income offered by 23.67 shares into which each bond is convertible (23.67 shares × 1.40/share) . . . . . . . . . . . . | 33.14 |
| Favorable bond income differential . . . . . . . . . . . . . . . . . | 55.56 |
| Favorable income differential per common share (55.56 ÷ 23.67 shares) . . . . . . . . . . . . . . . . . . . . . . | $ 2.35 |
| Break-even time equals the conversion premium per share dividend by the favorable income differential per share (2.61 ÷ 2.35) . . . . . | 1.11 years |

A break-even time exceeding five years is widely regarded by analysts as excessive, other things being equal. The Weyerhaeuser preferred have a significantly longer break-even time, though neither security suggests an excessive break-even time.

### Dilution of the convertible privilege

A large common stock split or stock dividend could markedly dilute the value of the conversion privilege, unless adjustment of the number of shares received in conversion is made. For example, assume a bond is convertible into 20 shares, and the company undergoes a two-for-one stock split. Recognizing this, the conversion privilege is typically protected by a provision in the bond identure providing for a pro rata adjustment of the conversion price and/or the conversion ratio, so the exchange ratio would increase to 40 shares after the stock split.

### When should a convertible be converted or sold?

If the prospects for favorable growth in the underlying common stock or the relative prices and yields of the convertible security and the common stock change significantly, a sale or conversion may be suggested. For example, the dividend obtainable by converting into the common stock of AT&T from the $4 convertible preferred rose to $4.20 a share during 1977. A conversion was then desirable, assuming the investor still wished to retain a claim on the further potential growth of AT&T, since current yield would be increased through conversion by 20 cents per share.

### Summary of convertibles

Some fixed-income securities are convertible into common stock, offering the basic advantages of a senior security (bond or preferred stock) while allowing the holder to participate in potential corporate growth. The investor pays for the conversion privilege by accepting a significantly lower yield than could be obtained by purchasing nonconvertible bonds or preferred stocks. A convertible, moreover, usually sells at a premium over the value of the underlying common stock. If the anticipated growth in the value of the common stock is not realized, the purchaser will have sacrificed yield and may well also see the value of the convertible instrument fall sharply.

There are three distinct areas of analysis that should be undertaken when evaluating a convertible security:

1. The quality of the security should be assessed in the same way as for other nonconvertible senior securities. This requires assessing the ability of the issuing company to meet the fixed charges mandated by the issue under reasonably conceivable adverse economic circumstances.
2. The growth potential for the underlying common stock must be evaluated, since that growth potential offers the basis for generating the added yield necessary to offset the yield sacrifice incurred at the time of purchase and provide a return that makes purchase attractive.
3. Special calculations developed in the illustrative analysis in this chapter should be used to assess the relative attractiveness of the many convertible securities available in the market.

Conversion should be considered when the annual total dividends that would be received from the common shares obtained through conversion exceeds the annual coupon payments offered by the convertible bond. Sale of the convertible security should also be considered when the price of that security exceeds the estimated value of the underlying stock into which it is convertible and/or the prospects for favorable growth in the underlying common stock deteriorate.

# SIXTEEN

## Mortgages

**Dexter Senft**
*Managing Director*
*Fixed Income Research*
*The First Boston Corporation*

### WHAT IS A MORTGAGE?

By definition, a mortgage is a "pledge of property to secure payment of a debt." Typically, property refers to real estate, which is often in the form of a house; the debt is the loan given to the buyer of the house by a bank or other lender. Thus, a mortgage might be a "pledge of a house to secure payment of a bank loan." If a homeowner (the *mortgagor*) fails to pay the lender (the *mortgagee*), the lender has the right to foreclose the loan and seize the property to ensure that it is repaid.

The form that a mortgage loan takes could technically be anything the borrower and lender agree upon. Traditionally, however, most mortgage loans were structured similarly. There was a fixed rate of interest on the loan for its entire term, and the loan was repaid in monthly installments of principal and interest. Each loan was structured in such a way that the total payment each month (the sum of the principal and interest) was equal, or *level*. We shall refer to this type of loan arrangement as a *traditional* mortgage loan. (There is a growing trend away from this traditional structure, but this is getting ahead of the story.) In a traditional mortgage loan, the terms to be negotiated are the interest rate and the period to maturity. Interest rates vary with the general economic climate, and maturities range from 12 to 40 years, depending on the type of property involved. Most mortgages on single-family homes carry 30-year maturities.

Exhibit 1 illustrates the breakdown of monthly payments between principal and interest on a 30-year, 10 percent traditional

---

**EXHIBIT 1**    Monthly mortgage payments–Interest/principal (30-year 10 percent conventional loan)

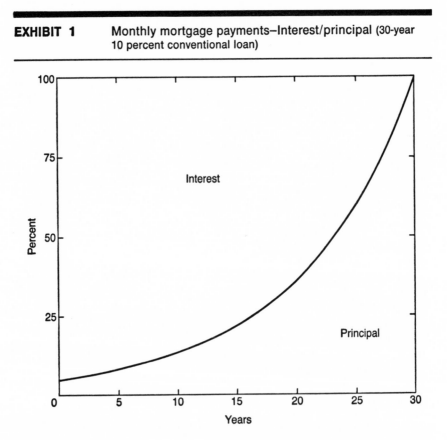

mortgage. At first, the mortgage payment is mostly interest. The principal portion increases over time until, at maturity, the payment is almost entirely principal. At all times, however, the sum of the principal and interest payments is the same. Notice that, over the course of the loan, the borrower pays more dollars as interest than as principal—in fact, total interest is more than twice total principal in this example.

The principal portion of each monthly payment is used to reduce the amount of the loan outstanding. In mortgage terms, the loan is *amortized* over 30 years, and the principal payments each month are known as amortization payments. The amount of the loan that is outstanding at any time is known as the *mortgage balance*. In any month the interest payment equals the interest rate (expressed monthly) times the mortgage balance at the beginning of the month (see Exhibit 2). Often the mortgage balance is expressed as a ratio or percentage of the

**EXHIBIT 2**    Sample payment schedule: Traditional mortgage (10 percent interest rate, 30-year [360-month] term)

| Month | Mortgage balance Dollars | Mortgage balance Decimal | Monthly payment | Interest | Principal |
|---|---|---|---|---|---|
| 0. . . . . . | 50000.00 | 1.00000 | | | |
| 1. . . . . . | 49977.88 | .99956 | 438.79 | 416.67 | 22.12 |
| 2. . . . . . | 49955.58 | .99911 | 438.79 | 416.48 | 22.30 |
| 3. . . . . . | 49933.09 | .99866 | 438.79 | 416.30 | 22.49 |
| 4. . . . . . | 49910.41 | .99821 | 438.79 | 416.11 | 22.68 |
| 5. . . . . . | 49887.55 | .99775 | 438.79 | 415.92 | 22.87 |
| 6. . . . . . | 49864.49 | .99729 | 438.79 | 415.73 | 23.06 |
| 7. . . . . . | 49841.24 | .99682 | 438.79 | 415.54 | 23.25 |
| 8. . . . . . | 49817.80 | .99636 | 438.79 | 415.34 | 23.44 |
| 9. . . . . . | 49794.16 | .99588 | 438.79 | 415.15 | 23.64 |
| 10. . . . . . | 49770.33 | .99541 | 438.79 | 414.95 | 23.83 |
| . . . | . . . | . . . | . . . | . . . | . . . |
| 100. . . . . . | 46567.88 | .93136 | 438.79 | 388.48 | 50.30 |
| 101. . . . . . | 46517.16 | .93034 | 438.79 | 388.07 | 50.72 |
| 102. . . . . . | 46466.02 | .92932 | 438.79 | 387.64 | 51.14 |
| 103. . . . . . | 46414.45 | .92829 | 438.79 | 387.22 | 51.57 |
| . . . | . . . | . . . | . . . | . . . | . . . |
| 200. . . . . . | 38697.88 | .77396 | 438.79 | 323.44 | 115.34 |
| 201. . . . . . | 38581.57 | .77163 | 438.79 | 322.48 | 116.30 |
| 202. . . . . . | 38464.30 | .76929 | 438.79 | 321.51 | 117.27 |
| 203. . . . . . | 38346.05 | .76692 | 438.79 | 320.54 | 118.25 |
| . . . | . . . | . . . | . . . | . . . | . . . |
| 300. . . . . . | 20651.61 | .41303 | 438.79 | 174.30 | 264.48 |
| 301. . . . . . | 20384.93 | .40770 | 438.79 | 172.10 | 266.69 |
| 302. . . . . . | 20116.01 | .40232 | 438.79 | 169.87 | 268.91 |
| 303. . . . . . | 19844.86 | .39690 | 438.79 | 167.63 | 271.15 |
| . . . | . . . | . . . | . . . | . . . | . . . |
| 355. . . . . . | 2140.13 | .04280 | 438.79 | 21.31 | 417.47 |
| 356. . . . . . | 1719.18 | .03438 | 438.79 | 17.83 | 420.95 |
| 357. . . . . . | 1294.72 | .02589 | 438.79 | 14.33 | 424.46 |
| 358. . . . . . | 866.72 | .01733 | 438.79 | 10.79 | 428.00 |
| 359. . . . . . | 435.16 | .00870 | 438.79 | 7.22 | 431.56 |
| 360. . . . . . | 0.00 | .00000 | 438.79 | 3.63 | 435.16 |

Note: Each month, the interest payment is $\frac{1}{12}$ of 10 percent of the mortgage balance. The principal payment is the total payment less the interest due. The principal balance is reduced by the amount of the principal payment.

original loan amount, in which case the mortgage balance runs from 1 (or 100 percent) initially to 0 at maturity. Exhibit 3 shows how the mortgage balance for several possible loans would decline over time. Another way to view the mortgage balance is as

**EXHIBIT 3**    Examples of mortgage balances for various loans

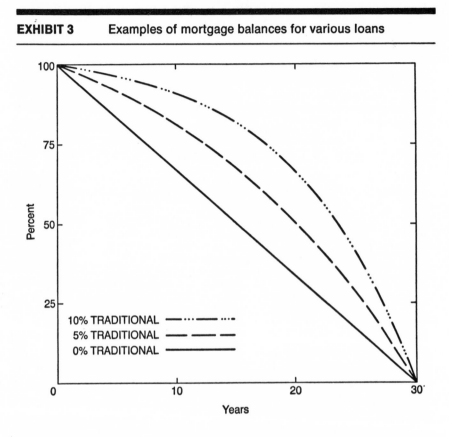

the amount of the house value the home buyer does not yet own. The amount of a home's value that is owned is referred to as the homeowner's *equity*. Equity can be defined as the difference between the current value of the home and the mortgage balance; as the mortgage balance declines, the equity rises. Equity also increases if the current value of the home increases, due to home improvements, inflation, etc.

Sometimes a mortgagor may want to make a monthly payment that is greater than the amount actually due, with the idea of applying the excess payment to further reducing the loan. Such excess principal payments are called *prepayments* and may be made for several reasons. Prepayments result in a direct reduction of the mortgage balance and a direct increase in the amount of equity. Another way to define mortgage balance is that it equals the original loan amount less the total amount of amortization and prepayments to date.

A mortgagor who fails to make a mortgage payment is said to be *delinquent*. Delinquencies can have a variety of causes—the homeowner may have died, become unemployed, bounced a check, or simply forgotten to make the payment. The mortgagee then reminds the homeowner that the payment is overdue and attempts to collect the money. If the matter is not resolved quickly, the mortgagee may assess the mortgagor with a late payment charge. Sometimes there is no quick solution, and the mortgagor may become more than one month in arrears. Although most lenders are willing to allow a borrower a few months leeway, in extreme cases it may be necessary for the bank to foreclose the loan, in which case the property is taken from the mortgagor and sold to pay off the loan.

## QUALIFYING FOR A MORTGAGE

Borrowers who are interested in obtaining mortgage loans must meet certain standards set by the lender in order to be considered creditworthy. The first thing a lender checks is whether the borrower has any other loans or obligations outstanding; if so, these will diminish the borrower's ability to make mortgage payments. Next the lender determines the income and net worth of the borrower. Many mortgage lenders use these classical rules of thumb to determine whether or not a borrower's income is adequate for the mortgage:

1. The total mortgage payment (principal and interest) should not exceed 25 percent of the borrower's total income less any payments owed for other obligations.
2. Total mortgage payments plus other housing expenses should not exceed 33 percent of the borrower's income less payments for other obligations. Other housing expenses include such items as taxes, insurance, utilities, and normal maintenance costs.

Of course, these percentages may vary depending on the lender and the circumstances. In particular, borrowers with relatively high net worth and/or liquid assets will find lenders to be more flexible. Also, in times of high interest rates and tight money, lenders have been known to bend these rules somewhat to maintain a certain level of business.

The buyer is usually required to make a down payment on the property in order to qualify for the mortgage. The down payment might range anywhere from 5 to 25 percent of the purchase price. The reason for requiring a down payment is that, in the event the lender is forced to foreclose the loan and sell the property, the mortgage balance will be more easily recovered. In other words, there is room for error if the property is sold—even if it cannot bring the original purchase price on the market, there can still be enough to cover the debt.

Lenders use the term *loan to value ratio,* or LTV, to express the amount of protection on the mortgage. LTV is calculated as the ratio of the mortgage balance to the market value of the property and is expressed as a percentage. The lower the LTV, the less the loan amount relative to the property value, and the greater the safety.

The LTV ratio tends to decrease over time. For example, if a buyer makes a 10 percent down payment on a property and mortgages the rest, the LTV is initially 90 percent. Over time, the mortgage balance declines from amortization and prepayments, while the property value tends to increase due to inflation. Both of these changes serve to lower the LTV.

As with income requirements, down payment and LTV requirements depend on certain circumstances. These include not only the net worth of the borrower but the condition and marketability of the property and the availability of credit. Higher LTV ratios are associated with newer, more marketable properties and with easier credit and lower interest rates.

An important (if not obvious) conclusion about qualifying for a mortgage is that it becomes harder when interest rates rise. Because of the income and LTV requirements, smaller mortgage balances are affordable when rates rise, and yet this is also the time when inflation and, therefore, home purchase prices are rising. As a consequence, all but those buyers with large amounts of cash or equity are squeezed from the market.

## MORTGAGE INSURANCE

Two types of mortgage insurance may be used when borrowers obtain mortgage financing. One type is originated by borrowers and the other by lenders. Although both have a beneficial effect on the creditworthiness of the borrowers, the latter is of greater importance from the lender's point of view.

The first type of mortgage insurance is taken out by the borrower (borrowers) usually with a life insurance company. The policy provides for the continuing payment of the mortgage after the death of the insured person, thus enabling the survivors to continue living in the house. In the sense that the mortgage might just as well have been paid off with part of the proceeds of ordinary life insurance, this form of mortgage insurance is really only a special form of life insurance. It is cheaper than ordinary life insurance, however, because the death benefit, which is equal to the mortgage balance, declines over time.

The other type of mortgage insurance is taken out by the lender, although borrowers pay the insurance premiums. This policy covers some percentage of the loan amount and guarantees that in the event of a default by the borrower(s) the insurance company will pay the amount insured or pay off the loan in full.

An example of how this type of mortgage insurance works is shown in Exhibit 4. Suppose a borrower finances $60,000 of property with a $5,000 down payment and a $55,000 mortgage. The initial LTV ratio is fairly high (91.7 percent) so mortgage insurance is obtained in the amount of $11,000 (20 percent of the loan). Suppose the borrower defaults after five years (the mortgage balance having been paid down to $52,000 by then). Suppose further that the property has deteriorated in condition (or perhaps has been partially destroyed), and its market value falls to $50,000. The bank then turns to the insurance company.

Several options are open to the insurance company, perhaps the simplest of which is that it can assist the borrower financially so that the amount in arrears can be paid and no foreclosure is necessary. Assuming this fails, there are two other alternatives. First, the insurance company could pay the claim of $11,000 and let the bank foreclose. The bank, which gets $50,000 for the property and $11,000 insurance, actually makes a profit of $9,000 over the mortgage balance outstanding. A better alternative for the insurance company, however, is to pay off the mortgage balance ($52,000), take title of the property, and sell it (for $50,000). The insurance company thereby loses only $2,000, instead of $11,000. Of course, the insurer could hold the property or even make improvements to it in hope of making a future gain instead of selling it immediately.

The net effect of mortgage insurance from the lender's stand-

**EXHIBIT 4**

Situation initially:

$$LTV = \frac{55,000}{60,000} = 91.7\%$$

$11,000 Mortgage insurance obtained

| | | Property |
|---|---|---|
| Mortgage: | $55,000 | value: |
| Down payment: | 5,000 | $60,000 |
| Total | $60,000 | |

Situation after 5 years:

Borrower defaults
Property value falls

| | |
|---|---|
| Mortgage balance: | Property |
| $52,000 | value: |
| | $50,000 |

**Option 1:** Insurance company pays claim

| | | | |
|---|---|---|---|
| Lender has | $50,000 | Property | Insurance company has |
| | 11,000 | Insurance | ($11,000) loss |
| | (52,000) | Bad debt | |
| | $ 9,000 | Net profit | |

**Option 2:** Insurance company takes title to property

| | | | | |
|---|---|---|---|---|
| Lender has | $52,000 | From insurer | Insurance company has | |
| | (52,000) | Bad debt | 50,000 | Property |
| | 0 | Net profit | (52,000) | Payment to lender |
| | | | (2,000) | Net loss |

point is to reduce its risk. The exposure of a lender to loss equals the amount loaned less property value and mortgage insurance. In a sense, the insurance has an effect similar to having a higher down payment, because both reduce the lender's exposure to loss. Mortgage insurance is advantageous to borrowers who do not have enough money for a large down payment but who can afford enough down payment and insurance to satisfy the lender.

The cost of the insurance can be passed on to the borrower in several ways. Traditionally, the cost was added to the mortgage rate as an extra one-eighth percent or one-fourth percent, depending on the amount of coverage. As mortgage rates escalated, however, increasing the rate further became less attractive. (In a sense, the insurance company would be increasing the chance of the default it was insuring against.) It has become increasingly common to pay for mortgage insurance in one lump sum at the time of mortgage origination.

It is not necessary to have mortgage insurance in effect for the entire term of a loan. Because the mortgage balance amortizes and the LTV tends to fall over time, the lender may deem mortgage insurance to be unnecessary when the mortgage balance has declined to some predetermined level. At that point, the policy is either cancelled or allowed to expire.

## SERVICING

Among the jobs that mortgage lenders must perform to ensure that borrowers make timely and accurate payments are sending payment notices, reminding borrowers when payments are overdue, recording prepayments, keeping records of mortgage balances, administering escrow accounts for payment of property taxes or insurance, sending out tax information at year-end, and initiating foreclosure proceedings. These functions are collectively known as *servicing* the loans. Many times the original lender, known as the mortgage *originator,* is the one who services the loan, but this is not always the case. Sometimes the mortgage is sold to someone else, and the servicing of the loan may or may not go along with the mortgage.

In the event that one party owns a mortgage and another services it, the servicer receives a fee (the *servicing fee*) for the trouble. Servicing fees usually take the form of a fixed percentage of the mortgage balance outstanding. Although the percentage may vary from one servicer to the next, it is usually in the area of .25 percent to .50 percent. Small servicing fee percentages are usually associated with larger commercial property loans and larger percentages with smaller residential loans. From the point of view of the owner of the mortgage, the servicing fee comes out of the interest portion of the mortgage payment. For example, if party A owns a 10 percent mortgage being serviced by party B for a three eighths of 1 percent fee, then A is really earning 9⅝ percent (10 percent minus three eighths of 1 percent) on the loan.

In addition to servicing fees, there are occasionally other fees that the servicer may keep. For example, some servicers are entitled to keep late-payment penalties paid by the borrower, foreclosure penalties, and certain other penalty fees. The specific types and amounts of fees that servicers are entitled to receive are set forth in a servicing agreement between the mortgage owner and the servicer.

## WHERE DOES MORTGAGE MONEY COME FROM?

The largest single originating group is the savings and loan industry. Savings and loans, together with savings banks and credit unions constitute the "thrift industry"—so-called because its funds come from the savings accumulated by thrifty depositors. Commercial banks make up the second largest group of originators, and like thrift institutions, the money they put into mortgages comes primarily from deposits. The third major source of mortgage loans is the mortgage company sector, or mortgage banks. Unlike savings banks or commercial banks, mortgage banks do not have depositors. They are in the business of finding other sources of mortgage money, such as thrifts or insurance companies, and making it available for housing construction and ownership; mortgage bankers' profits come from servicing the loans they originate, plus any profit that can be made from buying and selling the mortgages. The lesser originators of mortgages are the insurance companies, pension funds, and various federal, state, and local entities empowered to make mortgage loans.

Knowing who originates mortgages, however, does not really answer the question of where mortgage money comes from. The real lenders of mortgage money are those who *own* mortgages, who are somewhat different from those who create them. Mortgage bankers, for example, generally do not want to own mortgages at all—once they create them, they sell the mortgages to someone else. Thrifts and commercial banks prove to be the major holders of mortgages, but there are several other notable ones, such as life insurance companies and households. The owner category with by far the largest growth is mortgage pools and trusts.

What are these pools and trusts? Essentially, they are collections of mortgages of which shares, or participations, are resold to someone else. (In this sense, mortgage pools and trusts as an ownership category is not very informative.) Mortgage trusts can be created by securities dealers or investment advisors who offer shares in the trust as a form of investment for their clients. Mortgage pools, however, have the lion's share of this category.

## NONTRADITIONAL MORTGAGES

The decade of the 1970s saw the advent of many new and different varieties of mortgages. Unlike traditional mortgages, most of these alternative mortgage instruments (AMIs) do not have level monthly payments, but employ some other (often complicated) scheme. One AMI even provides a way for the homeowner to continually take cash out of equity, as opposed to continually putting cash into it.

What was the impetus for the creation of AMIs, and in what ways are they superior to traditional mortgages? The answers to these questions are related to level and behavior of mortgage interest rates. In the 15 years ending in 1979, mortgage rates doubled from roughly 6 percent levels to 12 percent levels, and by 1981 they had almost tripled to 17 percent. More importantly, the volatility of these rates increased tremendously. Moves of 1 percentage point between the time a loan application was made and the time the loan was closed were not unheard of in 1979. The interest climate resulted in a great deal of risk to both borrower and lender—the rate that seemed plausible one week might be out of line the next week. (Not to mention the next 30 years.) High interest rates combined with the rapid inflation in housing prices to make home financing difficult in general and all but impossible for the first-time buyer. AMIs were created as a way of coping with these problems.

There are literally dozens of different types of AMIs, each with its own peculiar twist. Their names, which are often abbreviated, include GPMs, ARMs, RAMs, ROMs, RRMs, ARMs, FLIPs, WRAPs, and SAMs. The remainder of this chapter will discuss some of the salient features of the more popular AMIs, except ARMs. The next article will discuss ARMs.

### Graduated-payment mortgages (GPMs)

The only essential difference between the GPM and the traditional mortgage is that the payments on a GPM are not all equal. Graduated payment refers to the fact that GPM payments start at a relatively low level and rise for some number of years.

The actual number of years that the payments rise and the percentages increase per year depend on the exact type or plan of the GPM. The five major GPM plans work as follows:

| Plan | Term to maturity (years) | Years that payments rise | Percentage increase per year |
|---|---|---|---|
| I | 30 | 5 | 2.5% |
| II | 30 | 5 | 5.0 |
| III | 30 | 5 | 7.5 |
| IV | 30 | 10 | 2.0 |
| V | 30 | 10 | 3.0 |

At the end of the graduation period, the monthly payment is held at its existing level for the remainder of the mortgage term. Exhibit 5 shows the payment schedule on a $50,000, 10 percent, Plan III GPM.

**EXHIBIT 5** Mortgage payment schedule for a $50,000 plan III GPM (30-year term, 10 percent mortgage rate)

| Year(s) | Monthly payment |
|---|---|
| 1 | $333.52 |
| 2 | 358.53 |
| 3 | 385.42 |
| 4 | 414.33 |
| 5 | 445.40 |
| 6–30 | 478.81 |

Note: Plan III GPMs call for monthly payments that increase by 7.5 percent at the end of each of the first five years of the mortgage.

The attraction of a GPM is the small payment in its early years. A first-time home buyer who might not be able to afford payments on a traditional mortgage might be able to afford the smaller payments of the GPM, even if both loans were for the same principal amount. Eventually, when the graduation period has ended, homeowners with GPMs make up the difference by paying larger monthly amounts than the traditional mortgages require. The originators of GPMs reason that most home buyers, particularly young, first-time home buyers, have incomes that will increase at least as rapidly as the mortgage payments increase. Thus, they should always be able to afford their monthly payments. Exhibit 6 compares the initial and fi-

| EXHIBIT 6 | Comparison of initial and final payments: Traditional mortgages versus GPMs ($50,000, 10 percent, 30-year mortgages) |

| Loan type | Initial payment | Final payment |
|---|---|---|
| Traditional . . . . . . . | $438.79 | $438.79 |
| GPM Plan I . . . . . . . | 400.29 | 452.88 |
| GPM Plan II . . . . . . | 365.29 | 466.22 |
| GPM Plan III . . . . . | 333.52 | 478.81 |
| GPM Plan IV . . . . . | 390.02 | 475.43 |
| GPM Plan V . . . . . | 367.29 | 493.60 |

nal payments of a traditional mortgage with the five GPM plans, assuming all mortgages have a $50,000 balance and a 10 percent interest rate. Notice that the lowest initial payment is on the Plan III GPM, and in this example it is about $100 less per month than the traditional mortgage in the first year. The Plan III GPM is the only plan to offer a 7.5 percent graduation rate; this is the maximum graduation rate that federally chartered banks can currently offer.

Because GPMs have smaller initial payments than do traditional mortgages, they do not pay down their mortgage balances as quickly. The interesting feature of GPMs is that, in their early years, they do not pay down any principal at all—in fact, their mortgage balances actually *increase* for a short time. Technically, we would say that they experience "negative amortization" at the outset. To see how this works, consider the first-month payment on the GPM in Exhibit 5.

Interest due for month one is 10 percent per year for one-twelfth year on $50,000 balance
= $50,000 × $1/12$ × $10/100$ = $416.67
Payment on GPM = $333.52
Principal paid = $333.52 − $416.67 = −$83.15
New mortgage balance = $50,000 − (−83.15) = $50,083.15

Another way of viewing this situation is: The amount paid on the mortgage ($333.52) was insufficient to cover even the interest due on the loan ($416.67), so the shortfall ($83.15) is lent to the mortgagor. Thus, the new mortgage balance is the sum of the original balance plus the new loan:

$$\$50,000 + \$83.15 = \$50,083.15$$

Of course, the mortgage balance must eventually be reduced to zero. The annual increases in the mortgage payment eventually catch up to and overtake the amount of interest due, and at that time the mortgage balance begins to decrease. In Exhibit 7 the

---

**EXHIBIT 7**   Graduated payment mortgage (GPM) factor comparison for 10 percent, 30-year loans

| Year-end factors | Ordinary mortgage | Plan I 5-year, 2.5 percent | Plan II 5-year, 5.0 percent | Plan III 5-year, 7.5 percent | Plan IV 10-year, 2.0 percent | Plan V 10-year, 3.0 percent |
|---|---|---|---|---|---|---|
| 0. . . . . . | 1.00000 | 1.00000 | 1.00000 | 1.00000 | 1.00000 | 1.00000 |
| 1. . . . . . | .99444 | 1.00412 | 1.01291 | 1.02090 | 1.00670 | 1.01241 |
| 2. . . . . . | .98830 | 1.00615 | 1.02258 | 1.03769 | 1.01214 | 1.02335 |
| 3. . . . . . | .98152 | 1.00582 | 1.02845 | 1.04949 | 1.01614 | 1.03258 |
| 4. . . . . . | .97402 | 1.00281 | 1.02987 | 1.05526 | 1.01853 | 1.03985 |
| 5. . . . . . | .96574 | .99678 | 1.02612 | 1.05383 | 1.01909 | 1.04484 |
| 6. . . . . . | .95660 | .98734 | 1.01640 | 1.04385 | 1.01759 | 1.04725 |
| 7. . . . . . | .94649 | .97691 | 1.00567 | 1.03282 | 1.01376 | 1.04669 |
| 8. . . . . . | .93533 | .96539 | .99381 | 1.02064 | 1.00732 | 1.04277 |
| 9. . . . . . | .92300 | .95266 | .98071 | 1.00719 | .99796 | 1.03504 |
| 10. . . . . . | .90938 | .93860 | .96623 | .99233 | .98532 | 1.02299 |
| 11. . . . . . | .89433 | .92307 | .95025 | .97591 | .96902 | 1.00606 |
| 12. . . . . . | .97771 | .90591 | .93258 | .95777 | .95101 | .98736 |
| 13. . . . . . | .85934 | .88696 | .91307 | .93773 | .93111 | .96670 |
| 14. . . . . . | .83906 | .86602 | .89151 | .91559 | .90913 | .94388 |
| 15. . . . . . | .81665 | .84289 | 86770 | .89113 | .88484 | .91867 |
| 16. . . . . . | .79189 | .81733 | .84140 | .86412 | .85802 | .89082 |
| 17. . . . . . | .76454 | .78910 | .81233 | .83427 | .82838 | .86005 |
| 18. . . . . . | .73432 | .75792 | .78023 | .80130 | .79564 | .82606 |
| 19. . . . . . | .70094 | .72347 | .74477 | .76488 | .75948 | .78851 |
| 20. . . . . . | .66407 | .68541 | .70559 | .72464 | .71953 | .74703 |
| 21. . . . . . | .62333 | .64336 | .66230 | .68019 | .67539 | .70120 |
| 22. . . . . . | .57833 | .59692 | .61449 | .63108 | .62663 | .65058 |
| 23. . . . . . | .52862 | .54561 | .56167 | .57684 | .57277 | .59466 |
| 24. . . . . . | .47370 | .48892 | .50332 | .51691 | .51326 | .53288 |
| 25. . . . . . | .41303 | .42631 | .43885 | .45071 | .44752 | .46463 |
| 26. . . . . . | .34601 | .35713 | .36764 | .37757 | .37491 | .38924 |
| 27. . . . . . | .27197 | .28071 | .28897 | .29678 | .29468 | .30595 |
| 28. .    . . | .19018 | .19629 | .20207 | .20752 | .20606 | .21394 |
| 29. . . . . . | .09982 | .10303 | .10606 | .10892 | .10816 | .11229 |
| 30. . . . . . | .00000 | .00000 | .00000 | .00000 | .00000 | .00000 |

mortgage balances (expressed as ratios to the original loan amount) are shown at the end of each year, for all five GPM plans as well as for a traditional mortgage. Notice that a Plan III GPM has a balance that rises through the end of the fourth year, at which point it declines to zero over the next 26 years. It is interesting to note that the mortgage balance does not go below 1.0 until some time in the 10th year. Exhibit 8 is a graph of the mortgage balances for a traditional mortgage and a Plan III GPM.

**EXHIBIT 8**      Comparison between Plan III GPM and a traditional mortgage

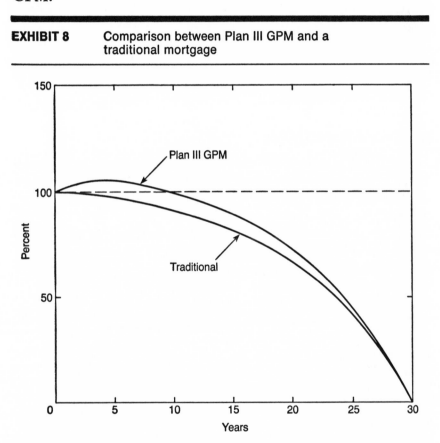

GPMs were first introduced by the Federal Housing Administration (FHA) in November 1976, although various legal and technical matters prevented any large-scale issuance until late 1978. In April 1979, GPMs became eligible for pooling into GNMA pass-through securities, and since that time GPMs have accounted for roughly 25–30 percent of all FHA-insured mortgages. In early 1979, the Mortgage Bankers Association of

America had predicted that by the end of 1981 GPMs could grow to half of the FHA-insured mortgages; the disarray of the mortgage market since 1979 has postponed such an event, but it still appears feasible.

As interest rates continue to rise, the need for GPMs and similar vehicles becomes increasingly important to the first-time home buyer or those with low cash flows. New varieties and plans of GPMs have been proposed that increase the period that payments rise and/or the graduation rate, thereby making the initial payment progressively smaller. One GPM proposal called for delaying the time at which payments would begin to rise—making the payments have a flat-rising-flat pattern. Such a scheme called for a mortgage balance that would rise for nine years and not become less than 1.0 until half of the term to maturity had elapsed.

### Rollover mortgages (ROMs)

The ROM is one of the more recent AMIs to be used in the United States and is seen by many economists and mortgage-market analysts to be the trend of the future for the domestic mortgage market. The ROM is hardly a U.S. innovation, since it has been a major financing vehicle in Canada for at least 50 years. In fact, ROMs are often referred to as Canadian-type mortgages or Canadian rollover mortgages. Occasionally these loans are called RRMs, for "renegotiated-rate mortgages."

In essence, ROMs offer long-term amortization with short-term financing. This means that the lender gives money to the borrower to be repaid over a long period (e.g., 30 years) at an interest rate that is periodically renegotiated (e.g., every 3 to 5 years). Because ROMs are just now making headway into the United States, there is no single model one can refer to as the typical ROM. One prototype ROM proposed by the Federal Home Loan Bank Board in January 1980 called for the renegotiation of rates every three to five years (to be determined at the time of origination), a maximum change in mortgage rate of one half of 1 percent for each year in the renegotiation period (e.g., 2.5 percent for five-year periods) and a guarantee by the lender to provide new financing to the borrower each period at either the going rate on similar loans or at a rate based on an index, such as with adjustable rate mortgage (ARMs), which are discussed in the next article. Other proposals call for guaranteeing the borrower a new loan only for one additional period and not thereafter.

There is no way to predict the amortization schedule of a ROM ahead of time, since it will depend on the mortgage rates to be negotiated in the future. Exhibit 9 shows a possible ROM over the course of 30 years. It begins at a 10 percent mortgage

**EXHIBIT 9**    Possible $50,000 rollover mortgage (ROM)

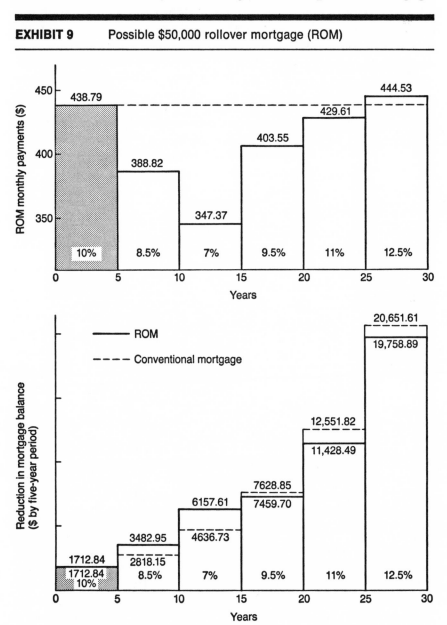

rate with renegotiation to occur every five years. In years one through five, the payment schedule on the ROM exactly corresponds to a traditional 30-year, 10 percent mortgage from both borrower's and lender's points of view. After five years we assume that interest rates have declined, and the new mortgage rate is negotiated to be 8.5 percent. At this point and until year 10 the payment schedule exactly matches that of a 25-year, 8.5 percent mortgage. Over its 30-year term, the ROM always resembles a traditional mortgage, but the particular mortgage that it resembles changes five times. Exhibit 10 graphs the mortgage balance of this hypothetical ROM versus that of a traditional mortgage.

---

**EXHIBIT 10**        Comparison between a ROM and a traditional mortgage

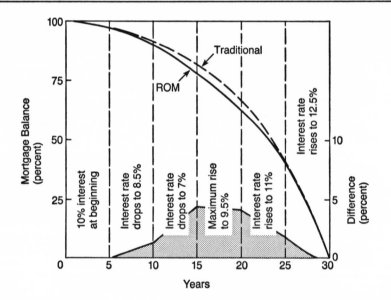

Notice that the mortgage rate on the ROM is always described as negotiated rather than determined (as with an ARM). *This is because the borrower has no obligation to keep the loan with the same lender after each period elapses,* but is free to find a new lender who can provide a lower mortgage rate or superior services, or both. It would be common, however, for the borrower to use the same lender for the entire mortgage term. Not only would this be more convenient, but taking the loan elsewhere would probably mean paying a mortgage origination fee, whereas keeping the same lender would probably cost only a small amount for the paperwork involved.

As with the ARM, the ROM has the advantage of reducing interest-rate risk to both borrower and lender (most especially to the lender). Unlike the ARM, however, the ROM takes on the flavor of a short-term asset, which is so badly needed to offset the short-term liabilities of the banks. Indeed, ROMs have been described as the key to the survival of the thrift industry in the United States in the coming years.

### Reverse-annuity mortgages (RAMs)

The key word to remember when discussing RAMs is *reverse* because, unlike any of the mortgages discussed so far, RAMs do not call for the homeowner to make payments to the bank. Rather, the homeowner (who is still the borrower) receives monthly payments *from* the bank, while the equity in his or her home *decreases*.

Young and first-time borrowers are not the only groups that tend to have cash flow problems from lack of income. Another such group is the elderly, often retired and on a fixed income. In the event that such a person owns (or has substantial equity in) a house, then a RAM provides a way of converting that equity into an income stream. Traditionally, this equity could be converted to cash in one of two ways: (1) by selling the house and paying off any outstanding mortgage balance, the homeowner realizes the entire equity in the home in cash; or (2) by taking out a new or second mortgage, the homeowner realizes part of the equity in cash. The RAM goes one step further by allowing homeowners to realize part of their equity in a cash stream, paid to them in monthly installments.

Exhibit 11 illustrates a possible RAM. It involves a homeowner who originally bought her home for $25,000—with a $5,000 down payment and $20,000 mortgage, which has been paid down to a $5,000 balance. The price of the house has risen, due to inflation, to $60,000. The equity in the home is $60,000 less the $5,000 mortgage balance, or $55,000. The homeowner decides to get a RAM for $40,000 for 10 years at an interest rate of 10 percent. The RAM provides her with a monthly payment of $195.27, which she then uses for food, utilities, home improvements, and other expenses. Each year the mortgage balance on the RAM rises to reflect additional payments to the

---

**EXHIBIT 11**     Example of a RAM

---

Original mortgage:

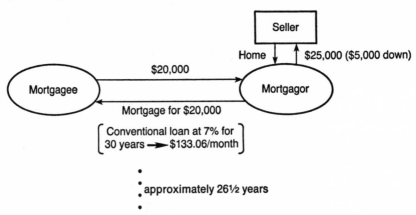

approximately 26½ years

At origination of RAM:

| | |
|---|---|
| Current value of home. . . . . . . . . . . | $60,000 |
| Mortgage balance . . . . . . . | 5,000 |
| Homeowner's equity. . . . . | 55,000 |

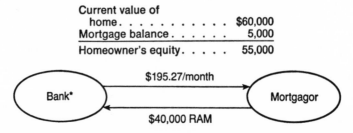

The mortgagor will owe a total of $40,000 to the bank after 10 years.

Cash flows associated with mortgage and RAM:

| | | |
|---|---|---|
| Before RAM: | −133.06 | (outflow = monthly mortgage payment) |
| For 3½ years after RAM: | +62.21 | (net inflow) |
| For remaining 6½ years of RAM: | +195.77 | (RAM monthly payment received) |

---

*The "Bank" may or may not be the original mortgagee.

homeowner plus interest on the money lent so far; at the end of 10 years, the mortgage balance is precisely $40,000. Of course, monthly payments on the original mortgage must still be made until it matures. (Often there is no outstanding mortgage when the RAM is originated, so this proviso would not apply.)

From the bank's point of view, the RAM is a continuous series of loans to a homeowner against which the house serves as collateral. Assuming the property keeps the same value, the LTV ratio is continually increasing because the mortgage balance is continually rising. Banks would probably not allow the LTV to get as high as they would for traditional mortgages (i.e., the RAM could not be made for a very high amount relative to the equity) because of the uncertainty of the property value at the end of the RAM's term; as far as the bank is concerned, the property could decline in value and/or deteriorate in condition and marketability.

### Shared-appreciation mortgages (SAMs)

The SAM loan is another innovation of the early 1980s brought about by high interest rates, and it uses inflation as a way of paying for part of the property. The basic terms are fairly simple. The mortgage lender agrees to provide funds at a greatly reduced rate of interest. In return, the borrower agrees to share part of the increase in the property value with the lender when the loan matures, when the property is sold, or at some other specified time.

At the inception of the SAM program, a one-third participation was popular—the lender would reduce the interest rate by a third (e.g., in a period of 15 percent interest rates the home buyer would obtain a loan at 10 percent) in return for one third of the appreciation in the property value. Over time, the formulas behind SAMs have varied somewhat from the one-third mix. In periods such as 1981, when interest rates were rising in concert with inflation falling, SAM lenders needed to compensate for the imbalance by lowering the percentage reduction in the interest rate, raising the percentage of property appreciation to be shared, or some combination of both.

Exhibit 12 shows the consequences of a SAM loan, assuming the home buyer remains in the home for five years. If the actual percentage increase in the property value (the inflation rate) is close to the prevailing level of interest rates, the cumulative savings over the first five years for the home buyer are roughly the same as the value surrendered at the end of the period. (This example assumes the one-third-type SAM and expresses all costs and benefits in comparable terms.) If inflation turns out to be lower, the homeowner wins in the long run because there is less appreciation in value to surrender; if actual inflation is

---

**EXHIBIT 12**     Traditional loan versus shared-appreciation mortgage (SAM)

---

- Traditional loan: $50,000 for 30 years @ 15 percent.
- One-third SAM: $50,000 for 30 years @ 10 percent one third of appreciation due on sale.

Assume: Inflation rate = 12 percent (1 percent per month).
Homeowner sells after five years.
Original down payment = $10,000.

|  | Traditional loan | SAM | SAM benefit |
|---|---|---|---|
| A. Monthly payment . . . . . . . . . . . | ($632.22) | ($438.79) | $193.43 |
| B. Total value of payments for five years (assuming 15 percent time value) . . . . . . . . . . | (55,998.58) | (38,865.61) | 17,132.97 |
| C. Value of house today . . . . . . . . . | 60,000.00 | 60,000.00 | — |
| D. Value of house in five years . . . . . . | 109,001.80 | 109,001.80 | — |
| E. Mortgage balance in five years . . . . | (49,360.31) | (48,287.16) | 1,073.15 |
| F. One third of appreciation due to bank on SAM . . . . . . . . . . | — | (16,333.93) | (16,333.93) |
| G. Net benefit of SAM in five years (B + E − F) . . . . . . . . | | | 1,872.19 |

---

greater, the homeowner loses. Of course, the homeowner will never have a problem coming up with the funds to pay the lender if the property is sold, because they can be taken from the proceeds of the sale. In the event that the SAM matures or whenever the lender must be repaid without the property being sold, it may be necessary for the homeowner to obtain new financing on the property to get the required funds.

The attractions of the SAM loan are great to both borrower and lender—the borrower is able to purchase the otherwise unaffordable home, and the lender has the potentially lucrative equity kicker, depending on the rate of inflation. Two factors, though have prevented SAMs from becoming more popular than they already are. First, although the SAM is simple in concept, the fine print can be onerous. The complications created by property additions or home improvements, for example, can cloud the issue of which portion of the overall increase in property value is really due to inflation and shareable with the lender. Second, SAMs are difficult to package into units and sell as securities, bcause there is such a broad range of formulas and other parameters being used to create them. It is difficult to have mass production of an item for which there is no standardization of parts. Access to the securities markets, which is vital as a liquidity source for mortgage originators, is effectively denied without a fungible product.

# SEVENTEEN

---

## Adjustable-rate mortgages

**Joseph C. Hu, Ph.D.**
*Vice President*
*Salomon Brothers Inc*

---

Recently, originations of adjustable-rate mortgages (ARMs) have flourished, exceeding those of long-term fixed-rate mortgages (FRMs). This surge in originations has resulted from aggressive marketing, mainly on the part of thrift lenders (savings and loan associations and mutual savings banks), and a confusing array of ARMs is now being offered to prospective home buyers. Because of the low initial rates of ARMs, many prospective home buyers are opting for these mortgages over FRMs, including some who would not have been qualified for FRMs. This article summarizes the complex features of ARMs.

### VARIETY OF FEATURES

The periodic adjustment of interest rates on ARMs creates uncertainty in the stream of their monthly payments. To make ARM financing more attractive, lenders have added various features to reduce this uncertainty. Different combinations of these features have created a wide variety of ARMs in the marketplace. These features are described below.

### Term of adjustment

One of the most important features of an ARM is the frequency of its interest rate adjustment. According to surveys done by the Federal Home Loan Mortgage Corporation and the Federal Home Loan Bank of San Francisco, the most popular term of adjustment is one year. Other terms are usually one month, six months, three years, and five years.

### Index of adjustment

An index of adjustment is an interest rate series whose maturity usually coincides with the term of adjustment. For one-year ARMs, the index has most frequently been the yield on one-year constant-maturity Treasuries. However, it is not necessary that the term of adjustment match the maturity of the index. The Federal Home Loan Bank Board's (FHLBB) national average mortgage contract rate on the purchase of previously occupied homes, which does not have any definite maturity, has also been used as an index for one-year ARMs. Exhibit 1 shows the interest rate series most often used as indexes: six-month Treasury bill rates (bond-equivalent yield), one-, three-, and five-

**EXHIBIT 1**  Historical yields on six-month Treasury bills, one-, three-, and five-year constant-maturity Treasuries and average mortgage contract rate on the purchase of previously occupied homes, 1974–1983

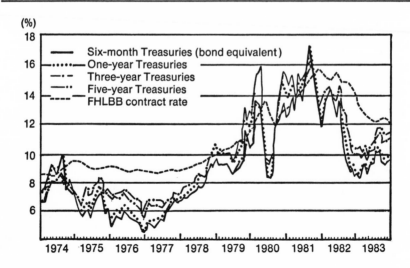

year Treasuries and the FHLBB's national average mortgage contract rate. The FHLBB's average contract rate covers all newly originated mortgages—ARMs as well as FRMs; consequently, as ARM originations expand, the index is becoming heavily weighted by the initial rates on ARMs.

### Initial rate

The initial rate is the rate at which the monthly payment for the borrower is established during the initial period before the first adjustment. Among all the features of ARMs, the initial rate is probably the most important one for the borrower. It enables some borrowers who would not have been qualified for FRMs to purchase homes. In the current pricing of ARMs, discounts or buydowns have often been provided to qualify borrowers. As a result, the initial rate can be lower than risk-free short-term Treasury yields.

### Margin

The margin is used to determine the new rate on the mortgage at the adjustment dates. For some ARMs, the new rate is established by adding the margin to the interest rate of the index at the time of adjustment. For others, the margin is added to the index only to establish the initial rate; subsequent new rates are then determined by simply adding the change in the index to the initial rate with no further reference to the margin.

### Fees

Lenders charge fees that are a certain percentage of the loan amount (or points) for originating ARMs. Fees for nondiscounted ARMs are slightly lower than those for FRMs currently being offered.

### Caps

Many lenders impose caps on the adjustment of either the interest rates or payments of ARMs to reduce the uncertainty in their payment stream. The caps can be applied to each adjustment period or to the total adjustments for the life of the mortgage, or both. For instance, an interest rate cap of one or two percentage points can be applied to each interest rate adjustment, or a 7.5 percent annual payment cap can be applied to each payment adjustment. Some ARMs are also subject to a total interest rate adjustment of, for example, five percentage points. Thus, the maximum possible interest rate on the mortgage for some ARMs is the initial rate plus the lifetime cap. For other ARMs (mostly with discounted initial rates), however, the maximum interest rate is the mortgage rate at the first adjustment plus the lifetime cap.

### Negative amortization

For some ARMs with payment caps or for which the payment is held constant for a longer time than the interest rate adjustment period, negative amortization could occur. In other words, if the monthly payment is held constant so that it becomes insufficient to amortize the loan at the newly established interest rate, the loan balance will not only cease to decline but will begin to increase. In effect, this is equivalent to the lender making additional loans to the borrower. As a result, the loan-to-value ratio is likely to increase as the outstanding loan balance increases during the period of negative amortization. Like FRMs, the ratio of the loan amount to the house price determines the bulk of the underwriting risk of the loan. Historical evidence indicates that, all other things equal, the higher the loan-to-value ratio, the higher the potential risk of the loan and vice versa.

### EXAMPLES OF PAYMENT STREAMS

Given the wide variety of ARMs, the stream of monthly payments can be vastly different on two mortgages even if they have the same initial rate. The following example, which is illustrated in Exhibit 2, shows the streams of monthly payments for the first 10 years for five 1-year ARMs, each with an original loan balance of $50,000. All five start with an initial rate of 7 percent with no discounts, but they differ in the following respects: (1) the selection of an index, (2) the limitations placed on the interest rate or payment adjustment, and (3) the possibility of negative amortization. The new interest rate for each adjustment is assumed to be the level of interest rate on the index plus a margin of 150 basis points. We assume that the five ARMs were originated with the same fees in the beginning of 1974.

**EXHIBIT 2**     Monthly payment streams of five hypothetical one-year ARMs, 1974–1983

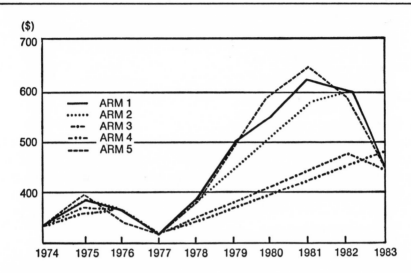

### ARM1

The interest rate and monthly payment are adjusted annually, based on one-year Treasury yields, with no caps of any kind and no possible negative amortization.

### ARM2

The interest rate and monthly payment are adjusted annually, based on one-year Treasuries with an interest rate cap of two percentage points per adjustment period but no possible negative amortization. There is no cumulative feature for the interest rate cap; that is, any movement in the index in excess of the two-percentage-point interest rate adjustment cannot be retained and applied to future interest rate adjustments.

### ARM3

This loan has the same features as ARM2, except that the interest rate cap is limited to one percentage point per adjustment.

### ARM4

The interest rate and payment are adjusted annually based on one-year Treasuries with a payment cap of 7.5 percent per adjustment period. Any necessary payment adjustment in excess of the 7.5 percent limit will be added to the loan balance, or, in other words, negatively amortized. The total negative amortization, however, can not exceed 25 percent of the original loan balance. When the 25 percent limit is reached, the 7.5 percent cap will no longer be in effect.

## ARM5

The interest rate is adjusted every six months, based on the six-month Treasury bill bond equivalent rate. The payment, however, is adjusted annually with no caps. Negative amortization is possible in the second six-month period when the adjusted interest rate exceeds the rate for the first six-month period.

Several observations can be made from Exhibit 2, which charts the monthly payment streams of the five ARMs, and Exhibit 3, which illustrates the unpaid principal balances.

---

**EXHIBIT 3**    Unpaid principal balance of five hypothetical one-year ARMs, 1974–1983

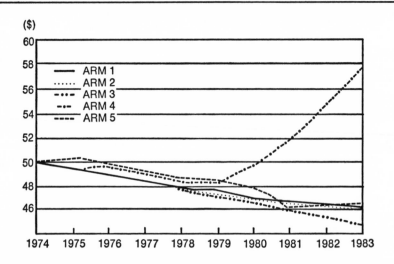

First, the payment stream of ARM1, whose rate floats freely according to the index, fluctuates almost as widely as that of ARM5, which is indexed by the more volatile six-month Treasury bill rate. Unlike ARM5, however, ARM1's unpaid principal balance declines steadily without any irregular increases caused by negative amortization.

Second, when the initial rate is at 7 percent, a one-percentage-point cap (ARM3) is much less restrictive than a 7.5 percent payment cap (ARM4), let alone a two-percentage-point cap (ARM2). In fact, unless the initial rate increases to 12 percent, a one-percentage-point cap will always be less restrictive than a 7.5 percent payment cap. As a result, in a rising interest rate environment, the payment streams of ARM2 and ARM3 are likely to accelerate much faster than that of ARM4, which resembles a graduated-payment mortgage.

Third, ARM5, which is indexed by the six-month Treasury bill rate, has the widest monthly payment fluctuation despite its one-year constant payment and negative amortization.

And last, mortgages with a combination of payment caps and negative amortization (ARM4 and ARM5) are likely to have higher year-end unpaid principal balances than those with interest rate caps. Moreover, ARMs with more restrictive interest rate caps are likely to have lower unpaid principal balances, because principal paydown is slightly faster at lower mortgage rates.

# EIGHTEEN

## Mortgage pass-through securities

**Kenneth H. Sullivan**
*Managing Director*
*Mortgage Research and Product Development*
*Drexel Burnham Lambert, Inc.*

**Bruce M. Collins**
*Analyst*
*Mortgage Research and Product Development*
*Drexel Burnham Lambert, Inc.*

**David A. Smilow**
*Analyst*
*Mortgage Research and Product Development*
*Drexel Burnham Lambert, Inc.*

The largest class of mortgage-related securities is the mortgage pass-through certificate. While pass-throughs existed as a legal investment form for decades, they first made sense on a broad scale when several federally supported entities assumed the role of providing credit support and standards of uniformity, which together made the pools of mortgages underlying the pass-throughs more readily marketable. The standardization of mortgage characteristics within pools made the resulting securities easier to analyze, thereby making them more suitable for nontraditional mortgage investors, while the credit support alleviated investor concerns about timely and ultimate collection of amounts due.

Because there are many types of mortgages (e.g., conventional 30-year fixed-rate mortgages, graduated payment mortgages, and 15-year mortgages, among others) a large number of pass-through types have been created. In the following section the principal types traded today are described and compared.

This article is designed to serve as a general introduction to mortgage pass-through securities. We present an overview of the structure of these securities by analyzing the factors that affect price, yield, and average life. In the final section, we compare them with other fixed-income instruments such as Treasury and corporate securities.

## TERMS AND FEATURES OF THE DIFFERENT TYPES OF MORTGAGE PASS-THROUGHS

Pass-through securities are formed when mortgages are pooled together and undivided[1] interests in the pool are sold. The sale of a pass-through security represents a sale of assets and is not a debt obligation of the originator.[2] The cash flow from the underlying mortgages is "passed through" to the holders of the securities in the form of monthly payments of interest, principal, and prepayments. Prepayments occur when the holder of an individual mortgage prepays the remaining principal before the final scheduled payment month. Critical to the pricing of pass-throughs are the specific features of that particular pass-through security. In this section, we describe in detail the similarities and differences of various pass-throughs.

Mortgage originators (savings and loans, commercial banks, mortgage companies) are among the most active in pooling mortgages and issuing mortgage-backed securities.[3] The originator can either issue a private pass-through security or file the necessary documents with a guarantor to issue a pass-through security backed by the guarantor. A GNMA (Government National Mortgage Association) security is an example of the latter

---

[1] Undivided means that each security holder has a proportionate interest in each cash flow generated in the pool.

[2] The reason is that the obligation continues to be that of the borrowers collectively, not the originator through whom the loans were made. Payments on the mortgages never become obligations of an originator unless some kind of explicit "first-loss" arrangement is formalized.

[3] Pass-throughs are often an attractive alternative to S&Ls in situations where the loans in a pool would trade below par because of their low coupons. By establishing a pass-through security, an S&L can more readily replenish its funds through reverse repurchase agreements. Also, in situations where an S&L wishes to sell assets, the backing of one of the federal agencies and liquidity of the trading markets for pass-throughs can often result in the realization of a higher price for the assets sold.

case. GNMA (commonly called Ginnie Mae) guarantees to the investor the timely payment of interest and principal.

A summary of the terms and features of different types of mortgage pass-throughs is found in Exhibit 1. There are four basic types of mortgage pass-through securities—GNMA pass-throughs, FHLMC participation certificates, FNMA mortgage-backed securities, and private pass-throughs. While all have similar underlying structures, there are several differences among the four types of pass-throughs.

### Government National Mortgage Association pass-through securities

The first group of securities is guaranteed by the Government National Mortgage Association. The mortgage pools underlying GNMA pass-through securities are made up of FHA-insured or VA-guaranteed mortgage loans. GNMA pass-throughs are backed by the full faith and credit of the United States government. GNMA is a wholly owned U.S. government corporation within the Department of Housing and Urban Development (HUD) and has the authority to fully guarantee the timely payment of principal and interest on its securities. The pass-through securities guaranteed by GNMA differ according to the nature of the mortgages that comprise the underlying pool.

The GNMA pass-through security is a fully modified pass-through security, which means that, regardless of whether the mortgage payment is received, the holder of the security will receive full and timely payment of principal and interest. The original GNMA pass-through is the most common and liquid pass-through security. It constitutes 80 percent of those outstanding in the market. The GNMA II is the most recent GNMA security. While providing the same guarantees as all GNMA certificates, GNMA II has some differences from GNMA I. First, GNMA IIs are based on multiple-issuer pools,[4] while the original GNMAs are based on single-issuer pools. In addition, the mortgage coupon requirements have been relaxed (a wider range of coupons is permitted in a pool), and there is an additional delay of five days in passing through principal and interest payments because of centralization of the payment facility.

---

[4] Multiple-issuer pools can be arranged by GNMA to accommodate many smaller issuers who may not individually generate the minimum volume of $1 million required to participate in GNMA I.

**EXHIBIT 1**   Features of selected mortgage pass-through securities

| | GNMA | | | | | | FHLMC PCs | FNMA MBS |
|---|---|---|---|---|---|---|---|---|
| | GNMA I | GNMA II | GNMA Midgets | GNMA GPM | Mobile Homes | FHA Projects | | |
| Type of mortgages | Level payment FHA/VA | Level payment FHA/VA | Level payment FHA/VA | Graduated payment loans (mostly 7.5%) | Level payment FHA/VA | FHA project FHA/VA | 95% single family (conventional) | Level payment single family |
| | New originations | New originations | New originations | New originations | New originations | New originations | New or seasoned conventional loans | New or seasoned conventional loans |
| Term | 90% must be 20 yrs. + | 90% must be 20 yrs. + | 15 years | 30-year original term | 4 types ranging from 12–20 yrs. | Most are 40 years | 97½% level payment, mostly 30 years (also, a relatively new 15-year term) | 30-yr. original term 20-yr. original term (also, a relatively new 15-year term) |
| Minimum original purchase price | $25,000 ($5,000 increments) | $25,000 ($5,000 increments) | $25,000 ($5,000 increments) | $25,000 ($5,000 increments) | $25,000 ($5,000 increments) | $25,000 ($5,000 increments) | $25,000 ($25,000 increments) | $25,000 ($5,000 increments) |

| Minimum pool size | $1 million, 12 loans | $7 million | $1 million | $1 million | $.5 million | $.5 million, 1 loan | $100 million (except Guarantors Program—$5 million) National | $1 million National |
|---|---|---|---|---|---|---|---|---|
| Geographic characteristics | Highly regional | May be regional or national | Highly regional | Highly regional | Highly regional | Highly regional | National | National |
| Mortgage coupons allowed (Max. Servicing and Guarantee Fee) | 0.5% over P-T rate | 0.5% to 1.5% over P-T rate | 0.5% over P-T rate | 0.5% over P-T rate | 3.25% over P-T rate (approx.) | 0.25% over P-T rate | 0.5% to 2.5% over P-T rate | 0.5% to 2.5% over P-T rate |
| Approximate number of pools outstanding | 73,000 | 3,300 | 1,925 | 8,600 | 5,100 | 600 | 12,450 | 8,150 |
| Approximate dollar amount outstanding (billions) | 151.0[a] | 8.7[b] | 3.4 | 14.3 | 3.3[c] | 3.0 | 75.3[d] | 33.6[e] |
| Range of coupons in the market | 5.25% to 17.000% | 8.00% to 14.50% | 7.25% to 13.50% | 9.00% to 17.50% | 6.00% to 16.75% | 8.00% to 14.25% | 4.25% to 16.50% | 4.00% to 17.00% |
| Stated delay | 45 | 50 | 45 | 50 | 45 | 45 | 75 | 54 |
| Actual penalty (days) | 15 | 20 | 15 | 20 | 15 | 15 | 45 | 24 |

[a] Includes $1.7 billion of buydown pools.
[b] Includes $1.1 billion of GPMs, $661 million of 15-year GNMA-IIs, $25 million of Adjustable GNMA-IIs, and $17 million of Mobile Homes.
[c] Includes $17 million of GNMA II Mobil Home pools.
[d] Includes both Regular and Swap/Guarantor PCs, $1.5 billion of 15-year Midgets, $790 million of FHA/VAs, and $385 million of Multi-Family PCs.
[e] Includes $3.0 billion of FHA/VAs, $395 million of Intermediate-Term, and $570 million of Long-Term Assumables.

The four additional GNMA securities summarized in Exhibit 1 include the GNMA Midget, GNMA GPM, Mobile Homes, and Projects. The GNMA Midget is an intermediate-term (15 years) security with an assumed average life of 7 years for purposes of quoting yields, it is similar in structure to the original 3-year GNMA security. The maturity of the underlying mortgages is the primary difference. Because of the maturity difference, which translates into a much shorter average life, the Midget will normally trade at a premium price to a regular GNMA with an equal coupon.

Another security backed by GNMA is the GNMA GPM.[5] The GNMA GPM pass-through security is based on graduated payment mortgages. This market is smaller and less liquid than fixed-rate single-family GNMAs. In addition, the cash flows are more complex, and amortization is initially negative. These features have translated into higher yields for the GNMA GPM. It should be noted that the GPM becomes the equivalent of a fixed-rate, fully amortizing, level-payment mortgage after five years. The demographics of the borrowers, however, may be materially different.

The major distinguishing features for GNMA Mobile Home (MH) pass-through securities from the other GNMA pass-through securities lies in the servicing fee. The servicing fee is the difference between the mortgage interest rate and the pass-through coupon rate. The higher servicing fee is the result of several factors. The first is that the "natural" rate for mobile home mortgages is higher than the current production rate for conventional loans. The second factor is that the payments are more difficult to collect from the borrowers, and policing the borrowers can be more costly. Finally, it is important to note that, despite the higher underlying coupons on the mortgages, the GNMA MH pass-through does not show a consistent record of higher prepayment rates than conventional pass-throughs. This, once again, highlights the importance of understanding all of the applicable demographic variables.

The GNMA FHA Projects security is based on longer-term (40 years) multifamily project mortgage loans. Pricing is based

---

[5] As explained in the previous article, graduated payment mortgages (GPM) differ from conventional mortgages because all payments are not level. Payments start out low and rise for a number of years. GPMs are designed to make housing affordable for first-time home buyers. Because of the low payments in the initial years, GPMs do not pay down as quickly as traditional mortgages. In fact, the smaller payments in the beginning will cause the mortgage balance to increase. This is known as *negative amortization.*

on an average life assumption of 18 years. An additional feature of these securities is that most of the mortgages in the project pools currently outstanding are "putable"[6] back to HUD 20 years from the date of insurance endorsement. Thus, the mortgage loans have what may be interpreted as a minimum return. GNMA projects have historically traded 10 to 40 basis points above the original GNMA yields. Today, however, the put option is no longer available. This should have the effect of increasing the yield differential.

### Federal Home Loan Mortgage Corporation participation certificate

Another type of pass-through is the Federal Home Loan Mortgage Corporation (FHLMC) participation certificate, or PC. This is commonly known as the "Freddie Mac" PC. The FHLMC is the second-largest issuer of pass-through securities. Its PC is based on conventional mortgages (i.e., single-family residential mortages that are *not* guaranteed by VA or insured by FHA). Some of the features that characterize PCs are (1) prepayments are often more consistent than those of GNMAs because the underlying mortgage pools are often larger; (2) the PC is also a relatively liquid market, although not as liquid as GNMAs; and (3) FHLMC securities have for most of their history traded at higher yields than GNMAs in the secondary markets. PCs can be purchased in the capital markets and can serve as collateral for other activities (e.g., repurchase agreements). Furthermore, FHLMC guarantees the timely payment of interest and ultimate payment of principal on all conventional mortgages that make up the pool.

Whereas GNMA and FNMA (discussed next) guarantee the timely payment of interest and principal, FHLMC guarantees only the timely payment of interest and ultimate payment of principal. This means that FHLMC passes through whatever principal it collects and guarantees payment of the remainder within a year.

The guarantee depends on the ability of FHLMC to satisfy the obligation. Most market participants perceive the credit worthiness of FHLMC PCs as similar, but not identical, to that of GNMAs despite the fact that GNMAs are backed by the full-

---

[6] A putable security is one in which the holder is granted the option to sell the security back to the issuer at a predetermined price.

faith and credit of the U.S. government while FHLMC PCs are not. The higher yield on FHLMC PCs reflects this slight difference in quality.

### Federal National Mortgage Association mortgage-backed security

A third type of pass-through security is Federal National Mortgage Association Mortgage Backed Security (FNMA MBS). FNMA, commonly known as "Fannie Mae," is the newest player in the pass-through security market. It offers a pass-through security similar to the FHLMC PC. FNMA guarantees the timely payment of principal and interest for all securities it issues. This means that there will be no delay in the receipt of either interest or principal. Although FNMA MBSs are not backed by the full-faith and credit of the U.S. government, as are GNMAs, it is felt that the U.S. government will not permit FNMA to default. The yields on FNMAs are comparable to that of FHLMC PCs and slightly higher than those of GNMAs. The liquidity of FNMA MBSs is comparable to that of FHLMC PCs.

More recent programs initiated by FNMA include a FHA/VA swap program, an intermediate-term (15-year) pass-through program, and an adjustable rate mortgage pass-through program.

### Private pass-through securities

The fourth type of pass-through security is a private pass-through. Because of the low volume of private pass-throughs, they have not been included in Exhibit 1. Approximately $3.3 billion of private pass-throughs have been issued through year-end 1983 by nine different issuers. Private pass-throughs can be issued without guarantees by independent companies, such as commercial banks. This differs from government-related institutions, such as GNMA and FHLMC.

## MORTGAGE AND MORTGAGE PASS-THROUGH CASH FLOWS

Before one can compare pass-throughs with other fixed-income instruments, one must master the details of how the payments work. The analysis of a pass-through security begins with an examination of the cash flow pattern of the mortgages underlying the pass-through, assuming there are no prepayments. This is the simplest case to analyze. In subsequent examples, the effects of servicing fees (an amount retained by a servicer out of the mortgage cash flow, which therefore reduces the cash flow to pass-through holders) and simulated prepayments are incorporated into the analysis. The mortgage pool generally used in the following examples to illustrate points is a $1 million pool of 11 percent mortgages with 30-year maturities. The corresponding pass-through certificate has a 10.5 percent pass-through rate and a .5 percent servicing fee typical of a GNMA pass-through. The servicing fee is retained by the originator of the loans, both to compensate for the cost of collecting the payments and to ensure that the originator has a continuing interest in monitoring the status of the loans.

As explained in the previous article, traditional mortgages are fixed-rate loans, which are repaid in equal monthly installments of principal and interest. In the early stages of repayment, most of the monthly installment consists of interest. Over time, the interest portion of each payment declines as the principal balance declines until, near maturity, almost all of each payment is principal.

Given the assumption that mortgages are homogeneous, the cash flow patterns from a mortgage pool are consistent with individual mortgages. Exhibit 2(A) shows scheduled cash flow patterns for a $1 million pool of 11 percent, 30-year mortgages under the assumption of no prepayments. Because there is a fixed rate of interest on the loan and no prepayments, the mortgage cash flow is level over all periods.

The cash flow patterns of pass-through certificates are related to, but not identical to, the cash flow from the underlying pool of mortgages. The differences are the deduction of servicing fees and a delay in the receipt of payments. While the minimum monthly cash flow from the mortgage pool is level, the corresponding pass-through cash flow is not. The servicing fee is a percentage of the outstanding principal and, thus, the dollar amount (of servicing fees) is reduced as principal declines. As a consequence, the minimum cash flows for pass-through certificates increase slightly over the term. The cash flow from a pass-through certificate with a 10.5 percent coupon (the difference between the 11 percent and the .5 percent servicing fee) is presented in Exhibit 2(B), which shows that the decline in servicing fees leads to slightly increasing cash flow.

**EXHIBIT 2**     Scheduled cash flow patterns for a $1 million pool of 11 percent, 30-year mortgage and a 10.5 percent pass-through certificate

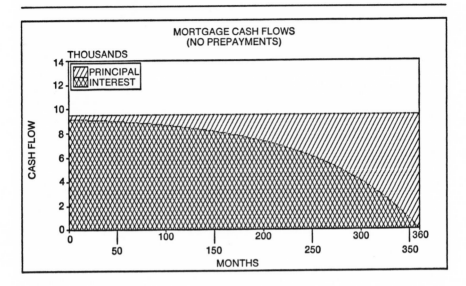

(A)

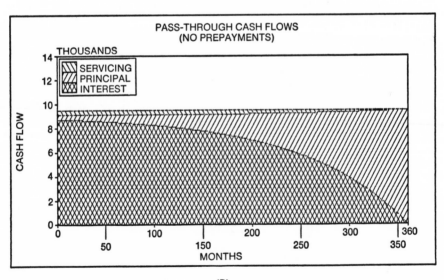

(B)

Analysis of the cash flow of both mortgages and pass-through certificates would be straightforward in the absence of prepayments. Since the possibility of prepayments introduces an additional and unpredictable component to cash flow patterns, assumptions must be made concerning the likely prepayment pattern.

Exhibit 3(A) depicts the cash flow patterns for the mortgage pool when prepayments are introduced. Specifically, the cash flow pattern shown in the diagram is based on the assumption of a 12-year prepaid life, which is the "industry standard" for quoting mortgage yields. Under this convention, the first 12 years of the mortgage pool are characterized by cash flows that consist of amortized principal and interest on each of the mortgages in the pool. At the end of the 12th year, the remaining principal balance is assumed to be paid in full. Mortgage-yield calculations are made on the assumption of a single prepayment "event," much like the maturity of a bond, which takes place at the end of the 12th year.

The 12-year life assumption was derived from and serves as an approximation for the mortgage termination data compiled by the Federal Housing Administration, beginning with 1957 originations. The FHA's analysis of mortgages indicated that mortgages were prepaid on average in the 12th year. Since the mean (or average) life to prepayment was 12 years, mortgage cash flows have traditionally been evaluated on this basis. The 12-year life assumption was adopted by the pass-through certificate market as well. Mortgage yield is, by definition, the calculated yield based on a 12-year life assumption. GNMA quotes, for example, refer to mortgage yield and not cash flow yield, which is dealt with in detail below. Exhibit 3(B) shows the cash flow patterns for a pass-through certificate based on a 12-year life assumption.

The mortgage yield convention was not unrealistic prior to the 1970s. The 1970s, however, brought dramatic increases in the level and volatility of interest rates—as well as demographic changes. Higher and more volatile interest rates altered the prepayment process and led to substantial increases in prepayments in the first 12 years. After a period of high interest rates, such as the most recent experience, any reduction in rates will speed up prepayments of mortgages originated near peaks, because of the benefits of refinancing at a lower rate. Although the application of the 12-year life assumption may have been

**EXHIBIT 3**   Scheduled cash flow patterns for a $1 million pool of 11 percent, 30-year mortgage and a 10.5 percent pass-through certificate assuming a 12-year prepaid life

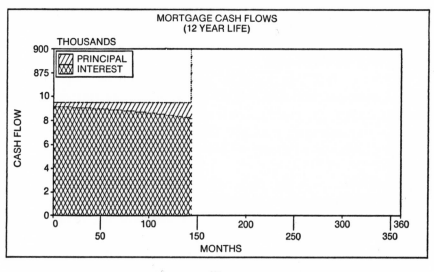

(A)

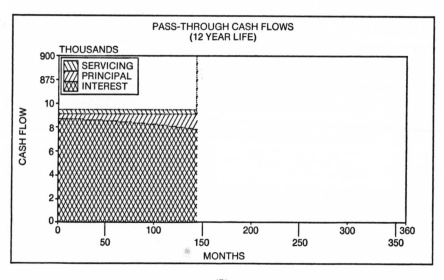

(B)

appropriate for the past periods of stable interest rates with few refinancing opportunities, this is not the case today because the volatility of interest rates is likely to produce highly volatile prepayment rates. For a mortgage pool, prepayment is not a single event, as is the case for an individual mortgage; the prepayments are spread out over time. The shortcoming of the conventional mortgage calculations is that it invariably imposes the same prepayment assumptions, regardless of the age and coupon of the mortgage or the interest rate environment. For example, the conventional mortgage calculation would prescribe the use of a 12-year prepaid life to both of the following GNMAs: a GNMA originated in 1974 with a 7 percent coupon and a GNMA originated in 1981 with a 16 percent coupon. In the first case, the effect of seasoning—the 10 years that have passed since origination—is that the remaining average life is likely to be substantially less than 12 years. In the latter case, the high prepayment rate one could expect, based on current experience, indicates that the "correct" life assumption may be as low as five years. The conventional calculation does not allow the analyst to determine a yield based on a probable economic life of the pass-through.

Changes in prepayment rates are fundamentally important for pass-throughs, as they are for mortgage pools, because of their effect on the yield and pricing of these instruments. Accelerating prepayments have an adverse impact on yields for pass-throughs purchased at a premium. The opposite is true for discounts. In the GNMA pass-through market, for example, it is known that high-coupon GNMA securities have a faster paydown (prepayment) rate than low-coupon GNMAs; therefore, it is highly misleading to compare high- and low-coupon GNMA yields if both are calculated on a 12-year life.

In summary, the fundamental problem of applying mortgage yields to pass-through certificates is that the cash flow pattern implied by the 12-year life does not conform to the prepayment pattern expected by the marketplace.[7]

---

[7] There are several alternative methods of addressing the problems associated with the 12-year life assumption. Such measures as a constant prepayment assumption are attempts to deal with the inherent problem of predicting future prepayment rates. Meanwhile, attempts to improve the method of modeling prepayments is to define a more realistic cash flow pattern than the single prepayment assumption and, thereby, generate more meaningful calculations of the rates of return. A yield calculation based on modeled prepayments is called a *cash flow yield*. For a further discussion, see Frank J. Fabozzi, ed., *The Handbook of Mortgage-Backed Securities* (Chicago: Probus Publishing, 1985).

## COMPARISON OF FEATURES OF MORTGAGE
## PASS-THROUGHS WITH TREASURIES
## AND CORPORATES

Mortgage-backed securities have certain features that distinguish them from Treasury or corporate fixed-income securities. The differences are described in Exhibit 4.

There are two basic differences between Treasury or corporates and between mortgage-backed securities. The most significant difference—and what makes the mortgage-backed security unique—is prepayments. The prepayment patterns inherent in mortgage-backed securities create uncertainties for maturity and yield that are not present in Treasuries and that are limited in corporates. The range of average lives available for pass-throughs, for instance, is limited by the ability to select pools with expectations of higher or lower prepayments. The average life must be estimated for mortgage-backed securities, while it is quite predictable for Treasuries and corporates.

The second principal difference is the frequency of payments. Pass-through securities pay monthly, while Treasuries and corporates pay semiannually. This has present-value implications for mortgage-backed securities. Several other factors must be incorporated into an analysis of pass-throughs as fixed-income investments. The most important are discussed in the following sections.

Throughout this section we use average life, as opposed to duration, half life, or other measures of term to compare securities and measure effects of changes in other variables.[8] Duration has gained broad acceptance since it is more easily used to describe the sensitivity of prices to changes in yields; however, it is more difficult to use when comparing mortgage-backed instruments to Treasuries. Treasuries, which are generally bullets (i.e., securities that repay the entire principal at maturity), have maturities and average lives that are equal; thus, no special calculations are required to derive the average life.

---

[8] Average life is the weighted average time to principal repayment. It is useful as an approximation of a single maturity where the mean or average maturity is used to describe the life of the instrument. Duration is calculated by taking a weighted average of the time periods to receipt of the present value of the cash flows from an investment. (The computation of a bond's duration is illustrated in the appendix to Article Nine.) Half life is the period until half of the original principal amount of the pool is repaid.

**EXHIBIT 4**    A comparison of the features of pass-throughs with those of treasuries and corporates

| Feature | Mortgage pass-through securities | Treasuries | Corporates | Stripped Treasuries |
|---|---|---|---|---|
| Range of coupons (premium and discount securities) | Full range. | Full range. | Full range for a few issuers. | Zero coupon; all are discount securities. |
| Maturities available | Limited to ability to select fast-paying pools or seasoned (short maturity) pools. | Full range. | Full range. | Full range. |
| Average life | Must be estimated; securities can be prepaid. | Very predictable; most are noncallable. | Minimum average life is predictable and a prepayment penalty helps if called. | Predictable. |
| Call protection/prepayments | Complex prepayment pattern; coupon selection can help limit the negative effects of prepayments. | Noncallable (except for certain 30-year bonds). | Usually callable after an initial period of 5 to 10 years. | Noncallable. |
| Frequency of payments | Monthly payments of interest and a portion of principal. | Semiannual interest payments. | Semiannual (except for Eurobonds which pay annual interest payments). | None until maturity. |
| Credit risk spectrum | Generally high grade; range from government-guaranteed to A (private pass-throughs). | All are government-guaranteed. | High-grade to speculative. | All are backed by government guarantees. |
| Liquidity/trading market | Good for many pass-throughs, particularly GNMA, FHLMC, FNMA. | Excellent. | Limited in most cases. | Fair. |
| Basis for quoting yields | Mortgage yield: monthly payments and a 12-year life (7-year life in certain cases). | Semiannual bond equivalent based on a 365-day year. | Semiannual bond equivalent based on a 360-day year of 12 30-day months. | Semiannual bond equivalent based on either a 360-day or 365-day year depending on the sponsor. |

## Payment delay

The first issue to examine is the fact that there is an initial payment delay with mortgage pass-through securities. The first mortgage payment is not due from the homeowner until the beginning of the second month after origination. The holder of the corresponding pass-through does not receive his or her first payment, however, until some time into the second month.

An investor in a GNMA single-family pass-through, for example, does not receive payment until the 15th day of the second month from origination. A GNMA trader will express this 15-day delay as a 45-day delay, indicating the time from origination to first payment. The FNMA security has a stated delay of 54 days. This means the first payment takes place on the 24th day of the second month. A FHLMC security has a 75-day delay.

For a given mortgage yield, as the delay in payments increases, the price of a pass-through declines. At a specific price, a greater delay will decrease the yield.

## Monthly payments

One feature that increases the value of a pass-through of a given coupon, compared to traditional corporate or government debt, is the monthly, rather than semiannual, payment frequency. This feature provides investors with reinvestment opportunities to compound interest monthly, which are not accorded investors in most corporate or government securities. This monthly compounding gives pass-through securities an advantage over other securities. The quoted mortgage yield, however, does not reflect the advantage.

To compare pass-through yields with yields on other securities it is necessary to adjust the mortgage yield upward to its corporate bond equivalent yield (CBE).[9] The CBE allows a standard of comparison for securities with different payment frequencies. In essence, the monthly coupons are treated as if they are collected and reinvested at the mortgage-yield rate until the end of each semiannual or other period. The accumulated amount is larger than the face amount of six monthly coupons.

---

[9] See Article Ten for more discussion on CBE.

**EXHIBIT 5**   Upward adjustment of mortgage yield due to monthly payments

| Mortgage yield (percent) | Semiannual bond equivalent* (percent) | Increase in yield (basis points) | Increase in yield (percent change) |
|---|---|---|---|
| 6.0% | 6.08% | +8 | +1.33% |
| 8.0 | 8.13 | +13 | +1.63 |
| 10.0 | 10.21 | +21 | +2.10 |
| 12.0 | 12.30 | +30 | +2.50 |
| 13.5 | 13.89 | +39 | +2.89 |
| 14.0 | 14.41 | +41 | +2.93 |
| 16.0 | 16.54 | +54 | +3.38 |
| 18.0 | 18.69 | +69 | +3.83 |

* The higher semiannual bond equivalent reflects monthly compounding of the mortgage yield at the mortgage-yield rate to an equivalent semiannual payment which includes reinvestment income.

Exhibit 5 shows the upward adjustment of the mortgage yield. The last column indicates the magnitude of the adjustment. The adjustment is absolutely essential for comparing relative performance of pass-through securities for anyone engaged in intermarket transactions.

A crucial assumption is made when the yield to maturity is used as a measure of how attractive an investment is. The yield to maturity, including both mortgage yield and corporate bond equivalent, assumes that the contractual periodic payments are reinvested at the yield rate. The reinvestment rate subsequently realized could vary considerably from the yield to maturity. Exhibit 6 shows the effect of various reinvestment rates on the yield realized on a security with monthly payment frequency.

When the reinvestment rate is below the quoted yield to maturity, the realized yield to maturity (also known as the *adjusted yield to maturity*) will be less than the corporate bond equivalent yield. The opposite is true when reinvestment rates exceed the quoted yield to maturity. The last column in Exhibit 6 shows how far the realized yield is likely to vary across a range of reinvestment rate assumptions that do not coincide with the mortgage yield. Careful assessment of mortgage yields

---

**EXHIBIT 6**   The effect of reinvestment rates on the realized increase in yield from monthly payment frequency (10.5 percent pass-through; 13.5 percent mortgage yield)

---

| Realized reinvestment rate (percent) | Semiannual bond equivalent[1] (percent) | Semiannual reinvestment rate of return[2] (percent) | Yield relative to semiannual bond equivalent (basis points) |
|---|---|---|---|
| 0% | 13.89% | 13.50% | −39 |
| 6 | 13.89 | 13.67 | −22 |
| 8 | 13.89 | 13.72 | −17 |
| 10 | 13.89 | 13.78 | −12 |
| 12 | 13.89 | 13.84 | −5 |
| 14 | 13.89 | 13.90 | +1 |
| 16 | 13.89 | 13.96 | +7 |

---

[1] Semiannual bond equivalent is not affected by the reinvestment rate, since its assumed reinvestment rate is the mortgage yield.
[2] Assumes monthly payments of interest and principal are compounded at the realized reinvestment rate to arrive at a semiannual equivalent payment.

---

requires consideration of the impact reinvestment rate assumptions have on realized return.

### Prepayment effects

The cash flow pattern of a pass-through security is strongly influenced by prepayments. When the prepayment rate is increased, this shortens average life and skews the cash flow to earlier years. This reduces the investment horizon and affects the realized yield.

If the pass-through security is trading at a premium (i.e., above par), an increase in prepayment rates will reduce the yield because the principal is being returned at par which is less than the initial price. It is beneficial for the investor to retain the high coupon interest for as long as possible. In general, for high-coupon (premium) pass-throughs, as prepayment rates rise, average life falls, which reduces rates of return and yield. When pass-through securities are purchased at a discount, increased prepayment rates serve to enhance the yield. This occurs because average life is shortened, which results in the early return of principal at par, which is more than the initial price.

## Seasoning

Seasoning refers to the time since origination or age of a mortgage or the mortgages in a pool. The average age of the mortgage pool is important because of the implications for average life and yield. Seasoning also affects the assumptions made about prepayment rates.

Consider, for example, a typical 12 percent GNMA pass-through security priced at 91 and expected to prepay at .01 percent per month. When the underlying mortgage pool consists of new originations, the security has an average life of 22.45 years and a cash flow yield of 12.23 percent. If, however, the underlying mortgages are seasoned 5 years (i.e., 5 years old) and we expect the prepayment rate to increase to .50 percent per month, then the average life falls to 10.72 years while the cash flow yield increases to 13.79 percent. The prepayment assumption is revised upward for the seasoned case, because we anticipate an increase in prepayment activity over the low levels associated with the first few years of a mortgage pool. Average life is lower and cash flow yield higher, because there are fewer years remaining in the term and principal is recovered more quickly.

## SUMMARY

Mortgage pass-through securities represent the largest class of a general category of securities that are mortgage-related. The cash flows of underlying mortgages are securitized and "passed through" to the investor in a pass-through security. The market for these securities has grown rapidly, due to the participation of three government agencies: GNMA, FHLMC, and FNMA. Today's market is characterized by pass-through security types backed by one of these agencies. The cash flow patterns of pass-throughs differentiate them from other securities, such as Treasuries or corporates. Payments are received monthly and there is an option for prepayment of principal. Monthly cash flows provide an opportunity for higher yields through reinvestment. The prepayment option creates uncertain cash flows and, thus, requires careful consideration when estimating performance of the security. These two features explain why, for example, pass-through securities historically have traded at a yield above comparable Treasuries.

# NINETEEN

## Financial futures and options

**Frank J. Fabozzi, Ph.D., C.F.A., C.P.A.**
*Walter E. Hanson/Peat, Marwick, Mitchell*
  *Professor of Business and Finance*
*Lafayette College*
*and*
*Managing Editor*
*The Journal of Portfolio Management*

With the advent of financial futures and options, active and offensive-minded risk management, in its broadest sense, assumes a new dimension. The money manager and the individual investor can achieve new degrees of freedom. It is now possible to alter the market risk profile of a portfolio economically and quickly. These derivative contracts, as they are commonly known because they derive their value from the underlying security, now offer money managers and individual investors risk and return patterns that were previously unavailable.

In this article, we will discuss these contracts and explain how they can be used in portfolio management. Whether the strategies that can be employed by using futures and options are permitted for a particular investment account may depend on client preference and applicable state statutory or regulatory provisions.

### FUTURES

A futures contract is a firm legal agreement between a buyer (seller) and an established exchange or its clearing house in which the buyer (seller) agrees to take (make) delivery of *something* at a specified price at the end of a designated time period. Prior to 1972, the *something* that the parties agreed to take or make delivery of was either traditional agricultural commodities (such as meat and livestock), imported foodstuffs (such as coffee, cocoa, and sugar), or industrial commodities. Collectively, such futures contracts are known as *commodity futures.*

Futures contracts based on a financial instrument or a financial index are known as *financial futures* and referred to by some as "pork bellies in pinstripes." It was not until 1972 that financial futures contracts were introduced. In that year, the International Monetary Market (IMM) of the Chicago Mercantile Exchange initiated trading in several foreign currencies. In October 1975, the Chicago Board of Trade (CBT) pioneered trading in a futures contract based on a fixed-income instrument—Government National Mortgage Association certificates. Three months later the IMM began trading futures contracts based on 90-day Treasury bills. Other exchanges soon followed with other interest rate futures contracts. In 1982, three futures contracts on broadly based common stock indexes made their debut. A unique aspect of stock index futures contracts is that they are cash settlement contracts.

### Mechanics of futures trading

**Taking and liquidating a position.** When an investor takes a position in the market by buying a futures contract, the investor is said to be taking a *long position.* If, instead, the investor's opening position is the sale of a futures contract, the investor is said to be in a *short position.*

The investor has two choices to liquidate a position. To liquidate a position prior to the delivery date, the investor must take an offsetting position. For a long position this means selling an identical number of contracts; for a short position this means buying an identical number of contracts. The alternative is to wait until the delivery date. At that time the investor liquidates a long position by accepting delivery of the underlying instrument at the agreed-upon price and liquidates a short position by delivering the underlying instrument at the agreed-upon price. It is rare for positions to be closed out by actual delivery. In the case of stock index futures, there is a cash settlement.

The broker is required to provide confirmation of the execution of an order as soon as possible. The confirmation form that is filled out when a position is taken indicates all the essential information about the trade. When the order involves the liquidation of a position, the confirmation form shows the profit and loss on the position and the commission costs.

It is not uncommon to purchase a security through one brokerage firm and sell it through another. However, this is usually not done with futures contracts. The brokerage firm that executes the order to establish the initial position also executes the order to liquidate the position.

When an investor takes a position in the market, another party is taking the opposite position and agreeing to satisfy the commitment set forth in the contract. But what if that party defaults on the obligation? Is the investor's only recourse to sue the defaulting party? If so, does that mean an investor must be concerned with who the other party is before taking a position in the futures market? Moreover, if the investor wants to liquidate a position before the final settlement date, must the investor do so only with that party?

The answer to those questions is that the investor need not worry about the financial strength and integrity of the other party to the contract. Once the order is executed, the direct relationship between the two parties is severed. A *clearing corporation* associated with each exchange interposes itself as the buyer to every sale and the seller to every purchase. Thus, each of the parties to the contract is free to liquidate his or her position without being concerned about the other party.

Like the commissions on common stock transactions, the commissions on executions of futures contracts are fully negotiable. The commissions charged on futures contracts are based on a round trip.

**Types of orders.** When an investor wishes to buy or sell a futures contract, the price and conditions under which the order is to be executed must be communicated to the account representative.

The simplest type of order, yet the most dangerous from the investor's perspective, is the *market order*. When a market order is placed, it is executed at the best price available as soon as it reaches the trading pit.[1] Market orders are fine for security

---

[1] The trading pit is the trading area on the floor of a futures exchange where all transactions for a specific contract are made.

trades, because security prices usually do not fluctuate substantially between the time the investor decides to trade and the time the order reaches the trading floor. Over 75 percent of stock transactions are placed as market orders. However, futures prices jump around a great deal during short intervals of time. Coupled with the higher leverage associated with futures, an adverse movement of just a few ticks[2] between the time the investor decides to transact based on prevailing market prices and the time the order reaches the trading pit could make the difference between a successful strategy and a disastrous one.

To avoid the dangers associated with market orders, the investor can place a *limit order*. With a limit order the investor may designate a price limit for the execution of the transaction. A buy limit order indicates that the futures contract may be purchased only at the price designated or at a lower price. A sell limit order indicates that the futures contract may be sold at the price designated or at a higher price.

The danger with a limit order is that there is no assurance it will be executed. The designated price may not be reached. Even if it is reached at a later time, the order may not be fulfilled because there is no one on a futures exchange to assume the role of the specialist on a stock exchange, who keeps a book on unfilled limit orders and executes them when the designated price is reached. Nevertheless, the dangers of a limit order are far less than the dangers of a market order. The investor can exert greater control with a limit order than with a market order because he or she can always revise the price designated in the limit order based on prevailing market prices.

The limit order is a conditional order: it is executed only if the limit price or a better price can be obtained. Another type of conditional order is the *stop order*. A stop order specifies that a transaction is not to be executed until the market price reaches a designated price, at which point it becomes a market order. A buy stop order specifies that the order is not to be executed until the market price rises to a designated price. A sell stop order specifies that the order is not to be executed until the market price falls below a designated price.

A stop order can be employed by an investor to protect a profit or to limit a loss. To understand how a stop order can be

---

[2] For each futures contract, a minimum price change is specified by the exchange. The minimum price change is a "tick."

used and how it differs from a limit order, consider the following examples. Suppose that an investor purchased an S&P 500 futures contract for 126 and that the futures price is now 139. The investor wants to protect the paper profit. To do so, the investor could place a sell stop order at, say, 132. This means that, when the futures price falls to 132 or lower, the futures contract is to be sold at the best price possible. To see how an investor can use a sell stop order to limit a loss, suppose that the investor purchased a NYSE Composite Index futures contract for 80 and that the position was taken in the expectation that the futures price would increase. To limit the loss should the futures price decline instead, the investor could place a sell stop order at, say, 75.

The two examples of a sell stop order show how it can be used by an investor in a long position. An investor in a short position can utilize a buy stop order to protect a paper profit or limit a loss.

Notice that in a sell stop order the designated price is less than the current market price of the futures contract. In a sell limit order, however, the designated price is above the market price of the futures contract. In a buy stop order the designated price is above the market price. In a buy limit order it is below the market price.

There are two dangers associated with stop orders. First, since the futures market exhibits abrupt price changes, it is possible that the direction of the change in the futures price may be only temporary, resulting in the premature closing of a position. Second, once the designated price is reached, the stop order becomes a market order and is subject to the uncertainty of the execution price noted earlier for market orders.

A *stop-limit order*, a hybrid of a stop order and a limit order, is a stop order that designates a price limit. For example, in our example of the S&P 500 futures contract that was purchased at 126 and is now priced at 139, the investor can place a sell stop-limit order that goes into effect at a futures price of 132 and has a limit price of 129. The stop-limit order has the same potential problem as the one we noted for a limit order. That is, the limit price may never be reached and, therefore, the order will not be executed. This defeats the purpose of the stop order, which is to protect a paper profit or limit a loss.

Conditional orders, such as the limit order or the buy order, must designate the time period for which the order is effective.

The order may be designated as good for a day, week, or month. An *open order,* however, is good until the order is canceled.

**Margin requirements.** An important consideration in determining whether to employ any of the strategies involving futures that will be discussed later in this article is the margin requirements. When a position is first taken in a futures contract, the investor must deposit a minimum dollar amount per contract as specified by the exchange. This amount is called the *initial margin.*[3] As the price of the futures contract fluctuates, the value of the investor's equity in the position changes. At the close of each trading day, an investor's position is "marked to market" so that any gain or loss from the position is reflected in the investor's equity account. *Maintenance margin* is the minimum level specified by the exchange by which an investor's equity position may fall as a result of an unfavorable price movement before the investor is required to deposit additional margin. The additional margin deposited is called *variation margin.* If there is excess margin, that amount may be withdrawn by the investor.

To illustrate the margin requirements, suppose that Trader X purchased four S&P 500 contracts on *Day 1* for 140. Since for the S&P 500 contract the value of the contract is equal to 500 times the futures price, the value of the four S&P 500 contracts would be $280,000 (4 × $500 × 140). Suppose, for purposes of this illustration, that the minimum initial margin requirement for this contract is $6,000 per contract, or $24,000 for four contracts. If the brokerage firm that Trader X is using for this transaction does not have a higher initial margin requirement, then Trader X must deposit $24,000 in cash or its equivalent. We will assume that Trader X deposits $24,000 in cash but will return later to alternative deposits that Trader X could make. The maintenance margin for this transaction is assumed to be $2,500 per contract, or $10,000 for four contracts.

The second column of Exhibit 1 presents the assumed settle-

---

[3] Individual brokerage firms are free to set margin requirements above the minimum established by the exchange. Although there are initial and maintenance margin requirements for buying securities on margin, the concept of margin differs for securities and futures. When securities are acquired on margin, the difference between the price of the security and the initial margin is borrowed from the broker. The security purchased serves as collateral for the loan and interest is paid by the investor. For futures contracts, the initial margin, in effect, serves as "good faith" money indicating that the investor will satisfy the obligation of the contract. No money is borrowed by the investor.

**EXHIBIT 1**   Margin requirements and account equity for the purchase of four S&P 500 contracts

Initial margin per S&P 500 contract = $6,000.
Initial margin for four S&P 500 contracts = $24,000 (4 × $6,000).
Maintenance margin per S&P 500 contract = $2,500.
Maintenance margin for four S&P 500 contracts = $10,000.

| Day | Assumed settlement price | Value of four contracts | Mark-to-market | Equity in account | Equity in excess of initial margin | Variation margin |
|---|---|---|---|---|---|---|
| 1. . . . . . . . | 140 | $280,000 | — | $24,000 | — | — |
| 2. . . . . . . . | 144 | 288,000 | $ 8,000 | 32,000 | $ 8,000 | — |
| 3. . . . . . . . | 142 | 284,000 | −4,000 | 28,000 | 4,000 | — |
| 4. . . . . . . . | 137 | 274,000 | −10,000 | 18,000 | −6,000 | — |
| 5. . . . . . . . | 138 | 276,000 | 2,000 | 20,000 | −4,000 | — |
| 6. . . . . . . . | 133 | 266,000 | −10,000 | 10,000 | −14,000 | — |
| 7. . . . . . . . | 130 | 260,000 | −6,000 | 4,000 | −20,000 | $20,000 |
| 8. . . . . . . . | 128 | 256,000 | −4,000 | 20,000 | −4,000 | — |
| 9. . . . . . . . | 134 | 268,000 | 12,000 | 32,000 | 8,000 | — |

Note: The contract value is $500 times the futures price. Since there are four contracts, the per contract value is multiplied by 4.

ment price of the S&P 500 futures contract and the value of four contracts for eight trading days following the purchase of the contracts by Trader X. Let us examine each trading day following Day 1. Trader X's account for each trading day is summarized in Exhibit 1.

*Day 2.*   The futures price increased from 140 to 144, resulting in a gain of $8,000. The increase in the contract value is added to the equity in Trader X's account. This is what is meant by "marked-to-market." The equity in Trader X's account is the initial margin plus the $8,000 gain. The equity in excess of the initial margin requirement is $8,000. *Trader X may withdraw the $8,000 from the account.*

If Trader X withdraws the entire excess of $8,000 in Day 2 and on Day 3 the equity in the account falls below $24,000, the initial margin requirement, there will be no margin call as long as the equity is at least $10,000, the minimum maintenance margin requirement. This will reduce the amount of funds tied up by the trader from $24,000 to $20,000.

*Day 3.* Although the futures price is higher than it was when Trader X purchased the contracts, it closed lower than on the previous trading day. Trader X lost $4,000 from the previous trading day's settlement price. The equity in Trader X's account declined from $32,000 to $28,000. The equity in excess of the initial margin is now $4,000 if Trader X did not withdraw any cash from the account in Day 2. Now $4,000 may be withdrawn from the account.

*Day 4.* The futures price closed below the purchase price on this trading day. The result is a loss of $6,000 from the purchase price and a further decrease in the equity in the account from that of the previous trading day. The $10,000 loss on this trading day reduced the equity to $18,000, assuming that no withdrawals of cash were made at the close of the two previous trading days. Although the equity in the account declined to a value that is less than the initial margin of $24,000, it is not less than the $10,000 maintenance margin. Hence, there is no margin call.

*Day 5.* The increase in the settlement price from 137 to 138 added $2,000 to the equity account. Since the equity in the account is still greater than the maintenance margin required, no margin call is required.

*Day 6.* The decline in the futures price to 133 reduced the equity in the account to $10,000. The equity is now equal to the maintenance margin requirement. Any further decline in the settlement price will result in a margin call.

*Day 7.* The settlement price of the futures contract fell to 130. The loss of $6,000 from the previous day's settlement price reduced the equity to $4,000. This is less than the maintenance margin requirement of $10,000. Consequently, there is a margin call to bring the equity in the account up to the *initial margin* of $24,000. This means that Trader X must deposit an additional $20,000 or its equivalent.

If Trader X fails to do so, the contracts will be sold and Trader X will realize a loss of $20,000 ($280,000 − $260,000). Since Trader X deposited $24,000, $4,000, the amount of equity in the account at the close of Day 7, is available to Trader X.

Let us assume that Trader X deposits $20,000 into the account. The $20,000 is the *variation margin.* Note how the amount of the margin call differs for stock index futures, compared to stocks purchased on margin. In the latter case, the amount of the call margin would be the amount necessary to bring the equity into the account up to the *maintenance margin,* not the initial margin.

To avoid bringing the equity up to the initial maintenance margin, a trader could *voluntarily* deposit funds if he or she anticipates that the equity will fall below the maintenance margin. For example, if Trader X had deposited $6,000 in the account on Day 7, the equity in the account on Day 8 would have been $10,000. Hence, there would not have been a margin call of $20,000.

*Day 8.* After the $20,000 variation margin was deposited, the settlement price declined further, to 128. This reduces the equity in the account by $4,000, to $20,000. Since the equity in the account is greater than the $10,000 maintenance requirement, there is no margin call.

*Day 9.* The settlement price increased to 134, increasing the equity in the account to $32,000. Since the equity in the account is $8,000 greater than the initial margin, Trader X may withdraw the excess.

The foregoing illustrated the purchase of a stock index futures contract. What would happen if four S&P 500 contracts were sold rather than purchased? The excess equity in the account is the opposite of that shown in Exhibit 1. In this illustration there would be no variation margin. *However, a trader must always make provision for the possibility of variation margin, lest he or she be forced to close a position at an inopportune time.*

In our illustration we have assumed that Trader X deposited cash to meet the initial and variation margins. As an alternative, Treasury bills or letters of credit may be used for initial margin. *Variation margin must be satisfied with cash.*

## Hedging with futures

Hedging is the employment of a futures position as a temporary substitute for transactions to be made in the cash market at a later date. Hedging attempts to eliminate price risk by trying to fix the price of a transaction to be made at a later date. If cash and futures prices move together, any loss realized by the hedger from one position (whether cash or futures) will be offset by a profit on the other position. When the profit and loss from each position are equal, the hedge is called a *perfect hedge*.

In practice, hedging is not that simple. The amount of the loss and profit from each position will not necessarily be identical. As will be explained below, whether there is an overall profit or loss from a particular hedge will depend on the relationship between the cash price and the futures price when a hedge is placed and when it is lifted. The difference between the cash price and the futures price is called the *basis*. *Consequently, hedging involves the substitution of basis risk for price risk.*

Some commodities do not have existing futures contracts. When a hedger assumes a futures position in a commodity different from that in which a cash position is held or will be held, the hedge is referred to as a *cross-hedge*. A hedger who seeks protection against potential adverse price movement for a commodity that does not have an existing futures contract will use a futures contract on an underlying commodity that he hopes will track the price of the commodity being hedged. For example, a party seeking to hedge against adverse price movements in okra will use a futures contract for some agricultural product, rather than a futures contract on a precious metal, such as gold or silver.

Consequently, cross-hedging adds another dimension to basis risk. The future cash price of the commodity that is being hedged may not be tracked well by the commodity that is being used for the hedge.

Cross-hedging with futures is the name of the game in portfolio management. Other than the few interest rate futures contracts currently traded, there are no futures contracts for specific debt instruments and common stock shares. For example, suppose that a portfolio manager wants to hedge a position in a long-term corporate bond of a particular issuer against adverse price movements due to an increase in market yields. He would have to use an existing futures contract on long-term Treasury bonds, since exchange-traded futures contracts on corporate bonds are not available. Because interest rates for all fixed-income obligations move in the same direction, the future cash price of the Treasury bond may track the future cash price of the corporate bond well. The only way to use a futures contract so as to hedge the price of a given issuer's common stock or the price of a common stock portfolio is by using a cross-hedge. Underlying a stock index futures contract is a specific index. How well the price of a stock or the price of a portfolio of common stocks tracks the index will determine the success of the hedge. Unlike debt obligations that have price movements in the same direction as interest rates change, the price of an individual stock or a portfolio of stocks may move in a direction opposite to that of the overall market.

The foregoing points will be made clearer in the illustrations presented later in this article.

**Short hedge and long hedge.** A *short hedge* is used by a hedger to protect against a decline in the future cash price of a commodity or a financial instrument. To execute a short hedge, the hedger sells a futures contract (agrees to make delivery of the underlying commodity or financial instrument). Consequently, a short hedge is also known as a *sell hedge*. By establishing a short hedge, the hedger has fixed the future cash price and transferred the price risk of ownership to the buyer of the contract. Three examples of who may want to use a short hedge follow:

1. A corn farmer will sell his product in three months. The price of corn, like the price of any commodity, will fluctuate in the open market. The corn farmer wants to lock in a price today at which he can deliver his corn in three months.
2. A client expects to liquidate a portion of her bond portfolio in three months to obtain funds to pay a substantial tax liability that will come due at that time. The proceeds received from the bond will depend on interest rates three months from now. Like all investors, the client is uncertain of the interest rates that will prevail three months from now and wants to be sure that any rise in interest rates will not result in a decrease in the proceeds obtained when the bonds are sold.
3. A client will retire eight months from now. He has a substantial amount in common stock accumulation units of his retirement plan. The value of these units will fluctuate with the movements of the stock market. He plans to liquidate a portion of the units eight months from now and place the

funds into fixed-income securities but wants to lock in the value of the units today.

A *long hedge* is undertaken to protect against an increase in the price of a commodity or financial instrument to be purchased in the cash market at some future time. In a long hedge, the hedger buys a futures contract (agrees to accept delivery of the underlying commodity or financial instrument). A long hedge is also known as a *buy hedge*. The following three examples are instances where a long hedge may be used:

1. A food processing company projects that in three months it must purchase 30,000 bushels of corn. The management of the company does not want to take a chance that the price of corn may increase by the time the company must make its acquisition. It wants to lock in the price of corn today.
2. A client knows that in two months $100,000 of par value of the bonds in his portfolio will mature. Prevailing interest rates are high now but are expected to decline dramatically by the time the funds are to be reinvested. The client wants to lock in a reinvestment rate today.
3. A client expects to receive proceeds from the sale of her business four months from now. She plans to invest those proceeds in a diversified portfolio of common stock. The stock market is expected to rise dramatically four months from now. She therefore wants to lock in the price of those stocks.

### Hedging illustrations

To further explain hedging, we shall first present several numerical illustrations from the commodities area.

Suppose that a corn farmer expects to sell 30,000 bushels of corn three months from now. Assume further that the management of a food processing company plans to purchase 30,000 bushels of corn three months from now. Both the corn farmer and the management of the food processing company want to lock in a price today. That is, they want to eliminate the price risk associated with corn three months from now. The cash or spot price for corn is currently $2.75 per bushel. The futures price for corn is currently $3.20 per bushel. Each futures contract is for 5,000 bushels of corn.

Since the corn farmer seeks protection against a decline in the price of corn three months from now, he will place a short or sell hedge. That is, he will promise to make delivery of corn at the current futures price. The corn farmer will sell six futures contracts, since each contract calls for the delivery of 5,000 bushels of corn.

The management of the food processing company seeks protection against an increase in the price of corn three months from now. Consequently, management will place a buy or long hedge. That is, it will agree to accept delivery of corn at the futures price. Since protection is sought against a price increase for 30,000 bushels of corn, six contracts are bought.

Let's look at what happens under various scenarios for the cash price and futures price of corn three months from now when the hedge is lifted.

Suppose that, when the hedge is lifted, the cash price declines to $2.00 and the futures price declines to $2.45. Notice what has happened to the basis under this scenario. At the time the hedge was placed, the basis is −$.45 ($2.75 − $3.20). When the hedge is lifted, the basis is still −$.45 ($2.00 − $2.45).

The corn farmer, at the time the hedge was placed, wanted to lock in a price of $2.75 per bushel of corn, or $82,500 for 30,000 bushels. He sold six futures contracts at a price of $3.20 per bushel, or $96,000 for 30,000 bushels. When the hedge is lifted, the value of the farmer's corn is $60,000 ($2.00 × 30,000). The corn farmer realizes a decline in the cash market in the value of his corn of $22,500. However, the futures price declines to $2.45, so the cost to the corn farmer to liquidate his futures position is only $73,500 ($2.45 × 30,000). The corn farmer realizes a gain in the futures market of $22,500. The net result is that the gain in the futures market matches the loss in the cash market. Consequently, the corn farmer does not realize an overall gain or loss. When this occurs, the hedge is said to be a *perfect* or *textbook* hedge.

Because there was a decline in the cash price, the food processing company would realize a gain in the cash market of $22,500 but would realize a loss in the futures market of the same amount. Therefore, this buy or long hedge is also a *perfect* or *textbook* hedge.

This scenario illustrates two important points. First, for both participants there was no overall gain or loss. The reason for this result was that we assumed the basis did not change when the hedge was lifted. Thus, if the basis does not change, a perfect hedge will be achieved. Second, notice that the management of the food processing company would have been better off if it had not hedged. The cost of corn would have been $22,500 less in the cash market three months later. This, however, should not be interpreted as a sign of poor planning by management. Management is not in the business of speculating on the price of corn in the future. Hedging is a standard practice to protect against an increase in the cost of doing business in the future.

Suppose that the cash price of corn when the hedge is lifted increases to $3.55 and that the futures price increases to $4.00. Notice that the basis is unchanged at −$.45. Since the basis is unchanged, the cash and futures price we have assumed in this scenario will produce a perfect hedge.

The corn farmer will gain in the cash market since the value of 30,000 bushels of corn is $106,500 ($3.55 × 30,000). This represents a $24,000 gain, compared to the cash value at the time the hedge was placed. However, the corn farmer must liquidate his position in the futures market by buying six futures contracts at a total cost of $120,000, which is $24,000 more than when the contracts were sold. The loss in the futures market offsets the gain in the cash market and we have a perfect hedge. The food processing company would realize a gain in the futures market of $24,000 but would have to pay $24,000 more in the cash market to acquire 30,000 bushels of corn.

Notice that the management of the food processing company under this scenario saved $24,000 in the cost of corn by employing a hedge. The corn farmer, though, would have been better off if he had not used a hedging strategy and simply sold his product on the market three months later. However, it must be emphasized that the corn farmer, just like the management of the food processing company, employed a hedge to protect against unforeseen adverse price changes in the cash market.

In the previous two scenarios we have assumed that the basis does not change when the hedge is lifted. In the real world, the basis does, in fact, change between the time a hedge is placed and when it is lifted. Now we shall illustrate what happens when the basis changes.

Assume that the cash price of corn decreases to $2.00, just as in the first scenario; however, assume also that the futures price decreases to $2.70 rather than $2.45. The basis has now widened from −$.45 to −$.70 (2.00 − $2.70). For the short (sell) hedge, the loss in the cash market of $22,500 is only partially offset by a $15,000 gain realized in the futures market. Consequently, the hedge resulted in an overall loss of $7,500.

There are two points to note here. First, if the corn farmer had not employed the hedge, the loss would have been $22,500, since the value of his 30,000 bushels of corn is $60,000, compared to $82,500 three months earlier. Although the hedge is not a perfect hedge because the basis widened, the loss of $7,500 is less than the loss of $22,500 if no hedge had been placed. This is what we meant earlier in the article when we said that hedging substitutes basis risk for price risk. Second, the management of the food processing company faces the same problem from an opposite perspective. An unexpected gain for either participant results in an unexpected loss of equal dollar value for the other. That is, the participants face a "zero-sum game." Consequently, the food processing company would realize an overall gain of $7,500 from its long (buy) hedge. This gain represents a gain of $22,500 in the cash market and a realized loss of $15,000 in the futures market.

The results of this scenario demonstrate that when *(a)* the future price is greater than the cash price at the time the hedge is placed, *(b)* the cash price declines, and *(c)* the basis widens, then: *the short (sell) hedger will realize an overall loss from the hedge, and the long (buy) hedger will realize an overall gain from the hedge.*

Exhibit 2 summarizes the impact of a change in the basis on the overall profit or loss of a hedge when the futures price is greater than the cash price at the time the hedge is placed.

---

**EXHIBIT 2**    Summary of basis relationships for a hedge

| Price | | Absolute change in basis | Overall gain (+) or loss (−) when at time hedge is placed cash price is less than futures price | |
|---|---|---|---|---|
| Cash | Futures | | Short hedge | Long hedge |
| Decreases | Decreases by same amount | No change | 0 | 0 |
| Decreases | Decreases by a smaller amount | Widens | − | + |
| Decreases | Decreases by a greater amount | Narrows | + | − |
| Increases | Increases by same amount | No change | 0 | 0 |
| Increases | Increases by a smaller amount | Narrows | + | − |
| Increases | Increases by a greater amount | Widens | − | + |

## Cross-hedging illustrations

Not all commodities have a futures market. Consequently, if a hedger wants to protect against the price risk of a commodity in which a futures contract is not traded, the hedger may use a commodity that he believes has a close price relationship to the one he seeks to hedge. This adds another dimension of risk when hedging. The cash market price relationship between the commodity to be hedged and the commodity used to hedge may change.

Since hedging financial instruments using futures frequently involves cross-hedging, we will first illustrate the key elements associated with a cross-hedge for a commodity.

Suppose that an okra farmer plans to sell 37,500 bushels of okra three months from now and that a food processing company plans to purchase the same amount of okra three months from now. Both parties want to hedge against price risk. However, okra futures contracts are not traded. Both parties believe that there is a close price relationship between okra and corn. Specifically, both parties believe that the cash price of okra will be 80 percent of the cash price of corn. The cash price of okra is currently $2.20 per bushel and the cash price of corn is currently $2.75 per bushel. The futures price of corn is currently $3.20 per bushel.

Let's examine various scenarios to see how effective the cross-hedge will be. In each scenario, the difference between the cash price of corn and the futures price of corn at the time the cross-hedge is placed and at the time it is lifted will be assumed to be unchanged at −$.45. This is done so we may focus on the importance of the relationship between the two cash prices at the two points in time.

We must first determine how many corn futures contracts must be used in the cross-hedge. The cash value of 37,500 bushels of okra at the cash price of $2.20 per bushel is $82,500. To protect a value of $82,500 using corn futures with a current cash price of $2.75, the price of 30,000 bushels of corn ($82,500/$2.75) must be hedged. Since each corn futures contract involves 5,000 bushels, six corn futures contracts will be used.

Suppose that the cash price of okra and corn decrease to $1.60 and $2.00 per bushel, respectively, and the futures price of corn decreases to $2.45 per bushel. The relationship between the cash price for okra and corn assumed when the cross-hedge was placed holds at the time the cross-hedge is lifted. That is, the cash price of okra is 80 percent of the cash price of corn. The basis for the cash price of corn and the futures price of corn is still −$.45 at the time the cross-hedge is lifted.

The short cross-hedge produces a gain in the futures market of $22,500 and an exact offset loss in the cash market. The opposite occurs for the long cross-hedge. There is neither an overall gain nor a loss from the cross-hedge in this case. That is, we have a perfect cross-hedge. The same would occur if we assume that the cash price of both commodities increases by the same percentage and the basis does not change.

Suppose that the cash price of both commodities decreases but the cash price of okra falls by a greater percentage than the cash price of corn. For example, suppose that the cash price of okra falls to $1.30 per bushel while the cash price of corn falls to $2.00 per bushel. The futures price of corn falls to $2.45 so that the basis is not changed. The cash price of okra at the time the cross-hedge is lifted is 65 percent of the cash price of corn, rather than 80 percent as assumed when the cross-hedge was constructed.

For the short cross-hedge the loss in the cash market exceeds the realized loss in the futures market by $11,200. For the long cross-hedge the opposite is true. There is an overall gain from the cross-hedge of $11,200. Had the cash price of okra fallen by less than the decline in the cash price of corn, the short cross-hedge would have produced an overall gain while the long cross-hedge would have generated an overall loss.

The appendix to this article illustrates how to hedge with stock index futures.

## OPTIONS

An option is a contract in which the writer of the option grants the buyer of the option the right to purchase from or sell to the writer a designated instrument at a specified price within a specified time. The writer, also referred to as the seller, grants this right to the buyer for a certain sum of money called the *option premium*. The price at which the instrument may be bought or sold is called the *exercise* or *strike price*. The date after which an option is void is called the *expiration date*. An *option* may be exercised any time before the expiration date.

When an option grants the buyer the right to purchase the designated instrument from the writer, it is called a *call option.* When the option buyer has the right to sell the designated instrument to the writer (seller), the option is called a *put option.* In the case of options on a stock index, settlement is in cash.

An option on a futures contract gives the buyer the right to buy from or sell to the writer a designated futures contract at a designated price at any time during the life of the option. If the option on a futures contract is a call option, the buyer has the right to purchase one designated futures contract at the exercise (strike) price. That is, the buyer has the right to acquire a long futures position in the designated futures contract at the exercise (strike) price. If the call option is exercised by the buyer, the writer (seller) acquires a short position. A put option on a futures contract grants the buyer the right to sell one designated futures contract to the writer at the exercise (strike) price. That is, the buyer has the right to acquire a short futures position in the designated futures contract at the exercise price. If the put option is exercised, the writer acquires a long position in the designated futures contract at the exercise price.

Notice that, unlike a futures contract, the buyer of an option has the *right* but not the obligation to perform. It is the option seller (writer) that has the obligation to perform. Both the buyer and seller are obligated to perform in the case of a futures contract. In addition, in a futures contract, the buyer does not pay the seller to accept the obligation as in the case of an option where the buyer pays the seller the option premium.

Most investors are familiar with exchange-listed options on common stock. Options on common stock were first listed on the Chicago Board Options Exchange (CBOE) in 1973, followed by trading on the American Stock Exchange in January 1975. Since then, common stock options have traded on several regional exchanges.

In early 1983, options on stock index futures contracts began trading on the Chicago Mercantile Exchange (S&P 500) and the New York Futures Exchange (NYSE Composite). By midyear these options on futures contracts had been joined by cash settlement options for two synthetic stock indexes. Options on fixed-income securities are traded on two exchanges—the American Stock Exchange and the Chicago Board Options Exchange. The underlying fixed-income securities for the options traded on these two exchanges are U.S. Treasury obligations. The Chicago Board of Trade is the only exchange that currently trades an option on an interest rate futures contract. The fixed-income instrument underlying the interest rate futures contract is also a U.S. Treasury obligation.

In this article we shall discuss the basic elements that an investor who is contemplating using options should be familiar with. No matter how intricate an option investment strategy the investor may adopt, *the principal result of any option purchase or sale is to modify the risk characteristics of an investor's position.*

### The option premium (price)

The cost to the buyer of an option is primarily a reflection of the option's *intrinsic* value and any excess over its intrinsic value.[4] Each is discussed below.

Intrinsic value.  The intrinsic value of a call option is the difference between the current price of the underlying instrument and the exercise price. For example, if the exercise price for a call option is 78 and the current price of the designated instrument is 81, the intrinsic value is 3 (81 − 78). That is, if the option buyer exercised the option and simultaneously sold the underlying instrument, the option buyer would realize 81 from the short position, which would be covered by acquiring an offsetting long position at 78 through exercise of the option—thereby netting 3 points.

When a call option has intrinsic value, it is said to be "in the money." When the exercise price of a call option exceeds the current price of the underlying instrument, the call option is said to be "out of the money" and has no intrinsic value. An option for which the exercise price is equal to the current price of the underlying instrument is said to be "at the money."

For a put option, the intrinsic value is equal to the amount by which the current price of the underlying instrument is below the exercise price. For example, if the exercise price of a put option is 78 and the current price of the underlying instrument is 71, the intrinsic value is 7. When the put option has intrinsic value, the option is said to be in the money. A put option is out

---

[4] Intrinsic value is sometimes referred to as *parity value.*

of the money when the current price of the underlying instrument exceeds the exercise price.

**Time value.** The time value is whatever amount buyers are willing to pay over and above any intrinsic value that the option may have. The option buyer hopes that at some point prior to expiration, changes in the price of the underlying instrument will further increase the value of the rights conveyed by the option. For example, if the option premium (price) for a call option with an exercise price of 78 is 9 when the current price of the underlying instrument is 81, then the time value for this option is 6 (9 minus the intrinsic value of 3). If the current price of the underlying instrument is 72 instead of 81, then the time value for this option is 9, since the option has no intrinsic value.

There are two ways in which an investor may realize the value of a position taken in the option. He may exercise the option giving him a position in the underlying instrument and simultaneously take an offsetting position in the cash market for the underlying instrument. For example, for our hypothetical call option with an exercise price of 78 and an option price of 9 and in which the current price of the underlying instrument is 81, the option buyer can exercise the option. This will give the option buyer a long position in the underlying instrument at 78. By simultaneously selling the underlying instrument for 81, the option holder will realize 3. Alternatively, the option buyer may sell the call option for 9. Obviously, the latter is the preferable alternative. Because the exercise of an option will cause the immediate loss of any time value that the option has left (in this case 6), options are not likely to be exercised very often. Furthermore, unlike the analogous exercise of an option on common stocks, which results in ownership of (or a short position in) a lasting asset, for an option on futures contract, exercise results only in a futures position that is itself due to settle.

### Margin requirements

There are no margin requirements for the option buyer once the premium has been paid in full. Because the premium is the maximum amount that the investor can lose, no matter how adverse the price movement of the underlying instrument, there is no need for margin.

Because the writer (seller) of an option has agreed to accept all of the risk (and none of the reward) of the position in the underlying instrument, the writer (seller) is required to put up not only the margin required on the futures contract position in the case of an option on a futures contract, but, with certain exceptions, the option premium that he has received for the option. In addition, as prices adversely affect the writer's position, the writer would be required to deposit additional margin on the increased premium as it was marked to market. An exception occurs when the option is out of the money, in which case the margin requirement is reduced, depending on the particular option.

### Risk-return trade-off for basic option strategies

In this section the risk-return trade-off associated with the four basic option strategies—buying call options, buying put options, writing (selling) call options, and writing (selling) put options—will be explained. We shall use the following hypothetical option in our illustrations: A December call (and put) option on some underlying instrument with an exercise price of 88 and an option premium of 5. The current price of the underlying instrument is 88. For purposes of the illustrations, let's assume that each one point is equal to $100. Hence, an option premium of 5 is equal to $500. The exercise price is $8,800 ($100 times 88). *In the illustrations, we shall assume that the option is held to expiration and not exercised early.*

Buying call options.    The most straightforward option strategy for participating in an anticipated increase in the price of the underlying instrument (decrease in interest rates in the case of fixed income options) is to buy a call option. The investor who buys a call option is said to be in a "long call" position.

Suppose the investor purchases the December 88 call for 5. The option premium of $500 represents the maximum loss that the option buyer faces by buying a call. If the price of the underlying instrument is 88 or less at expiration, the buyer of this call option will lose the entire option premium, $500. The investor will break even if the price of the underlying instrument at expiration is 93 (the exercise price plus the premium). Any price between 88 and 93 reduces the investor's loss to an amount less than the option premium. However, should the price of the underlying instrument at expiration exceed 93, the option buyer will realize a profit of $100 for each point by which the price exceeds 93.

**Buying put options.** The most straightforward option strategy for benefiting from an anticipated decrease in the price of the underlying instrument (increase in interest rates in the case of fixed-income options) is to buy a put option. The investor who purchases a put option is said to be in a "long put" position.

Suppose an investor buys the at-the-money put option for a premium of $500. Should the price of the underlying instrument at expiration be greater than the exercise price of 88, the put option will expire worthless and the investor will lose the entire premium of $500. The investor will recover the premium but show no profit or loss if the settlement price of the underlying instrument is 83 (the exercise price of 88 minus the premium of 5). This value is known as the *break-even point*. For any price for the underlying instrument between 83 and 88 at expiration, the investor will reduce his loss below the premium of $500. The investor will realize a $100 profit for each point by which the price of the underlying instrument at expiration is below the break-even price of 83. As in the case of call options, there is limited risk for the buyer of a put; the return for the buyer is limited to the maximum price by which the underlying instrument can fall at expiration.

**Writing (selling) call options.** An investor who believes that the price of the underlying instrument will decline or remain unchanged, if his expectations are correct, can realize income by writing (selling) a call option. A call writer is said to be in a "short call" position.

For our hypothetical call options, the maximum profit that the call writer can realize is the amount of the premium, $500. As long as the price of the underlying instrument is less than 93 (exercise price of 88 plus the premium of 5), the writer will realize a profit. If the price of the underlying instrument at expiration is greater than 93, the call writer will realize a $100 loss for each point above 93. That is, the profit position of the writer is of the same dollar magnitude but in the opposite direction of the buyer.

**Writing (selling) put options.** An investor who believes that the price of the underlying instrument will increase or remain unchanged, if his expectations are correct, can realize income by writing (selling) a put option. A put writer is said to be in a "short put" position.

For our hypothetical put option, the maximum profit that the option writer can realize is the amount of the premium. As long as the price of the underlying instrument is greater than 83 (exercise price of 88 minus the premium of 5), the put writer will realize a profit. If the price of the underlying instrument at expiration is 83, the put writer will break even. Any price for the underlying instrument at expiration that is less than the break-even price will produce a $100 loss for each point below 83.

### Hedging with options

When an investor uses futures to reduce downside risk, she sacrifices upside potential. Options and options on futures also can be used to provide downside risk protection; however, the cost of this protection is known and leaves any remaining upside potential intact.

The purchase of put options provides protection against a decline in the price of the instrument currently owned and to be hedged, because it locks in the price of the instrument. The locked-in price is the exercise price of the put. Such a strategy is referred to as a *protective put*. However, when the price of an instrument is expected to rise and an investor seeks protection against such a situation, the purchase of a call option would be an appropriate strategy. This is because the buyer locks in the price at which he would purchase the instrument. Once again, the locked-in price is the exercise price of the option. The cost of insuring a minimum price in the case of a put and a maximum price in the case of a call is the option premium.

In applying the two strategies just mentioned to hedge against adverse price movements of an instrument that is not the underlying instrument of an options contract, it is necessary to create a cross-hedge. Constructing a cross-hedge requires that the investor (1) determine the appropriate exercise price and expiration date and (2) as in the case of hedging with futures, determine the appropriate risk equivalent position. The risk equivalent position is the number of contracts, in this case options, that must be bought or sold per dollar amount of the instrument being hedged to equalize the dollar magnitude of the cash and options market position.

The first issue, the appropriate exercise price and expiration date, depends on the degree of protection the portfolio investor seeks. The cost of the protection is a function of the option premium, which, in turn, depends on whether the option is in, at, or out of the money, and the time to expiration.

## APPENDIX

### Hedging with stock index futures

In this article we have demonstrated that a successful hedge strategy will depend on what happens to the basis between the time the hedge is placed and the time it is lifted. The basis is a function of the pricing of the futures relative to the cash price. Moreover, when cross-hedging is employed, the cash price relationship between the product to be hedged and the product underlying the futures contract will determine the degree of success of a cross-hedge.

How successful stock index futures will be for hedging the price risk of an individual stock or a portfolio of common stocks will depend on the pricing of the futures relative to the underlying cash or spot stock index. Since a stock index futures contract may be used to hedge a stock or a portfolio of common stocks that is not identical in composition to the underlying stock index, any hedge employing stock index futures is a cross-hedge. Therefore, a relationship between the value of the stock index and the individual stock or portfolio of common stocks must be estimated.

The statistical technique of regression analysis is used to estimate the relationship between the price of an individual stock or a portfolio of common stocks and a market index. The relationship estimated is as follows:

Percentage change in price of a stock (or value of a portfolio) in period $t$

$$= \text{Alpha} + \text{Beta} \left( \begin{array}{l} \text{Percentage change in} \\ \text{the value of the market} \\ \text{index in period } t \end{array} \right) + \begin{array}{l} \text{Error term in} \\ \text{period } t \end{array}$$

This relationship is known as the *market model.*

The parameter of interest is beta, the slope of the market model. This parameter tells us how volatile the individual stock or the portfolio of common stocks is relative to the market index. A value of beta greater than one indicates that the stock or the portfolio is more volatile than the market index. If beta is less than one, the stock or portfolio is less volatile than the market index. If beta is one, the stock or portfolio mirrors the market index. It is rare to find a beta that is negative.

However, the value of beta is not the only important piece of information that we must have to assess the likelihood of success of a hedge. We must know how good the relationship is. Look at the last term in the expression for the market model. The size of the error term indicates how well the stock or portfolio tracks the movement of the market index. If there is a strong relationship between the movement of the stock or portfolio and the market index, the error term will be small.

A statistical measure of the strength of the relationship is the coefficient of determination, or "R-squared" ($R^2$). This measure indicates the percentage of the variation in the movement of the stock or portfolio explained by the market index. The coefficient of determination can range from zero to one. The closer the coefficient of determination is to one, the stronger is the statistical relationship. The coefficient of determination is directly related to a concept that most individuals are familiar with—the correlation coefficient. The correlation coefficient is equal to the square root of the coefficient of determination. Whether the correlation coefficient is positive or negative is determined by the sign of beta. For example, if the coefficient of determination is .7 and the beta is 1.2, the correlation coefficient is +.84.

A major problem with the market model for individual common stocks is that the coefficient of determination is small, typically between .01 and .65. As the number of stocks in a portfolio increases, the error term tends to decrease. In the jargon of modern portfolio theory, price movements not associated with the movement in the market, the error term, are diversified away as the number of issues in the portfolio increases. Studies have shown that only 12 to 18 issues are needed to diversify the risk not associated with the movement of the market. Consequently, a diversified common stock portfolio does a better job of tracking the market index than does an individual stock issue. In statistical terminology, the coefficient of determination approaches one as the number of issues in the portfolio increases. However, keep in mind that even if the coefficient of determination is one for a portfolio relative to a market index, this does not mean that the beta for the portfolio will equal one. The beta tells us how volatile the portfolio is relative to a market index. The coefficient of determination and the correlation coefficient indicate how good the relationship is.

When a hedge is constructed, the beta will tell the investor the contract value of the futures position that should be taken to hedge the stock or portfolio. It plays the same role in hedging a stock or portfolio that the relationship between the cash price of okra and the cash price of corn did in our cross-hedging example earlier in this article. The coefficient of determination will indicate how good the relationship is and will allow the hedger to assess the likelihood of success of the hedge.

To demonstrate how stock index futures can be used to hedge the price risk of an individual stock or a portfolio, an actual case will be used. Suppose that on May 17, 1982, an investor owned 10,000 shares of Crown Zellerbach. On that day the closing price of the stock was $21 per share and, therefore, the market value of 10,000 shares was $210,000. Suppose that the investor needed to hold the shares until August 9, 1982, to qualify for long-term capital gain treatment. However, the investor anticipated that the market and, therefore, his stock, will decline in value by August 9. To protect himself against a decline in the price of the stock, the investor decided to enter into a sell or short hedge using the September S&P 500 futures contract.

The first thing that the investor has to determine is how many contracts to purchase. This depends on Crown Zellerbach's beta and on the dollar value of the cash index at the time the hedge is placed. The steps for determining the number of contracts are as follows:

**Step 1.** Determine the "equivalent market index units" of the market by dividing the market value of the stock (portfolio) by the current cash index underlying the futures contract.

$$\text{Equivalent market index units} = \frac{\text{Market value of stock (portfolio)}}{\text{Current cash index value}}$$

**Step 2.** Multiply the equivalent market index units by beta to obtain the "beta-adjusted equivalent market index units."

$$\text{Beta-adjusted equivalent market index units} = \text{Beta} \times \left[ \begin{array}{c} \text{Equivalent market} \\ \text{index units} \end{array} \right]$$

**Step 3.** Divide the beta-adjusted equivalent market index units by the multiple specified in the futures contract. Since stock index futures contracts are for $500 times the value of the index, divide by $500.

$$\frac{\text{Number of}}{\text{contracts}} = \frac{\text{Beta-adjusted equivalent market index units}}{\$500}$$

In our illustration, since the S&P 500 index on May 17, 1982, was 118.01 and the beta for Crown Zellerbach was estimated to be equal to 1.614, the number of S&P 500 futures contracts required to hedge 10,000 shares of Crown Zellerbach was 5.7443, as shown below:

**Step 1.**

$$\text{Equivalent market index units} = \frac{\$210,000}{118.01}$$
$$= \$1,779.5102$$

**Step 2.**

$$\frac{\text{Beta-adjusted equivalent}}{\text{market index units}} = \$1,779.5102 \times 1.614$$
$$= \$2,872.1295$$

**Step 3.**

$$\text{Number of contracts} = \frac{\$2,872.1295}{\$500}$$
$$= 5.7443$$

Although it is not possible to purchase fractional portions of a futures contract, in the illustrations presented in this appendix fractional portions will be used.

The value of the futures position of the investor is equal to the number of contracts times the current futures price of the contract times the contract multiple ($500). Suppose that the investor sold 5.7443 S&P 500 futures contracts for 118.30 on May 17, 1982. Then the value of the investor's short futures position would be $339,775 (5.7443 × 118.30 × $500).

On August 9, 1982, the time the stock was to be sold, the price of Crown Zellerbach declined to $16.50 per share. Consequently, the market value of the shares declined $45,000, from $210,000 to $165,000 ($16.50 × 10,000).

The futures price of the September S&P 500 contract on August 9, 1982, was 102.60. Hence, 5.7443 contracts could be purchased for $294,683; therefore, closing out the futures position produced a profit of $45,092 ($339,775 − $294,683). Since the loss in the cash market was $45,000 and the gain in the futures market was $45,092, the overall result of the short hedge was a trivial gain of $92.

Let us analyze this hedge to determine why it was successful. As explained earlier in this article, in a cross-hedge there are two risks—basis risk and the risk that the relationship assumed between the product used for the hedge and the product to be hedged fails to materialize precisely as hypothesized. Consider the basis risk. At the time the hedge was placed, the cash price was 118.01 and the futures price was 118.30. The basis at the time the hedge was placed was −.29 (the futures price sold at a premium to the cash price). Had the basis been unchanged at −.29 at the time the hedge was lifted, the futures price would have been 104.00 (103.71 + .29). The cost of closing out the futures position would have been $298,704 (5.7443 × 104.00 × $500), and the profit from the futures position would have been $41,071 ($339,775 − $298,704).

At the time the hedge was lifted, the cash value for the index was 103.71, so the basis was 1.11 (103.71 − 102.6). That is, the futures price sold at a discount to the cash price. The change in the basis was 1.40 (1.10 − (−.29)). The change in the basis was in favor of the short hedger, resulting in a gain in the futures market of $700 per contract (1.4 × $500), or $4,021 for 5.7443 contracts.

In the cash market, the S&P 500 index declined by 12.11762 percent, from 118.01 to 103.71. Since the beta of Crown Zellerbach is 1.614, the price of the stock should have decreased by 19.55783 percent (12.11762 percent × 1.614) to $16.8929 per share, or $168,929. This would have resulted in a loss of $41,071 in the cash market. Notice that the loss of $41,071 in the cash market had the price of the stock declined by the hypothesized relationship (as indicated by beta) would have been exactly equal to the gain in the futures market had the basis remained constant. That is, there would have been a perfect hedge.

The stock, in fact, declined by more than the amount suggested by its beta. It fell from $21 to $16.50, or $0.3929 more per share than was predicted by its beta. Thus the loss in the cash market was $3,929 more than it would have been if the stock price had fallen to only $16.8929. Since the additional gain in the futures market because of a change in the basis was $4,021 and the additional loss in the cash market because the stock price fell more than predicted by its beta was $3,929, there was an overall gain of $92 ($4,021 − $3,929). This, of course, agrees with our earlier analysis of the outcome of the hedge.

Because of the higher correlation between a diversified portfolio of common stock and the market index, one would expect a hedge to perform better for a diversified portfolio than for an individual common stock. To see this, suppose that on May 17, 1982, a portfolio consisting of 10,000 shares of each of the following 19 randomly selected stocks was to be hedged against an adverse price movement:

| | | |
|---|---|---|
| Amerada Hess | Ford | Scott Paper |
| American Brands | Procter & Gamble | G. D. Searle |
| American Broadcasting | Rohr Industries | Sears Roebuck |
| CP National | Rollins | Stokely-Van Camp |
| CSX | Schering Plough | Eastman Kodak |
| Crown Zellerbach | Schlumberger Ltd. | Eaton |
| Crum & Foster | | |

The beta for the portfolio was estimated to be 0.94, and the correlation with the S&P 500 was .93. The market value of the portfolio on May 17, 1982, was $6,337,500. The number of September S&P 500 futures contracts that had to be sold to hedge this portfolio was 100.9618. The value of the futures contracts was, therefore, $5,971,891 (100.9618 × 118.30 × $500).

On August 9, 1982, the market value of the portfolio was $5,737,500, resulting in a loss in the cash market of $600,000. Since the futures price of the September S&P 500 declined to 102.60, the futures position could be closed out for $5,197,340 (100.9618 × 102.60 × $500), for a gain in the futures market of $792,550 ($5,737,500 − $5,197,340). The overall result of the hedge was a gain of $192,550. Considering the dollar value of the portfolio that was hedged, the short hedge performed well. The portfolio value increased by only +3 percent compared to a decline of 9.5 percent that would have occurred had the short hedge not been placed. Had a long hedge been placed, the hedged position would have produced a portfolio value 3 percent less than the market value at the time the hedge was placed. The transaction costs are trivial. These costs would not have exeeded $11,000 ($100 round-trip commission per contract).

An analysis of the outcome of the hedge would be insightful. Because of the change in the basis in favor of the short hedger, there was a gain in the futures market of $70,673 (100.9618 × 1.4 × $500). Based on a portfolio beta of 0.94, the market value of the portfolio should have declined by 11.39056 percent, since the market declined by 12.11762 percent. Had the decline been 11.39056 percent, the market value of the portfolio on August 9, 1982, would have been $5,615,623. The predicted market value for the portfolio was less than its actual market value of $5,737,500 by $121,877. The reduced loss in the cash market by $121,877 and a gain of $70,673 in the futures market due to a favorable change in the basis produced an overall gain of $192,550 for the short hedge.